W9-DAT-778

JERUSALEM
THE CONTESTED CITY

MENACHEM KLEIN

JERUSALEM

The Contested City

TRANSLATED BY HAIM WATZMAN

NEW YORK UNIVERSITY PRESS
WASHINGTON SQUARE, NEW YORK

*in association with the
Jerusalem Institute for Israel Studies*

#45958010

© the Jerusalem Institute for Israel Studies, 2001
All rights reserved

First published in the U.S.A. in 2001 by
NEW YORK UNIVERSITY PRESS
Washington Square
New York, NY 10003

A CIP catalog record for this book is available
from the Library of Congress

ISBN 0-8147-4754-X

Typeset in Bembo by Bookcraft Ltd, Stroud, Gloucestershire
Printed in England

ACKNOWLEDGEMENTS

Many fine people have assisted me in preparing this book for publication and all deserve my heartfelt thanks. Ora Ahimeir, director of the Jerusalem Institute for Israel Studies, initiated the project and followed its progress both closely and from a distance. She is to be thanked together with the entire staff of the Institute, led by Prof. Avraham (Rami) Friedman, head of the Institute, Prof. Shlomo Hasson, Yisrael (Lulik) Kimchi, Dr. Maya Choshen, and Reuven Merchav. I also received much assistance from Dr. Ron Pundik of the Economic Cooperation Foundation (ECF); attorney Dani Seideman; Col. (ret.) Shalom Goldstein, political adviser to the mayor of Jerusalem; Yaffa Rosenberg of the American Cultural Center in Jerusalem; Dr. Gershon Baskin of the Israel/Palestine Center for Research and Information (IPCRI); and from Muhmad al-Nakhal. I owe special thanks to Dr. Riad al-Malki of the Panorama organization; to Rami Nassarallah of the International Peace and Cooperation Center; and to the staff of Orient House, especially Dr. Khalil al-Tafugji, director of the Mapping Division of the Arab Studies Society, and to the staff of the Orient House library and document center. The chapter on the political profile of East Jerusalem's inhabitants could not have been written without the assistance of the Center for Palestine Research and Studies under the directorship of Dr. Khalil al-Shikaki. The director of the Center's survey unit, Dr. Nader Said, and Mrs. Raja Taher, were kind enough to make available to me findings that were not included in the survey papers they published. I received similar help from Jamil Rabah, who is responsible for surveys at the Jerusalem Media and Communication Center (JMCC), which is headed by Ghassan al-Khatib.

This book was translated into English by Haim Watzman, whose contribution can be felt in every word. Of course, none of these helpful people bears any responsibility for the contents of the book. The analysis of events, the interpretation of survey findings, and the errors are all mine.

Jerusalem   M.K.
January 2001

CONTENTS

Contents

INTRODUCTION

Jerusalem is hardly just another city and is far from being a local urban phenomenon. Nor is it just one more national capital. It is also more than just the most political city in Israel and the West Bank. The cliché is that Jerusalem is a mosaic of sparkling gem-stones, a splendid city whose inhabitants live side by side in harmony. The reality, as everyone knows, is far less idyllic. All the fault lines that cut through Israeli society intersect in Jerusalem, and as if that were not enough, the city lies on the front line of the conflict between Israel and the Palestinians. It is the capital of Israel, but East Jerusalem is the future Palestinian state's capital-in-the-making. Most Palestinians feel a personal relationship with Jerusalem even if they have not visited it for years (Segal & Sa'id, 1997). This is much the same as Jews feel about the city. Quoting the Jewish poet Zelda, Meron Benvenisti called the city "a place of fire" (Benvenisti, 1996).

The front lines in Jerusalem are not only national and ethnic. The city's holiness to Jews, Muslims, and Christians adds a religious dimension to its tangle of conflicting and contradictory identities, making the city a focus of worldwide interest. The city's holiness to the monotheistic religions is often inseparable from its national sanctity, and these two forms of the sacred feed each other's flames. Jerusalem is also saturated with historical memories, with existential anxieties and utopian hopes, all bubbling together in a steaming stewpot.

Jerusalem is a frontier city, even though it has not been thought of as such since 1967. The physical barrier, the fence that divided Israeli and Jordanian Jerusalem over which Israeli and Jordanian army outposts faced each other, no longer exists. But the city's national and ethnic barriers have remained in place, and have become even more impervious since 1967. The confrontation, which was intercommunal between 1917 and 1948, became international between 1948 and 1967. During these years Jerusalem was a frontier city divided between two countries. In many ways,

1

the confrontation between Israel and the Palestinians has returned since 1967 to its previous intercommunal form. Since Israel annexed East Jerusalem, the city has had two ethnic-national groups ranged against each other without any physical barrier separating them. As a frontier city, Jerusalem was, and to a large extent still is, a locus of competition for control of the city, with each group being unwilling to accept the governance of the other. The opposite side is a rival, not a partner. The Palestinian Authority's partial penetration of Jerusalem since September 1993 has inserted a dimension of statehood into East Jerusalem. Unlike the chaotic nature of intercommunal relations, relations between countries have a more institutionalized and ordered character. It is much easier to locate and manage conflicts between states than between communities. The resolution of the confrontation between Israel and the Palestinians, and its stabilization, requires institutionalization, and institutionalization cannot be built without political foundations.

When this book was written, the Oslo accords were the most important factor in shaping Israel–Palestinian relations. The Oslo process reached its climax at the Camp David summit of July 11–24, 2000. It was there that Jerusalem's status in the permanent settlement was first discussed at a decisive stage of the negotiations. Expectations were high, so there was great disappointment when the top-level Israeli–Palestinian–American talks produced no agreement. Subsequent talks, which went on for about a month after Camp David ended, were also fruitless.

When violence – the Al-Aqsa Intifada – broke out it demonstrated, in a way not seen since 1967, that Jerusalem was the center of the conflict, and that it is a frontier city. Shots were fired from the Palestinian city of Beit Jala at the southern Jerusalem neighborhood of Gilo, where the Israeli army deployed tanks both as a deterrent and to return fire. Many roads leading into Jerusalem and in East Jerusalem itself were closed off to Israeli Jews. The tight closure cut off the eastern city's links to the Israeli interior, and Israel severely limited Palestinian access to the Al-Aqsa Mosque for Friday prayer services.

The Camp David conference produced several oral understandings, not put into writing. It also focused the points of dispute in Jerusalem: the Temple Mount/al-Haram al-Sharif; the Old City; the crescent of Palestinian neighborhoods adjacent to the Old City that constitute the historical and religious cores of Jerusalem, and the city as defined by the Jordanians between 1949 and 1967. The dispute focused less on the management of these areas and more on the symbolic and political issue of sovereignty. In contrast, the two sides reached understandings about a significant number of questions of principle. These understandings are based on irreversible geographic and demographic reality and on the national interests of each side. On a fundamental level, then, this was a win-win situation.

First of all it was understood, as Israel demanded, that there was no returning to the reality of Jerusalem prior to the war of 1967. At the same time, it was understood that the municipal boundary unilaterally established by Israel as Jerusalem could not remain.

Secondly, all agreed that Jerusalem would grow in both directions. The Jewish city would be larger than that defined by Israel immediately after the 1967 war, and the Palestinian city would also grow to include the suburbs of Jerusalem that, in 1967, were villages not physically connected to the city. The two parts of the city would be larger than its current territory.

Third, this enlarged Jerusalem was seen to be a single metropolitan unit with common characteristics and needs, and would remain open. An international border, in the common sense of the word, would not run through it. In order to avoid damaging the common fabric of the city and the two-way flow between the two parts of the city, appropriate security measures would have to be taken that would keep Jerusalem from turning into a focus of terror, crime, and violence. Furthermore, a series of agreements would have to be reached to lay out the day-to-day functioning of the metropolitan area. Some of these arrangements will apply to the entire area and will require coordination between the two sides in solving problems that span the administrative borders – for example, air pollution and sewage. Another kind of special arrangement grows out of the need to preserve common interests such as the appearance of the Old City and its sites. Legal and economic arrangements are required because of the freedom of movement between the eastern and western cities. These special arrangements will apply largely to the seam where the two populations will be in intensive contact.

Fourth, both sides agreed to the establishment of two municipalities in the enlarged territory of Jerusalem. A Palestinian municipality will be established as a separate administrative unit under full Palestinian sovereignty. It will serve as the capital of the Palestinian state (Barak to the *Jerusalem Post*, 28 Sept. 2000). The debate at the Camp David conference centered on the powers of the Palestinian municipality in the historical and religious heart of the city, the municipal commercial center, and the adjacent neighborhoods. Everyone agreed, however, that the Palestinian municipality would have full powers in most parts of metropolitan East Jerusalem. Agreement on the principle of establishing two municipalities and an open municipal space requires, in turn, agreement on the establishment of a super-municipal administrative framework, whether it is a coordinating committee or umbrella municipality.

Fifth, both sides realized that an exchange of neighborhoods is necessary. Israel will exclude from its sovereign territory neighborhoods in its outer belt, such as Sur Baher in the southeast and Sho'afat and Bait Hanina in the north. These will be joined to the suburbs that now lie outside the municipal boundary drawn by Israel in 1967.

In exchange, Israel will receive sovereignty over settlements adjacent to Jerusalem – Ma'aleh Adumim, Givat Ze'ev, and Gush Etzion. Israel can decide whether Gush Etzion will remain an independent entity or whether it will be integrated into the Jewish Jerusalem municipality. In addition, the Palestinians will officially recognize the Jerusalem neighborhoods that Israel built after 1967 on former Jordanian territory. As far as the Palestinians are concerned, these neighborhoods are illegal settlements just like any other in the West Bank and Gaza Strip. It will be hard for the Palestinians to make the distinction between the Jerusalem neighborhoods and other settlements, but, realistically, this is what they must do. About half of the residents of the former Jordanian area are Israeli Jews, and their inclusion in the Palestinian city, even if they were to remain Israeli citizens, would give the eternal capital of Palestine a binational character. The same is true in Israel's case. As hard as it will be for Israel to retract its unambiguous and determined statements about Jerusalem in its 1967 borders being the united Israeli capital forever, the fact that a third of the city's residents are Palestinian Arabs makes such rhetoric hollow.

In short, both sides reached the conclusion that it is people, more than anything else, that determine the identity of the land on which they live. In this sense, the foundation laid at Camp David will constitute a reference framework for all future agreements, since its base is solid. When guns are blasting and people dying it is hard to see how the two sides can begin to negotiate again, in order to complete what they began at Camp David. The Camp David conference closed a period in which Jerusalem was discussed with the use of slogans. The national agenda of Israel and the Arabs now includes the understanding that in Jerusalem mutual concessions will have to be made. Without a resolution of the Jerusalem question and the inclusion of an arrangement for Jerusalem in the general Israeli–Palestinian agreement, there can be no peace.

Many books have been written about the conflict in Jerusalem and some of their authors believe that the antagonism prevailing in the city has long since become a law of nature. In contrast with the prevailing view, this book's subject is how the Israelis and Palestinians in Jerusalem have moved closer to each other despite their differences. It chronicles the attempts that have been made since 1977 to resolve the conflict and find a solution that will enable the communities to live together. Even though each side to these negotiations has declared that Jerusalem cannot be bargained for or be the subject of compromise, agreements have been made and understandings have been reached. The search for a political arrangement acceptable to all parties to the conflict is a new experience, coming after long years of fanning the flames of hostility in the city. This book follows these attempts at resolution and notes what differences remain.

It is not my intention to write a history of Jerusalem since June 1967 or to present the reader with the entire spectrum of solutions that have been proposed over the years. I begin where the theoretical proposals turn into political facts laid face up on the negotiating table, or where both sides have adopted them. This book differs from others on the same subject in two ways. First, it integrates the political status of the city on the negotiating table with the urban reality that influences the negotiations; second, it examines both parties to the conflict in Jerusalem.

I have tried to provide the reader with the most comprehensive and reliable information I could gather on what has been done in East Jerusalem. There still is no reliable information resource for this; my hope is that the data contained here is sufficiently reliable for my purposes. I will happily correct in the future what is distorted or missing.

The reader enters the gates of Jerusalem through my first chapter, which presents the geographical and urban reality and its historical background. The remaining chapters address the political reality that has taken shape on the negotiating table. Chapter 2 describes how the Jerusalem question was handled during the peace negotiations between Israel and Egypt from 1977 to 1979. Chapter 3 analyzes the negotiations between Israel and the Palestinians from the beginning of the 1980s to the Declaration of Principles signed by Israel and the PLO in September 1993. Chapter 4 discusses the status of the Arab League and the Organization of the Islamic Conference, as well as the status of Jordan in the negotiations on Jerusalem and on the Islamic holy sites in the city.

The final chapters return to the urban reality and analyze the patterns of competition and the *de facto* arrangements that Israel and the Palestinians have reached in Jerusalem since September 1993. Chapter 5 analyzes the Palestinians' moves in Jerusalem and the tension between the local and national institutions. Chapter 6 examines whether the uniqueness of East Jerusalem also finds expression in its politics by analyzing the political profile of East Jerusalem's inhabitants and of their representatives in the Palestinian Authority's Legislative Council.

Chapter 7 addresses Israeli policy and actions, first under the Labor and then under the Likud administrations. The concluding chapter follows the permanent status negotiations, including the unofficial understandings that were reached between Yossi Beilin and Abu-Mazin. Whatever the final shape of the permanent settlement, it will largely be molded to fit the prevailing reality in Jerusalem. This reality, I believe, will impose itself on the negotiators, including those who unsuccessfully try fundamentally to change it.

TRANSLITERATION AND TERMINOLOGY

Arabic and Hebrew terms and place names have generally been transliterated according to the accepted rules in works of general scholarship. Exceptions have been made, however, when transliteration according to these rules might confuse the reader or where there is a familiar English spelling. I have spelled proper names according to the preferences of the person bearing them. This seems only fair, despite the inconsistencies it produces (for example, Yitzhak Rabin, but Itzchak Mordechay). Finally, all apostrophes before Arab and Hebrew names have been omitted as have most occurrences of al- before well-known names.

I have tried to be even-handed in my terminology as well, even though East Jerusalem terminology is inevitably laden with political implications. The Arabs tend to emphasize the fact that East Jerusalem is populated largely by Arabic-speaking Palestinians. Their official documents largely call the area "Arab Jerusalem" in English, in order to distinguish it from the other part of Jerusalem where Hebrew rules. Israelis habitually call the Arab-inhabited part of Jerusalem "East Jerusalem," since it lies on the east side of a single large entity, Jerusalem. So, with regard to the city's name, I have adopted three rules: 1. In texts translated from Arabic the city's name will remain as it was in the Arab source. "Sublime Jerusalem" is my translation of the Arabic *"Al-Quds al-Sharif,"* which occurs frequently in Palestinian texts. This literal translation enables it to be distinguished from *"al-Madina al-Muqadasah"* – the Holy City – which also appears in Palestinian texts. 2. I have generally used the term "East Jerusalem" for the Arab part of Jerusalem, because this is the familiar term in English. In fact, even Arafat uses "East" rather than "Arab" in his speeches. I have, however, preferred to use the term "Jewish Jerusalem" instead of the misleading "West Jerusalem," since a number of the Jewish neighborhoods built since 1967 are not actually west of East Jerusalem. 3. The holy site where the Dome of the Rock and the Al-Aqsa Mosque are located is called *Har Ha-Bayit* in Hebrew (whence the common English term, "the Temple Mount"), and *al-Haram al-Sharif* in Arabic. Each of these names is historically charged and significant in the present. I have therefore used both terms, each where the context seemed to require it.

MAPS

This first map shows the changes in Jerusalem's, municipal boundaries made by Jordan and Israel. In the period 1949–67 each state ruled its own share of the divided city and implemented boundary changes in that part. In 1967 Israel occupied Jordanian Jerusalem, and decided unilaterally to enlarge the city's municipal boundaries. The most far-reaching and dramatic change was made on 28 June 1967, when Israel decided to increase the former 6 sq. km of the Jordanian city by some 70 sq. km of West Bank territory and annex the whole to the Israeli city. By this act Israel laid down the geographical foundation of metropolitan Jerusalem. The following maps show the demographic components of the metropolitan area and its undesigned results.

In the thirty years between the annexation and 1997 the population of Jerusalem grew by 126%. During this period the Jewish and Arab populations increased by 113% and 164% respectively. The more rapid increase of the Arab population was due both to natural increase (a higher birth rate among the Arabs) and migration movements (lower Arab migration from the city and many new arrivals). The Arab growth was also driven by the large job market open to Arab blue-collar workers due to the massive building of Jewish neighbourhoods. Since 1988, there has been a sharp rise in the negative Jewish migration balance of Jerusalem *vis-à-vis* its environs. Parallel to this, more Arabs returned from the suburbs outside the municipal boundaries to live in the city under Israeli jurisdiction.

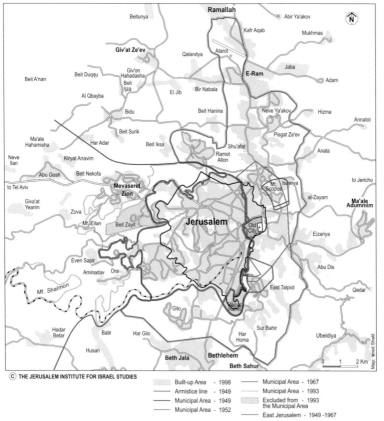

Beitunya · **Ramallah** · Abir Ya'akov
Kafr Aqab · Mukhmas

Giv'at Ze'ev · Qalandya · Atarot
Jaba
Beit A'nan · Beit Duqqu · Giv'on Hahadasha · **E-Ram** · Adam
Beit Iiza · El Jib · Bir Nabala
Al Qbayba · Bidu · Beit Hanina · Hizma
Neve Ya'akov · Annatot
Beit Surik · Pisgat Ze'ev
Ma'ale Hahamisha · Har Adar · Beit Iksa · Shu'afat · Anata
Neve Ilan · Kiryat Anavim · Ramot Allon
Abu Gosh · Beit Nekofa · Mt. Scopus · Isawiya · to Jericho
to Tel Aviv · **Mevaseret Zion** · al-Zayam · **Ma'ale Adummim**
Giv'at Yearim · Zova · **Jerusalem** · Old City · Eizariya
Mt. Eitan · Beit Zayit
Even Sapir · Abu Dis
Aminadav · Ora · East Talpiot · Qedar
Mt. Shalmon
Gilo · Sur Bahir · Ubeidiya
Hadar Betar · Batir · Har Gilo · Har Homa
Husan · **Beth Jala** · **Bethlehem** · **Beth Sahur**

Map: Vered Shatil

© THE JERUSALEM INSTITUTE FOR ISRAEL STUDIES

Built-up Area - 1998   Municipal Area - 1967
Armistice line - 1949   Municipal Area - 1993
Municipal Area - 1949   Excluded from - 1993 the Municipal Area
Municipal Area - 1952   East Jerusalem - 1949 -1967

0   1   2 Km

1. Changes in the Municipal Area

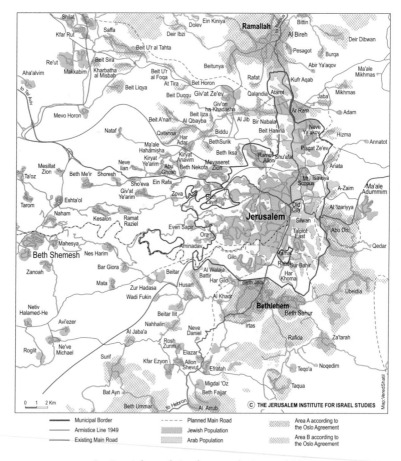

2. Jewish and Arab populations, 1997

Municipal Border   Planned Main Road   Area A according to the Oslo Agreement

Armistice Line 1949   Jewish Population   Area B according to the Oslo Agreement

Existing Main Road   Arab Population

© THE JERUSALEM INSTITUTE FOR ISRAEL STUDIES

Map: Vered/Shalit

0 1 2 Km

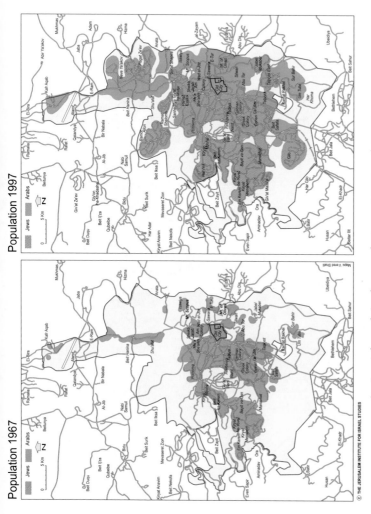

3. Jewish and Arab populations, 1967 and 1997

© THE JERUSALEM INSTITUTE FOR ISRAEL STUDIES

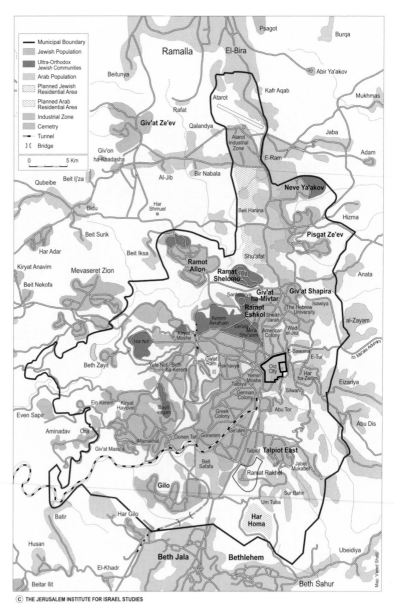

4. Distribution of Jewish and Arab population, 1997

1

THE ARENA

A FRONTIER CITY

Frontier cities and multicultural cities

According to the common wisdom in Israel, on June 4, 1967, the
eve of the Six Day War, the country had boundaries; during that
war the state stood on its frontiers and expanded them. It settled
Jerusalem, the "desolate city," and improved the lot of its Arab
inhabitants by bringing them progress and prosperity.

The term "frontier" is characteristically distinct from the term
"boundary." "Frontier" suggests open spaces available for settlement and conquest. "Frontierity" motivates people and states to
expand their borders. A state's frontiers lie not only at its geographical and physical limits; there is also, for example, a frontier
of outer space and a frontier of knowledge. A frontier is thus any
place where the state seeks to expand or extend itself, where it
seeks to move a geographical or intellectual boundary. From this
perspective, the movement is unidirectional – forward in the
name of enlightenment, civilization, and progress. At some frontiers, the state is a more salient presence than it is on its home
ground because it is exerting a national will to expand. At other
frontiers, the state's control is looser than it is in the center, since
the expansion is being accomplished by individuals or by groups
acting on their own initiative. In both cases, however, the frontier
region lacks a local character and is rather an extension and operational instrument of national policy. In contrast, the term
"border" designates something static, a place where one must halt.
A border is inward directed and marks the existing situation and
the limit of current possibilities. The frontier faces outwards, and
marks the place at which a stationary, limiting border can be

moved. A frontier is inclusive and implies an open future, while a border is exclusive, a buffer between foreigners and ourselves (Barth, 1969; Gal-Nur, 1995; Hasson, 1996; Kerwin, 1997; Kimmerling, 1977; Kotek 1997b).

According to more recent thinking, however, there is little difference between a frontier and a boundary. The frontier is now thought to mark confrontation between conceptions or communities, not finality or unidirectional movement. In contrast with the classical view, the new conception no longer assumes a confrontation between the enlightened and the uncultured, the ignorant, or the primitive, but rather a confrontation between two cultures. A boundary, according to this new view, marks the point to which each collective reaches, while the frontier directs its gaze to the other side of the boundary, to encounter and confrontation with an opposing entity or culture. Each side has an empiric history and a mythic past; each has its own religion and values, norms and aspirations. Each group defines how it distinguishes itself from others, and each group continually revises or updates its worldview in the light of political and historical circumstances. The confrontation on the frontier does not take place on a broad front, but rather is concentrated in a specific territory. Each of the contending groups seeks to control or defend its territory against being physically taken over by the "other," the "invader." In the conflict over territory, each group develops holy sites of its own and turns certain sites into symbols of struggle and defense, or enhances the value of the territory and defines it as a strategic asset. Territory thus has symbolic value, in the name of which the group can mobilize its members in defense of their territory against the "other" that threatens it. The iconographic characteristics of a territory carry great weight in a frontier area. The community creates a set of sacred symbols that link its members to each other and motivate them to defend and hold fast to their homeland. This is a static situation that is opposed to the activity that takes place in "regular" areas, which are characterized by mobility and cyclicity. In "regular" areas there is a constant flow of ideas, people, commerce, capital, and knowledge, and the connection with the territory is secondary. According to this view, in East Jerusalem there is a confrontation between two cultures and communities that are competing for a single space, yet also divide it between them. Jerusalem, as will be shown, has several boundary lines that separate the Arab east from the Jewish west. The two sparring entities in the city have developed mutual relations of exchange alongside confrontation and animosity (Hasson, 1977a; Hasson, 1996; Hasson, 1998; Kimmerling, 1989; Kotek, 1997a; Stotkin, 1996).

The term "frontier" also designates the relations between those in the rear and those who bear the burden of the confrontation. The term "frontier city" denotes not only the confrontation between Arab and Jewish Jerusalem, but also the connection that each of them has to its center. The place held by Jewish Jerusalem in the State of Israel, and the place held by East Jerusalem in Palestinian consciousness and action, reflects the distinction between the frontier and the center. In order to close the distance between frontier and center, the national leadership will turn the frontier area, and the confrontation with the other side, into unifying axes around which the nation and the state are constructed, thus achieving "national unity." Despite vows of loyalty and declarations about the mobilization of the entire center behind the people of the frontier, the lines of contact and friction – the borderlines – lie in the frontier area not in the interior. The lines of confrontation distinguish the heartland from the frontier and passionate declarations cannot bridge that gap.

The concept of the frontier designates a deeper fissure than that of a multicultural and multi-ethnic city. Today, all modern cities in the Western world, such as Paris, New York, and London, are multinational because of the large-scale immigration of members of other national groups and speakers of other languages. Multicultural cities are composed of different linguistic–cultural minorities and of one dominant culture, whereas a frontier city is a city in which there is an ethnic–national confrontation between two communities. Unlike a multicultural city, in which the minority feels disadvantaged because of its linguistic–cultural difference, in a frontier city the minority group does not see itself as inferior. First of all, this distinction derives from the fact that in a multicultural city the minorities view themselves as part of a common system that they share with the majority. Their dispute with the majority is about the legitimacy of their minority status, about the regime's policy towards them, and about the just division of resources. The members of the minority do not seek to break away from the system, but rather to integrate into it as a legitimate entity with equal rights. In a frontier city, by contrast, the minority seeks to delegitimize the rule of the majority, and to disengage itself in one way or another from that rule. Each of the communities in a frontier city sees itself to be of equal, if not higher, status than the other groups. Therefore, in a frontier city the principal question preoccupying the rivals is who the ruler is and who has the right to define the government's agenda. For the minority, the majority's policies, aimed at stability and continuity, are simply a means for perpetuating the majority's pre-eminence. In many cases, the government of the majority is incapable of dividing assets equitably, thus reinforcing the minority's demand for separation. Furthermore, in a frontier city, the demographic minority's case against the majority is not local, but rather represents one facet of the national confrontation. The national–ethnic gap prevails over the municipal boundaries defined by urban management, borders, the supply of services, demographics and territory. It takes on national significance, and becomes part of the identities of each side. In contrast, the multicultural city does not embody a confrontation between national groups – at most it reflects a social problem that characterizes the country itself. The multicultural city is heterogeneous and there can be different coalitions between the ethnic groups that comprise it. These coalitions vary according to the issue at hand. In a frontier city, however, the polarization is deep and dichotomous, and the fissures that characterize it largely coincide with national fissures (Bollens, 1998a; Kotek, 1997b; Roman, 1997a). Some of these sources call the frontier city the "polarized city" but this is only a difference in terminology; all the characteristics of a polarized city are shared by the frontier city.

Jerusalem, a frontier city, differs from Brussels, which is divided along linguistic–cultural lines. The tension there is between speakers of Flemish, who are a majority in the region though not in the city itself, and speakers of French, whose numbers have grown from 13.5 per cent of the city's population in 1846 to 66.5 per cent in 1968. In Brussels there is a mechanism for compromise, a superstructure that bridges the gaps and formally organizes the confrontation.

In Jerusalem, in contrast, there are no official compromise arrangements and there are no institutions whose goal it is to manage the confrontation; the result is that the level of tension between the two ethnic national groups is much higher. Public institutions function as two entirely separate systems in the two parts of the city. They have different days off, different currency laws, and different dominant languages. The minority group has a different legal–civil status than the majority group. In Brussels, bridging and compromise mechanisms have reduced disputes to questions such as whether French should be recognized as the primary language in the new suburbs and in additional neighborhoods outside the 16 suburbs in which it is already the official language. The segregation between Jews and Arabs in Jerusalem, which has its origins in the Mandatory period (when Britain ruled Palestine between 1917 and 1948) is more profound than the separation of the two national groups in Brussels, where both sides enjoy equal status and divide the positions of power. In Brussels there is a tendency for Flemings to adopt French as their language, but in Jerusalem there is no such flow from one identity to another. There are no intercommunal marriages, as there frequently are in Brussels, where there are also mixed residential neighborhoods. In Jerusalem there is almost complete ecological segregation between Jews and Arabs, and the two sectors maintain separate public and private institutions and professional organizations. There are no partnerships in the ownership of land nor between commercial and economic organizations, and day-to-day contact is largely utilitarian rather than social. The Jewish sector enjoys demographic, economic, and political supremacy and takes advantage of this to establish facts unilaterally in its favor. In Brussels the bilingual identity is grounded in law and is reflected in local symbols. It is consensual and explicit and has developed in to a political culture of compromise. In Jerusalem the situation is completely different. There are no institutions in which the minority enjoys equal status. The city is dominated by Jews, and Arabs are relegated to the margins. Critically, the French-speakers in Brussels are a majority in the city but a minority in the country, whereas the Palestinians in Jerusalem are a minority in both the city and the state (Demant, 1997; Gutmann & Klein, 1980; Roman, 1997a).

Another example of a divided multicultural city that is very different from Jerusalem is Montreal, Canada's largest municipality. Metropolitan Montreal is home to 44 per cent of the residents of the province of Quebec, where French is the language of law, administration, and business. The metropolitan area also contains most of the province's English speakers, whose language is that of the country's majority. On the municipal level, Montreal has a minority of English speakers surrounded by a French-speaking majority on the provincial level, who are themselves surrounded by English speakers on the national level. Unlike Brussels, where bilingualism was consolidated after the minority language was reinforced, Montreal has seen attrition in the status of both languages. In the one hundred years between 1871 and 1971, with the influx of immigrants whose native language was neither English nor French, the percentage of English speakers in Montreal declined from 38 per cent to 26 per cent. That was even though 10 per cent of the latter were immigrants whose native language is English. French has not fared much better. It has lost about four per cent of its 64 per cent of speakers, as well as its exclusive status. Furthermore, European French speakers consider Quebecois French inferior, while the English of the Canadian English-speaking majority is considered standard by other speakers of the language; its speakers benefit from the increasing dominance of English in the world and from its proximity to the United States. Montreal has thus gradually become bilingual and has established official and unofficial arrangements to institutionalize this. The result is that the points of dispute between the two linguistic-cultural groups have been reduced to questions of detail – for example, whether the legal primacy of French is compromised if children who are not native English speakers are allowed to enroll in English-language schools, or whether the government can dictate the use of French as an official language in the private sector (Gutmann & Klein, 1980). Again, Jerusalem is not a divided city but rather a frontier city, and despite unofficial and semi-official arrangements that have developed there, as will be seen below, it is more different than similar to Montreal.

There are also several important differences between Jerusalem and Johannesburg in South Africa, during and after Nelson Mandela's presidency. In Jerusalem the goal of the regime is to rule in the eastern part of the city and to perpetuate Jewish dominance. Since 1991, in contrast, the goal in Johannesburg, where 60 per cent of the population is black and 31 per cent white, has been to achieve conciliation, to erase the reality of apartheid and the geography of black poverty. As Bollens (Bollens, 1998a) has shown, a strategy of aggressive urban planning has developed in Jerusalem. In his opinion, professionals were not disinterested, and they supplied decision-makers with technical methods of annexing the Arab space to Israel and of dominating it. According to Bollens, when professional urban planners became the tools of the politicians they were left frustrated and helpless from a professional point of view, but at the same time they were proud of their contribution to a national goal with which they identified. In contrast to the dominance in Jerusalem of the ethnic criterion in planning and in allocation of resources, in Johannesburg there has been an egalitarian planning approach. The city was replanned on that basis with the blacks empowered, their institutions upgraded, and their living conditions considerably improved (Bollens, 1998a).

On the other hand, Jerusalem as a frontier city is not physically divided, and its two populations are not at war. It is thus distinct from Belfast of 1968–98, from Beirut during the civil war of 1975–91, and from Nicosia since 1974. Belfast is the principal city in Northern Ireland, containing 23.6 per cent of the inhabitants of the province, which is part of the United Kingdom. The Irish Catholics, a quarter of the city's population, have wanted to become part of the Republic of Ireland, whereas the Protestant majority insists on preserving the ties with London. This has led to a confrontation between Protestants and Catholics on a long series of questions principally involving political loyalty, national identity, the division of resources, and equitable political representation. During the period of conflict Belfast was polarized and divided horizontally and vertically; it was impossible to remain neutral. There was a sharp ecological and institutional separation between Protestants and Catholics in their areas of residence, employment, and in the educational system. Armed militias and underground forces took responsibility for defense and public order, preventing effective action by the municipality. Gutmann and Klein concluded in their study of Belfast that, when faced with national–ethnic confrontation, a city cannot be disassociated from its surroundings. Implicitly referring to Jerusalem Mayor, Teddy Kollek, Gutmann and Klein stated that wise municipal management can reduce tensions, if only temporarily, but that the larger conflict will, in the end, impinge on the city and sweep it into the struggle. Even if the rule of the Jewish majority in

Jerusalem was established through democratic procedures and the majority did not overstep itself in using its power, and even if we assume that in the future the structural discrimination against the Arab minority in Jerusalem is rectified and the Jewish majority supplies effective services to the Arab minority and treats it fairly, the conflict in Jerusalem will not be resolved. At most, there will be a temporary respite. There will be no peace unless the conflict is dealt with on the level of politics and symbols. In contradiction of the Israeli slogans to the effect that Jerusalem has, since 1967, maintained exemplary Jewish–Arab coexistence under Israeli rule, Jerusalem cannot be an island of peace in a sea of war between Israel and the Arabs (Gutmann & Klein, 1980). The peace accord in Northern Ireland, signed in 1998, opens new opportunities for comparative study of Belfast and Jerusalem, especially if the Northern Ireland pact is realized with fewer difficulties than the Oslo accords between Israel and the PLO.

The Turkish invasion of Cyprus in 1974 turned Nicosia into the heart of the conflict between Greece and Turkey, a conflict that has its roots in the Greek struggle for independence from the Ottoman Empire in the 1820s. Cyprus is not a case of a politically divided nation, as Korea is and as were Germany and Vietnam. Instead, it suffers from a conflict between two national, ethnic, and religious communities that involves their connection to their mother countries, their historical memory and culture, and to the control of financial systems, territory, and resources. Nicosia was first divided by the British military demarcation line of 1963–64; the division was perpetuated by the links that Turkey established in the 1960s with its loyalists in Cyprus, and by the provision of Turkish services such as drivers' licenses, building licenses, commercial licenses, and postal facilities, as preparation for the possible failure of the Greek-dominated federation. Afterwards, a dual regime was created and, with the Turkish invasion, Nicosia was divided physically into two parts. Major population movements created large areas of demographic homogeneity in Cyprus, and in Nicosia specifically. The two parts of the city are divided by impassable border check posts and there is animosity between the two national leaderships. Not only are the languages, the religious and social institutions, and the regimes different in the two parts of the city, so is collective memory and public space. Fostering the expectation that the northern part of the island will be liberated from the Turks, the public space in the south preserves a historical memory of the Turkish presence by retaining the names of parks, houses, and streets. In the north, in contrast, there has been a Turkification and Islamization of the region, from which Greek and Christian markings have been removed. Despite this, Nicosia is not a completed divided city. There is cooperation between the two municipalities in certain areas. The supply of electricity to the north depends on the Greek-ruled south, the supply of water to the south on the Turkish north. There are common sewage, drainage, and sanitation systems; and there is coordination in the planning of urban space and in certain health services (Kliot & Mansfield, 1997). The case of Nicosia leads to the conclusion that a broad and profound conflict that divides a city into two parts, even physically, does not prevent cooperation in defined professional fields. The inverse is also true – professional cooperation in several areas connected to the joint management of the metropolitan area does not bridge the fissures of the physically divided city.

Beirut shows that under certain circumstances a multicultural and heterogeneous city can deteriorate to become a physically divided city. In the 1960s, Beirut enjoyed economic prosperity and a cultural flowering. It became a center for many intellectuals and a focal point for Arab media, literature, and culture. The flourishing economy broke down ethnic divisions; economic liberalism, as well as a lack of restriction on banking activities and on political and cultural expression, made Beirut into the Paris and Geneva of the Middle East. While residential patterns were not based exclusively on ethnicity, in many neighborhoods a single ethnic group had a sizeable majority. Yet in no few neighborhoods there were pockets of different ethnic or religious groups; these became death traps for outsiders during the civil war. Until the civil war, Beirut reflected the openness of the entire country and Lebanon's multicultural character. It demonstrated how members of different religious groups could live in a common political framework that was culturally progressive and Western in character. Integration in Beirut was at its strongest in the city center and became attenuated towards the periphery. The newer neighborhoods on the city's expanding edge, inhabited mostly by recently arrived immigrants to the city, were the most segregated. Paradoxically, Beirut's prosperity, which was coterminous with Lebanon's prosperity, upset the fragile existence of the city and the state.

Beirut's flowering attracted hundreds of thousands of immigrants, including Sunni Muslims from Syria, Maronite Christians
from the villages of Mount Lebanon seeking employment and
higher incomes, and Shi'ites from the south who were fleeing
from the conflict between Israel and the Palestinians. Of course,
there were also numerous Palestinian refugees who had fled to the
Lebanese coastal cities and to Beirut in the wake of the war of
1948.

In a census conducted in 1932, two-thirds of Beirut's inhabitants were Christians, but Christians were but a narrow majority in
the country as a whole. The results of this census were used to
establish an ethnic key dividing up the country's positions of
political power and administration. There had clearly been demographic changes in the country since the 1932 census and these
were especially evident in Beirut, where more and more elements
sought to undermine the existing order. The Muslim minority
and marginal groups, who constituted a demographic majority,
though not officially recognized as such, united in a bloc that
sought to reallocate the positions of power and the division of
resources in the country. They applied most of their pressure on
the political, economic, cultural, and symbolic fronts, all of which
were concentrated in Beirut. When fighting broke out in Beirut it
spread from the refugee camps and the poverty belt at the periphery to the urban center. The destructive force was so powerful that
it drew in all the country's ethnic groups, and the war turned into
a battle between sub-groups within each of the communities.
Terrorism and the geography of fear became a way of life (Hanf,
1993: 66, 97, 103–6, 160–8, 194–202, 223, 242–3, 328, 339–47,
357). Beirut showed that multiculturalism and integration cannot
be maintained when separated from their demographic and political base. An arrangement that establishes multiculturalism must
be updated and must answer to the dictates of reality, and the city
must adapt to the political context it finds itself in, lest it pay a
heavy price.

Soft, flexible and permeable borders

Jerusalem is the largest city in the State of Israel. It has the largest
population, the most Jews and the most non-Jews of all Israeli
cities. In 1967, in the wake of the Six Day War, Israel annexed East

Jerusalem and extended the municipal borders (Map 1). The annexed territory included not only what had been the Jordanian sector of the city, which covered 6.5 square kilometers, but also an additional 64.4 square kilometers of West Bank villages and some land within the boundaries of Bethlehem and Beit Jala. With the annexations, the Israeli government turned two peripheral cities – the Jordanian and the Israeli, which itself covered 38.1 square kilometers – into the country's largest city with an area of 108.5 square kilometers. Until then, both cities had been at the end of narrow corridors of territory. The Jordanian city had been a peripheral city, far from the capital in Amman and under its sway. The Israeli capital was located at the end of the Jerusalem corridor, a narrow strip of land that linked it to the coastal plain and the rest of the country. As will be seen below, the change in the area and status of Jerusalem had far-reaching consequences. In 1993 the city's territory was enlarged still more to 123 square kilometers (Benvenisti, 1996: 57; Choshen, 1998).

The expansion of Jerusalem's geographical and municipal borders was accompanied by the growth of its population. In June 1967, following the annexation, Israel conducted a census in East Jerusalem. All its inhabitants and their children, amounting to some 66,000 people, received the status of permanent residents. Only 2,700 to 5,000 East Jerusalem Arabs assumed Israeli citizenship and bear Israeli passports (*Ha'aretz*, 17 May 1996, 28 May 1996). Most East Jerusalem Arabs rejected the offer of Israeli citizenship, preferring to retain Jordanian citizenship. As residents of Jerusalem they received the right to hold Israeli identity cards and to participate in municipal elections. But they cannot bear Israeli passports or participate in Israel's general elections for the Knesset and prime minister. In 1999 the city's population, according to the Jerusalem Institute of Israel Studies, was 645,700, comprising 10.5 per cent of the Israeli total. There were 437,400 Jews (67.7 per cent) and 208,300 non-Jews (32.3 per cent). Table 1.1 presents data on the city's population.

The Jews of Jerusalem constitute 9.1 per cent of the Jewish population of Israel. This is a ratio similar to that of the inhabitants of East Jerusalem to the population of the West Bank and Gaza Strip, 8.6 per cent. For the most part, the non-Jewish population of Jerusalem is made up of people who are Muslim in religion and Palestinian Arab in nationality and culture. In 1997 the

Table 1.1.   JERUSALEM'S POPULATION

	Data of the Jerusalem Institute of Israel Studies, 1997	Israeli Population and Residential Census, 1995	Data of the Central Bureau of Statistics of the Palestinian Authority, 1997
Jews (000s)	421.2	417.1 (426.2★)	no data
Arabs (000s)	180.9	182.7 (187.49★)	210.0
Proportion (%)	70:30	68:32 (69:31★)	65:35★★
			58:42†

Notes

★ In parentheses: corrected figures from 1996 as a result of overcounting
★★ According to the number of Jews given by the Jerusalem Institute
† According to the number of Jews given by the Israel Central Bureau of Statistics

Sources: *Al-Quds*, 26 Feb. 1998, 27 Feb. 1998; Choshen & Shahar, 1998: 30; Chosen, 1998; State of Israel, Office of the Prime Minister, the Central Bureau of Statistics, 1998. Palestinian Central Bureau of Statistics.

city's Muslim inhabitants numbered 164,300, or 90.8 per cent of the non-Jewish population. There were 16,500 Christians, who constituted 9.1 per cent of the non-Jewish population of the city (Choshen, 1998; Choshen & Shachar, 1998: 30). The demographic data show that in the capital of the State of Israel there is a large population, a third of the city's inhabitants, who reject Israeli citizenship. This constitutes the largest geographical concentration of the Arab minority in the entire country.

The central principle that guided the authors of the 1967 annexation was to add as much territory to the city as possible, including strategic high points in the region, while at the same time holding the additional Arab population at a minimum. Their assumption was that the ethnic–national composition would determine whether the annexation would endure or become merely a brief episode in history. The ratio of Jews to Arabs was 74.2 to 25.8 per cent at the time that the annexation boundaries were drawn. The boundaries were drawn in accordance with the above principles, creating a number of interesting distortions. Settlements such as Al-Azaria and most of Abu-Dis in the east and Hizma and Al-Za'im in the north, only five kilometers from Jerusalem's city center, remained outside the municipal territory.

Until the Palestinian Authority entered them at the end of 1995, Abu-Dis and Al-Azaria were under the Israeli civil administration of Bethlehem, ten kilometers away, while Hizma and Al-Za'im were under the civil administration district of Ramallah, some 15 kilometers away (Benvenisti, 1996: 47–8, 57–60; Cheshin, 1992: 179).

The Israeli establishment has mobilized itself, since the annexation, to preserve the Jewish demographic advantage. A Jewish majority of 74.2 per cent was almost identical to the situation that prevailed in Jerusalem when the State of Israel was established. At this time, after the first stage of the war of 1948, the percentage of Jews rose from 66.3 to 74 per cent (Cheshin, 1992). After the annexation of 1967 the Israeli authorities hoped to enlarge the percentage of Jews in the city to 80 or even 90 per cent by providing incentives for them to move to Jerusalem, and by encouraging a construction boom. But the hoped-for influx of Jews did not materialize. Nor did the idea of settling large numbers of immigrants from the former Soviet Union in Jerusalem in the early 1990s produce results. As early as 1973 the Israeli authorities had realized that they would not be able to achieve their objective of a significant change in the demographic balance in Jerusalem. In consequence, the government accepted the recommendation of an inter-ministerial committee that the goal should be to preserve a ratio of 74.5 per cent Jews to 25.5 per cent Arabs (State of Israel, 1973: 12). This became the primary justification for the Jewish building boom on the east side of the city.

Israel's policy meant that the rate of growth of the city's Jewish population had to be brought in line with the rate of increase of the Arab population, and this demographic imperative took precedence over all other considerations. In this respect it can be said that Israel did not have the success it had hoped for. In the 31 years since the annexation, the demographic balance has changed for the worse for the Jews, whose numbers had declined to 70 per cent of the city's population by 1997, perhaps even less. Moreover, according to estimates of the Israeli authorities, there are some 10,000 to 30,000 Arabs living in East Jerusalem who remain uncounted in the official figures. This means that the real balance is even worse for Israel. Two factors have influenced this. The first is the reversal, since 1988, in the Jewish immigration balance to Jerusalem. In the five years from 1973 to 1978 and in the period from 1979 to 1987, the number of Jews coming to Jerusalem was larger, on average, than the number leaving it by some 5,600. But in the decade that followed, 1988–1997, a total of 35,341 more Jews moved out of the city than moved in – some 6,000 a year. The second factor is the growth of the Palestinian Arab population in Jerusalem. From 1967 to 1995 the Jewish population grew by 110.9 per cent and the Arab by 154.2 per cent (Choshen and Shachar, 1997: 34–5). The demographic data has severe implications for Israel: it represents the failure of a long-standing policy in which the country had invested a great deal of effort, and it cast doubt on the state's claim to sovereignty in East Jerusalem. For this reason the municipality and government ministries have begun to take steps to reduce the number of Arab residents in East Jerusalem (see below).

The major factor in the growth of Jerusalem's Jewish population has been the establishment of new neighborhoods in the eastern part of the city, while the Arab population has grown as a result of natural increase and immigration. Paradoxically, the building boom and the annexation have abetted the growth of the Arab population of East Jerusalem. These two factors have turned East Jerusalem into a metropolitan center, and inhabitants of the surrounding area have been drawn to it as settlers or day laborers in a search for employment. According to figures from the mid-1980s, when employment of Arabs was at its height, the Bethlehem and Ramallah districts supplied most of the day laborers to Jerusalem. Of the West Bank residents employed in the capital, 99 per cent came from the two districts (Cohen and Mazor, 1994). At the end of the 1980s some 20,000 people from the Jerusalem metropolitan area worked in the western part of the city, constituting some 15 per cent of the combined Jewish–Arab workforce. In 1994 an estimated 12,000 Arabs were employed by Jews in the Jewish part of the city, making up some 40 per cent of the Arab workforce in Jerusalem (Kimhi, 1997).

The annexation made the economy of East Jerusalem dependent on resources in the western part of the city, such as employment and income from labor, as well as tourism. In the period of Jordanian rule, too, the East Jerusalem economy was based on commerce, services, and tourism. But, unlike the West Bank, where a third of the workforce was employed in agriculture, in Jerusalem a third was employed in services. Also, commercial

Table 1.2.   BREAKDOWN OF THE WORKFORCE BY SECTOR (%)

	East Jerusalem, 1961	Arabs in East Jerusalem, 1994	Jews in West Jerusalem, 1994
Agriculture	1.0	—	—
Industry	19.0	16.6	11.0
Construction	7.4	15.6	3.7
Water and sanitation	1.4	—	—
Commerce	15.7	22.1	12.4
Transport	5.0	6.9	5.6
Public and private office workers, banks, services, and tourism	33.0	37.8	65.0
Other	17.5	1.0	2.3

Sources: Data from the Jerusalem Institute of Israel Studies, 1996; Kimhi, 1997; Dumper, 1997: 214–16.

employment was twice as high as in the West Bank as a whole (Dumper, 1997: 214–16). After 1967 the East Jerusalem economy continued to be based on these activities, but it became dependent on the Jewish sector for much of its business. Table 1.2 presents the breakdown of the workforce in Jerusalem, by sector.

The workforce in East Jerusalem is young – some 79 per cent of the workers are between the ages of 18 and 44 (Cohen & Mazor, 1994). In the age cohorts of 25–34 and 45–54 employment is higher in the Palestinian district of Jerusalem (an administrative unit established by the Palestinian administration that includes East Jerusalem and outlying areas) than in other Palestinian regions (Awartani, 1998). Unlike these other districts, the Jerusalem district has fewer employees without formal education (0.5 per cent uneducated, as opposed to 4.3 per cent in the rest of the country) and more with an elementary-level education (31.9 per cent as opposed to 26.2 per cent) (Awartani, 1998).

According to the 1995 data, some 90 per cent of the employed in Jerusalem are wage earners, both among Jews and Arabs. But the Jewish rate of participation in the workforce is higher than that of the Arabs – 53.2 per cent of Jews as opposed to a range of 35.3 per cent to 36.1 per cent among Arabs. An even larger gap between Jews and Arabs is evident in the unemployment rate: 5.3 per cent of Jews as opposed to a rate ranging from 10.9 per cent to 11.1 per cent for Arabs. This gap is largely due to the fact that the supply of workplaces for Arabs in Jerusalem is smaller than that for Jews, and because the rate of participation of Arab women is much smaller than that of Jewish women (Friedman, 1998). According to Samir Hazboun, the 1995 unemployment rate in the Palestinian district of Jerusalem was 15 per cent, and the rate of participation in the workforce in this district was 37 per cent (Hazboun, 1998).

Employment for Arabs in Jerusalem's Jewish sector is in blue-collar fields such as construction, automobile repair, sanitation, and cleaning. In these fields, youth is an advantage, and an academic education is not required. The incomes of workers in the Jewish sector are higher than those of persons who are employed in East Jerusalem and they are high in comparison to what they were in the past. But the Arabs nevertheless earn less, and have lower status, than do Jews in the same fields. In part this is because the Jews are generally on a higher professional and management level than they are. The informal relations between worker and employee in the west are also very much affected by ethnic affiliation and by the inferior political status of the Palestinians (Benvenisti, 1996: 153–4).

The fact that Jerusalem is an open city has an effect on the incomes of the Arabs who live there. Tourists can move freely from one side of the city to the other, creating mutual, though asymmetric, dependence between Jewish and Arab service providers in this field. The strong Israeli sector needs Arab manual laborers, and the Arabs are dependent on incomes from workplaces in Jewish Jerusalem. As a result, the average daily income in the Palestinian district of Jerusalem is higher than in the rest of the West Bank and Gaza Strip; in 1997 – NIS (New Israeli Shekels) 82.6 in Jerusalem as opposed to NIS 61 elsewhere (Awartani, 1998). Moreover, the health and welfare services that residents of East Jerusalem receive from Israel leave them with more take-home income than the Palestinians who are living under the Palestinian Authority. Even though inhabitants of East Jerusalem constitute only 8.6 per cent of the Palestinian population in the West Bank and Gaza Strip, the income per person in East Jerusalem is 55 per cent higher than in the West Bank and 70 per cent higher than in the Gaza Strip. It is, however, some 20 per cent lower than incomes in Israel (Jerusalem Institute of Israel Studies 1996).

Indices of local production also underline the economic dependence of Arab Jerusalem on Jewish Jerusalem. The gross local product in the Palestinian district of Jerusalem is more than 13 per cent higher than in other Palestinian districts. The principal sectors on which the gross local product is based in the Jerusalem district consist of services, 23 per cent in 1995; real estate and business services, 18.3 per cent; and manufacturing, 15 per cent (Hazboun, 1998; Jerusalem Institute of Israel Studies, 1996). The economic dependence of Jerusalem's Arabs on the income that they receive from Jewish Jerusalem is particularly evident in the tourism sector. By the number of direct employers such as hotels, tour guides, travel agencies, and so on, and indirect employers such as stores and vendors, this is the largest employment sector in East Jerusalem. But tourism in East Jerusalem also depends on west Jerusalem. The number of hotel rooms in East Jerusalem has not grown since 1967 from 2,061, while in the Jewish sector the number of rooms increased from 1,193 in 1967 to 6,500 in 1997. During this period the number of travel agencies in East Jerusalem declined from 46 to 36, while in Jewish Jerusalem it rose from 35 to 436 (Hazboun, 1998). Palestinian dependence on tourism and on work in Jewish Jerusalem has direct implications for public security. Hamas, the Muslim fundamentalist movement, has not been, for the most part, active in Jerusalem in a direct way. The terrorist acts it has perpetrated in Jewish Jerusalem have been carried out not by Hamas activists from Jerusalem but rather by outside agents infiltrated into the city with the help of local confederates.

In addition to applying Israeli law and administration, Israel has conducted a large-scale construction operation surrounding the Arab city with the goals of establishing control over the mountain ridges that circle East Jerusalem and creating an irreversible demographic change in the former Jordanian area of Jerusalem. Israel has maintained that control of the territory requires control of the ridges, the blocking of Arab construction, bringing as many Jewish settlers as possible to the former Jordanian area, and the connection of the new Jewish neighborhoods to the heart of the Western city with a well-developed road system. These goals have indeed been realized. While Israel continues to strive to achieve a belt of contiguous built-up areas around East Jerusalem, it has succeeded in linking the new neighborhoods to the city center in terms of demographics and transportation. This makes up, to some extent, for the fact that they are residential areas rather than sources of employment, commerce, culture, and leisure activities. In 1995, 55 per cent of Jerusalem's inhabitants were living in the part of the city that was annexed in 1967. Of this number, 48.9 per cent (125,000) were Jews. Most of them lived in the new satellite neighborhoods that Israel had built around the Arab city. In other words, the city's population was equally divided between the former Jordanian territory and Israel's pre-1967 city, and in the former Jordanian areas there was roughly an equal number of Jews and Arabs. This silver lining was, however, beclouded. Israel still has not succeeded in breaking down the religious, national, and ethnic dividing lines between Jews and Arabs in the eastern city. The new Jewish neighborhoods are functionally part of west Jerusalem, while East Jerusalem is an Arab city. Jewish residents of the Arab neighborhoods enjoy the benefit of a road system that links them to west Jerusalem while circumventing the Arab-populated areas. Arab inhabitants use a separate road system to link them with their own compatriots. Geographically and topo-graphically (with its command of the heights), the Jewish pres-ence beyond the June 4, 1967 borders is massive, dominant and expressive of ownership. Israel has won Jerusalem with construc-tion, but victory is imperfect. The two populations on the eastern side of the city do not mix, nor is the minority assimilating into the majority.

The Israeli national government and the municipality have employed a variety of bureaucratic and administrative devices to stamp Jerusalem as a Jewish city. In March 1973 the Israel Lands Administration established a unit called Igum, whose goal in Jeru-salem was to crack the nut of Arab–Muslim residency in the Old City by purchasing properties that would become Jewish–Israeli public institutions and a counterweight to Muslim and Christian institutions in the Old City. Igum purchased property from pri-vate individuals via straw men who presented themselves as having a purely private interest in the property. In contrast with actions taken by the Likud governments of the 1980s and mid-1990s, Igum did not intend to purchase residential units in order to house individuals, since Labor governments and Mayor Teddy Kollek pursued a policy of separation between Jewish and Arab residential areas. Igum had only partial success in Jerusalem, in contrast with extensive purchases it made in the West Bank. When the Likud came into power in 1977, the unit's activity came almost to a halt. There was no need for a government agency to continue the purchases because the Likud governments allowed Jews to privately purchase land and houses in the Arab part of the city, and to live on property there owned by the state (*Kol Ha-Ir*, 29 Nov. 1996). However, organizations that established a goal of settling in the Palestinian neighborhoods of East Jerusalem copied Igum's methods. A committee headed by Ministry of Justice Director-General Haim Klugman, revealed that the private organizations that operated in East Jerusalem until the beginning of the 1990s cooperated with officials in the Ministry of Construction and Housing, the municipality, the Israel Lands Administration, the Office of the Trustee of Abandoned Properties, the Jewish National Fund, and the Ministry of Justice. Illegally, and without any oversight, these bodies had handed money and buildings over to the settlement organizations and granted them additional benefits as well (*Ha'aretz*, 26 May 1998, 29 May 1998).

The Israeli construction operation could not have been accomplished without large-scale land confiscation from the Arabs. A confiscation of lands and assets in May 1968 was intended to allow construction of the new Israeli neighborhoods of Ramot Eshkol and French Hill, and to expand the Jewish Quarter of the Old City. It is interesting that the initial Israeli expansion plan was similar to that conceived by the Zionist movement and the young State of Israel – linking west Jerusalem to Mount Scopus via French Hill and Ramot Eshkol, and providing a firm foundation for the Old City's Jewish Quarter. Even earlier, a few days after the Old City was occupied, Israel had demolished the Mughrabi neighborhood that adjoined the Western Wall. This action had a functional goal – creating a large open space for prayer and mass events in front of the Wall. Yet it was no less intended to express Israeli sovereignty and to get rid of what had been a physical obstruction to the Jewish sacred site, a humiliating reminder for many Jews of the restrictions imposed on worship there during the Mandatory period. Surrounding East Jerusalem on all sides with Jewish neighborhoods came later. It was not until 1970 that Israel expropriated the land on which the neighborhoods of Ramot, Gilo, and East Talpiot were built; Pisgat Ze'ev was founded on land expropriated by the Likud government a decade later, in 1980; the land on which the neighborhood of Har Homa is now being built was expropriated from Jews and Arabs in 1991. Between 1967 and 1994 a total of 24.8 square kilometers of land were expropriated, out of 70.5 square kilometers annexed by Israel in 1967. All the expropriated land is in East Jerusalem, and 80 per cent of it was taken from Arabs. The great majority of the Arabs refused to accept compensation, so as not to acknowledge the legitimacy of the Israeli move and give it the stamp of being final. These Arabs paid a high price for this, because the Israeli authorities thus did not have to pay large sums in compensation, making the expropriations much simpler (Ir Shalem, 1998). From 1967 to 1997 there was public construction of 38,350 housing units for Jews on more than 25 per cent of the area of East Jerusalem that was expropriated from Arabs (not including Har Homa); not a single apartment for Arabs was built on this land. Only 8,890 housing units were erected for Arabs during this period, amounting to only 12 per cent of total construction in the city. Only 600 of these were public housing units for Arabs, built at the beginning of the 1970s (Seideman, 17 Aug. 1997). The small scale of Arab construction was first and foremost a consequence of the political–demographic situation and the subdivision of ownership of Arab land, combined with the lack of a modern title registry and the absence of procedures for unification and reparceling. Also, the policy of allocating open public spaces, an accepted practice in construction plans in the Jewish sector, was alien to the Arab sector. At the beginning of the 1990s Arabs in Jerusalem faced a shortage of some 20,000 housing units. Since then there has been a widening gap in construction for the city's two populations. From a multi-year average of 12 per cent the proportion of construction for Palestinians has declined to 4.8 per cent (B'tselem, 1995: 32–6).

Moreover, zoning plans have been completed for only 39 per cent of the 45.5 square kilometers that were left under Arab ownership in East Jerusalem after the expropriations. Since 1967 there has been no general master plan for the Arab part of the city, and this makes it difficult for Palestinians to receive building permits. Until the 1980s *ad hoc* building permits were granted, and since then neighborhood zoning plans have been prepared. Yet there is no master plan integrating the East Jerusalem neighborhoods into the municipal system that answers the needs of the population above the neighborhood level. In addition, 40 per cent of the planned area is defined as open space, with less than 37 per cent designated for housing. In order to actualize residential construction, some of this land needs plans for unifying and reparceling, a complex process that takes a great deal of time because of the bureaucratic maze it must go through and the legal problems it presents. It is also problematic because of the special conditions in East Jerusalem, which has large areas in which there is no modern title registry and where not all landowners are registered. The residents are not willing to acquiesce in the process of unifying and reparceling the land, and many landowners submit objections to these plans. As a result only 7.3 per cent of East Jerusalem is, in practice, available for construction for Palestinians. This land lies largely in built-up areas, concentrated in a region defined geographically as "northeast." In terms of available housing units, it is generally permitted to build only one or two floors, so, according to the approved plans, it is possible to add fewer than 5,000 housing units (*Ha'aretz*, 4 Jan. 1996; Seideman, 17 Aug. 1997). Low construction density is an aspect of the building plans for East Jerusalem because of design considerations, a desire to preserve its village character, and political and demographic considerations – that is, in order to keep a lid on the Arab city's population capacity (*Ir Shalem*, 1998). The average housing density in East Jerusalem is 2.21 housing units per dunam (quarter acre), as opposed to 6.1 units in Jewish areas. It may be concluded that the residents of East Jerusalem are relatively rich in land, but poor in floor space (*Ha'aretz*, 15 Aug. 1995, 3 Sept. 1995, 17 Aug. 1997; *Ir Shalem*, 1998).

As noted, Israel imposed building restrictions on the Arabs when it declared available land reserves in East Jerusalem to be public or green areas. In most of the plans, some 40 per cent of East Jerusalem is designated as open spaces where construction is forbidden. There are legitimate planning reasons for leaving this land open, for example, the desire to preserve valleys as green space as well as the overall vista of the Old City basin, but without a doubt another reason is the desire to keep control of the demographic ratio in Jerusalem (Ir Shalem, 1998) and to ensure land reserves for construction for Jews. The green area in East Jerusalem covers some 35,000 dunams, and since 1967 the Jewish National Fund has planted 11 million trees there. In the national consciousness and according to Israeli myth, tree planting is a central Zionist ritual, since it points up a contrast with the desert and the wasteland that symbolizes the Arab area. In response to Israel's actions, Palestinians in the West Bank and Jerusalem environs began to plant olive trees, which for them symbolize their enduring roots in the land and in their villages (Cohen, 1993: 5–8, 112–31, 186–9).

The story of the building plan for the northern side of the city, near the Arab neighborhoods of Sho'afat and Beit Hanina, on the last large reserve of land that remained for the growing Arab population, demonstrates very well the Israeli bureaucracy's method. The municipality prepared the first plan in 1980, proposing the construction of 18,000 housing units, but the Ministry of the Interior rejected it, as well as a reduced plan for the construction of 11,500 housing units. In 1991, a plan for erecting only 7,500 units was approved, at a time when it was generally believed that there was a shortage of some 21,000 housing units in East Jerusalem. Even this minimal Arab construction program did not receive final approval. Likewise, preparations for drawing up a zoning plan for the Arab neighborhood of Jabel Mukaber began in the 1980s and the plan was approved in 1996. According to this plan, 70 per cent of neighborhood's land was designated as green areas, with only 20.5 per cent remaining for construction, most of which had already been used. The residents of Jabel Mukaber were allowed to build only at 25 per cent housing density level at a time when the adjacent Jewish neighborhood was allowed 140 per cent (*Ha'aretz*, 6 May 1999).

The use of building plans to block the growth of the Arab population was also demonstrated in the neighborhoods of Um Tuba and Sur Bahir. According to the initial plans, the housing density in these neighborhoods was to be 0.6 units per dunam, while the plans for the adjoining Jewish neighborhood, Har Homa, stipulated 3.5 units per dunam. The construction density assigned to the Arabs ranged from 10 to 50 per cent, while Jews were allotted 100 to 200 per cent. It was only in the wake of the international crisis caused by the construction of Har Homa that percentages in one part of Sur Bahir were raised to 70 per cent. To put it another way, the object of the plans for Jewish neighborhoods is to settle the maximum number of people on a given piece of land, while for the Arabs it was the precise opposite (Benvenisti, 1996: 132–3; B'tselem, 1995: 65–81).

The restrictions on the Arabs created a severe housing shortage in East Jerusalem. In 1995 the average housing density in East Jerusalem was twice as high as in west Jerusalem – 2.1 people per room in the Arab sector as opposed to 1.1 in the Jewish sector. In East Jerusalem, 27.8 per cent of the Arabs live in homes where there are three or more people per room, as opposed to only 2.4 per cent in Jewish Jerusalem (Benvenisti, 1996: 133; Choshen & Shachar, 1998: 130; *Ha'aretz*, 17 Aug. 1997). In 1994 only 95 building permits were granted to East Jerusalem Arabs, in 1995 only 86 permits, and in 1996 only 108 permits. All of these were for private construction, and in the absence of a zoning plan it took a very long time to process the requests. In comparison, the building commission of the Jerusalem district of the Palestinian Authority in 1996 issued more than 20 permits a week to residents of the suburbs of Jerusalem that are under its jurisdiction (*Ha'aretz*, 2 June 1997).

The demographic growth of the city's Arabs, the low construction density that the municipality has approved for them, and the skyrocketing cost of housing in Jerusalem have pressured members of the Arab middle class to leave the city or to build illegally. Many Palestinians have moved out of Jerusalem, converting the villages at the city's margins into suburbs. This process has been taking place since 1982. Since that year, most Arab construction in the Jerusalem area has been in its suburbs (between 1967 and 1982 there was large-scale unlicensed construction within the city) (Kimhi, 1997). There are varying estimates of the number of Palestinians who have moved from Jerusalem into the suburbs. According to Sabella, between 1967 and 1997, some 12,000 members of the middle class have moved to the West Bank or out of the country (Sabella, 1997b). Al-Nakhal estimates 32,000, while the conventional estimate in East Jerusalem is 80,000 (al-Nakhal, 1996: 7, 33; Friedland & Hecht, 1996: 175–92, ARIJ 275). The large-scale construction in the suburbs, which Israel sees as part of the West Bank, has been abetted by the weak enforcement of regulations in these areas, which were under the control of the Israel civil administration. Another factor attracting Palestinians from the city to the suburbs has been the low tax rates in the West Bank as compared to Jerusalem and the fact that the cost of land in the suburbs is about a tenth of that in the city. The demand for housing and land in the suburbs has altered the status of the established residents. They have enlarged their capital by selling their land for housing and have thus become middle class, more strongly linked than in the past to the urban business and service center. Thus, Jerusalem's surroundings have become more strongly linked to the urban focal point, despite the movement to the suburbs. The growth in the numbers of former East Jerusalem residents in the suburbs has brought about a historic change in that it has weakened the previous connection that the suburbs had with the Arab cities around Jerusalem. These links were established during the nineteenth and twentieth centuries because of large movements from these cities, especially Hebron, into Jerusalem and its suburbs. The migration from Hebron began in the 1920s, at the same time that East Jerusalem's social, economic, and political elite were leaving the Old City for the prestigious new neighborhoods around it, such as Sheikh Jarah. Another wave of migration from Hebron to Jerusalem occurred after the war of 1948, which led many members of the old elite to move to Jordan's East Bank, other Arab countries, and to the West. The newcomers from Hebron were people of the lower middle class and below. Their arrival, along with the arrival of a large number of war refugees, changed the city's character. The Hebronites brought with them a conservative Islamic bent that expressed itself in things such as separate Muslim social institutions and the use of customary law in resolving and mediating civil disputes. Over time, the Hebronites were absorbed into the city, and today they are a significant component of the merchant class. Their representatives have filled key positions in religious institutions and in the Jerusalem Chamber of Commerce (al-Nakhal, 1994; Zilberman, 1997).

Officially, there was no change in Jerusalem's demographic balance as a result of this movement to the suburbs because the new residents did not declare their change of address. They wished to continue to receive the benefits they were entitled to as residents of Israel, especially social security payments, health insurance, and free passage during closures. These were rights they would have lost if they had changed their status to that of residents of the West Bank (Cheshin, 1992: 182–4). Moreover, it is reasonable to assume that immigrants from the West Bank were filling the vacuum left by the emigrants. By one estimate, there were about 10,000 such immigrants (B'tselem, 1995: 31; Zilberman, 1997). According to unofficial estimates in Israel, some 20,000 people returned from the West Bank to live in East Jerusalem, making houses more crowded and providing an impetus for illegal construction. According to Palestinian estimates, some 30,000 people were involved (*Ha'aretz*, 17 June 1998; *Kol Ha-Ir*, 22 Aug. 1997; Rubinstein, 12 Feb. 1998).

As noted, along with the migration to the suburbs, East Jerusalem began to see a rise in illegal construction. Yisrael Kimhi of the Jerusalem Institute of Israel Studies compared aerial photographs from 1968 and 1995 as well as figures provided by the municipality and reached the conclusion that, during this period, the number of homes in East Jerusalem has nearly doubled. His figures do not include the Old City and the neighborhood of Silwan, where buildings are not easily discernible in aerial photographs. During this period 13,600 houses were added to the 8,890 houses that existed in 1968 in East Jerusalem and a belt of about three kilometers around it. On average, 2,000 new houses were built each year. According to Kimhi, this is the equivalent of about 15,000 housing units; Ir Shalem says it equals 12,500 housing units. Since 1968, Kimhi found that 40 per cent of the construction starts were in areas around the Old City, such as Isawiya, Silwan, and Ras al-Amud; 30 per cent were in the northern part of the city; 20 per cent in the south and 10 per cent in Beit Safafa. But in recent years construction starts have been concentrated solely in the city's north, and in northern Jerusalem there is a contiguous Arab built-up area reaching to Ramallah (*Ha'aretz*, 6 June 1997; Kimhi, 1997). In the absence of building permits, and for nationalistic reasons, Arab construction has been without legal sanction. It should be noted that illegal construction is widespread, too, because of a desire to save the time required for completion of the bureaucratic procedures, and the fees involved. In the areas where there is a master plan, the policy of the municipality and the courts is to "grandfather" in this construction in exchange for a fine that is smaller than the fees (Ir Shalem, 1998; Shalom Goldstein to the author, October 1998). Israel cannot entirely prevent illegal construction. It cannot demolish it all, but neither can it be ignored. Israeli government authorities have sounded the alarm – Mayor Olmert claimed that between the summers of 1995 and 1997 the city identified 2,600 violations; the Ministry of the Interior in May 1996 announced the discovery of an additional 1,291 violations (*Ha'aretz*, 25 March 1997, 9 April 1997, 20 May 1997, 1 June 1997,

6 June 1997, 23 July 1997). But, paradoxically, the higher the estimate of illegal construction, the deeper the bankruptcy of Israeli policy, which has sought to preserve the 1967 demographic ratio. Despite Israel's original intentions, Palestinian construction has turned into a burden that the country does not know how to bear.

It is important to note that the municipal boundary that Israel established in 1967 is different from the metropolitan boundary as defined by the geographic distribution of the population and by its economic, employment, and transportation networks. The legal boundary established by the Israeli annexation is sharply defined, but there are *de facto* boundaries that are more numerous and less sharp. Since 1967 Jerusalem has been a focus of employment, shopping, commerce, services, leisure, and education for a large population that lives in the area around it, from the outskirts of Hebron in the south to those of Ramallah in the north and from the edge of Jericho in the East to Beit Shemesh in the West. The annexation of East Jerusalem has helped turn Jerusalem into a metropolis.

Over the years the June 4, 1967 line, which divided the city physically and politically, has become smudged, as has the annexation line that Israel established just a few days later. The extent to which the annexation has become a fact of daily life is testified to by the fact that even Palestinians recognize the Israeli definition of Jerusalem. According to a public opinion poll conducted in mid-1996, nearly 30 years after the annexation, 69 per cent of the Palestinians consider the Jewish neighborhoods built in the eastern part of the city after 1967 to be part of East Jerusalem, and 84 per cent also include the Palestinian villages that Israel annexed, but which were not included within the city's boundaries before 1967. Among the residents of East Jerusalem, the findings are even clearer: 74 per cent of them consider the new Jewish neighborhoods to be part of the city, and 91 per cent also include the Palestinian residential areas that were annexed after 1967 (Segal, 1997: 39–42; Segal & Sa'id, 1997: 37). Day-to-day reality has thus vanquished the law books, and it has blurred Israel's annexation lines. The border set by Israel in 1967 did not encompass the functional space of Jerusalem, nor did it match the consciousness of many Palestinians. Even though Israel's annexation is of questionable status under international law (Blum, 1971; Blum, 1972–73; B'tselem, 1997: 20–3; Dinstein, 1971; Lapidot, 1997; Lustick,

1997), daily life has functionally expanded the city's borders, and this in fact is the perception of Israelis, as well as that of most Palestinians, especially those who live in Jerusalem.

The most obvious fissure in Jerusalem is the national–ethnic divide between Jews and Arabs. This cleavage spans not only the city itself, but also the metropolitan area. While extensive data concerning this divide are lacking, an observer of the functioning of the Jerusalem area would conclude that the city's metropolitan services and activities are divided geographically and ethnically. The public transportation lines from Hebron and Ramallah lead to the central bus station at the Nablus Gate in East Jerusalem, while the bus lines that serve the Israeli settlements extend to the central bus station in west Jerusalem. Jews refrain from using the Arab transportation system because its destinations are not theirs. In contrast, Arabs who have no car and find that Arab public transportation does not go to their destinations make use of the Jewish public bus system to get to and from work, despite periodically having to undergo security checks when traveling on a Jewish bus (al-Nakhal, 1993). The interaction between the two ethnic groups in the metropolitan area is very similar to the relationship that exists between them in the city itself, where there is, for all practical purposes, a division between east and west.

From the point of view of the Palestinians, the importance of the metropolitan area increases when one considers demography, because Arab Jerusalem within the Israeli municipal boundaries contains only 30 per cent of the total number of Arabs in the metropolitan area. In contrast, in the area extending from Ramallah in the north to Bethlehem in the south and from Ma'aleh Adumum in the east and the June 4, 1967 border in the west, the Arab and Jewish populations are almost equal. In 1992, the Jerusalem metropolitan area contained 489,000 Jews and 467,000 Arabs. The Arabs become a majority if the area is expanded to include Gush Etzion in the south, Jericho in the east, Shilo in the north, and Beit Shemesh in the West (Cohen & Mazor, 1994; Hasson, 1997). Ma'aleh Adumim, Beitar, Efrat, and Beit Shemesh are highly dependent on Jerusalem, but Bethlehem, Beit Jallah, and Ramallah have developed as independent Palestinian cities on the margins of the metropolitan area. However, the existence of independent, important Arab cities of distinct character on the edges of the East Jerusalem metropolitan area poses no challenge to East

Jerusalem's pre-eminence in Palestine eyes. Most of the Palestinian elites are concentrated in East Jerusalem: the religious elite, the Waqf administration (which governs Islamic holy places and properties, and which is a wealthy and powerful religious, economic, and social organization), the central Palestine cultural institutions, and the important political institutions. East Jerusalem links the northern West Bank to the southern West Bank, and Amman, the capital of the Kingdom of Jordan, to Gaza, in which the offices of the Palestinian Authority are located.

The lengthy closure that Israel has, since 1993, imposed on the West Bank and Gaza Strip severely hindered operations in the East Jerusalem metropolitan area. The closure lines were almost identical to Jerusalem's municipal boundaries, with the exception that the Atarot airport was left outside the city for this purpose. The closure cut East Jerusalem off from the interior and the suburbs, and triply hurt the Palestinians in Jerusalem. First, just as Jewish Jerusalem is not industrial, so East Jerusalem is a city of services, public offices, and commerce, and the closure cut off its ties with the larger area it serves. Close to 90 per cent of the employees of large East Jerusalem workplaces, such as the Arab electric company, the Al-Magased Hospital, and the Waqf offices are Palestinians who live outside the city. These institutions could not function properly because of the inability of employees to get to work regularly. Second, there was a loss of income because of the blow to the tourist industry delivered by the terrorist attacks of Hamas, the Muslim extremist group, in the winter of 1996 and the summer of the following year. Third, the level of services and income for the residents of the suburbs was also severely affected. As a way of overcoming at least some of these problems, several East Jerusalem companies opened branches in those parts of the West Bank close to the city. The Arab electric company opened branches in Ramallah and Bethlehem in mid-1996, and East Jerusalem professional people did the same. Since clients could not get to the offices of their lawyers, doctors, engineers, pharmacists, and accountants, the professionals went to their clients. Owners of restaurants and halls understood that if one had a wedding in East Jerusalem the guests from the rest of the West Bank would not be able to attend, so facilities were established in the suburbs, in the neighborhoods of Al-Ram and Dahiat al-Barid, to which people could get without a special permit. Transportation services also had to adjust. The number of people using the central bus station at the Nablus Gate, the major business center in East Jerusalem, declined by 60 per cent. The result of this was that the surrounding businesses, which had benefited from the influx of travelers, were also severely affected. At the beginning of 1996, improvised bus stations were set up next to the Israeli roadblocks in the south, east, and north of Jerusalem, which compensated in part for the central station in the city center. The closure also hurt the residents of the suburbs that depend on the city. They found it difficult to maintain their connections with the city center. For this reason, many of them circumvented the roadblocks, and only a few sought alternative employment or services in the nearby Palestinian cities, Ramallah and Bethlehem (*Ha'aretz*, 26 March 1998; Rubinstein, 19 Sept. 1996). But one central facility could not be transferred elsewhere – the Muslim sacred center of al-Haram al-Sharif, the Temple Mount. The sanctity of Jerusalem for Islamic believers could not change because of the closure. On the contrary, Israeli policy induced Palestinian Muslims to rally around holy places as evidence of the Palestinian–Arab identity of East Jerusalem, which they insisted could not and should not be abandoned. This explains the extreme sensitivity of the Palestinians and the Arab states at the opening of the Western Wall Tunnel in September 1996 (see chapter 7), and the fact that 250,000 Muslims took part in the prayer service on the last Friday of Ramadan in the Al-Aqsa mosque. Israel acted with restraint and overlooked the entrance into Jerusalem of masses of worshippers without permits and with disturbances from the Palestinian Authority lands, as Israel had done during the previous Fridays of Ramadan.

Aside from the effects of the closure, the entry of the Palestinian Authority into Ramallah in December 1995 led to increased status for the Ramallah/Al-Bireh region. Ramallah became a city of offices, commerce, culture, art, and leisure, and in several ways an alternative center to Jerusalem. Central offices of the Palestinian Authority dealing with the affairs of the West Bank were established in Ramallah. The Legislative Council convenes there at regular intervals, and the police and security services have their main offices there. Two daily newspapers put out by the Authority are published in Ramallah: *Al-Ayam* and *Al-Hayat al-Jadida*. The large Arab banks in the Authority have located their administrative offices in Ramallah, as have insurance and financial firms.

Bir Zeit University, near Al-Bireh, attracts young people from around the West Bank and Gaza Strip, and the city also houses three teachers' colleges. This transformation of Ramallah into the administrative and financial center of the West Bank has brought about immediate economic results, an increase in employment and income. Between December 1995 and the summer of 1996, a total of 669 new companies and businesses opened; restaurants, coffee houses, bakeries, supermarkets, and even a small industrial zone have been established (Algazi, 19 Aug. 1998; Litani, 3 Sept. 1996; Rubinstein, 27 Oct. 1995).

The developments surveyed so far emphasize from two points of view the importance of the political dimension in shaping Jerusalem's boundary lines. First, the entrance of the Palestinian Authority into cities bordering on Jerusalem to the south – Bethlehem – and north – Ramallah – has curtailed East Jerusalem's metropolitan operations and the extent of its influence. Second, the closure line is not simply a municipal boundary but also a political one, marking the area of Israeli sovereignty in Jerusalem. The damage the closure has caused to the Palestinian status of East Jerusalem serves the purposes of the Israeli government. While closure was not imposed for this purpose, the longer it has lasted the more have the Palestinians come to perceive this as the major reason for its persistence. True, the people of East Jerusalem have not abandoned their desire to become part of the Palestinian Authority, nor have they accepted the Israeli annexation, but their connections with the Palestinian hinterland have been loosened and have been made more difficult than they were in the past. The pressure on the Arab inhabitants of Jerusalem has increased and they have found themselves caught between, on the one hand, the annexation line and the closure that has cut them off from the West Bank, and on the other, the national–ethnic line that divides the city.

Ever since Israel and the Palestinian Authority began implementing the Oslo agreements in May 1994, the political map of Jerusalem and its environs has changed. Until then there was a single border as far as Israel was concerned, the annexation boundary which was also the Jerusalem municipal limit. The establishment of the Palestinian Authority and its penetration into Jerusalem made the Jerusalem political border less than straightforward. Officially, the Palestinian Authority is forbidden to operate within Israeli Jerusalem, but as will be shown below the Authority has found ways of circumventing this prohibition, and this has brought into sharper relief the political–national boundary line that passes through the city. Alongside this boundary, additional boundary lines have been added – electoral district lines for the Palestinian Authority's legislative council and the Palestinian administrative district (*Muhafzat Al-Quds*) of Jerusalem. These two lines coincide and are identical with those of the Jerusalem district (*Liwa Al-Quds*) that existed when East Jerusalem and the West Bank were under Jordanian sovereignty (Map 1).

The Oslo II agreement, signed in September 1995, divides the Jerusalem area into four zones of control. The Israeli zone includes the city of Jerusalem and Israeli settlements around it. The Palestinian area is divided into Zones A and B. Zone A is under complete Palestinian control, including the cities of Jericho, Bethlehem, Beit Jala, Ramallah, and Al-Bireh, which are on the periphery of the Jerusalem area. In Zone B the Palestinians have civil and police control, while Israel has the overriding responsibility for security. Zone B includes villages that are, in terms of urban geography, suburbs of Jerusalem, such as Al-Azaria, Abu Dis, and Hizma. A large block of territory defined as Zone B lies to the east and southeast of Jerusalem and extends, unbroken, from Al-Azaria to the outskirts of Bethlehem. In the north, by contrast, there are only small islands of Zone B, reaching to Ramallah. The neighborhood of Al-Ram to Jerusalem's north is split. Its eastern part is in Zone B, its center in Zone A, and the neighborhood's western part, adjacent to the main road leading to the Atarot airport, has a special status since the airport is within the city limits. Between the different islands of Zone B that dot the suburbs of the Jerusalem metropolitan area lie swathes of Zone C. Its size, and the powers the Palestinians are to receive there, are subject to additional negotiation (Map 2). In the wake of the Oslo accords the Palestinian Authority made East Jerusalem part of its District (*muhafaza*) of Jerusalem, which is one of the nine Palestinian administrative districts of the West Bank. In 1995 Al-Ram was accorded special status for the purposes of planning and construction, but the rest of the regions in the Jerusalem area remained subject directly to the District Planning Committee in Abu-Dis, whose members include representatives from East Jerusalem (Choshen et al., 1998).

One important aspect of the Oslo II agreement was that it defined parts of the Jerusalem area as Zones B and C. The Oslo agreements prohibit, at Israel's insistence, the Palestinian Authority from operating in Jerusalem, but from the Palestinian point of view, Zones B and C, and even more so the Palestinian cities in Zone A, are jumping-off points or anchors to which East Jerusalem can be attached in the lead-up to discussions over the permanent settlement. This is the essence of Israel's motivation to establish the Har Homa neighborhood as a wedge between the Al-Azaria/Abu-Dis block and Bethlehem. Furthermore, in North Jerusalem, the area with the land reserves for Palestinian construction, the Palestinian Authority has not achieved territorial contiguity between the regions under its control. Also, the A and B zones have cut off Jerusalem from the settlements on its southern periphery, from Efrat and Gush Etzion, which according to the Israeli plan are supposed to be part of an Israeli-ruled Greater Jerusalem. The link with Ma'aleh Adumim to the east has also been narrowed because of the assignment of the Al-Azaria block to Zone B. For this reason the municipality is trying to launch a construction plan and to expropriate land from the Arabs in order to create a physical connection between Ma'aleh Adumim and the new Jewish neighborhoods in the eastern part of the city (see map). Finally, the line that the map shows is temporary in nature and cannot be made permanent. The Oslo II lines make it difficult for inhabitants of the Arab space, which from an urban point of view had previously functioned as a single unit, to live as they used to live. For example, the border between Israeli Jerusalem and the Palestinian district of Jerusalem runs straight through the neighborhood of al-Sawahra. The residents find this unacceptable, especially with regard to the closure, which prevents residents of the Palestinian Authority from entering the city (Benvenisti, 2 Nov. 1995; Rubinstein, 15 Oct. 1995).

Jerusalem thus has ethnic–national, demographic, political, and metropolitan borders. Since it is on the frontier, the borderlines divide the city and also enclose it. On the face of it, this multiplicity of borderlines should intensify the conflict between Israel and the Palestinians, but in fact it moderates the conflict. Instead of a single deep fissure in a single place, the Israelis and the Palestinians have, unintentionally, made the national–ethnic–geographic confrontation run along several faults. As will be shown below, this division of the borders cushions rather than sharpens the conflict. The borderlines in Jerusalem are permeable, soft, and flexible.

The division of Jerusalem.   A borderline has run through Jerusalem ever since the prospective Jewish state appeared on the horizon. As early as 1937, when the Peel Commission discussed the partition of Palestine between Jews and Arabs, it was clear to the Zionist leadership that Jerusalem would be a frontier city. The leadership reasoned that there was no escaping a division of the city between the two states that would be established in Palestine, and it submitted to the Peel Commission a plan for the partition of Jerusalem. The dividing lines in the Zionist plan were geographic, ethnic–national, and functional–religious. Geographically, the Zionist leadership supported separating the eastern city from the western city, with Mount Scopus, where the Hebrew University and Hadassah Hospital were located, being under Israeli sovereignty. Ethnically, its proposal was to separate the Jews and the Arabs, with the Jews becoming citizens of the Jewish state even if they remained in the eastern – Arab – part of the city. Functionally–religiously, the Zionist leadership proposed giving the holy places international status (Golani, 1994: 32–3; Golani, 1998: 268–72). The proposal was indicative of the thinking and priorities that guided its formulators. Winning control of the Jewish population and establishment of the state were more important to the Zionists than sovereignty over the territory of East Jerusalem. Moreover, title to Mount Scopus was more vital than sovereignty on the Temple Mount (Paz, 1997). The symbols of Zionism, its culture, and the desire to establish a state took precedence over the Jewish symbols in Jerusalem. The dominant part of the leadership, headed by Ben-Gurion, was prepared to give up the Old City and historic Jerusalem in order to establish a state with New Jerusalem as its capital. In principle, this was the policy that Israel followed until 1967 (Golani, 1998: 270).

The Palestinians and the British rejected the partition plan. The mufti of Jerusalem, Haj Amin al-Husseini, made Jerusalem and its religious significance for Islam the focus of a political confrontation with Zionism; he and the rest of the Palestinian leadership wanted a unitary state ruled by an Arab majority. Britain would not agree to parcel out the Christian sites in the Holy Land,

and so abdicate entirely its imperial status. The Peel Commission ruled that Jerusalem and Bethlehem would remain under the British Mandate, as well, perhaps, as Nazareth and the Sea of Galilee. Likewise, the Peel Commission proposed that Jerusalem and Bethlehem be given an eastern corridor leading to the Dead Sea and the Jordanian emirite, later to be the Hashemite Kingdom of Jordan. The holy cities' principal ties would be to Jordan and not to the Jewish state to be established to their west (Laqueur & Rubin, 1995: 48). Between 1937 and 1967 the two generally accepted alternatives regarding Jerusalem were the internationalization of the city or the partition of it.

At first, internationalization was considered the better option. The United Nations commission of inquiry on Palestine, UNSCOP, established in May 1947, and which at the end of August submitted its recommendations to the UN General Assembly, did not accept the Zionist position that West Jerusalem should be under Israeli sovereignty and East Jerusalem under international rule. The recommendation of the majority was to divide Palestine into two states, Jewish and Arab, and to put Jerusalem in its entirety under an international regime; a minority preferred to designate Jerusalem as the capital of the independent federal state (Laqueur & Rubin, 1995: 92–5). The Zionist leadership had to choose at this early stage between two options, neither of them simple – having a Jewish state without Jerusalem or being part of a Jewish–Arab federal state that included Jerusalem. In the plan it submitted to UNSCOP, the Zionist leadership tried to obtain a part of the capital, the western part, with the state. In order to accommodate the international institutions, the Zionist leadership thought it would be wise on its part to propose putting the eastern part of Jerusalem under international protection. However, an inequitable proposal of this sort had no chance.

Getting a state was the most urgent need, especially after the Holocaust. In order to obtain the support of the UN General Assembly for UNSCOP's majority opinion, recommending the partition of Palestine, the Zionists had to accept the internationalization of Jerusalem, including Jewish Jerusalem, in exchange for international support for a Jewish state. There was no point in insisting on Jerusalem as the capital if the future of the state itself was not ensured. Nevertheless, the Zionists were not prepared to accept the internationalization plan unilaterally. They would do so only if the Arabs also agreed (Golani, 1994).

On November 29, 1947 the UN accepted the majority recommendation, and linked the plan for internationalizing Jerusalem to the overall solution of the Palestine question. In that decision to divide Palestine into Jewish and Arab states, Resolution 181, the General Assembly recommended putting Jerusalem under an international regime sponsored by the UN. This regime was meant to ensure the demilitarization and neutrality of Jerusalem, to make arrangements for religious observances at the holy sites, and to resolve disputes concerning Jerusalem between the Jewish and Arab states in Palestine. According to the decision, the city would have a legislative council chosen by proportional representation; there would be autonomous municipalities for Jews and Arabs. After ten years of international control there would be a plebiscite on the city's future. Resolution 181 states, however, that the results of the vote would be advisory only. The international regime reserved the right to decide whether to accept the majority's will. For all practical purposes, the General Assembly ruled that internationalization would not be for a definite period, but on the other hand that it need not necessarily be permanent (Hirsch, Hausen-Koriel & Lapidot, 1994: 10; Lapidot, 1997; Laqueur & Rubin, 1995: 97–103). This cold and logical compromise was based on the demographics of the city and Mandatory Palestine. When the partition resolution was passed, there were 102,000 Jews living in Jerusalem as opposed to 65,000 Muslims and Christians (a 66 per cent majority for the Jews). In the territory of the British Mandate there were, however, about a million Palestinian Arabs and about 600,000 Jews. To put it another way, the demographic situation in Jerusalem was the reverse of that in Mandatory Palestine as a whole. A different logic, however, reigned in the region, a reality of war in which each side sought to shuffle the deck and deal out the cards again to win an advantage for itself.

The Arabs immediately rejected the entire partition plan because they did not want to see the establishment of a State of Israel. As a result, the leaders of the Jewish national institutions considered themselves absolved of their consent to the partition and to the internationalization of Jerusalem. The war between the Jews and Arabs of Palestine, which began immediately after passage of the partition resolution, prevented enforcement of the decision and improved the Jewish advantage in the city. On May 15, 1948, when the independence of the State of Israel was declared, there were 80,000 Jews as against 30,000 Muslims and Christians in the city (a Jewish majority of 74 per cent). The course of combat after May 15, 1948 led to the division of the city between the two population groups and made it even more difficult for the UN to implement the resolution. The General Assembly reaffirmed the decision after the war, in November 1949 (Laqueur & Rubin, 1995: 115–16). Since then, UN institutions have deliberated over the question of Jerusalem several times, but they have not reaffirmed the internationalization decision, and between 1953 and 1967 the question of the city's status was not raised at all. There were two reasons for removing the question of Jerusalem in general, and the question of its internationalization specifically, from the agenda. First, the internationalization idea was no longer relevant. Israel and Jordan divided Jerusalem by force of arms during the 1948 war. It was no longer possible to return to a proposal based on the dividing lines in Jerusalem prior to the war. Second, after the 1948 war an understanding developed between Israel and Jordan, with both parties seeking to torpedo the UN initiative while partitioning the city between them. They succeeded.

In fact, the emerging Jewish state and the Emirate of Transjordan had already begun discussing Jerusalem before the 1948 war. The issue was raised during the 1947–48 contacts between King Abdullah and the head of the Jewish Agency's political department, Golda Meyerson (Meir). Evaluation of these negotiations has been a contentious issue among historians, but it is generally agreed that nothing had been settled concerning Jerusalem until the 1948 war. Although the Jewish Agency and the Jordanian Emir arrived at some sort of understanding about non-belligerency and a quiet partition of Palestine between them, they did not come to an agreement regarding Jerusalem. When the fighting began, the Jordanian Legion sought – for political reasons – to refrain from military involvement in the city itself (in contrast to its northern and eastern approaches and the Arab quarters surrounding it), assuming that the Israeli army would also abstain from occupying the city. This assumption was realistic as far as the Old City of Jerusalem was concerned, but not as to the western city.

   The Jewish Agency, and later the Israeli Government, decided to establish west Jerusalem as the capital of Israel by force of arms. In early 1948, the Haganah and the Israeli army (IDF) fought several battles for control of the road leading into Jerusalem from the west – from Tel Aviv and the coastal area – and conducted several military operations in order to lift the Arab blockade imposed on the city from April 20 to June 2. Lifting of the blockade was intended not only to allow transport of food and supplies to the besieged Jews of the city, but also to establish Israeli sovereignty in west Jerusalem. However, Israel did not invest the same effort in the conquest of the Old City as it did in west Jerusalem. It assumed that the conquest of the eastern part of Jerusalem, with its Christian and Islamic holy places, would eventually lead to the ouster of Israel from the western city as well. Israel therefore conducted only two military operations in the eastern city, both directed at relief of the Jewish Quarter. The first of these was made on May 17–19, when the IDF entered the quarter but left it a few hours later. The Jordanian Legion immediately entered the Old City on May 19, occupying the Jewish Quarter on May 28. The Israeli attack thus gave Abdullah the legitimization he had been seeking to invade the Old City and to turn it into the religious–spiritual capital of his kingdom. Incidentally, he acted against the military advice of John Glubb, commander of his army, and of Kirkbride, the senior British representative in Jordan. In conquering the Old City, Abdullah wished to extend the understanding on partition reached on the eve of the war between himself and the Jewish Agency and divide Jerusalem as well. The Israeli leadership was not bound by any such agreement, and in July 1948 a second attempt was made to liberate the Jewish Quarter. This attempt also failed, and following the first cease-fire agreement on June 11, 1948 a borderline was drawn, dividing the city: west Jerusalem, including the Arab quarters of Baq'a, Talbbiyeh, Qattamon, and part of Abu Tor came under Israeli rule, while Jordan controlled the east, including the whole of the Old City (Morris, 1996: 13–17; Pundik, 1994: 105–10; Rabinowitz, 1991; Sela, 1990; Shlaim, 1988: 217–18).

   Israel's foremost aim directly after the fighting ceased was to be accepted as a member of the United Nations, thereby bolstering the legitimacy of the newborn state. Israel faced a dilemma: its acceptance by the United Nations required that it agree to some form of internationalization of the whole of Jerusalem, in keeping with the decision of the UN General Assembly. However, the Jewish leaders wished to preserve the gains of the war – to seal the partition of the city between Israel and Jordan and to declare west Jerusalem the capital of Israel. Israel therefore rejected Abdullah's overtures at the end of 1948 to agree on a partition of Jerusalem; it offered instead international rule over the holy places only. However, since they were situated mostly in a small area of the Old City, this was just another way to distinguish west from East Jerusalem. As this offer naturally did not gain international support (Bialer, 1985; Golani, 1994; Karpel, 13 Oct. 1995), Israel then turned to Jordan in order to reach a quick understanding which would block the internationalization of Jerusalem. This suited the intentions of King Abdullah, whose primary aim was to maintain his sovereignty over the areas he had occupied during the war: the West Bank and East Jerusalem (Pundik, 1994: 156–7, 170, 242).

Israel portrayed the partition of Jerusalem as being in the interests of both itself and Jordan: Abdullah could gain legitimization of his rule and justify annexation of the West Bank through his control over the Islamic holy places in Jerusalem; and Ben-Gurion could declare west Jerusalem the capital of Israel. This joint interest in blocking the internationalization plan brought about Israel's surprising and radical offer to Jordan in January 1949, in talks conducted by Moshe Dayan, the military commander of Jerusalem, with his Jordanian colleague Abdullah al-Tal. Dayan offered to reach a quick agreement over Jerusalem, which would form part of an overall agreement between the two countries. He openly admitted that Israel wanted a quick resolution of the issue, and was thus willing to make significant concessions. Israel offered to cede the Arab quarters it had conquered in 1948: Qattamon, the German Colony, Baq'a and Malha; its military posts in Mount Zion and Abu-Tor; the Israeli Kibbutz Ramat Rachel, and the two Jewish neighborhoods of Talpiot and Mekor-Haim. This would give Jordan territorial continuity from east to west and southwest Jerusalem, as well as a broad strip of land connecting the Arab city of Jerusalem with Bethlehem. In return, Israel asked for the Ofel Hill, in order to gain a narrow corridor to the Jewish cemetery on the Mount of Olives, and the Jewish Quarter in the Old City, which abuts the Ofel hill to the east and with Mount Zion in west Jerusalem to the west. Mount Scopus, according to Dayan, would remain under Israeli rule, as would the road leading to it. In contrast to the sites in the Old City with which there was territorial continuity, Mount Scopus was a Jewish enclave. Israel suggested connecting it to the Jewish city via a new road that would circumvent the Arab quarters (American Consul in Jerusalem Burdett to the Secretary of State, 13 Jan. 1949, *Foreign Relations of the United States (FRUS)*, 1949: 661–3).

The Jordanian king could not reject such a generous offer outright, since it would win for him through political means much more than his army had achieved. However, he was in no hurry, and he raised the ante. In addition to the Arab quarters, he demanded full Jordanian sovereignty over the Jewish Quarter in the Old City. Neither was he to be satisfied only with control of the military posts in Abu-Tor and Mount Zion; he demanded full sovereignty over both quarters. These demands, although made for the sake of bargaining only, kept Israel from gaining the time advantage it had sought. Talks conducted later with Abdullah al-Tal also led nowhere (*FRUS*: 667, From Amman to Washington, 15 Jan. 1949).

Dayan's offer was discussed informally by the consuls of the United States, France and Great Britain in Tel Aviv and Amman, and between them and the Jordanian king. The American position at the end of January 1949 was that partition of the city by mutual agreement was better than coerced internationalization. The United States supported the partition of Jerusalem according to the lines drawn by Dayan without, however, granting either Israel or Jordan sovereignty over their parts of Jerusalem. In order to appease the United Nations, Washington stated that any bilateral agreement would need the ratification of the UN General Assembly. The American position was acceptable to Jordan, as it tacitly confirmed Jordan's gains. Jordan did not intend to transfer its capital from Amman to Jerusalem, and it stood to lose less than Israel from not gaining sovereignty over the city. It went even one step further than the Americans, proposing to enlarge the international zone of the city. In direct talks with Israeli delegates at the end of January 1949, Jordan suggested that the city be partitioned according to the American plan, allowing loose international supervision. This did not appeal to Israel at all, and two weeks after Dayan's generous proposal, Israel again demanded sovereignty over west Jerusalem and the internationalization of East Jerusalem, with its holy places (*FRUS*: 710, Burdett to the Secretary of

State, 29 Jan. 1949; McDonald to the Secretary of State 3 Feb. 1949: 721, 740). The Americans received the impression that Israel's foreign minister, Moshe Shertok, was ready for a UN stamp of approval on an Israeli–Jordanian agreement for the partition of the city (see meeting of Dean Rusk with Shertok, 4 April 1949: 890). At the same time, Israel blocked the realization of Dayan's offer by starting to settle the southern Arab quarters it had conquered (American Consulate in Jerusalem to the Secretary of State, 29 Jan. 1949, *FRUS*: 711; Krystall 1998).

Jordan had two other reasons for rejecting Dayan's proposal, as well as all other Israeli offers about Jerusalem. First, Jordan noticed Israel's eagerness to reach a settlement on the partition of Jerusalem, and wanted to capitalize on the Jerusalem issue to pressure Israel for concessions in other areas, such as a solution of the refugee problem and the future of the southern Negev region. The Negev was a bone of contention between Abdullah and the British government, their priorities being different. Britain saw the Negev as a strategic asset, whereas Abdullah placed a higher priority on the West Bank and Jerusalem than on using the Negev as a corridor to the Gaza Strip and the Mediterranean. He did not view territorial demands in the Negev as a "must," since he thought he could find an alternative Jordanian corridor to the Mediterranean (there were talks about providing access to Haifa port) (Pundik 1994: 156, 173–4, 194, 197, 278–9). Second, Israel's insistence on establishing its capital in Jerusalem raised Jordan's apprehensions that Israel would not long tolerate a divided capital, with Jordanian rule in the Old City and the Jewish holy places. Jordan also feared that Mount Scopus would serve as a base for an Israeli attack on East Jerusalem, in which the Jordanians would be caught in a vice that might squeeze East Jerusalem from the west and northeast. Jordan saw an intimation of this in Israel's demand for sovereignty over the road to Mount Scopus. Abdullah therefore linked the Jerusalem issue with a solution to all outstanding questions between the two countries. He made a proposal similar to that of the U.S.: autonomy to both Israel and Jordan in Jerusalem without sovereignty to either, as well as minimal internationalization (*FRUS*: 729–30, Burdett to the Secretary of State 5 Feb. 1949).

Meanwhile, the *de facto* status created by the fighting led to a tacit, practical agreement between Israel and Jordan on partition of Jerusalem according to the alignment of the Israeli and Jordanian armies at the end of the war.

The next attempt to anchor the partition of Jerusalem in a written agreement between the two countries, including territorial alterations in their sovereignty in the city, was made at the end of 1949 and the beginning of 1950. It was again a proposal for internationalization that brought Israel and Jordan to the negotiating table. In November 1949, the UN General Assembly decided to ratify once more the internationalization proposal of two years previously (Golani, 1994), and it was time to renew vigorous political contacts in order to reach an overall agreement between Israel and the Hashemite Kingdom of Jordan. Israel had territorial demands in Jerusalem. On the eve of the talks between the two countries in November 1949, Ben-Gurion's aim was to achieve territorial continuity with the Western Wall through the Jewish Quarter in the Old City, as well as with Mount Scopus. In exchange, he was willing to cede to Jordan a certain area in the southern part of the city, the size of which was not clearly stated.

On December 13, a joint Israeli–Jordanian document was drawn up, outlining an agreement between them. The document promised Israel sovereignty over the Jewish Quarter in the Old City and over the adjacent Western Wall; however, Israel would not gain a territorial link to Mount Scopus. In order to allay Jordanian apprehensions that it would use such a link as a staging ground for an attack on the Jordanian city, Israel was asked to agree with Jordan on the passage to Mount Scopus through Jordanian territory. In return, Jordan would receive, in accord with Ben-Gurion's original plan, territorial continuity from the eastern side of the city to its south (Rabinowitz, 1991: 119–24; Shlaim, 1988: 233–4, 440).

It was not the issue of Jerusalem that caused the failure of this agreement, but the lack of consent on other territorial issues, such as the Negev and the Latrun area. Thus, between December 1949 and February 1950, the two sides strove to reach an agreement at least about Jerusalem and then to consider less controversial issues. However, negotiations began at a much lower level, and the former understanding seemed to have dissipated. Israel proposed the partition of the city into a northern district that would belong to Jordan, and a southern district, including the Old City that would belong to Israel. This was, of course, rejected outright by Jordan. Israel reiterated as an alternative its demand for sovereignty over the area from the Western Wall, through the Jewish Quarter, to the western city; as well as territorial continuity from west Jerusalem to Mount Scopus. The Jordanians rebutted with a demand to be given the Arab quarters held by Israel in the western city, and it was Israel's turn to refuse outright. Instead, though, Israel agreed to negotiate about an exchange of territories in Jerusalem and about financial compensation for the Arab neighborhoods that would stay under its rule. But these negotiations also reached a dead end.

This failure has been much discussed by historians, who have tried to ascertain why it happened and who was to blame. Rabinowitz (1991: 111–67) and Pundik (1994: 280–1) believe that the King of Jordan was responsible. The king's immediate move to annex the West Bank required him to include members of his government in the negotiations, and these included West Bank Palestinians. The government opposed any territorial concession to Israel on the issue of Jerusalem. These historians also believe that King Abdullah's maneuverability within his government had weakened since he had begun the process of annexation, and that he lacked energy and dynamism at that time. The weakness of the king *vis-à-vis* his government and the socio-political reality in the West Bank were held responsible for the failure of the agreement. Shlaim (1988: 111–67), on the other hand, believes that the blame must be laid on Israel, which made excessive demands in order to stall the agreement. He held that the Israelis did not want a definite and agreed borderline in Jerusalem because they wanted to change it by force later on. Shlaim claims that Israel preferred to wait for an opportune time to conquer the whole of Jerusalem. However, on July 20, 1951, a radical Palestinian and partisan of the mufti murdered King Abdullah, and the option of reaching an Israeli–Jordanian agreement – whether comprehensive or partial – became but another historical footnote.

In the absence of a broader agreement, the *de facto* partition of the city remained in force, along with the cease-fire agreement signed at the end of the war. On July 7, 1948, Israel and Jordan agreed, among other things, to seek the "resumption of the normal functioning of the cultural and humanitarian institutions on Mount Scopus [i.e. the Hebrew University of Jerusalem and the Hadassah Hospital], and free access thereto; free access to the Holy Places and cultural institutions [e.g. synagogues], and the use of the cemetery on the Mount of Olives" (Hirsch, Hausen-Koriel & Lapidot, 1994: 4). However, this paragraph was not honored by Jordan. The agreement also stipulated that Mount Scopus would be demilitarized; that a small force of policemen and civilian workers would be present there; that the UN would ensure provision of water and scientific equipment, and would regulate a semi-weekly provisioning. In effect, Israel sent soldiers dressed as police officers, smuggled arms and military equipment to Mount Scopus, and turned the mountain into an observation post and a main stronghold for its planned conquest of East Jerusalem (Narkis, 1975; 1991).

During the 19 years between 1948 and 1967, Jerusalem was divided between Israel and Jordan, both of which came to accept this partition. The border areas between the two grew into neglected no man's lands, not into springboards for eastward or westward expansion. On December 5, 1948, Ben-Gurion claimed Jerusalem as part of Israel and eight days later the Knesset declared it the capital of Israel. East Jerusalem was annexed to the Kingdom of Jordan about one week thereafter, on December 13, 1948. The West Bank was also annexed *de facto* to Jordan. This was made *de jure* in May 1950. Only Pakistan and Great Britain recognized the acquisition, with the latter declaring that it did not recognize Jordan's sovereignty over Jerusalem, only its administration of it. International recognition of the reality of a divided Jerusalem was conferred in 1952, when the UN General Assembly decided that Israel and Jordan would be responsible for reaching an arrangement about Jerusalem in accordance with the UN resolution. Thus, the UN recognized Israel and Jordan's joint authority to decide the future of the city, and directed them to do so according to the UN resolution on internationalization, without stating how the two would implement a decision that both opposed. In other words, the UN recognized Israel and Jordan as the governing authorities in Jerusalem, and tacitly accepted the demise of the notion of internationalization. The Arab League recognized Jordan's annexation on May 15, 1950, the latter having confirmed its commitment that the annexation of the West Bank would not prejudice in any way the final settlement of the Palestine problem. From that time until the war of 1967, Jordan was recognized as controlling the West Bank (Hirsch, Hausen-Koriel & Lapidot, 1995: 3–6).

Jordan governed Jerusalem in the same way that it governed the West Bank as a whole. As was the case during the British mandate, under Jordan the social elite – notables whose influence was based on kinship, and who also happened to have property and capital – controlled the centers of political power. They dominated the chambers of commerce and the religious establishment (the Waqf and the Sharia' courts), and their financial positions ensured their children access to modern schools, higher education, and to senior positions. After 1948 the members of the traditional elite were integrated into Jordanian institutions. The Jordanian establishment exploited for its own benefit the old Palestinian elite's loss of property and prestige and the dissolution of its political organization in the 1948 war. Also playing into the hands of the Jordanian establishment was the fact that many members of the old elite had moved to other Arab countries and to the West because of the Second World War. The status of the local elite in the West Bank was weakened and its authority in the eyes of other inhabitants was diminished. Nevertheless, many of its members, such as the sons of the Nusseibeh, al-Khatib, al-Alami, and Barakat families, were given senior positions in parliament, in the cabinet, and in the top level of Jordanian officialdom, giving them the means to perpetuate their positions. In the framework of the Hashemite dynasty, an owner–client relationship was developed between the Jordanian elite on the East Bank and the Palestinian elite in the West Bank, and between the Palestinian elite and the larger public (Sabella, 1997a).

On July 13, 1951, elections were held for positions of municipal office in Jordanian Jerusalem, and on April 1, 1952 the borders of the Jordanian city were extended to include adjacent areas (e.g. Silwan and Ras-al-Amud). The area of the Jordanian city was thus six and a half square kilometers, while the built-up area was only half of that, three square kilometrers. In February 1958, the Jordanian municipality of Jerusalem initiated the extension of the city's area north towards the airport in Kalandia. This plan was not implemented, nor was the 1963 plan to expand the city's area to 75 square kilometers. Discussions concerning these plans ceased in 1967, with the outbreak of the war (al-Tafugji, 1996: 363; 1997). On the other side, west Jerusalem consisted at that time of 38 square kilometers, after its area had been extended west. This reflected the difference in status between the capital of Israel and

Jordanian Jerusalem, which remained an outlying town with symbolic religious importance only. West Jerusalem's status in Israel was higher than East Jerusalem's in Jordan, although the center of Israeli economical, cultural and social life, the political parties, trade unions and main newspapers were all in Tel Aviv.

The war of 1967 was not premeditated, and the parties involved – other than the PLO and the radical wing of the Syrian government – entered it against their will. On the day the fighting began, Israel sent a message to Jordan asking it not to enter the war, stating that it would, however, accept Jordan's token participation in the fighting, such as diffuse light weapons fire on the borders of Jerusalem. However, Jordan did not respond to this request. This was after communication between the two heads of state was disrupted as a result of the extensive Israeli military action in Samo'a in November 1966, in which the Jordanian army suffered heavy losses (Klein, 2000).

In accordance with accepted Israeli strategic military thinking prior to the establishment of the state, Israel did not, in the 1960s, have military contingency plans for the conquest of the Old City of Jerusalem. There were plans only for taking possession of the road to the Israeli outpost on Mount Scopus. Israel's first step during the war was in this direction; at the same time in the south, the UN headquarters at the old British high commissioner's residence and the area surrounding it were occupied in order to keep Jordanian fire away from adjacent Jewish neighborhoods and to prevent Jordan's occupation of the strategic site. The next step was to surround the Old City; only when this maneuver had been completed, without producing an international outcry, was the command given to invade the Old City (Zak, 1996: 106, 115). Zak recounts that Israel's anger with King Hussein for opening fire was so intense that Israeli warplanes bombed the king's palace on the first day of the war in an attempt to kill him (Zak, 1996: 116).

Immediately after the war, the government considered the possibility of establishing Palestinian self-rule in parts of the West Bank outside Jerusalem, but this idea was shelved in September 1968 (Pedhatzur, 1995). After the Palestinian option had been dormant for 20 years, the Jordanian option surfaced. On September 27, 1968, Israeli foreign minister, Abba Eban, met with King Hussein, specifying the Israeli principles for negotiation. In contrast to its position before the war, Israel was not now ready to share sovereignty of Jerusalem with Jordan. It demanded that Jerusalem stay united under Israeli sovereignty, through which it was ready to grant to the Arab section of Jerusalem, including the Temple Mount, a special Jordanian–Muslim status. Eban also mentioned the possibility of providing Jordan with a territorial corridor connecting this part of Jerusalem to other parts of the West Bank, which would be returned to Jordanian sovereignty. In other words, Israel intended to retain its sovereignty over the city, but was willing to grant Jordan a foothold in East Jerusalem, provided that its presence and authority be religious only.

Jordan demurred politely; at most, it was willing to consent to Israeli sovereignty over the Jewish holy places in East Jerusalem, excluding al-Haram-al-Sharif, which it viewed as holy to Muslims but not Jews. Jordan agreed with Israel that the city must remain open, with free movement, trade and passage between its two parts; but it would not agree that the city that was united *de facto* should remain *de jure* under Israeli sovereignty. At most, it would agree to a special status for East Jerusalem (Zak, 1996: 157–9). This was King Hussein's consistent policy throughout his subsequent secret negotiations with Israel.

In 1972, King Hussein proposed to the Palestinians the establishment of an equal status federation of the East and West Banks of Jordan, once the latter had been liberated from Israeli occupation. East Jerusalem would be the capital of the Palestinian region of this federation. Prime Minister Golda Meir gave the Israeli reaction to this proposal in a secret meeting with King Hussein. She would, she said, be prepared to recognize the king as custodian of the Islamic holy places in Jerusalem, but would not under any circumstance relinquish Israeli sovereignty over East Jerusalem. Hussein insisted on sovereignty over East Jerusalem, or at least to extricate the city from Israeli sovereignty and establish a special regime. Hussein's longing for the city he had lost in the war of 1967 was so intense that on March 7, 1974 he refused the offer of the minister of defense, Moshe Dayan, to hand back to Jordan all of the West Bank except East Jerusalem. Hussein was willing to leave negotiations on Jerusalem to the last, as Dayan suggested, but demanded a prior Israeli commitment to return sovereignty over Jerusalem to Jordan (Zak, 1996: 161–6, 180).

The broad gap between Israel and Jordan from the beginning of the secret dialogue between them diverted their efforts away from finding an overall agreement – what the Israeli political discourse called the Jordanian option – into a number of limited understandings and *ad hoc* arrangements (Garfinkle, 1992). Israel allowed Jordan to consolidate its position in East Jerusalem via its control of the Muslim religious bodies there. Until it repealed its annexation of the West Bank in 1988, Jordan had appointed the chief of the Supreme Muslim Council and the mufti of Jerusalem, controlled the Waqf and its assets, and paid the salaries of the officials (teachers, doctors, municipal and government employees etc.), who were employed by the Hashemite Kingdom. Jordan financed schools, colleges, graveyards, mosques, social and welfare services, supplied employment to its supporters and developed patronage networks and political influence in the West Bank and in Jerusalem via the various properties of the Waqf and state appropriations. With an annual budget of $17 million, including $5 million for Jerusalem alone, the Jordanian Waqf managed some 950 mosques in the West Bank (180 in Jerusalem and environs), and paid the salaries of 2,500 employees (1,000 in Jerusalem and environs). Between the years 1953 and 1994, Jordan invested in the West Bank, through the Waqf, about $485 million, and in 1967–89 another $250 million. In addition, in the summer of 1998 King Hussein donated $8.2 million for refurbishing the golden dome on the Dome of the Rock, prompting the King of Saudi Arabia to donate a similar sum to the holy places on the Haram al-Sharif. The Jordanian donation was handled through the official channels of the Hashemite Kingdom, with the Saudi donation by UNESCO in coordination with the PLO (Friedland and Hecht, 1996: 286–8; Giladi and Merchav, 1998; Musallam, 1996: 97–8, 107; Reiter, 1997; Zak, 1996: 175–8).

Israel approved the Jordanian steps as they were in accordance with its policy of granting Jordan religious standing in Jerusalem. The moves bolstered Hussein's political control over other parts of the West Bank, limiting the influence of the PLO and suppressing all outcrops of local Palestinian autonomy.

In June 1967, immediately after the annexation, Israel wanted to put the Sharia' courts under the authority of its religion ministry, but the religious leaders in East Jerusalem rejected the idea outright. In July 1967 they re-established the Supreme Muslim Council, which had been founded in the early 1920s under the leadership of Haj Amin al-Husseini, putting the religious courts under its provenance. Israel did not recognize the Council, but with Jordan exerting its influence and directing the operation of the religious institutions in the eastern city, a way was found of arranging for the activity of the Sharia' courts there as well. They remained an independent institution whose decisions did not obligate the Israeli establishment. Judgments dealing with personal status that required official state registration, such as that of marriages and births, were handed over for ratification by the Sharia' courts in Israel, first the one in Jaffa, then the one in West Jerusalem. The Sharia' court in East Jerusalem is not responsible for sending the records to the Israeli courts; this is done by the applicant. This arrangement does not require mutual recognition and thus constitutes a technical solution that each side relates to from its own point of view. The Israeli administration credits the authorization of a court it recognizes, and the East Jerusalem court remains independent of the Israeli Ministry of Religious Affairs (al-Qaq, 1997; Roman, 1997a; Sabella, 1997b). Jordan's involvement in directing the religious institutions behind the scenes made it easier to reach this arrangement. The confrontation was regulated and managed in pragmatic ways, also with regard to oversight of Al-Aqsa's religious preachers. When a Jewish official asked a Muslim preacher, on July 24, 1967, to seek prior approval of the contents of his upcoming Friday sermon, the request was rejected by Sheikh Hassan Tahbub, director of the Waqf in Jerusalem and later minister of religious endowments in the Palestinian Authority. The Supreme Muslim Council issued a declaration that it was forbidden for non-Muslims to supervise Islamic affairs. In response, Israel deported some of the signatories to the declaration, most prominently Sheikh Abd al-Hamid Sa'ih, then chairman of the Supreme Muslim Council, and later, from 1983 to 1993, the speaker of the Palestinian National Council (al-Qaq, 1997; Benvenisti, 1996: 84; Zak: 1996; 175–8). Jordan intervened to organize religious life, thus preserving its standing in the West Bank. As the status of the PLO rose in the West Bank and Gaza Strip and its competition with Jordan intensified, the religious institutions, and in particular the management of the Waqf, became targets for the PLO. In the 1980s the PLO insinuated several of its men into the Waqf directorship, and the ups and downs in the relations between the PLO and Jordan during these years were reflected in this body, which was headed by Sheikh Sa'ad al-

Din al-Alami, and afterwards by Sheikh Hassan Tahbub. In the mid-1990s this entity, along with the other religious bodies in Jerusalem, came under the control of the Palestinian Authority (al-Qaq, 1997).

Jerusalem versus the Temple Mount

East Jerusalem has been blessed with historical assets and sites sacred to the three monotheistic religions. These include the sites of the crucifixion and resurrection of Jesus in the Church of the Holy Sepulcher, according to most Christian traditions; of the binding of Isaac, according to the Jews and Christians, and of Ishmael, according to most Muslim traditions; the site of the First and Second Temples of the Jews; of the Prophet Mohammed's ascent to heaven, according to Muslim tradition; and the focal point of Muslim prayers before that was transferred south to Mecca (all these are on the Temple Mount, called al-Haram al-Sharif by the Muslims); the Western Wall, part of the retaining wall of the Temple Mount from the Second Temple period and the most holy site for Jews in the absence of the Temple; and any number of churches, mosques, synagogues, cemeteries, and historical sites scattered around the city. This lodges a great responsibility with the ruler. Of all these holy sites in East Jerusalem, al-Haram al-Sharif – the Temple Mount – is the one with the greatest potential for an explosion. It is a holy place for two religions whose adherents in Jerusalem are in the midst of an intense political confrontation. The more pious they are, the more interest they have in the site and the more importance they attribute to it (Segal and Sa'id, 1997). Furthermore, in the twentieth century, the age of Middle East nationalism, each controlled the area in turn. The problem of who should control the site became acute with the appearance of groups of believers, Jewish extremists on one side and Muslim extremists on the other, for whom control of and sovereignty over the Temple Mount are the litmus test of religious devotion. In short, these groups believe that the Middle East conflict is not political, but religious, and the side that controls the Temple Mount can prove that God is on its side and that it is bringing redemption to the world.

In order to regulate religious tension and prevent it from sliding into and exacerbating the already present national tension in the city, the Israeli authorities have, since 1967, given the Muslim and Christian authorities autonomy in managing their holy sites. In the law for their preservation, enacted in 1967, Israel promised to afford full protection from desecration and harm, free access to visitors and tourists, and freedom of religious practice in all these places. Entry to the Temple Mount is permitted to all during the visiting hours that have been set by managers of the site in keeping with Muslim ritual requirements. In fact, Jewish freedom of worship on the Temple Mount was seriously restricted after the occupation in 1967 out of fear of strong Muslim protests. On August 22, 1967, "legal scholars, teachers, and muftis in Jerusalem and in the West Bank" went so far as to issue a warning that any change in the *status quo* would be "a gross violation of the sanctity of the sites holy to the Muslims, and serious aggression that would have far-reaching results, not only within the Muslim community in Jerusalem, but throughout the Muslim world and in the international community" (Benvenisti, 1996: 222). Israeli Defense Minister Dayan ruled, in June 1967, that Jews could visit the Temple Mount but not conduct public prayers there or pray individually in a provocative way. The government approved Dayan's decision. On August 16, 1967 the ministerial committee for holy sites decided to forbid the chief rabbi of the Israel Defense Forces (IDF), Shlomo Goren, from bringing thousands of Jewish worshippers to the Temple Mount on the Sabbath following the fast of the Ninth of Av. From 1967 onwards, the Temple Mount was at the center of Rabbi Goren's religious world and his activity. While the final shots of the battle were still whistling through the Old City in June 1967, he proposed to the general of the central command, who had directed the battle, that he blow up the Dome of the Rock. The general, Uzi Narkis, rejected the idea categorically, but Rabbi Goren did not remain silent. He called Dayan's measures "handing the Temple Mount over to the Muslims" and "desecration of the Temple Mount." While he was still in uniform he sought, in a variety of ways, to have the decision revoked, but never succeeded (Shragai, 31 Dec. 1997). The vote of the ministerial committee acquired the force of a cabinet decision, and it has served as the basis for all subsequent government determinations about the *status quo* on the Temple Mount. As is usual in politics, the government has tried to refrain from making an explicit decision forbidding Jewish prayer on the Temple Mount, or from declaring the place a site holy to Muslims alone. Instead, ministers have preferred to rule that entry to the site is forbidden to Jewish worshippers on a given date. Similarly, they have preferred to use affirmative phraseology for this purpose, stating that Jews asking to pray on the Mount be directed by the police to the Western Wall. This was justified by what was said to be a need to preserve public order (Shragai, 25 Feb. 1997).

Since 1967, the Israeli police and the municipality have been conducting an ongoing dialogue with the Waqf, which administers the Temple Mount. The police have forbidden Jews to engage in public prayer on the Mount on the grounds of security and preservation of public order. They ignore Jews who pray individually and inconspicuously on the margins of the compound. Israeli ministers of religion have chosen not to exercise their authority to permit Jewish prayer on the site. The government has been aided by the orthodox rabbinate, which forbids Jews to ascend to the Temple Mount on religious grounds. According to Jewish law, since the cessation of Temple sacrifices, Jews cannot reach the level of purity required for entering the Temple area, and since the precise location of the Temple is unknown, most rabbinical authorities ban entry to the Temple Mount entirely. A minority permits Jews to enter a certain part of the Mount where, in their opinion, the Temple was not located. These restrictions have led certain right-wing religious groups to attempt to establish a synagogue on the Temple Mount in this area. But Israel's chief rabbis have consistently opposed such an initiative (*Ha'aretz*, 13 Oct. 1996).

During the 1990s there have been changes in the *status quo* on the Temple Mount, as well as in its legal, political, and national status. First, while in the 1970s the Israeli Supreme Court rejected on formal grounds the right of Jews to pray there, in the 1980s it ruled in principle that the government could not enforce, on the grounds of preservation of public order, a blanket prohibition against Jews worshipping on the site. The state, the court ruled, had to provide concrete and near-certain proof in each instance that Jewish worship would create a disturbance. Second, the Oslo accords and the peace treaty with Jordan made the ultimate status of the site open to negotiation. This was a matter of great concern to the national religious camp in Israel. The Committee of Rabbis of Judea, Samaria, and Gaza issued a call for "every rabbi in whose

opinion going up [to the Temple Mount] is permitted to himself
go up to the Mount and also to instruct the members of his community on how to go up in accordance with all the stipulations of
Jewish law" (Shargai, 19 Feb. 1997). These rabbis' political–religious
impulses moved them to challenge the chief rabbinate's prohibition against Jews entering the Mount. Their religious–political
outlook overtook their loyalty to the chief rabbinate, and they
began to take measures to obtain sanction for going up to the
Mount. Third, Israeli and Waqf authorities no longer permit individual Jews to pray on the Mount in inconspicuous solitude. In
order to ensure that they not engage in provocative activity, religious Jews are allowed to enter the Temple Mount only alone or
in pairs, solely in order to visit the site, and only with police or
Waqf chaperones (Ramon, 1997; Reiter, 1997).

In addition to modulating religious tension, guaranteeing freedom of worship and access to holy sites serves as a political tool for
the Israeli government in its struggle to obtain recognition of its
sovereignty over East Jerusalem and the Temple Mount. The
government advertises its guarantee of free access and worship in
East Jerusalem to the world at large, contrasting it to the situation
that prevailed between 1948 and 1967. During this period, the
Jordanian authorities did not allow Israelis to go to the Western
Wall or the Jewish cemeteries on the Mount of Olives, even
though the armistice agreement between Israel and Jordan in
1949 required Jordan to do so (Hirsch, Hausen-Koriel & Lapidot,
1994: 131–58). In fact, Israel's sovereignty is not recognized by
any international body, and no flag flies over the buildings on the
Temple Mount. There is an Israeli flag inside the Israeli police
station on the site, and the Palestinians hoist their flag during
demonstrations that occasionally break out in the compound.
Officially, security and public order are Israel's responsibility, but
in practice the Waqf also plays a role in this, with its employees
policing, protecting, and supervising the site. The police are the
sole guardians of the Mughrabi entry gate adjacent to the Western
Wall, and they guard the external walls. The Waqf guards are
solely responsible for the rest of the gates and for guarding the
interior of the compound (Reiter, 1997).

Since 1967 some ten extremist nationalist and religious groups
have been asking for authorization to conduct religious ceremonies on the Temple Mount, but the Israeli police and courts have

prevented them from doing so. There are regular confrontations between these groups and the police on holidays and days of commemoration related to the Mount: the Ninth of Av, the anniversary of the destruction of the Temple; and the three pilgrimage holidays, Pesach, Shavu'ot, and Sukkot, during which the Torah commands Jews to appear at the Temple. In general, this is an internal Israeli affair that comes to a head at the gates of the holy compound. It is not an interreligious conflict between Jewish and Arab nationalist extremists, nor does it take place on the Mount itself. Such a confrontation occurred on the Ninth of Av in 1995. In general, the police have allowed Israeli right-wing activists to enter the compound as visitors, in pairs, on this day. As in the past, on this particular day the police relied on the understanding that had been reached with Faisal Husseini, who is the PLO official responsible for Jerusalem affairs, and with the vice-chairman of the Supreme Muslim Committee, which supervises the management of the site. But flaring tempers and the preparations made by young Muslims for physical confrontation with the Israeli visitors and with the police who accompanied them undermined the understanding and led the police to close the Mount to both Jews and Muslims (*Ha'aretz*, 7 Aug. 1995).

As a rule, Israeli governments have managed to neutralize the Mount's potential to spark an uncontrollable religious–national conflagration. The attempts at the establishment of a common front by extremist Jewish groups that are active on this issue have failed. In the years since 1967 there have been very few cases in which the joint Jewish–Israeli and Muslim–Palestinian supervision of the site holy to both groups has not worked. These episodes can be divided into three categories. The first involves a combination of religious fundamentalism and mental illness. In June 1968 an Australian Jew set fire to Al-Aqsa; on August 28, 1969 a Christian messianic fundamentalist did the same; on April 11, 1982 a Jew took cover in the Dome of the Rock and went on a shooting spree, killing two Palestinians and wounding 44 others. The group that came physically closest to blowing up the Islamic holy sites also falls into this category. Its members were less developed ideologically and less expert operationally than those of some of the other groups that have tried to do the same, and for this reason Israel's security services gave them scant attention. Yet on January 26, 1984 Waqf guards discovered members of the Bnei

Yehuda cult, consisting of one-time criminals from the aban-
doned neighborhood of Lifta in Jerusalem, trying to infiltrate the
Temple Mount under the direction of their leader, Shimon
Barda.

The second category is one in which religious fundamentalism
and political goals are combined. In 1974, 1977, and 1982, the
extreme rightist religious Zionist Yoel Lerner gathered around
him groups of enthusiastic young men who conspired to blow up
the Al-Aqsa mosque and the Dome of the Rock. Israel's under-
cover General Security Service (GSS – the so-called Shin Bet)
became attuned to these plots at an early stage, and the conspirators were tried and convicted. On the Sukkot holiday, October 12,
1990, there was a violent Palestinian–Muslim demonstration
against the intention of some extremist Jews to lay a cornerstone
for a new Temple on the Mount. The Temple, this group
believed, would be built on the ruins of the Islamic holy places,
and they concluded that laying the cornerstone would expedite
destruction of the Muslim shrines. Matters got complicated when
the Israeli authorities decided not to allow the Jews to bring the
stone into the Temple Mount compound, but to permit them
only to pray there. In response, there was a general call-up of
young Muslims to defend their holy site. Tempers flared and a
demonstration broke out during which stones were thrown from
al-Haram al-Sharif down onto the Jewish worshippers at the
Western Wall below. When police entered to restore order, they
killed 21 Palestinians and wounded 150 (Shragai, 1996: 292–8,
343–60). In December 1997 the Israeli security services frustrated
the plan of a Jewish group to outrage Muslim worshippers on a
Friday during the Muslim holy month of Ramadan by throwing a
pig's head wrapped in pages of the Koran into the compound. The
intention was to create a bloody riot that would stymie the government's intention of making an additional restricted withdrawal
from the West Bank, as it had obligated itself to do (*Ha'aretz*, 25
Dec. 1997).

The third category consists of individuals with a messianic theology according to which the redemption of the Jewish people
and the world will be brought about by human action, and that, as
a result, the Islamic shrines should be forcibly removed from the
Temple Mount. Indeed, God, they believe, has assigned this task
to his faithful so that they can prove that they desire and deserve

redemption. Unlike beliefs in the second category, which are characterized by a political ideology consistent with its religious–fanatic principles, the thinking in this third category is based entirely on the messianic theological principle. The most dangerous and best-known of the extremist Jewish attempts to destroy the Muslim shrines was the plan designed by members of the Jewish underground organization of the early 1980s, a case which can be seen as falling into both of the last two categories. In January 1984, members of this group sought to blow up the Muslim shrines on al-Haram al-Sharif. The plot originated in the heart of the religious Zionist establishment in Israel and some 80 people knew of it, at one level or another. These were not individuals on the lunatic fringe; rather, they were people who had profoundly internalized the dominant religious–Zionist ideology and messianic theology. They concluded that God was angry with his people and that he had punished them with the evil of the withdrawal from the Sinai and with the peace agreement with Egypt. God was also angry, they believed, because of the State of Israel's failure to expel the Muslims from the Temple Mount. Purging the Temple Mount of the Islamic shrines was, in their view, a revolutionary act that would redeem the Jewish people and change the world. The redemptive explosion would mitigate God's wrath, and from then on His loving kindness towards His people would prevail. Ironically, they did not view the pan-Islamic holy war and the international actions that would surely follow their act as being punishment for a nefarious deed. Instead, they saw these as an expression of divine grace, a messianic world order that would turn back the wheels of history and pave the way for renewal of the Israeli kingdom and rebuilding of the Temple. Other members of the group sought through this dramatic, war-precipitating act, to achieve the political goal of halting the Israeli withdrawal from the Sinai and from the rest of Greater Israel. The Jewish Underground's plot integrated messianic religious–mystic with political violence. The plan was never, however, put into action, and the entire Underground was arrested over the course of six months in 1984. The operational competence and ideological motivation of its members marked this as the most highly developed of the groups that had planned to attack the Islamic shrines. Its failure grew out of ideological–religious doubts, which led to repeated postponements of the operation. During the delay, other targets were given priority, as being less problematic for the conspirators. These operations included attacks on Palestinian leaders and civilians in revenge for the murder of Israeli settlers. The Underground carried out several such actions before its members were rounded up (Ramon, 1997; Shragai, 1996; Shragai, 30 Dec. 1997; Sprinzak, 1991; Sprinzak, 1995).

In summary, since 1967 Israel has succeeded in keeping the issue of Jerusalem a political rather than a religious problem. Pathological religious phenomena have not damaged the political frameworks. So far, politics has won out over religion. It has enlisted religion in its service while keeping it under control. The problem of Jerusalem is not congruent or identical with the problem of the Temple Mount, and the question of the Temple Mount will not prevent political negotiations on Jerusalem. The status of the Temple Mount is one of the disputed issues to be dealt with in those negotiations, one that the politicians hope to neutralize if they cannot resolve it.

On March 7, 1995, Binyamin Netanyahu, then running for prime minister, committed himself in a letter to Yehuda Etzion to allow Jewish worship on the Temple Mount. Etzion is one of the most extreme and unrelenting activists working for the removal of Muslim shrines from the Temple Mount and for the construction of a new Jewish Temple in their place, and he was the moving force behind the Jewish Underground's plot to blow up the mosques. But, once elected, Netanyahu took no steps to keep his promise. The National Religious Party, the parliamentary incarnation of the religious Zionist worldview, proposed that the Netanyahu government's program read as follows: "The government will arrange for the Jewish right to worship on the Temple Mount in accordance with the restrictions of Jewish law." But Netanyahu decided to leave out any mention of the Temple Mount and to declare instead his government's commitment to "the right of Jews to pray in all places holy to them in accordance with the restrictions of Jewish law." He also moved the declaration from the section of the government program dealing with Jerusalem to the section on religion and the state (*Ha'aretz*, 4 July 1996). So politics has not acceded to the messianic religious demand; quite the opposite is the case. Politicians have used the religious importance of the Temple Mount as a means of enlisting support. Once that is accomplished, however, the issue is neutralized.

A city united in theory and divided in practice

On June 27, 1967, after its crushing victory in the war, Israel decided unilaterally to apply its law and administration to East Jerusalem. The shock of the war and the sharp psychological transition from a sense of being caught in an inescapable state of siege to a consciousness of having won a historic victory, with its attendant conquest of biblical territories of the Land of Israel, provided the impetus for the annexation of East Jerusalem immediately after the battles in the city had ceased on June 9, 1967. Many people in Israel viewed the annexation as a continuation of the Zionist enterprise and a completion of the process that had begun in 1948. In addition, it should be remembered that Israel had asked King Hussein not to enter the war, and that there were Israeli leaders, such as Chief of Staff Yitzhak Rabin and General Uzi Narkis, who bore personal memories of Israel's military failure in Jerusalem's Old City in 1948 (Hirsch, Hausen-Koriel & Lapidot, 1994; Narkis, 1975; Narkis, 1991; Rabin, 1979).

The annexation was greeted harshly by 22 local Palestinian leaders, who on July 24, 1967 protested to the military governor of the West Bank about Israel's unilateral action. In their petition the leaders noted that "Arab Jerusalem is an integral part of Jordan." Affiliation with Jordan seemed to them legitimate since the international community accepted it. They therefore wrote that, "the annexation of Arab Jerusalem is a null and void act that the occupation authorities have imposed unilaterally, in opposition to the wishes of the city's inhabitants, who oppose this annexation and who believe in the unity of the Jordanian homeland" (Benvenisti, 1996: 216). The Basic Law: Jerusalem the Capital of Israel was passed by the Knesset on July 30, 1980. The law declared that "Jerusalem, complete and united, is the capital of Israel ... the seat of the President of the State, the Knesset, the Government, and the Supreme Court." The annexation thus became a basic law, the equivalent of being part of the country's constitution (Hirsch, Hausen-Koriel & Lapidot, 1994: 8). UN Security Council decision 478 ruled that Israel had violated international law, and called on the 14 countries that had diplomatic missions in Jerusalem to leave the city. In the wake of the decision all these countries moved their legations out of Jerusalem. El Salvador and Costa

Rica returned their embassies to Jerusalem in May 1982 and April 1984 respectively, and Burkina-Faso did so in September 1986.

Under Israeli law, the legal status of East Jerusalem is different from that of the rest of the territories occupied in 1967. Since the Six Day War Israel has maintained that the West Bank and Gaza should not be annexed officially. Instead, Israel has preferred to create *de facto* integration between these territories and the State of Israel. Israel understood that, in the absence of an option to transfer the Arab population, it should adopt a policy of encouraging Palestinian emigration and Jewish settlement in order to change the demographic balance between Jews and Arabs in the territories. This would be accomplished by administrative rules and means that are available to states when they determine who has the right to reside permanently in their sovereign and recognized territory. Israel made use of methods such as not granting permits to return to the West Bank to any Arabs who had not been there on June 5, 1967, and to those who had remained outside the West Bank for seven consecutive years without coming to visit at least once a year. Israel also made it difficult for Arabs residing elsewhere to move to live with their family members in the West Bank. It should be remembered that the dependence of the inhabitants of the West Bank and Gaza Strip on administrative permits from the Israeli authorities served primarily as a means of control and oversight, and were also intended, indirectly, to motivate them to leave the territories. Most of the Arabs, however, held fast to their land despite everything that was occurring, an action they called *sumud* – steadfastness in harsh conditions. Given the huge gap in demographic growth between Jewish Israelis and Palestinians in the 1967 territories (Gazit, 1985; Gilbar, 1992: 20–39; Grossman, 1987; Ma'oz, 1985), this policy of encouraging emigration by administrative means had little, if any, success, and since June 1967 has not been implemented consistently. The policy of *de facto* integration thus failed in the long run.

Even in Jerusalem, in which a policy of *de jure* rather than *de facto* integration was pursued, and where Israeli leaders were constantly declaring that the city had been united for eternity, the national–ethnic split remained a fact of daily life. While it is true, as Michael Romann and Alex Weingrod have proven (Romann & Weingrod, 1991), that Jerusalem is not physically divided between east and west as it was in the 1948–67 period, even after June 1967 it remained split between Jewish Israelis and Arab Palestinians on two planes. There was a vertical division between East and West in day-to-day affairs and a horizontal division, meaning that where there was contact between the two populations, Jews generally had the upper hand. The annexation did not narrow the ethnic–national divide or the cultural gap. The distinction between the residential neighborhoods of the two national communities in the city, their different city centers, the separate business and commercial centers, school systems, public institutions, public transportation, and medical services all created a notional borderline. This is not a small matter. It is a notional but concrete wedge between two groups that are very much aware of the division, and in fact they perceive it to be dangerous. Romann and Weingrod also found that moving from the territory of one side, "ours," to that of the "other" is not an everyday matter. The ethnic–national boundary that remains in Jerusalem has created profound segregation between East and West Jerusalem, and different ways of life and behaviors on both sides.

Exchange relations and economic contacts almost never occur across the ethnic–national border. Different levels of wealth divide commerce, economics, and the labor market, and this division coincides with ethnic–national affiliation. The Jewish side has resources and capital, and thus is in a controlling position in such economic cooperation as exists. Cooperation on an equal basis, if it exists at all, is *ad hoc*, fortuitous, opportunistic, limited in extent and brief in duration. These are, then, economic relations imposed by circumstances; they are not the result of free choice and preference. Furthermore, the relations between the two ethnic groups are in no way commensurate or symmetric. The ethnic–national divide in Jerusalem is a divide between ruler and ruled. There is a manifest inequality that favors the Jewish–Israeli side in access to resources, political power, and the ability to use force. Israel is able to operate systems of oversight and control over the weak Arab side. In practice, the Arabs in Jerusalem depend in every way on the Jews. Jews dictate the conditions, the place, and the manner of their exchange relations with the Arabs. So, for example, the Arabs are dependent on the employment market in the Jewish city, and are thus forced to adopt the Hebrew language. Jews are never in a situation where they must speak Arabic, nor are they dependent on vital services that can only be obtained in the Arab part of the city. Jews alone determine the municipality's policies and make its major decisions about East Jerusalem, and municipal authorities generally have minimal contact with the Arab population. While Arabs who must apply to the municipality are dealt with by Arab staff, these staff do not determine policy. The Jewish majority sees to it that the Arab side does not compete with it, and sets rules of the game that assist it in perpetuating its dominance. The reliance of East Jerusalem Palestinians on the Jewish sector has become more profound over the years; Palestinians are extremely dependent on their income from work in the Jewish sector and from commerce with Jews. This dependence has served to widen the economic and social gap between the two groups.

The Jewish–Arab differential has been maintained in education as well. Upon annexing East Jerusalem in 1967, Israel sought to impose the curriculum of Israel's Arab school system. This roused Palestinian opposition, both for national and practical reasons. For the former, they refused to consider themselves Israeli Arabs and to instill their younger generation with messages and content aimed at making them Israeli. The Israeli Arab curriculum was pro-Israel in its narrative and required knowledge of Jewish culture and history at the expense of Arab culture, which was emphasized in the Jordanian curriculum. So, for example, the Israeli curriculum devoted 156 annual school hours to the study of Jewish texts and only 30 hours to the study of Islam, as against 360 hours of Islamic literature in the Jordanian curriculum. There was also a practical objection to the Israeli program. Graduates of the Israel Arab system could not be accepted to universities in the Arab world, where most young East Jerusalemites preferred to get their higher education. The Palestinians boycotted the schools between June 1967 and January 1968, and the public schools were emptied of most of their pupils. Only about 50 per cent of the students in municipal elementary schools in East Jerusalem in the 1968–9 school year continued to study in the municipal schools the following year. In the summer of 1968 only four out of 96 East Jerusalem Arabs passed the Israeli high school graduation examination. In comparison, between 70 and 80 per cent of those who took the Jordanian high school graduation examination passed it. The result was that only a small number of students registered for municipal high schools where the Israeli examination was imposed on them. (Private Christian schools prepared their students for European examinations and college studies in the west, while private Muslim schools prepared their students for the Jordanian examination.) Private schools required the payment of tuition, so Jerusalem Arabs who could not afford private schools sent their children to study in public schools in Ramallah and Bethlehem. Since in 1971 this became common, the Israeli government forbade East Jerusalem Arabs to study in the West Bank. In 1969 the government tried to divert Palestinian protest in a different direction. Israel opened a program to prepare the students at municipal high schools in East Jerusalem for both the Israeli and Jordanian examinations. However, of 200 students who registered for this program, only five passed the Jordanian exams and none the Israeli. In 1975 Israel gave in and offered two separate programs, one following the Israeli Arab curriculum, to be taught in one school only, and the second following the West Bank – that is, Jordanian – curriculum. According to the municipality and the Palestinian Teachers' Association, since this time 50–60 per cent of East Jerusalem students have studied in private schools belonging to convents, churches, the Waqf, and other sponsors, with the rest studying in municipal schools. The movement from municipal to private schools and back again was also affected by economic factors. Recession, lowered incomes, and higher tuition fees in private schools have increased the number of students attending municipal schools (Cheshin, 1992: 180–1; *Kol Ha-Ir*, 2 Oct. 1998; Kutab & Kaminker, 1997; al-Qaq, 1997).

Israel excised several problematic components from the Jordanian curriculum, such as its treatment of the existence of Israel and the conflict between Israel and the Palestinians and its possible solution. No instructions were given on how to teach subjects, such as geography and history, in which the Palestinian narrative and point of view were entirely different from those of Israel. In addition to the Jordanian program, the East Jerusalem schools also teach Hebrew, civics, and road safety. But these subjects are optional and are not conditions for promotion of students from one class to the next, so the level of the classes, and of the teaching, is low. The municipality makes do with administrative responsibility for upkeep of the buildings and with paying salaries, but neglects the development of the system and does not provide it with the same services it gives to schoolchildren in the Jewish sector. In 1995, the Jerusalem municipality had only two and a half school inspector positions for the East Jerusalem school system. That system, according to figures from the municipality and the Palestinian Teachers' Association, numbered, in 1997, 26,153 pupils (alongside about 16,000 in private institutions). In 1998 there were 33 schools in East Jerusalem, or a total of 842 classes. Students in them received no psychological counseling from the municipality, no safety inspections, and no oversight of the appointment of teachers and principals, all services the city provides to the schools in the Jewish sector. In practice, the content of the teaching was not under the supervision of the Israeli Ministry of Education but rather of an officer of the military government. A report by the municipal education office in 1997 pointed out the long-standing pedagogical and physical neglect of municipal education in East Jerusalem. As a result of this the level of illiterates in the upper classes of elementary school reached 30 per cent, while the drop-out rate from secondary schools was about 40 per cent. Neglect shows itself also in the education gap between Jews and Arabs in Jerusalem, in elementary education and in higher education. In 1995, only 13.9 per cent of the population above the age of 15 in East Jerusalem had up to an eighth-grade education, as opposed to 35.2 per cent in the Jewish sector. The percentage of those with more than 13 years of education was 39.9 among Jews as opposed to 19.1 among Arabs. However, the percentage of those with 9–12 years of education was similar: 46.2 for Jews and 45.7 for Arabs (Choshen & Shachar, 1998: 266; *Ha'aretz*, 16 June 1998; Nesher, 6 Sept. 1996; Rubinstein, 11 Aug. 1995; Segev, 4 July 1995; State of Israel, Survey of Population and Housing, Central Bureau of Statistics, 1995).

The responsibility for determining the curriculum of the public schools in East Jerusalem was handed over to the Palestinian Authority on November 25, 1994; the Jerusalem municipality continued to be responsible for physical maintenance. Aside from replacing the seal of the Hashemite kingdom with the Palestinian seal, a symbolic action, the Palestinian Authority made no changes. The curriculum and textbooks remained Jordanian and are identical to those used in the rest of the Palestinian Authority. The course material contains no incitement against Israel or any information that opposes the Oslo accords. The imprinting of the Palestinian seal on the textbooks and graduation examinations put

Israel in an awkward position but, seeing no other way out, the Israeli authorities decided in 1995 to paste stickers bearing the seal of the city of Jerusalem over the Palestinian seal (*Ha'aretz*, 26 Aug. 1996; Nesher, 6 Sept. 1996; Rubinstein, 11 Aug. 1995; Segev, 4 July 1995).

In 1994, Jerusalem's mayor, Ehud Olmert, urged the Ministerial Committee for Jerusalem Affairs to ban the use of the Palestinian curriculum. In a document he submitted to the committee in October 1994, he stated:

Via the curriculum the road will be paved towards an absolute takeover by the Autonomy Authority of the entire school system in East Jerusalem ... There is a very real danger that under Israeli government financing ... the school system will in practice be run by the PLO and/or the Autonomy Authority ... including the history of the conflict from a Palestinian point of view, the status of Jerusalem, and so on.

(Jerusalem municipality, background paper for the discussions of the Ministerial Committee on Jerusalem Affairs, 25 Oct. 1994: 10)

Olmert's request was not accepted and neither did the Palestinian Authority implement its intention, in 1996, of replacing the Jordanian curriculum with its own (*Ha'aretz*, 15 Aug. 1995; Rubinstein, 11 Aug. 1995; Segev, 4 July 1995). In parallel, the new Israeli government elected in June 1996 did not impose the Israeli curriculum on East Jerusalem, despite its original intention of doing so. Neither did it prevent the Palestinian Authority's involvement in the high school graduation examinations in the summer of 1997 in both the municipal and private schools. The Palestinian Authority handed over examination papers without a Palestinian seal at the Israeli roadblocks at the city limit, and received the exams back, at the same locations, for grading. Supervision of the examination itself was in the hands of Israeli Arab instructors. The Israeli authorities presented this arrangement as temporary, just for a single year. It is similar in several aspects to the arrangements achieved for counting the votes in the ballot boxes placed in East Jerusalem during the elections to the Palestinian Authority in January 1996 (*Ha'aretz*, 26 Aug. 1996, 3 June 1997, 5 June 1997; *Kol Ha-Ir*, 6 June 1997, 13 June 1997). This compromise left Israel's right-wing Likud government frustrated, so it set up a committee of senior officials which proposed imposing the Israeli curriculum in East Jerusalem. In June 1998 the Ministerial Committee on Jerusalem Affairs rescinded the decision, after it became clear that it would be impossible to implement. The Ministerial Committee made do with a decision to oversee the curriculum in East Jerusalem, and stated that, "the textbooks there will be printed by an Israeli publisher," and not by the Palestinian Authority (*Ha'aretz*, 16 June 1998).

In the arena of higher education, the Palestinian Authority placed Al-Quds University, which operates in East Jerusalem without being part of the Israeli system of higher education, under the Palestinian Council for Higher Education. Al-Quds was founded in 1984. In 1996 it had 2,564 students, 41 per cent of whom (1,050) were residents of Jerusalem, and 247 faculty members. It is a small university, even by Palestinian standards, and certainly in comparison with the Hebrew University of Jerusalem, which in 1996 had 24,739 students and 1,249 senior full-time faculty members. The Israeli government helps fund the Hebrew University, as it funds all public universities in Israel, but it provides no funds to Al-Quds (Kamil & Reiter, 1998). In the wake of a petition to the High Court of Justice by the right-wing organization Be-Tzedek, Al-Quds announced that it had initiated the process of requesting a permit from the Israeli Council of Higher Education (*Kol Ha-Ir*, 3 July 1998, 24 July 1998).

Romann and Weingrod (Romann & Weingrod, 1991) note that the Arabs in Jerusalem have preferred to preserve, rather than to blur, the fundamental segregation of the two ethnic–national communities. From their point of view, this has been the only way to preserve their distinct national identity. In their desire to preserve their sectorial identity and not to recognize the annexation of East Jerusalem to Israel, they collectively boycotted Israeli institutions and thus the vast majority of them have not participated in municipal elections. This boycott was not, however, complete. A large number – some 1,500 – Palestinians have been employed by the municipality (Cheshin, 1992: 191), and many others have worked in other arms of the Israeli government, or have provided building services to Jews, even on expropriated Palestinian land. They have justified such activity as part of their *sumud*, in order to provide for Palestinian viability and presence in Jerusalem. The collective boycott has preserved their self-identity and has prohibited what might naturally and logically have been considered an outcome of the annexation to Israel, such as a collective demand for equality in the allocation of resources and in access to city control and supervisory functions. Even though this position created inequality that grew continually from 1967 onward, the Arabs in East Jerusalem were willing to pay the price in order to strengthen collective segregation and their covert struggle with Israel. In many respects, the Palestinians succeeded in this mission in Jerusalem. Since the annexation there has been an entire range of special Palestinian arrangements and institutions, such as the Jordanian curriculum, the independent Islamic courts, religious and welfare institutions (the Waqf), and the use of Jordanian currency. The Bank of Israel also allowed Palestinian moneychangers to operate there even when similar activity was prohibited in Israel. Many Palestinian institutions have been established in Jerusalem, under the protection of Israeli law, which allows more freedom of action than that prevailing in the rest of the 1967 territories, where military law applied. The Israeli authorities have looked the other way when confronted with violations of the law relating to arrangements with the internal institutions of the Palestinians. Israel has satisfied itself with imposing its authority on the legal level, and with regard to the contacts that East Jerusalem Palestinians have with the Israeli establishment. At the same time, the Israeli government has done little to reduce the gap between the large and strong Jewish sector and the weak and small Arab one. The huge gap in government services has been maintained even though, legally, East Jerusalem Arabs have equal status and rights, since the eastern city was annexed to Israel and its residents bear Israeli identity cards and pay municipal taxes.

In fact, the level of services East Jerusalem enjoyed at the time of annexation was a low one. Jordanian Jerusalem had only partial water and sewage systems, and the Jordanian territory that Israel added to Jerusalem included rural areas where people conducted their lives independently without any link to the Jordanian municipality of Jerusalem. The level of services and infrastructure in these rural areas was even lower than that in Jordanian Jerusalem. There was almost no system of roads linking these villages, the water system did not supply the needs of the inhabitants, and there were no sewage or telephone services at all. Bringing the services and infrastructure of these areas up to the Israeli level required huge investments, but for the reasons cited above Israel did but little in this area. Until the 1980s Israel refrained from preparing a master development and building plan for East

Jerusalem, thus supplying itself with an administrative excuse for preserving the gap between Arab East Jerusalem and Jewish West Jerusalem. Israel did link up all homes in Jerusalem to the water system, but the garbage removal service, the state of the roads and sidewalks, street lighting and sewage are all far inferior in Arab Jerusalem to that which exists on the Jewish side. Furthermore, in the years 1988–90, less than five per cent of all non-residential building starts were in the Arab areas of Jerusalem. This structural discrimination against the Arabs is also reflected in the city's workforce. Most of the workers responsible for East Jerusalem are from the western part of the city. In the 1990s Arab municipal workers were 17 per cent of the total municipality workforce, which is only half of East Jerusalem's proportion of the city population. Moreover, two-thirds of the Arab employees are employed in sanitation and maintenance work (Benvenisti, 1996: 102, 150–1; Cheshin, 1992: 178–84).

In 1995, the municipality prepared a report in which it acknowledged, for the first time, that there is a serious gap between the Arab and Jewish sectors in terms of infrastructure and municipal and national services. The lack of a detailed master plan approved by the authorities made it impossible to develop the road, water, and sewage systems, or to set aside land for the construction of schools, public institutions, and parks. There were serious difficulties in garbage collection, firefighting services, distribution of mail and of household gas, and in the development of the electric and telephone networks. In several areas the situation was particularly harsh – there was no street lighting in large areas, there was a shortage of 21 kilometers of roads, and of 150 kilometers of sewage and drainage pipes; there was no regular garbage collection. There was a shortage of 345 schoolrooms, a serious problem of adolescent drug use, overwhelming poverty and neglect of the elderly because of the lack of welfare services and failure to care for disadvantaged populations. There were no arrangements for the hospitalization of the mentally ill and the retarded. It should be remembered that the East Jerusalem Arabs make up 30 per cent of the city's population, but received, in 1995, only about seven per cent of funds budgeted by the city. In the national budget their share was even smaller. In 1995 the Arabs of East Jerusalem received less than one per cent – NIS 1.5 million – of the NIS 175 million allocated by the government to Jerusalem.

Ironically, most of this sum was directed to the Arab neighborhood of Beit Safafa in the western part of the city, in particular for
a new highway that ran through the neighborhood and which
would serve large numbers of Jews (*Ha'aretz*, 10 July 1995;
Rubinstein, 20 Nov. 1996). In 1999 less than ten per cent of the
municipality's development budget was designated for investment in East Jerusalem, most of it in projects connected to tourism. At a special cabinet meeting in 1999, the municipality
presented further data on the East–West gap in the city, gaps running from 300 to 1,000 per cent, depending on the area. In Jewish
Jerusalem there were 743 inhabitants per kilometer of sewage
pipe; in Arab Jerusalem 7,362 inhabitants. In Jewish Jerusalem
there were 690 inhabitants per kilometer of sidewalk, as opposed
to 2,917 in the East (*Ha'aretz*, 25 March 1999; *Kol Ha-Ir*, 16 April
1999). According to the report of 1995, the sum required to close
the gap between Arab and Jewish Jerusalem was NIS 520 million,
but according to municipality data from 1999, this will require
more than NIS 1 billion (*Kol Ha-Ir*, 16 April 1999).

Teddy Kollek, Jerusalem's mayor from 1965 to 1993, implemented Israel's annexation and discrimination policy, maintaining that in order to prevent friction between Jews and Arabs it was
necessary to develop a multi-confessional and multicultural fabric
in Jerusalem. But Kollek's policy, as he himself acknowledged,
was also "to make it difficult for the Arabs to live, not to allow
them to build. Maybe they will get out of their own volition,
ensuring the demographic balance in Jerusalem" (Benvenisti,
1996: 132). This institutionalized the discrimination against the
Arabs of East Jerusalem. The segregation and communal autonomy of the Arabs in Jerusalem in the areas of religion, education,
language, professional associations, communications, economics,
commerce, and culture led to neglect, despite the repeated asser-
tion that Jerusalem was a united city, and despite Israel's convic-
tion as to the correctness of this proposition. Teddy Kollek
confessed:

We said over and over again that we would make the rights of the Arabs
equivalent to the rights of the Jews in the city. These were empty words
… They were and remained second and third-class citizens … I did
something for Jewish Jerusalem during the last 25 years. For East
Jerusalem? Nothing! What did I do? Schools? Nothing! Sidewalks?
Nothing! Cultural institutions? Not at all! Yes, we built a sewage system

and improved the water supply. You know what? Do you think it was for their good? To improve their lives? Where have you been? There were a few cases of cholera there and the Jews got alarmed that they'd get it, too. Then we did the sewage and water system.

(*Ma'ariv*, 10 Oct. 1999; in: B'tselem, 1995: 49–50)

As noted, this policy did not arouse the wrath of the Arabs because it coincided with their national goal of keeping themselves separate from the Israeli framework and of not achieving equal rights within it.

In order to conduct day-to-day life, the Israeli establishment, and the municipality and the Palestinian public in particular, made use of a mediating institution in the form of the village or neighborhood leader, called the *mukhtar*; the heads of religious institutions; and the veteran elite. The mukhtar was the modern incarnation of an institution with Ottoman origins that Jordan had also exploited in order to create a mediating class (*wasta*) between the governing authorities and the population. Functioning alongside the mukhtars were members of the economic, academic, religious, and social elite, serving as intermediaries who obtained benefits and various permits for their institutions and families. This class of intermediaries enabled the central government, whose authority over the population was doubtful, to impose its will. The mukhtar and the intermediary presented the complaints and requests of the Arabs in their neighborhoods to the mayor's advisor on Arab affairs, and, when these requests were acted on, it gave the intermediaries authority within their communities. In exchange for the status they enjoyed from the Israeli authorities, the mukhtars and intermediaries were expected to legitimize Israeli rule, and to participate in official events as representatives of the East Jerusalem population. Since these were not political personages of the first order, there were no protests against their grant of legitimacy to Israel, and they were not considered to be collaborators (Benvenisti, 1996: 100–2, 104–7, 131–5; Hasson, 1996). The Israeli authorities thus made use of the veteran elite, which was adaptable and cooperative, and used traditional methods to ensure that they would help oversee the Arab population. This would help foster an enlightened image without equalizing the living conditions in East Jerusalem to those in Jewish Jerusalem. The Palestinians in East Jerusalem were annexed to Israel, but they did not become part of the Israeli community and collective.

They are not part of the same "public." The governmental and municipal authorities address the demands and problems of a specific civil consumer community, the Israeli Jewish public. Even when no deliberate policy of discrimination is implemented, the authorities tend to be unaware of the needs of a public that is not part of the "civil society." ... Benefiting this public gives no political profit to any decision-makers and there are elements that profit electorally from harming it (*Ir Shalem*, 1998: 49–50).

Labor Party governments and Teddy Kollek maintained that Israeli sovereignty would be determined in accordance with physical changes – the construction and habitation of Jewish neighborhoods on the eastern side of the city, and unequivocal preference for Jerusalem's Jews over its Arabs. As compensation, Arabs were allowed to maintain their own symbolic space in the form of the link with Jordan. This included the use of Jordanian passports and of the Jordanian dinar, maintenance of Jordanian citizenship, the operation of the Waqf and the Sharia courts that were not subject to Israeli law, and a measure of local freedom of action allowing the development of local Palestinian institutions and identity. The shortages and discrimination preserved the Palestinian uniqueness of East Jerusalem and reinforced its ties to the rest of the 1967 territories. This enabled energetic development of the Jewish sector in Jerusalem and its suburbs, from which Arabs in the metropolitan area also benefited. This benefit was, however, only indirect, especially in the form of the growth of employment and income. In infrastructure and services, construction and education, as well as in welfare services, their situation worsened as the gap between them and the Jews grew larger and as the Arab population of East Jerusalem increased dramatically. The discourse between Israel and the Palestinian public was a hegemonic one, characterized by Israeli dominance and the exclusion of Palestinians from positions of power and from resource allocation. This exclusion was not forced on the Palestinians; on the contrary, they chose it.

The Likud administrations in the municipality since 1993 and on the national level between 1996 and 1999 took an approach diametrically opposed to that of previous Labor administrations. They worked to impose symbols of Israeli sovereignty and governmental presence, and declared their intention of narrowing the gap between Arab and Jewish Jerusalem. The Likud governments assumed that improvement in day-to-day life would, for the Palestinians, serve as compensation for their losses on the symbolic level (*Ha'aretz*, 10 July 1995). The first step was made by the national government when it decided, at the beginning of January 1997, to add NIS 130 million to the municipal budget "in the framework of the program to strengthen Israeli sovereignty in the eastern city" (*Ha'aretz*, 27 Jan. 1997). This was an unprecedented decision, one that even the most "dovish" government in Israeli history, the Labor–Meretz government of 1992–6, had not made. During 1997 and 1998 some NIS 200 million was invested in East Jerusalem (*Ha'aretz*, 10 May 1999; *Kol Ha-Ir*, 16 April 1999). In May 1999, on the eve of the national elections, the Likud government decided to allocate approximately NIS 400 million over four years for infrastructure improvement in East Jerusalem. However, of the NIS 60 million designated for 1999, only NIS 18.1 million was actually budgeted (*Ha'aretz*, 10 May 1999). The decision was made over the opposition of the Ministry of Finance and it is reasonable to assume that it will not be implemented. In fact, no Israeli government will find it easy to provide the huge sums needed to close the gaps created by policies in existence for more than 30 years. After all, East Jerusalem Arabs are not Israeli citizens, are not Jews, and are linked politically to the institutions of the Palestinian Authority. At the same time, disadvantaged Jews and Arabs who are Israeli citizens are also knocking at the government's doors.

As will be made clear below, the East Jerusalem Palestinians reject Israeli national symbols and have no demands for the improvement of their daily life. They see Israeli government decisions to invest in the development of the East Jerusalem infrastructure as another type of conquest and of the imposition of Israeli identity, not as the government's obligation to the residents of its territory. The government commitment to build Arab housing as compensation for the construction of the Jewish neighborhood of Har Homa is an illustration of this. In February 1997, a month after the decision on the large investment in East Jerusalem, the national and municipal Likud administrations decided to commence the public construction of a Jewish neighborhood on the hill called Jabel Abu-Ghenem by the Arabs and Har Homa by the Jews. As compensation, national and local government leaders announced that they would proceed with infrastructure work that would allow the private sector to build thousands of housing units for Arabs in East Jerusalem (*Ha'aretz*, 27 Feb. 1997, 5 June 1997; *Kol Ha-Ir*, 9 May 1997). However, unlike on the Arab side, the infrastructure work for Jews on Har Homa was begun immediately since all the plans had already been completed and approved and contracts had already been signed. The work in the Arab sector was not able to begin, even if the decision makers had been overflowing with goodwill and had made the appropriate political decision and even if a private Arab contractor had turned up. In order to build, it was necessary to prepare detailed plans and to receive permits from city planning officials and from the Ministry of the Interior, permits that have been methodically denied to East Jerusalem. Thus the Likud government's decisions were no more than a declaration of intent, an attempt to improve the image that had been sullied by the decision to construct Har Homa (Shragai, 27 Feb. 1997).

The Intifada, which began at the tail end of 1987, turned the struggle between Israel and the Palestinians in Jerusalem from covert to overt. It is interesting that in several respects the Intifada in Jerusalem was different from that in the rest of the 1967 territories, all linked to the fact that Jerusalem was a frontier city. The economic dependence of the Arabs of East Jerusalem on the Jewish sector, and the geographical closeness of the two populations, made movement and the transfer from the rebellious East to the western part of the city easier. This also made several aspects of the patterns of the Intifada in Jerusalem distinct from those in the rest of the 1967 territories. First, there was only a limited response to the Intifada leadership's call to Arabs to detach themselves from Israel administration; the proportion of policemen and municipal workers from East Jerusalem who resigned their jobs was much lower than that of their colleagues in the rest of the 1967 territories. This was because the Jerusalem Arabs' economic dependence on income from employment from Israeli institutions was higher than in the West Bank; the public could not make such a sacrifice. In general, in Jerusalem a Jewish employer from the private sector hesitates to employ Arabs out of fear for his personal safety, while in other places Palestinian workers boycott the Jewish workplace. Second, their Israeli identity cards gave Jerusalem Arabs freedom of movement while their compatriots in the West Bank and Gaza Strip were under closure. The geographical proximity of the Jewish and Arab areas of Jerusalem made it easier for Jerusalem Arabs to get to their workplaces at times when there was a general Palestinian strike or when there was an Israeli-imposed closure. As a result, Jewish employers began to prefer Palestinians from Jerusalem to those from the rest of the territories. Third, the relatively easy access to the Jewish part of the city allowed Palestinians who were less fearful of Jewish violence, harassment, molestation, and security checks to go to the Jewish part of the city to relax and enjoy themselves, and of course also to make a living. Those who sought work in Jewish Jerusalem came from mobile sectors such as cab, truck, and bus drivers, as well as driving instructors who took advantage of their proximity to Jewish Jerusalem to supplement their incomes at times of strikes in East Jerusalem and as a result of the decline in tourism. There is much symbolism in the fact that, despite the attempt of the agitators to boycott everything connected to Israel, the souvenir shops in the Old City – both those owned by Christians and those owned by Muslims – continued to sell Jewish and Israeli symbols such as Hanukah menorahs and Star of David chains. Fourth, under the protection of Israeli law, which applied to East Jerusalem, the Palestinian leadership could foster independent institutions and take advantage of the relative freedom that prevailed there in comparison with the rest of the territories in order to lead the Intifada. With the institutionalization of the uprising it was easier to run it from Jerusalem, the location of professional associations, religious organizations, and other institutions of Palestinian civil society. The leaflets distributed throughout the territories by the United National Command, the Intifada leadership, providing instructions to the Palestinian public, were printed in and around Jerusalem. It was also easier to fax the leaflets to PLO headquarters in Tunis from East Jerusalem than from anywhere else. The political elite led the uprising in East Jerusalem, but there were also elements in the city that sought to restrict and moderate the expression of the Intifada in Jerusalem because of economic interests. The Intifada in East Jerusalem was largely the work of residents of refugee camps and the suburbs over the city line in the West Bank. In these places there was no economic interest in keeping things quiet. The leadership of the Intifada linked East Jerusalem to the West Bank, as did the connections between the veteran political elite and its counterparts in the rest of the West Bank. Fifth, in the second phase of the Intifada, once the mass demonstrations and commercial and employment strikes had played themselves out, and the Intifada was being run by select groups and not by organized masses, there were fewer terrorist actions in East Jerusalem than in other places in the 1967 territories. At the same time, it should be noted, the Intifada in Jerusalem has been characterized by spontaneous stabbings of Jewish civilians and policemen by individual Palestinian Arabs with nationalist, and sometimes personal, motives. The nationalist and religious reasons grew much stronger after the bloody incident of October 1990 on the Temple Mount. At this time, Jerusalem became a central theater for acts of vengeance by Muslim fanatics, who, at their own initiative, went out into the streets of West Jerusalem and stabbed Jewish civilians. In this frontier city, the lines of friction and contact became as close as the length of a knife blade. In February and March 1996 Jerusalem was hit hard by Hamas terror, harder than any other city in Israel. As retribution for the December 1995 slaying by the GSS of Yehiye Ayash, the commander of the organization's military arm, the Hamas carried out terrorist attacks against Israeli buses, and in Jerusalem 53 people were killed, 43 in a single week (Riedland & Hecht, 1996: 333–4; Roman, 1992; Zilberman, 1997).

Nevertheless, there is any number of points of similarity between the manifestations of the Intifada in Jerusalem and its pattern in the rest of the Palestinian areas. One of these is the boycott of Israeli products. This began as a total boycott that the Palestinian public was unable to live with, and was thus replaced with one of all products that could have Palestinian-produced replacements, such as cigarettes, soft drinks, and sweets. There was considerable evasion of the boycott, because of the financial temptation to make money by smuggling Israeli goods for which there was always a demand because of their higher quality. There was no boycott of Israeli raw materials purchased for use in local industry, and Palestinian products continued to be exported to the Israeli market.

Another similarity between Jerusalem and the rest of the Palestinian territories was the transition from the civil disobedience and mass demonstrations of the first stage of the Intifada to armed attacks by individuals. Others were the use of wall graffiti and leaflets as a channel of communication between the Intifada leadership and the Palestinian public; the boycott of the school system, with schoolchildren and students going out into the street to demonstrate and cause disturbances; and the severing of contact with Israeli authorities, even by the mukhtars who had mediated between the Arab populace and the municipality. There was a drastic decline in the number of East Jerusalem Arabs who participated in courses sponsored by the municipality, especially courses in Hebrew. There were also extended commercial and employment strikes, either full or partial; the adoption of a Palestinian calendar, an independent agenda which the Intifada leadership declared and for which it won impressive obedience by the Palestinian populace. There was also a sharp drop in the number of Jewish visitors and tourists in East Jerusalem, even at the Western Wall; Jewish Israeli tourists changed the paths of their walks so as to circumvent the Arab area of the city. Jews found alternatives to the cheap services that East Jerusalem had offered Jews, especially auto repair shops and restaurants. The organs of Israeli rule retreated to a large extent from East Jerusalem – business licensing regulations were not enforced, building and sanitation codes were not strictly observed, and traffic and parking laws went unenforced. East Jerusalem branches of Israeli institutions, such as banks and the telephone company, were closed, while Jewish industries moved from the Arab northeast of the city to its western side. Non-professional Arab workers in Jewish Jerusalem, in fields such as cleaning, maintenance, store clerks, and gas station attendants were laid off because of fear of terrorist attacks. Jewish workers, mostly immigrants from the former Soviet Union, were hired in their place. Jewish dependence on professional Arab workers, especially in the construction and auto repair sectors, prevented layoffs on a similar scale in these areas, despite the anxiety of Jewish employers. There was also sporadic and spontaneous Jewish violence against Arabs who crossed from East Jerusalem to the Jewish part of the city, along with frequent security checks by the police and the army. This reduced the number of Palestinians who crossed the city's seam (Cheshin, 1992: 188–92; Roman, 1992; Zilberman, 1997).

The conclusions are obvious. First, in most dimensions of time and space, the Intifada linked East Jerusalem even more strongly to the rest of the 1967 territories and deepened the gulf between it and the Jewish part of the city. At the time of the Intifada, the frontier city of Jerusalem was governed by a geography of fear. The close relations between the two populations and the well-developed contacts between them only made the fear more intense. Second, the special form the Intifada took in Jerusalem did not fundamentally change the previous system of relations, that between ruler and ruled, but in fact reinforced it. The two sides adjusted their previous relations to the conditions of the Intifada, and even broadened the gaps between them. While it is true that, from the beginning of the Intifada to the accession of the Labor government in 1992, Jewish settlers insinuated themselves, with the encouragement of the Israeli authorities, into more than 40 sites in the Arab areas of East Jerusalem, this did not in any fundamental way change the basic reality in East Jerusalem. The Palestinian Intifada was much more effective than were Israeli moves to make the Arab part of the city Jewish. Third, the Intifada underlined the unique position of East Jerusalem in the Palestinian space. From the Palestinian point of view also, Jerusalem is a frontier city with many connections to the "other" and the "enemy," leading to the unique form the Intifada took there.

It is important to note that the processes that the Palestinian citizens of the State of Israel has undergone since 1948 did not repeat themselves with the East Jerusalem Palestinians, and did not lead to their coming to terms with Israeli annexation. Such a development was impossible in the conditions of 1967 and thereafter. As Romann and Wingrod stress, there were many a priori differences between the Palestinians in East Jerusalem and the Palestinians residing in Israel. When, in 1948, Israel conquered areas in which there were large numbers of resident Arabs, the population was largely a rural one scattered over a wide area. Beyond this geographic aspect, and the low level of urbanization and modernization that characterized this population, the Palestinian population of 1948 lacked a political leadership and autonomous institutions that functioned more or less properly. This was apparently because the leadership dissolved with the flight of many of its members and the arrest, by the British, of others, and because it had been deeply divided since it had become tied up in the rebellion of 1936–9 (Arnon-Ohana, 1989; Nevo, 1977; Porat, 1978). None of this was the case in East Jerusalem in 1967, and all the more so thereafter. Jerusalem was home to a Palestinian community with a solid consciousness of itself, a local leadership, and a tradition of political leadership, both within the Palestinian institutions of the British Mandate period and in the Jordanian kingdom.

In the period that preceded the Israeli occupation, Jerusalem was not a remote rural area but rather a city of great religious importance, rule over which had granted legitimacy to the Hashemite dynasty, even if from an administrative and political point of view the city had been marginal. Beyond this, the lack of contact between the Arabs of Israel and their Palestinian and Arab brethren for 19 years had led to far-reaching changes among them. Unlike the Arabs of East Jerusalem, only a minority of the Palestinians in the State of Israel has social and family links to the inhabitants of the West Bank and Gaza Strip. The East Jerusalem Arabs are politically linked to the institutions of the territories, and the vast majority of them boycott Israel's municipal and political institutions. The Arabs of Israel, in stark contrast, are active participants in Israeli politics, and one of them, Knesset Member Azmi Bishara, was, in 1999, a candidate for Prime Minister. The ethnic–geographic boundaries between them and the dominant and ruling Jewish majority have been open since the dissolution of the military government over Israel's Arab population in 1966. In many cases, the Arabs in Israel even cross over the ethnic–cultural border and assimilate the norms of the majority as part of the process of Israelification they are undergoing (Mana' and Haj Yehiye, 1995; Rekhes, 1992: 127–99). Many of them have adopted Israeli identity, and the mainstream among them demand that their country's government treat them as citizens with equal rights.

In practice this is movement in two opposite directions. While the Palestinians in Israel are intensifying their demands for equal division of resources and access to the collective institutions, the process of separation has intensified among the Palestinians of East Jerusalem. The Palestinians in Jerusalem do not want to penetrate the heart of the political structure and change the division of power and resources, but rather to detach themselves from Israeli rule. Until the Oslo accords, the official demand of the Palestinians was to separate Jerusalem into two sovereign municipal entities while keeping the city undivided physically. Since then, the peace process has produced other ways to divide positions of control, administration, and resources in Jerusalem between Jews and Arabs.

2

THE CURTAIN RISES

JERUSALEM IN THE ISRAELI–EGYPTIAN PEACE NEGOTIATIONS

To Sinai via Jerusalem

When Israel and Egypt began sounding each other out on the possibility of an agreement, Jerusalem was one of the issues on the agenda. The discussions originated in secret contacts between Israel's foreign minister, Moshe Dayan, and President Sadat's emissary and deputy prime minister, Hassan Tohami, in Morocco in September 1977. The records of these talks have not yet been published, but the account provided by Dr. Eliahu Ben-Elissar, then director-general of the prime minister's office and later Israel's first ambassador to Egypt, can be presumed to be reliable, given his personal involvement and the fact that he quotes Dayan directly.

Tohami demanded of Dayan that he present a constructive program that would be considerate of Arab sensitivities about the city that was so holy to the Muslims. Dayan's reply, as Ben-Elissar reports it, was extremely interesting. "We have vested rights in the territories," Dayan said. He cited, "The settlements on the Golan Heights, the Western Wall, and the Jewish Quarter [of the Old City of Jerusalem], the Mount of Olives and the university, new population centers [in the southern Gaza Strip and northern Sinai] ... A solution to the problem of the Holy City could be easy and satisfactory to all parties" (Ben-Elissar, 1995: 40–1). Moshe Dayan seems to have gone a long way towards Tohami. He did not insist on the annexation to Israel of Arab East Jerusalem, or of the new Jewish neighborhoods built on the eastern side of the city after June 1967. Dayan stood firm on Israel's religious rights in

East Jerusalem, yet he refrained from naming the Temple Mount as a holy site for the Jews. He mentioned the new Jewish neighborhood in the Jewish Quarter in the Old City, but placed it in the same category as the settlements on the Golan Heights and in the Rafiah salient on the Sinai Peninsula. According to Ben-Elissar, Dayan made no distinction between the new Jewish neighborhoods in East Jerusalem and the Israeli settlements in the Golan Heights and in eastern Sinai, even though their status was different under Israeli law (because they were never formally annexed to Israel, as the East Jerusalem ones were). In Ben-Elissar's account, it was only at dinner, after the formal discussions had ended, that Dayan referred to the geographic, demographic, and municipal changes that Israel had made in Jerusalem. Ben-Elissar states that Tohami attached no importance to Dayan's remark. Indeed, there was no reason for him to do so, since Dayan's formulation during the formal discussion had given him what he was looking for – a foundation for a Sadat–Begin summit and more than an indication of Israel's conditions for peace with Egypt.

Dayan and Tohami's conversation paved the way for a diplomatic and historic event – Anwar Sadat's visit to Jerusalem. President Sadat addressed Israel's parliament, the Knesset, on November 21, 1977. At this early point in Egypt's open contacts with Israel, he stressed that Muslims attached great importance to the question of Israel's rule over East Jerusalem in general and over the Islamic holy sites in particular. Israel's annexation of East Jerusalem and its rule over the Islamic holy places were at the core of the Israeli occupation from the Muslim point of view, according to Sadat. His speech indicated that even the moderate camp in the Arab world, which he headed at that time, would not acquiesce in the annexation of East Jerusalem to Israel and in the perpetuation of exclusive Israeli rule there. From their point of view, Israel would have to change its policy – to turn from an aggressive entity threatening the Arabs into a state prepared to live in peace with its neighbors. This transition could take place only when East Jerusalem and the Islamic holy sites were returned to Arab sovereignty (Israeli, 1982: 79–80).

Israeli Prime Minister Menachem Begin's official reply did not address details. He refrained from repeating the points that Dayan had made in Morocco and emphasized the principle that everything was open to negotiation: "Do not say – there cannot be, and will never be, negotiations over any particular issue. I suggest, and this in the name of a majority in this parliament, that we shall discuss and negotiate about every point. ... Everything must be negotiated and can be negotiated" (*Jerusalem Post*, 21 Nov. 1977). In this declaration, Begin brought the issue of Jerusalem to the negotiating table without committing himself to the outcome. The two leaders were on parallel paths – Begin committed himself unambiguously to the process itself, while Sadat expressed a firm commitment to the results. They could not, however, continue in this way for long. Confrontation between the two, both on principle and on personal grounds, was not long in coming. It broke out when the process required the two sides to lay out in detail their positions on what the outcome of the talks should be.

Begin took a position that was not at all like the one Dayan had taken at his meeting with Tohami. East Jerusalem was excluded entirely from the autonomy framework that Begin offered the Palestinians, and thus the city's Arab inhabitants would not be allowed to participate in the elections for the autonomy's administrative council. Administrative arrangements for the holy sites in Jerusalem would be included, according to the Israeli program, in a separate arrangement that would ensure free access by the members of all religions to their holy sites. Begin wished, in fact, to detach the discussion of East Jerusalem from the talks about the rest of the West Bank. During the course of the negotiations he proposed removing East Jerusalem from the autonomy framework – that is, leaving it under Israeli sovereignty – and leaving the question of sovereignty over the West Bank open, with Israel's claim to sovereignty over this territory contending with "other claims." Sadat did not oppose postponing discussion of sovereignty over the West Bank, but he notified Begin, through U.S. President Jimmy Carter, that East Jerusalem could not remain under Israeli sovereignty (Ben-Elissar, 1995: 101–3, 109; Shiloah Institute, 1978). In other words, Menachem Begin put Jerusalem one notch above the rest of the 1967 territories. According to his plan, sovereignty over the 1967 territories was in dispute between the two parties, while Egypt had no claim regarding East Jerusalem, but rather acquiesced in the Israeli annexation. It hardly needs to be said that this position could not have been acceptable to the Egyptian president. Sadat stuck fast to his position – East Jerusalem was to have the same status as the rest of the 1967 territories. If the 1967 territories were in dispute, the same was true of the territory of East Jerusalem. This was the farthest Sadat could go towards Begin.

What was the special arrangement regarding the holy sites that Menachem Begin was thinking of? Ben-Elissar reports in his memoirs that Begin raised a "temporary" and "non-binding" proposal: "The holy sites will be handed over to the self-administration of each religion and its representatives. The Islamic holy sites will be administered by a representative of the administrative council of the autonomy and representatives of the neighboring states – one representative from each country." According to Ben-Elissar, Begin was willing to include representatives from countries that did not border on Israel, such as Saudi Arabia, Morocco, and Iran, in the Muslim body. He would not limit representation to the confrontation states on Israel's borders. Begin shared his thoughts with President Carter, and when the latter asked him if this meant giving the holy sites a status similar to that of the Vatican, Begin replied: "We will consider all kinds of possibilities. We haven't decided yet" (Ben-Elissar, 1995: 219–20).

This had serious implications, because Begin's approach confirmed that Israel had no exclusive political hold in Jerusalem, and that he was prepared to grant the political representatives of the Arab states informal standing in the body administering the Muslim holy sites in Jerusalem. Begin recognized that these sites were not solely religious; moreover, in his plan he granted the representatives of the Palestinian autonomy in the administrative body a standing equal to that granted to recognized countries. True, this was a special arrangement for limited functional representation and with a status inferior to that of Israel, but Menachem Begin created an opening for a non-Israeli political entity in Jerusalem.

While these were preliminary and non-binding proposals for the administration of religious affairs in the Islamic holy places, the fact that they were presented to the president of the United States proves that they were not meant to be taken lightly. It is important to remember that in 1967 Begin, then a minister without portfolio in the national unity government, furiously attacked the minister of labor, Yigal Allon, for proposing that the Israeli government give Jordan some measure of control over the Islamic holy places in Jerusalem. Begin argued then that a state could not have any kind of status that was not a political status. He was so firm on this point that he even rejected the possibility that Allon's proposal would state explicitly that Jordan's status in religious affairs would be subject to Israeli sovereignty. Begin reasoned that giving any standing at all to Jordan was tantamount to giving it political status, and that such status would necessarily compromise Israeli sovereignty over the site (Shragai, 1996: 372).

Begin did not reject the Vatican model in his conversation with Carter, and this had far-reaching political implications, for two reasons. First, in 1929 Italy recognized the sovereignty of the Holy See over the Vatican in the international theater, while the Holy See undertook to remain neutral in international disputes. On the Vatican model, the holy sites would be independent of Israeli sovereignty, and their status would be different from that of Begin's version of autonomy. The autonomous entity that Begin envisioned was not meant to be independent on the international level, while an "Islamic see" in Jerusalem would be. Second, citizenship in the Vatican state is dependent on position – that is, it is acquired by being appointed to a Vatican post and is thus linked to a job and not a person. On the model of the relations between Italy and the Vatican, an entity granting its own citizenship would be located in the heart of Jerusalem's Old City. Israeli sovereignty and citizenship would be withdrawn from the Islamic and Christian holy sites in Jerusalem and they would thus enjoy a higher status than that which Begin offered, in his proposal, to the rest of the 1967 territories (Hirsch, Hausen-Koriel & Lapidot, 1994).

In raising these ideas, Begin displayed, for a short time, a measure of pragmatism. In order to ensure that the Arabs and Muslims would come to terms with the annexation of East Jerusalem to West Jerusalem, and with the grant of autonomy to the inhabitants of the West Bank according to the parameters that he had sketched, Begin was prepared to consider removing the Temple Mount from the area of Israeli sovereignty and establishing an "Islamic State" in the heart of the Old City in Jerusalem. However, as will be seen, this was his position at the beginning of the negotiations, when he was still under the influence of Sadat's visit to Jerusalem, and before the beginning of the tough bargaining on the details of the agreement between Israel and Egypt. As the points of dispute with Egypt grew more serious, Begin's position became more rigid.

The Camp David conference: peace despite Jerusalem

The negotiations between Israel and Egypt on the details of the agreement between them ran into many difficulties even before there was a thorough discussion of Jerusalem. There was the question of Israel's withdrawal from the Sinai, the future of the Israeli settlements there, and Begin's proposal for administrative, non-territorial, and personal autonomy in the West Bank (Laqueur & Rubin, 1995: 400–3). All these were rocks that the negotiation wagon ran into even before the question of Jerusalem was addressed by the two parties. The dead end that Israel and Egypt reached after eight months of talks led to the Camp David Conference.

The conference opened on September 6, 1978, and by the next day it was clear that the starting positions of the two sides were diametrically opposed. Sadat sought to apply to Jerusalem the principles of sovereignty he had laid out in his speech to the Knesset – that is, the return of East Jerusalem to Arab sovereignty according to the borders of June 4, 1967. In the program he tabled at the conference, he proposed that Israel withdraw from Jerusalem to the lines of the armistice agreement of 1949, in accordance with the principle of non-recognition of the acquisition of territory by war. Arab sovereignty and government, Sadat said, would be restored to the Arab area. A joint municipal council, composed of an equal number of Palestinian and Israeli members, would be responsible for the provision of public services – traffic control, public transport, mails, telephones, and tourism. The parties would commit themselves to freedom of worship at and free access to holy sites without distinction and without prejudice (Ben-Elissar, 1995: 220).

In addition, Sadat demanded that an Arab flag of some sort be flown above the Islamic holy sites, while Begin, in response, wished to preserve East Jerusalem under Israeli sovereignty in accordance with the new borders that Israel had established in July 1967 (Ben-Elissar, 1995: 220; Kamil, 1986: 297; Quandt, 1988: 309).

Despite the dispute over the question of Jerusalem, the Camp David conference opened as planned. There were two principal reasons for this. First, the question of Jerusalem was set aside at Camp David because there were more burning issues for both sides. Just as had happened during the eight months of negotiation that had preceded the conference, at Camp David the bilateral issues between Israel and Egypt were more important than Jerusalem, because the latter was essentially an Israeli–Palestinian question. Instead of entering into a detailed discussion of Jerusalem and the West Bank, Israel and Egypt made do with a general treatment of the Palestinians.

Second, on September 11, 1978 President Carter asked President Sadat not to discuss the Jerusalem question for the present. This request, made when the Americans decided to begin active mediation, was an indication of the American inclination to take Jerusalem out of the framework of the talks so that it did not interfere with reaching an agreement on the Egyptian front (Quandt, 1988: 218–33). Sadat did not respond to the American request, but neither did he raise the question again at the conference. His priorities were similar to those of the Americans, because the American position on Jerusalem was closer to his own position than it was to the Israeli position. Sadat preferred to wait, and then raise the Jerusalem question at some time appropriate for the Americans. It was Begin, in fact, who raised the Jerusalem question the next day, when he met with the American team. Begin reiterated his commitment to Israeli sovereignty in Jerusalem, but this statement was drowned out by the commotion over other issues, which were more important for the bilateral agreement that was then crystallizing.

On September 14, 1978 Egypt proposed a goodwill gesture to the United States. Sadat told Carter that he would remove Jerusalem from the framework of the accords if Israel would agree to fly an Arab flag over the Islamic holy sites in Jerusalem. Carter asked Sadat to wait, and not make this proposal to Begin, preferring to put off confrontation over the question of Jerusalem in order to move forward on the agreement between Israel and Egypt (Benziman, 1978; Haber, Schiff & Ya'ari, 1980; Kamil, 1986: 29; Sofer, 1986). Only on the final day of the Camp David conference, on September 17, 1978, did a discussion of the Jerusalem question begin, and it was fundamentally a discussion between Israel and the U.S. and not between Israel and Egypt. Carter turned the dispute over Jerusalem into a personal argument between him and Begin. On other issues, the United States had functioned as an active mediator, taking positions and trying to reach an understanding with Begin about the interim arrangements, yet it had set aside resolving the permanent status of Jerusalem. When the Americans raised the issue, Begin was so angered that he adopted an inflexible position. He reiterated his refusal to include Jerusalem in the autonomy framework and even refused to discuss the issue, in complete contradiction of his previous undertaking that everything was open to negotiation. At this point he was not inclined to make any compromise and also categorically rejected the idea of flying a green flag (the color of Islam) above the Dome of the Rock, even if this was a plain flag that did not represent any particular Arab state. Furious, Begin threatened to leave the conference. In the face of the severe crisis that Begin had caused, the Americans had no choice but to satisfy the Egyptians. The Americans thus drafted a letter to President Sadat, quoting the statement of the American representatives at the UN, Ambassadors Goldberg and Yost that, in keeping with its past position, the United States saw East Jerusalem as occupied territory. In other words, the U.S. supported Egypt's stand on the autonomy and the future of East Jerusalem. This unambiguous U.S. position angered the Israeli representatives and they threatened to leave the conference. After an incisive discussion, unavoidable given the force of the dispute and the psychological pressure on the parties, the necessary compromise was achieved. It was agreed that the American president would send Begin and Sadat a general letter clarifying America's position. Carter's letter made it clear that "the position of the United States on Jerusalem remains as stated by Ambassador Goldberg in the UN General Assembly on July 14, 1967, and subsequently by Ambassador Yost at the UN Security Council on July 1, 1969" (Ben-Elissar, 1995: 221; Quandt, 1988: 219; Sofer, 1986).

What was the position of the United States in the documents that President Carter was referring to? In the UN General Assembly debate of mid-July 1967, Ambassador Goldberg explained his country's reasons for abstaining on Resolution 2254.

I wish to make it clear that the United States does not accept or recognize these measures [the annexation of East Jerusalem] as altering the status of Jerusalem ... We insist that the measures taken cannot be considered other than interim and provisional and not prejudging the final and permanent status of Jerusalem.

(American Foreign Policy, 1967: 579;
Near and Middle East Doc. VII-52)

The ambassador based his speech on President Johnson's declaration of June 28, 1967 that Israel should not take any unilateral steps of any sort in Jerusalem, and also on the announcement of the American State Department of that same day that the decision to annex East Jerusalem to Israel could not be a final determination of the status of the holy places or the permanent status of the city. Ambassador Yost's statement at the beginning of July 1969 was no less trenchant:

> The United States considers that the part of Jerusalem that came under the control of Israel in the June war, like other areas occupied by Israel, is occupied territory and hence subject to the provisions of international law regarding the rights and obligations of an occupying power. ... [T]he occupier has no right to make changes in laws or in administration other than those which are temporarily necessitated by his security interest, and that an occupier may not confiscate or destroy private property. ... I regret to say that the actions of Israel in the occupied portion of Jerusalem present a different picture. ...
>
> (Moore, 1974: 993–4)

Ambassadors Goldberg and Yost stressed Jerusalem's uniqueness as a city holy to the three monotheistic religions, and that as such it should remain open and free for the worship by all believers. Precisely because Jerusalem was holy not just for the Jews, Israel should not implement any unilateral measures of any kind.

In his letter, President Carter made no change in the fundamental American position on Jerusalem, and this satisfied Egypt. Egypt hoped to make use of the U.S. in the future, when the autonomy discussions began and the question of the connection between East Jerusalem and the autonomy would arise. On the other hand, the omission of a direct statement of the American position enabled Israel to argue that, in practice, nothing new had happened, and that the U.S. was simply repeating its known position. A similar claim was made by the Egyptian foreign minister, Ibrahim Kamil, a hawk. He believed that the U.S. had deliberately fudged his position on the status of Jerusalem in the permanent arrangement because it wished to perpetuate Israeli occupation of the city (Kamil, 1986: 297, 333, 345, 373). Israel, the U.S., and Egypt also agreed that, in their replies to Carter's letter, Begin and Sadat would state their differing positions on the question of Jerusalem.

The Israeli prime minister's letter was laconic and formal, and presented his position unambiguously – exclusive Israeli rule over East Jerusalem (Ben-Elissar, 1995: 222). The dry legalistic tone in which Begin chose to express himself was meant, quite properly from his point of view, to circumvent and dismiss the dispute. Camp David was enough for him.

In contrast to Begin's letter, Sadat's was detailed and proposed both partnership in and partition of Jerusalem. To the position in principle that he had presented to the Knesset, Sadat added a few practical sections on how, in Egypt's view, sovereignty over Jerusalem should be divided while preserving its physical unity, the unified administration of the city, and its vital activities, which were also to be carried out jointly. This exchange of letters thus continued the discussion of the status of East Jerusalem in the interim and permanent agreements. Begin did not succeed in removing the issue from the negotiating table, and it could be said that he jumped the gun. The serious differences of opinion on the question of Jerusalem came up prematurely, as did the serious differences of opinion between Begin and Carter. From the Egyptian point of view, this was a success, because the opening shot on the negotiations over the autonomy applying to East Jerusalem was fired on the last day of the Camp David conference.

Jerusalem and the autonomy negotiations: a dialogue in two languages

Officially, the negotiations between Israel and Egypt over the establishment of autonomy for the Palestinians began in May 1979. In these talks there were again disagreements over the question of whether East Jerusalem should be included in the autonomy as Egypt demanded, or whether it should remain outside the framework of the negotiations, as Israel demanded. Egypt did not see East Jerusalem as an inseparable part of Israel, but rather as part of the West Bank, so in its opinion the Palestinian inhabitants of Jerusalem would be able to exercise their political and national rights in the framework of the autonomy arrangements to be instituted there. The principles of the Egyptian position, as confirmed by the Egyptian Ministerial Committee on Autonomy Affairs on May 10, 1979, stated that "the autonomy as a whole will apply to all the Palestinian territories conquered in 1967. In other words, to the West Bank including Jerusalem, and the Gaza Strip" (Gemer, 1981: 3). Egypt's autonomy proposal of January 29, 1980, was based on these guiding principles (Gemer, 1981: 41–2).

As expected, the American position on the subject was close to that of the Egyptians, and this was also expressed in the American administration's contacts with Jordan. The Carter administration was, in October 1978, trying to tempt Jordan to get on the Camp David bandwagon. Jordan had questions; Harold Saunders drafted the American answers, which were written above President Carter's signature. With regard to Jerusalem, Saunders repeated the statements made by Ambassadors Goldberg and Yost, and emphasized that the United States would support the Egyptian position of allowing the inhabitants of East Jerusalem to participate in the elections to and activities of the autonomous authority, although the autonomy would not apply to the city during the interim period (Ben-Elissar, 1995: 134–5; Quandt, 1988: 336–9). The American position infuriated Begin, and in response he ordered that his office be transferred to the eastern part of the city (a decision that was never implemented) and that several settlements in the territories be enlarged. The United States did not want to impose its unambiguous position on Israel, so it left the problem of Jerusalem to the parties involved in the conflict. In the Reagan plan of September 1982 the United States would take a similar position.

The disagreements on Jerusalem caused the Egyptian president to bring up the subject in a series of summit meetings between the two leaders and also to refuse to visit the city again. The lack of communication between Sadat and Begin over Jerusalem soured relations between them. This lack of communication can be illustrated by an event that took place in July 1978, when Begin and Sadat met at El-Arish. At this meeting Begin understood Sadat to be proposing an exchange: an Israeli concession in Jerusalem in exchange for piping water from the Nile into the Negev (Ben-Elissar, 1995: 223–4). But Begin considered Jerusalem to have spiritual and symbolic value that could not be exchanged for something material, and was unable to appreciate the national and symbolic value of the Nile's waters in the Egyptian consciousness. This incident would be recalled later, when the autonomy talks ended and each side tried to share out the responsibility.

From this point forward the Egyptian government worked along two lines. First, the president made an effort to pry out of Begin a concession on the question of Arab sovereignty in Jerusalem. Second, on linking the city's Arab inhabitants to the autonomy, and his vice-president tried to persuade the Israelis to make a symbolic concession – to allow the flying of some sort of non-Israeli flag in Jerusalem. The Egyptian vice-president at the time, Husni Mubarak, tried, in March 1980, to persuade Ambassador Ben-Elissar to agree to this (Ben-Elissar, 1995: 224–5). Mubarak ignored the fact that Begin and the Likud administration he represented were advocates of the politics of symbols, as opposed to the political culture of the Labor Party, which emphasized action. Mubarak tried to persuade Ben-Elissar that, in exchange for a minimal, symbolic price, Israel and Egypt could gain the favor of Saudi Arabia and the support of the Muslim masses outside the Arab countries. These Arabs were important to Egypt because of the isolation that had been imposed on Egypt by the Arab world after the accords with Israel. Mubarak argued that the Muslim world was not able to challenge Israel's hold on East Jerusalem, so that the symbolic concession he was asking Israel to make was meaningless. The Israeli government of the time was very much attuned, however, to the politics of symbols, and saw any concession on the symbolic level as fundamental.

Mubarak did not give up. At the end of March he tried to explain directly to Ben-Elissar how important it was for Egypt to circumvent its isolation in the Arab world.

They can't be allowed to accuse us of having given up Jerusalem completely. You need to help us with that. … What do you care about a flag, an Arab flag. All we ask for is something external, something symbolic, that's all. Who knows what will be in five more years. After all, you are there. You will be there. No one will take you out of there.

In response to Ben-Elissar's question about which flag he was speaking, Mubarak said "any flag." "An Egyptian flag?" Ben-Elissar wondered. "Let it be an Egyptian flag," the vice-president answered (Ben-Elissar, 1995: 226). The Egyptians were almost on their knees. This shows how great their distress was, and to what extent the two governments did not understand each other's language and each other's dilemmas.

The issue came up for a third time on August 8, 1980, in a conversation between Ben-Elissar and Vice-President Mubarak

(Ben-Elissar, 1995: 233). Then, too, the Egyptian efforts were in vain. The politics of symbols that the Israeli government made great use of in both its foreign and domestic policy contradicted the pragmatic arguments of the Egyptian vice-president. For the Likud government, the symbol, the flag, played an important psychological role in creating consciousness. It was consciousness, not deed, that determined reality. What Egypt portrayed as a scrap of cloth covering the nakedness of the separate peace with Israel was seen by the Israeli regime as a symbol of foreign sovereignty in the entire city, not just at the Islamic holy sites in Jerusalem.

In parallel, Egypt tried to make progress in the talks to establish the autonomy administration, talks that were meant to be concluded on May 26, 1980. Egypt made every effort to guarantee a link between the inhabitants of East Jerusalem and those of the autonomy. It demanded, first, that the inhabitants of East Jerusalem participated in the elections to the autonomous authority's representative council; and second, that the institutions of the self-governing authority be located in Jerusalem. East Jerusalem would be designated in the agreement as the capital of the Palestinian autonomy (Ben-Elissar, 1995: 225; Gemer, 1981: 99; Legum, Shaked & Rabinivich, 1979–80: 131). Israel, of course, rejected Egypt's two demands, since Begin saw them as a redivision of sovereignty over the city. He was not prepared to discuss the issue without seeing the discussion itself as a declaration of division of the city. This was in contrast to his previous refusal to discuss East Jerusalem at all. Nevertheless, he would not agree to grant the inhabitants of East Jerusalem political ties to any entity other than Israel, because he feared that having the Arab inhabitants of Jerusalem vote for the autonomy council would create a political linkage to the Palestinian autonomy, and this would refute the annexation of the eastern part of the city to Israel.

As already noted, Menachem Begin was prepared to commit himself to the process but not to any outcome other than the one he wanted. When, later on, the dimensions of the gap between the desired results of the two sides became clear, as did the inability to bridge those gaps, the end of the process was near. But in the meantime the discussions continued. Israel explained its position again and again, assuming that its interlocutor had difficulty understanding it, and that the source of the problem was not Israeli policy but the way it was explained. At the same time, Egypt tried to broaden the circle of the talks and to involve outside actors in the discussions, in the hope that they would influence Israel to make its position more flexible.

At first Egypt turned to the United States. In April 1980, Sadat presented the dispute over the linkage of the inhabitants of East Jerusalem to the autonomy to President Carter. Carter raised the subject with Begin when they met in Washington a few days later. Carter supported the Egyptian position, justifying this by noting that Israel allowed Jordanian citizens who were residents of East Jerusalem to vote for the Jordanian parliament without seeing this as compromising Israeli sovereignty. But Begin was not persuaded and even cast doubt on whether Israel would in the future continue to allow Jordanian citizens from East Jerusalem to vote for the Jordanian legislature. Begin also rejected Carter's suggestion that East Jerusalem residents vote for the autonomy council by mail, as do American citizens who live outside their states (Ben-Elissar, 1995: 227). It is important to recall that Begin had once considered, as part of his autonomy plan, offering the Arabs of Judea, Samaria, and Gaza (though not, of course, the Arabs of East Jerusalem) a choice between Israeli and Jordanian citizenship. According to this proposal, the grant of citizenship would give its recipients the right to vote for the parliaments in their respective countries. Ben-Elissar testifies that this offer had been meant as a fundamentally tactical move, aimed at countering the charge that Israel intended to rule over the Arab minority. Begin believed that only a few Arabs in Judea, Samaria, and Gaza would choose Israeli citizenship, and that Israel would be able to cope with this when the time came (Ben-Elissar, 1995: 101–2 – Ben-Elissar unhesitatingly states that Begin was being naïve on this point). This proposal of Carter's reduced the size of the wedge that Begin had put between the Arabs of East Jerusalem and the inhabitants of the rest of the 1967 territories, and created a political link between the inhabitants of East Jerusalem and the autonomy authorities. Begin was not prepared to be party to this. Since Begin was proposing both administrative and personal autonomy in the territories, he ostensibly could have agreed to either one or the other kind of autonomy in East Jerusalem while still retaining its special status. Yet he refused. Begin did not want the elections to create a political–personal link between the inhabitants of East Jerusalem and the autonomy, while preserving their administrative link to Israel. He saw the elections themselves as no less than a redivision of the city. They were not a political–personal act that externalized the ties of the Arabs of East Jerusalem, but rather an incursion of the autonomy into the Israeli capital that would lead to its political division. The hard part of this approach is that Begin never proposed to impose Israeli citizenship on the Arabs of East Jerusalem. He preferred the existing situation in which only a small part of the Arabs of East Jerusalem voluntarily accepted Israeli citizenship, and another small portion kept their Jordanian citizenship. The majority was to remain without political rights, even without the minimal rights that Begin offered in the autonomy plan.

Since the attempt to involve Carter in the dispute failed, the discussions changed venue to the United Nations. After the Jewish Underground attacked the mayors of Nablus, Ramallah, and El-Bireh, and after it booby-trapped Arab buses and planned to blow up the Islamic holy places in Jerusalem, the UN General Assembly decided, in June 1980, to condemn Israel. Unlike previous proposals of this sort, the U.S. did not veto this decision and it included East Jerusalem in the list of occupied territories from which Israel had to withdraw. In response, the Begin government decided once again to transfer the prime minister's office to East Jerusalem. The American government was adamantly opposed to this decision and tried to prevent it. The Israeli government responded to these events by supporting the Basic Law: Jerusalem, a bill introduced to the Knesset by right-wing opposition member Ge'ula Cohen that changed the legal status of the annexation of East Jerusalem. The law was passed on July 30, 1980, with Begin voting in favor, even though the issue was still under negotiation with Egypt. Passage of the law led Egypt to declare that it was halting the autonomy talks. Egypt understood that, under the circumstances, the process was worthless, and it had no reason to prefer Palestinian interests over its own. The chasm between the goals of both sides was too wide for them to continue to be committed to negotiating autonomy for the Palestinians. Instead, they preferred to finalize their own peace treaty.

With the autonomy talks suspended, each side took stock. Begin and Sadat accused each other of responsibility for the failure. During August 1980 the two leaders exchanged personal letters setting out their reciprocal grievances (Ben-Elissar, 1995:

229–30; FBIS, Daily Report, 13 Aug. 1980, 18 Aug. 1980). Sadat claimed that dialogue and negotiation could not be accompanied by unilateral actions. A person who is committed to the process and who declares that everything is open to negotiation must prove the sincerity of his intentions and avoid acting unilaterally in accordance with his ideology. Sadat rejected Begin's approach of distinguishing between the rights of Jews in Jerusalem, which he claimed were national rights, and the rights of Christians and Muslims, which in Begin's view were solely religious rights. Sadat also rejected Begin's "it's all mine" attitude. He suggested Israeli–Palestinian partnership in the administration of the city and a division of sovereignty, instead of exclusive Israeli rule. Sadat believed that the division of sovereignty in Jerusalem and the preservation of its administrative and municipal unity through the joint management model offered a fair compromise between Israel's goals of not physically redividing the city and of having East Jerusalem as part of the Israeli capital, and the Arab goal of returning Arab sovereignty to Jerusalem and making it part of the Palestinian territories. In practice, Sadat was proposing *de facto* unity and *de jure* partition. This was the proposal of a pragmatic statesman to a statesman for whom the symbol and legal status were paramount and actually shaped daily life. Begin preferred a city that was unified *de jure* and divided *de facto* – although from his point of view, it should be noted, the *de facto* reality was a product of the *de jure* situation. The two leaders spoke different languages.

The suspension of the autonomy talks put an end to the negotiations between Israel and Egypt with the exception of the long wrangling over Taba, a small part of the Sinai Peninsula that was disputed by the two countries. Egypt made do with its achievements – a peace treaty and normalization in exchange for all of the Sinai Peninsula and the dismantling of the Israeli settlements there, Israeli commitment to autonomy for the Palestinians and acceptance of the statement that the permanent solution must, as the Camp David agreements stated, "recognize the legitimate rights of the Palestinian people and their just requirements." (Laqueur & Rubin, 1995: 404–10). From here on out Egypt would make no claim to be negotiating for the Palestinians or in their name, and would at most mediate between them and Israel, and between them and the U.S. – the moving force behind the diplomatic process in the Middle East.

The Camp David model: the indirect approach and its limitations

The peace talks between Egypt and Israel advanced the problem of Jerusalem towards a solution. First, Egypt recognized west Jerusalem as the capital of Israel, and the fact of the Egyptian president's historic visit to Jerusalem in November 1977 proves this. The negotiations with Egypt dealt only with East Jerusalem. Second, both sides agreed that Jerusalem would remain a physically undivided city. All the functions aimed at ensuring the unity of the city in practice, without which that unity would not be realized, were to be handed over to a city council with equal Israeli and Palestinian representation. Third, freedom of worship would be guaranteed, and the representatives of the religions would administer the holy sites. This was, in practice, recognition by Egypt of the reality that Israel had created in the holy sites immediately after the Six Day War in 1967, with the annexation of the city.

After identifying these points of agreement, Israel and Egypt defined the points of dispute as well. As expected, no agreement was reached on the question of sovereignty in Jerusalem. Egypt categorically rejected the Israeli annexation and Israel's measures in East Jerusalem after the occupation in 1967. There were other differences of opinion regarding the link that should be established or prevented between East Jerusalem and the rest of the 1967 territories. Israel rejected such a link, while Egypt insisted on applying all the arrangements regarding the rest of the 1967 territories to East Jerusalem as well. While the U.S. took Egypt's side in the fundamental debate on Jerusalem, it did not impose its position on Israel. The United States made great efforts to reach a positive conclusion on the point that it and the two negotiating parties placed first – a peace agreement and Israeli withdrawal from the Sinai.

Progress towards a solution of the question of Jerusalem did not receive any official expression in a consensual document. The reason was that, despite its importance, the two sides addressed it on a secondary level. The agenda between Israel and Egypt included manifestly bilateral issues such as the extent of the Israeli withdrawal from Sinai and its schedule; the question of the Israeli settlements in the Sinai; the security arrangements and the early warning stations; the stages of the normalization of bilateral relations, and the question of Taba. The two sides viewed these questions as being of extremely high importance, more than the question of Palestinian autonomy in general and the question of Jerusalem in particular. First and foremost, Egypt wanted to achieve peace with Israel and to return the entire Sinai to its sovereignty. Its involvement with the question of Jerusalem and the West Bank was of secondary importance, and was meant to pave the way to an arrangement in Sinai. Nevertheless, its duty as an Arab state and its own relation to Jerusalem should not be taken lightly.

The negotiations between Israel and Egypt at Camp David gave birth to the presumption that, in order to succeed and progress in peace negotiations, the subject of Jerusalem should be pushed to the end of the discussions. In this view, the question of Jerusalem is so momentous for the parties involved that dealing with it prematurely is likely to cause trouble. In order not to bring negotiations to a halt at their very beginning, Jerusalem should be addressed only at the end of the process. While this postponement will not solve the problem, when the parties get around to it there will be a mutual and equal risk involved in a stalemate that will lead them to a compromise. Failure to reach an agreement would threaten to destroy all the achievements of the negotiations and destabilize the peace that had been built with such great labor. On the positive side, the understandings and agreements achieved on lesser questions would produce mutual trust between the sides. This trust and understanding would broaden and spread from the periphery to the center and neutralize the reluctance to make concessions on Jerusalem. This approach can be called the indirect strategy.

This strategy was developed at Camp David by President Carter. It was adopted first by President Sadat and afterwards also by Prime Minister Menachem Begin, although never with the same enthusiasm as the Egyptian president. Begin, after all, frequently spoke on the question of Jerusalem and it was a matter of great importance in his politics of symbols. This model proved itself, since it led to the signing of the peace treaty between Israel and Egypt. Since then, it has been accepted as the only way to cope with the question of Jerusalem.

This assumption was appropriate for the negotiations between Israel and Egypt, in which the bilateral issues shunted aside detailed consideration of the Palestinian question, of which

Jerusalem was one aspect. It was also appropriate when those with a direct interest in the matter – the Palestinians – were not involved. Once Israel and the Palestinians conducted negotiations on the Jerusalem question, it was no longer possible to adopt the Camp David model in full. Moreover, at the time of the autonomy negotiations it was already clear that it was impossible to completely ignore the Jerusalem question, and a dispute arose over the status of Jerusalem in the interim period and on the connection between the residents of East Jerusalem and the autonomy institutions. The differences of opinion on these issues were expressed in blunt exchanges between Begin and Sadat.

The parties involved in the negotiations learned the limitations and advantages of the Camp David model for the solution of the problem of Jerusalem. Thus, from that point to the Madrid Conference of 1991, Jerusalem would be addressed on two parallel tracks. Israel would try to ignore the subject of Jerusalem completely in the plans it proposed, in order not to get into the same dispute it ended up with in the autonomy negotiations with Egypt, or in order to avoid internal disputes among the different components of the Israeli government. The Arabs and the U.S., for their part, understood that it was impossible to resolve the issue of the permanent status of Jerusalem for the time being. At the same time they demanded that the issue of Jerusalem not be ignored entirely. The U.S., the Palestinians, and Egypt would concentrate on searching for Jerusalem's place in the interim agreement and in the transition period leading to the permanent solution.

3

THE P.L.O.

FROM THE WINGS TO CENTER STAGE

The PLO: politics stops at the gates of Jerusalem

The PLO was founded in 1964 as a body with an entirely marginal political status. In 1968 the organization received a facelift and turned into a coalition of guerrilla and terrorist organizations. Diplomatic and political action was sidelined in favor of revolutionary activity – liberation via "armed struggle." For many long years the PLO was relegated to the wings on the political stage, fighting for a place under the lights. It strove, in various ways, to gain recognition as the sole representative of the Palestinian people and their goals. The story of the PLO's movement into the spotlight has been the story of the organization's changing attitude to the diplomatic process, from the time when it made its first moves in that direction in 1974. The turning points were in 1974 and 1993. In June 1974, the PLO accepted the "staged program," which in retrospect can be seen as the first step in the direction of a political solution. In October of that year, the Arab League summit conference recognized the PLO as the only legitimate representative of the Palestinian people. A month later, Arafat was invited to speak before the UN General Assembly, and nearly 20 years later, in September 1993, Arafat signed a declaration of principles with Israel on the White House lawn. This agreement, reached after the PLO recognized Israel towards the end of 1988, and after lengthy negotiations that began in Madrid in 1991, was the final development that made the PLO the major, if not the sole, Arab negotiator for Jerusalem.

The PLO, from its inception, considered itself to be tied to Jerusalem. In fact, its founding conference was held in Jerusalem from May 28 to June 2, 1964, in the Intercontinental Hotel on the Mount of Olives. The Jordanian authorities at first rejected the Palestinian's request to gather in the city, but acquiesced after reaching an understanding with the PLO on the organization's objectives and the relationship between Palestinian identity and Jordan's identity. To accommodate Jordan, the PLO's leadership agreed that it would represent only those Palestinians outside Jordan. This meant that its goal was to liberate only Israeli Jerusalem, not the Jordanian side of the city. The PLO's founding charter stated that Jerusalem would be the seat of the Palestinian National Council, the PLO's quasi-parliament (Harkabi, 1975: 24, 48). However, the Palestinian National Council has not convened in Jerusalem since the founding conference in 1965.

The PLO's position on Jerusalem is expressed in its sharp response to the Basic Law: Jerusalem the Capital of Israel, passed by the Knesset on July 30, 1980 (Hirsch, Hausen-Koriel & Lapidot, 1994: 8–9). The PLO's Executive Committee considered this law to be a violation of UN resolutions, and interpreted it as an additional aggression against the Palestinian people and its heritage, and against the Palestinian national and Muslim and Christian religious character of Jerusalem. The PLO considered the U.S. to be primarily responsible for this Israeli government action. The U.S., the PLO charged, had not restrained Israel and had continued to grant the country economic, military, and political assistance. The Executive Committee's statement emphasized that Jerusalem

has been the capital of our Arab–Palestinian homeland from the time it was built by our Arab Jebusite and Canaanite forefathers in the heart of Palestine, and which was also the first direction of prayer for Islam's believers [*qiblat al-muminin*]. Therefore, liberation of Jerusalem from the Zionist occupation that disavows the city's Christian and Muslim essence is a fateful mater for our people and nation, and this is the only way to ensure freedom of worship there for all believers.

(*Filastin al-Thawra*, 11 Aug. 1980)

(The PLO emphasizes its "Canaanite" roots as the foundation of its claim to modern Jerusalem, and in order to condemn the Israeli occupation of 1967. The PLO claims prior, Jebusite–Canaanite ownership, and thus implicitly also condemns the conquest of the city by King David. In order to prove its historical rights, the PLO names the Canaanites and Jebusites as its forefathers, even though they were in no way Arabs and even though the pre-Islamic *Jahilia* period is condemned by Islam as a period of idolatry and ignorance.)

The changes that took place in the PLO's political approach during the 1980s did not change its fundamental position on the future of East Jerusalem. Up until the 1980s, the PLO adhered to all the articles of the Palestinian National Covenant (1968) and all the articles of the "staged program" (1974), including their sections on Jerusalem. Between 1988 and 1993 the PLO accepted UN resolution 181, the partition decision, and recognized the State of Israel. It accepted UN resolution 242 while continuing to demand an independent Palestinian state, offering a conciliation plan based on peace in exchange for the territories that Israel occupied in 1967. This change, from hostility to peace and coexistence, did not modify the PLO's position on Jerusalem until Israel, in 1993, recognized the PLO and accepted it as a partner in negotiations over the city.

On November 15, 1988 the PLO declared Jerusalem the capital of its country. "By virtue of the natural, historical, and legal rights [of the Palestinian Arab people] ... the Palestine National Council in the name of Allah and in the name of the Palestinian Arab people hereby proclaims the establishment of the state of Palestine on our Palestinian territory, with its capital Holy Jerusalem" (Abdul Hadi, 1997: Vol. 1, 332).

In the wake of the decisions of the 19 Palestinian National Council, Arafat was invited to speak at a special session of the UN General Assembly in Geneva, held on December 13, 1988. In his speech, he reiterated the PLO's position on the Jerusalem question, and put it in the most moderate context that had ever been heard in the organization's history (*Ha'aretz*, 14 Dec. 1988). Immediately after Arafat's speech and after his press conference the next day, the United States launched an official dialogue with the PLO. The U.S. interpreted Arafat as having accepted UN Resolution 242, as having abandoned terrorism, and as having recognized Israel's existence. (The dialogue between the U.S. and the PLO was cut off in 1990, after the organization refused to issue an unambiguous condemnation of the May 30, 1990 attempt by Abu al-Abas's Palestinian Liberation Front to stage a terrorist attack against Israeli civilians.)

At this stage, the PLO had not yet conducted negotiations with Israel and the organization was in any case not at the center of the diplomatic stage. The moderation in PLO policy did not extend to Jerusalem. The organization's stand on Jerusalem at this stage was ideological rather than political – it was not willing to bargain. It had made a one-sided payment in order to join the negotiating process, but the price of entrance was not going to be paid in Jerusalem currency.

Israel's position on Jerusalem had not, however, become more flexible in the decade and a half following 1967. It maintained that the city in which it had wrought huge physical, demographic, and constitutional changes must remain unified under exclusive Israeli sovereignty, with Israel taking responsibility for ensuring freedom of worship for all religions at their holy places. From Israel's point of view, the status of Jerusalem is different from that of the rest of the 1967 territories, so arrangements that applied to them did not apply to Jerusalem. At the beginning of the 1990s, when the PLO pushed its way into the negotiating hall and took its place beside the table, Israel's position on Jerusalem changed. Henceforth, it would become more pragmatic about Jerusalem and more willing to view it as a political issue. By then Israel could no longer ignore the presence of the Palestinian "homeowner" facing it, and during the negotiations over Jerusalem there was a quantum leap. Until that happened at the Madrid Conference and in the Oslo agreements, the two sides had to overcome Israel's two nos – no negotiations with the PLO and no negotiations about Jerusalem. As expected, breaking these 'nos' became a challenge for the Palestinians.

Detouring around Jerusalem and the PLO

Republican Ronald Reagan was among the most friendly of American presidents in his attitude towards Israel, yet despite this he did not accept the Begin government's position on East Jerusalem. In the wake of the Lebanon War of 1982, Reagan decided to promote a continuation of the diplomatic process that had begun at Camp David. Reagan's administration understood that it could not ignore the Jerusalem question entirely, but that it was not worthwhile to awaken too many disputes over it. In the plan he proposed on September 1, 1982, Reagan addressed only what he thought was the necessary minimum: he said that the U.S. supported the proposal to allow Palestinian residents of East

Jerusalem to participate in the elections to the autonomy authority. Jerusalem would remain undivided, he maintained, with its
final status to be determined by negotiation. Reagan believed that
the territories-for-peace formula should be implemented in the
West Bank without it bringing about the establishment of a Palestinian state. The final solution in this arena, in his opinion, would
be achieved between Jordan and Israel. In the meantime, there
would be an interim arrangement of five years, during which
period a self-governing Palestinian regime would be administered
by an elected Palestinian authority. Reagan refrained from stating
in his plan that the principle of territories for peace applied also to
Jerusalem, or that it applied only to the rest of the West Bank, nor
did he say whether, in the permanent agreement, the autonomy
would be linked to Jordan or to Israel.

Begin and Arafat rejected Reagan's plan categorically. Begin
was angered that it had been issued without prior consultation,
and Arafat was not prepared to lend his hand to a plan that
rejected the establishment of a Palestinian state and which did
not accept the PLO as a party to the permanent settlement.
Moreover, Reagan's plan placed much hope in King Hussein of
Jordan taking the PLO's place, after the PLO's forces had been
beaten in the war and the organization had been deported from
Lebanon. Jordan said it would not take such a risk unless the
U.S. could pressure Israel at the very least, to freeze its settlement activity in the territories. In Jordan's view, the settlements
endangered the Hashimite character of the East Bank, because
they were liable to press the members of the West Bank to move
to the east. Jordan's desire to preserve the Hashimite character of
its kingdom was greater than its desire to regain control of the
West Bank.

Furthermore, the PLO's defeat in Lebanon had been military
but not in any way political. The organization enjoyed political
support from Egypt, and President Mubarak had reiterated to Secretary of State George Shultz that it was the PLO, not Jordan, that
should conduct the negotiations with Israel. For this reason,
Hussein stressed to the U.S. that it would be difficult for him to
act without the PLO's approval (FBIS, 2 Sept. 1982; Klein, 1988;
Laqueur & Rubin, 1995: 439–45; Susser, 1985: 22–5; Shultz,
1993: 85–100). The failure of Reagan's initiative proved that the
Lebanon War had not eliminated the PLO from the political map.

On the contrary, its veto power had actually grown stronger. The Reagan program was a non-starter.

The desire to break the diplomatic deadlock led the foreign minister in Israel's national unity government, Shimon Peres, to conduct a personal, secret diplomatic effort behind the back of Likud Prime Minister Yitzhak Shamir. On April 11, 1987, before the Intifada began, Peres's secret diplomacy led to the London agreement. The London agreement was the endpoint of a long series of contacts during 1986–87, in which the participants were Peres, Hussein, and American envoys. In these contacts, Peres tried to realize the Jordanian option, as he understood it. This meant convening an international conference in which the PLO would not participate, or at most would be a junior participant. Only eight years later, Peres led the negotiations with the PLO without Jordan's knowledge, but in the years 1985–87 he labored to bolster Jordan's standing in the West Bank and to weaken the PLO's status both there and in Tunisia. (The bombing of PLO headquarters and Arafat's residence in Tunis in October 1985 was presented as Israeli retaliation for the murder of three of its civilians in Cyprus, but at the same time it was meant to get the senior Palestinian actor out of the arena and make it easier for the King of Jordan to take his place.) In July 1985, Peres reached an understanding with Hussein that the United States would open a dialogue with a Jordanian delegation that would include Palestinian members from the PLO. Peres conditioned the participation of PLO representatives on the organization, disavowing terrorism immediately at the end of the meeting. He promised that in such a case Israel would only protest against opening a dialogue with PLO members without the organization having abandoned terrorism. Reagan, however, opposed this. In October and November 1985, several further important meetings were held between the parties and, according to the account of one of the participants, the problem of Jerusalem was also floated, indirectly. Because of the conflicting demands of the two sides for sovereignty over Jerusalem, everyone preferred to adopt Carter's approach and postpone seeking a solution to the problem until the end of the negotiations. In the meantime, Israel agreed that in the final arrangement there would be a Jordanian presence on the Temple Mount, and that a Jordanian flag would fly over the Islamic holy sites (Zak, 1996: 20, 201–2, 205).

Hussein and Peres signed the "London Agreement," and the Israeli cabinet was meant to approve it after the U.S. presented it to Shamir. The agreement stipulated that an international Middle East peace conference would be convened with the participation of a joint Jordanian–Palestinian delegation. The participants in the conference would be obligated to accept UN Security Council resolutions 242 and 388, to abandon terrorism and violence, and to conduct direct talks among them. It was, by and large, a procedural document that did not make any mention of the conference's agenda and which made no reference to Jerusalem. The non-inclusion of Jerusalem was something that Peres adopted, following Carter, with the goal of circumventing the differences between Israel and Jordan and the Palestinians, as well as the differences between the Labor Party and the Likud, the prime minister's party. This was not the only piece of creative diplomacy that Peres concocted, and it was ingenious to the point of being untenable. Peres tried to use Hussein to tempt Shamir to go to an international conference, and used the United States as the salesman who was supposed to market the goods to a stubborn client. Peres presented Shamir with a *menu fixé* at a bargain price, but the price didn't interest Shamir. What did interest him was that the meal had been prepared without his knowledge. The Likud ministers viewed Peres's actions as political subversion and this confirmed their image of the foreign minister and his party as unreliable. When the debate turned into a contention between the two parties, Peres's hope for a vote that would cross party lines – like the vote on withdrawing the Israeli army from Lebanon in 1985 – was dashed. The camps were clear, as were the rules of the coalition game. The national unity government was one in which the two large parties and their satellites had equal numbers of ministers, and a tie vote on any subject meant its rejection. That was the result of the vote on the London Agreement on May 13, 1988. The paralyzing parity and the mutual veto doomed in advance every proposal that became framed as a partisan dispute (Koren, 1994: 148–50, 188–93; Makovsky, 1996: 181–2; Shultz, 1993: 937–42; Zak, 1996: 267–8, 270–3).

This political paralysis was one of the factors leading to the outbreak of the Intifada in December 1987. A short time thereafter, in January 1988, the political leaders of the local inhabitants (the "internal" leaders, in Palestinian jargon, as opposed to the "external" leadership, the PLO in Tunis) issued a political program, laying out their demands in 14 points. The Palestinian position on East Jerusalem was unambiguous, and in contrast with Peres's desire to strike it from the diplomatic agenda, the Palestinians addressed the issue prominently. According to the Palestinian program, East Jerusalem was an inseparable part of the 1967 territories, and they therefore demanded that Israel desist from its construction, population, land confiscation, and settlement activity in East Jerusalem as in the rest of the 1967 territories. In any case, the Palestinians emphasized, Israel had to conduct negotiations with the PLO (Laqueur & Rubin, 1995: 505–7). In fact, the 14-point plan was a protest manifesto, the product of a political uprising more than a basis for meaningful negotiation. The importance of the plan is not its details, but in its presentation. The Intifada's success gave the inhabitants of the territories and their political leaders prominence and from this point onward this coterie of political leaders took its proper place as a mediating factor between Israel and the U.S. on the one side and the PLO on the other.

Despite the Reagan administration's bitter experience in presenting a plan for the resolution of the Middle East conflict, Secretary of State George Shultz was of the opinion that three months of the Intifada were a sufficient spur for the two sides to move towards each other. On March 4, 1988, Shultz wrote to King Hussein and Prime Minister Shamir asking for their response to proposals gathered in a framework that was already familiar to them from previous programs. This included an international peace conference and a joint Jordanian–Palestinian delegation; an interim arrangement and permanent agreement; the acceptance of resolutions 242 and 338; abandonment of terrorism and violence; and consent to direct talks between the parties as a condition for participating in the plenum. Shultz even set out a detailed schedule linking the interim arrangement to the permanent solution, and thought that this would attract the Palestinians. As for Shamir, Shultz tried to tempt him by stating that the Jordanian–Palestinian path would not be dependent on the other channels of negotiations, that the conference would not be able to force solutions on the parties, and would not veto agreements achieved in bilateral talks. This meant that the conference would not turn into a means of applying Arab pressure against Israel. Regarding

Jerusalem, Shultz adopted Peres's line, and he thus made no mention at all of the Jerusalem problem in his plan, just as he said nothing about the conference's agenda (Makovsky, 1996: 183; Shultz, 1993: 1,028–9).

As far as the Palestinians were concerned, Shultz succeeded in circumventing the Jerusalem problem on the way to the international conference, but he did not manage to circumvent the PLO. The PLO's leaders in Tunis were disturbed in particular by their absence from the negotiations picture, which they interpreted as a denial of their right to an independent state, and the duty to establish an independent Palestinian state and the installation of an alternative quisling leadership. The PLO had always identified itself with the Palestinian nation and with its demand for independence and it considered the Palestinian representation slated to participate in the conference to be a puppet delegation to whom the conditions for a settlement could easily be dictated. The issue of a state was a matter of principle for the PLO, more important than having the first meeting ever in East Jerusalem between an American secretary of state and prominent Palestinians. For this reason, the PLO made it clear that it would not permit the representatives of the territories to attend the meeting with Shultz at the American Colony Hotel in East Jerusalem. What seemed very dangerous to the Palestinians did not tempt Shamir. He was nauseated by the convening of an international peace conference and was not at all impressed by Shultz's roundabout way of achieving it.

While Shamir's fears were not the PLO's, paradoxically the fears of one party to the confrontation did not neutralize the fears of the opposing side. Shultz did not succeed in using the fears of each side as a way of sedating the opposite side. Shamir rejected the initiative, and the designated Palestinian delegation notified Shultz in advance of the PLO's veto. Despite this, the secretary of state insisted on showing up for the meeting at the American Colony Hotel. He wanted to be the first secretary of state to visit East Jerusalem and to make a statement before the world's press on the political rights of the Palestinians, and to proclaim that the Palestinians should receive political and economic responsibility for issues that touch them and influence their lives (Shultz, 1993: 1,024–5). Shultz's memoirs give the impression that Shamir's repeated rejections made Shultz all the more determined to go to

East Jerusalem, and spurred him to establish an official link with the PLO towards the end of his term at the State Department, in December 1988. It should be noted that the issue of Jerusalem was not raised in the official contacts between the U.S. and the PLO. From the point of view of the U.S., Jerusalem was not preventing the PLO from achieving legitimacy and status. The issue was raised only in the public pronouncements of PLO leaders (Abas [Abu-Mazin], 1995: 28–9).

Shultz was right about the incentive that the Intifada had created for the two sparring sides, Israel and the Palestinians, but some time had to pass before the Intifada produced political fruit. The Intifada's success caused the Israeli government to understand that it must initiate some sort of diplomatic program in order to minimize its losses. Israel's peace plan of May 14, 1989 was aimed at continuing the Camp David agreements via negotiations with a delegation of inhabitants of the territories. The big innovation in the plan was the section that stated that the Palestinian delegation would be elected, chosen by the Palestinian inhabitants of the West Bank and Gaza Strip. This recognized that Israel had to give the inhabitants of the territories something as a result of their uprising. In addition to making a necessary concession, Israel also sought to use the elections to create an alternative leadership to the PLO. Israel hoped the residents of the territories would use the Intifada to rid themselves of the PLO. The plan did not speak of an international conference, which was taboo for the Likud, but rather of direct negotiations with the elected delegation of the Palestinians. At first they would discuss an agreement for an interim period of five years, during which the inhabitants of the territories would enjoy self-government except in the areas of security, foreign affairs, and the settlements, and later there would be discussions for a final agreement. The plan explicitly rejected any sort of negotiation with the PLO, and noted that the permanent settlement and determination of Israel's eastern border would be agreed on with Jordan. However, the Israeli program refrained from proposing a clear outline of the permanent agreement. According to the accepted practice of Israeli governments of the 1980s, the plan did not mention Jerusalem (Laqueur & Rubin, 1995: 547–51). However, the minute the idea of elections had been broached, the question of Jerusalem could not be ignored, because the inevitable question was whether and how elections would be held in East Jerusalem. As if that were not enough, from here on out the question of Jerusalem was tied up with the question of the PLO's presence at the negotiating table.

The non-mention of Jerusalem in the Israeli plan was a compromise formulation of the members of the "prime ministers' club," comprised of Prime Minister Shamir and the two former prime ministers that served in his national unity cabinet – Foreign Minister Peres and Defense Minister Rabin. The plan had to paper over their differences of opinion, since during this period, the cabinet was equally divided between hawks and doves. While the Labor ministers were pressing for a positive decision on the participation of East Jerusalem's Arabs in the elections as voters, though not as candidates, Likud ministers Sharon, Moda'i and Levy were pressuring Shamir to oppose the plan. They opposed any participation at all by East Jerusalem's Arabs in the elections, as well as any negotiations with the PLO and the establishment of a Palestinian state (Koren, 1994: 219–24). The Likud thought that allowing East Jerusalem Arabs to vote for the autonomous authority would be tantamount to sanctioning a Palestinian political element in Jerusalem, which they viewed as a significant step towards redivision of the city. Labor, for its part, maintained that there was no evil in allowing East Jerusalem Arabs to vote, just as U.S. citizens living outside their country are allowed to vote in presidential elections from their place of residence. In order to differentiate the elections in Jerusalem from those in the rest of the territories, the Labor Party proposed placing the voting sites outside the city limits. The Labor Party opposed allowing East Jerusalem Palestinians to be candidates in the election, because it interpreted this to imply the application of Palestinian jurisdiction and law on East Jerusalem via their representatives in the legislative council (Makovsky, 1996: 31–2).

The only way around these opposing pressures within the Israeli government was to ignore the subject of Jerusalem entirely, knowing that on this issue there was a difference of opinion between the Likud and Labor. Even before a decision was needed, Labor and the Likud were divided on the issue of whether Israel would allow Palestinians from Jerusalem to participate even in the negotiations over the procedures for and implementation of the elections. The Likud unanimously vetoed this, seeing it as a first step towards the participation of residents of East Jerusalem in the elections, and rejected the Labor Party proposal to make a gesture to the Palestinians on this issue. An additional Israeli initiative for the advancement of the peace process was thus ground into powder by the national unity government.

The PLO officially rejected the Israel program, since it left out both the PLO and the question of Jerusalem. Unofficially, however, the PLO's leaders understood that via the elections they could get into the diplomatic process through the back door, even though the front door had been slammed in their faces. This was indeed the new reality created in the territories after the Intifada began at the end of 1987 and after Jordan severed its ties with the West Bank at the end of July 1988. It was no longer possible to ignore the PLO as a diplomatic actor, and it would be the PLO that would decide the results of the elections in the territories. The organization's leadership remembered that for four years they had been searching for a way to integrate themselves into the diplomatic process, but their wish had not been granted, even though in the Amman agreement of 1985 the PLO had accepted the principle of territory for peace. The position of Israel and the U.S. was that a solution of the Palestinian problem would be found in the framework of Jordan or in the framework of autonomy for the inhabitants of the West Bank and of the Gaza Strip. The Intifada indeed proved that it was no longer possible to ignore the Palestinians as an active element in the diplomatic scene, and Israel and the U.S. thus toyed with the thought that the PLO's place could be taken by local representatives of the Intifada rebels. This hope was, however, disappointed. While the Intifada did in fact elevate the status of the "inside" leaders, they could under no circumstances be an alternative to the establishment ensconced in Tunis; the leaders of the "outside" also made sure to prevent this by carefully controlling the grants they poured "inside." They encouraged the growth of several competing elite groups "inside," all of them looking to the PLO "outside," seeking to preserve their positions as granters of authority, legitimacy, and status. The PLO leadership in Tunis maneuvered astutely and successfully between the different elites. It knew that in order to be integrated into the diplomatic process it had to take advantage of the opening provided to the "inside" leadership, and at the same time turn the "insiders" to its emissaries. It had to give them rope to conduct talks while at the same time proving to the opposite side how short the reach of the insiders was; it must prove the seriousness of its intentions and be flexible without losing sight of its principal goals. This process was conducted between 1989–93 and reached its height in the period between the Madrid Conference and the Israel–Palestinian statement of principles.

The person who persuaded the PLO to raise the gauntlet that Israel had thrown down before it was Egyptian President Mubarak, who had a very good grasp of the importance of the planned elections – national political elections held for the first time in Palestinian national history, and specifically since Israel had occupied the West Bank and Gaza Strip. Mubarak helped the PLO become convinced that the endpoint of this detour around the PLO paved by Israel could be Yassir Arafat himself (later, the PLO, with the help of Secretary of State Baker, would reach the same conclusion about Jerusalem). Therefore, the Egyptian president devised, in September 1989, a ten-point plan, with elections in the territories at its center. The debate between Israel and Mubarak was conducted around the question of who would participate in the negotiations over the Israeli plan – who would represent the Palestinian side? It was clear to all that the Palestinian delegation would be composed of people from the West Bank and Gaza Strip. But what part would the PLO play in putting the delegation together? The PLO acceded to Mubarak's request to remain in the background, but demanded that all threads lead to it, and visibly – the PLO would appoint the delegation and declare that the Palestinians accepted the initiative, or at the very least would make it clear to the entire world that it had given the delegation a green light.

This, of course, intersected with the issue of the participation of East Jerusalem representatives in the Palestinian delegation and the question of whether and how the elections would be held there. In Mubarak's plan, Jerusalem was part of the West Bank, and the sections addressing the electoral process in the West Bank also applied to Jerusalem. All the inhabitants of the West Bank and Gaza, including "the Palestinians in East Jerusalem, will participate in the elections," both as voters and as candidates (*Filastin al-Thawra*, 17 Sept. 1989). President Mubarak thus maintained that, with regard to the elections, all the arrangements applying to the rest of the 1967 territories would also apply to East Jerusalem: all of Israel's security forces would have to retreat from the territories during the elections, no entry of Israelis would be allowed on election day, the elections would be held under international supervision, and the candidates would have complete freedom of expression during the election campaign. Even though Israel rejected the plan, President Mubarak's efforts were not in vain. His plan was coordinated with the United States, and Secretary of State James Baker, who would soon sire his own five-point plan, and later the Madrid Conference adopted several of the Egyptian leader's points.

In October 1989 Baker formulated his five points, which were meant to produce a consensus on the composition of the Palestinian delegation. Baker proposed that Israel approve the composition of the delegation, enabling it to ensure that it contained no PLO representatives; the agenda of the discussions would be open. Israel would come to the negotiations with its May 14, 1989 election plan, while the Palestinian delegation could put other subjects on the agenda or propose to broaden the circle of participants and include PLO representatives as well. Baker also stated that, in the framework of the negotiations, the Palestinians could express their position on the election arrangements; that is, they could demand to hold them in Jerusalem as well (Laqueur & Rubin, 1995: 556). This formulation made it possible to transfer the disagreements over elections in Jerusalem to the negotiating table, without allowing the difference of views to block the discussions themselves. This technical–procedural compromise was accompanied by a clarification made by the U.S. to Egypt and the PLO that, in its opinion, the East Jerusalem Arabs ought to participate in the planned elections. The U.S. refrained, however, from promising that it would impose its opinion on Israel.

Upon the presentation of Baker's five points, the Likud and Labor again began to argue over the issue of the participation of East Jerusalem Palestinians in the negotiating delegation. Like the U.S., Labor supported their participation, while the Likud was, of course, opposed. This dispute led to the dissolution of the national unity government in March 1990, but not before Labor and Baker made one last attempt to placate the Likud. Baker proposed that the Palestinian delegation include two or three Palestinians that Israel had in the past deported from the territories, alongside a person with two addresses, one of which was in East Jerusalem. Through this compromise Baker hoped to accommodate both the PLO leadership and Israel. Israel would claim that they were indigenous non-PLO Palestinians of the territories, while the PLO would claim that they represented the "external" PLO. This was a brilliant idea that caused a difference of opinion in the Likud. Foreign Minister Arens favored accepting the American compromise proposal, but Shamir and the other Likud ministers opposed it vociferously. Baker thought that the Likud's moderates would vote with the Labor ministers to accept his proposal, but when it became an internal Israeli political issue, it was no longer possible for the amenable Likud ministers to break ranks and vote against their party. The Likud only saw what it wanted to see – the political success of the Labor Party. For the Likud, Labor was a horrifying demon, worse than a diplomatic quagmire and worse than a confrontation with the U.S. Only when the Likud remained alone in government did its internal differences of opinion become a catalyst for the advancement of the peace process. But this happened only after the Gulf War of 1991, when, in parallel, the necessary changes in the world and the region took place that made convening the Madrid Conference possible (Arens, 1995: 124; Bentzur, 1997: 46–50; Shamir, 1994: 248–9, 258).

A consensual lie: the PLO does not function in Jerusalem

After the Gulf War, in 1991, Baker renewed his efforts to achieve a peace accord in the Middle East, taking advantage of the state of the Arab world at the end of the war. Arab unity had been shattered more severely than at any time since the Arab states of the Middle East had come into existence. A pro-Western block had consolidated, for the first time bringing together the oil states with their money and capital and Syria and Egypt, the strongest and most important Arab states that had in the past led the war against Israel. The Palestinians, who had supported Iraq, were stinging from their ally's defeat, and Jordan was eagerly knocking on the U.S.'s door after having taken an equivocal stance during the war. The international stage was weighted in the U.S.'s favor, especially after the collapse of the Soviet bloc and the end of the Cold War, on which the Israel–Arab dispute had been built as an upper floor. All this allowed the United States to get the wheels of the diplomatic process moving. Baker had the full support of President George Bush, the leader of the victorious war coalition, and it was hard to resist the brilliant move he planned. Baker, the energetic architect of the conference, entered the political history of the Middle East with his truly amazing diplomacy.

The major element was the American proposal on March 6, 1991 of a procedural framework for the convention of an international Middle East peace conference. According to the proposal, in the framework of the conference there would be negotiations between Israel and the Palestinians on a two-stage solution to the conflict. The first stage would be the establishment of self-government for a transition period of five years, with negotiations on a permanent settlement beginning in the third year. The Palestinians would be represented at the conference by a delegation of residents of the territories that would be part of a joint Jordanian–Palestinian delegation (this analysis of the actions leading to the Madrid conference is based on Abas [Abu-Mazin], 1995; Arens, 1995: 241–6, 271–2; Ashrawi, 1995: 81–130; Baker, 1995; Bentzur, 1997: 82–135; Makovsky, 1996: 443–67; Naufel, 1995).

In order to bring the different sides into the vicinity of his goal, Baker used a number of methods that he himself compared to hunting, his favorite hobby. First, Baker took elements from past plans. There was the international conference that Shultz and his predecessors had insisted on, the Israeli government's proposal for negotiations with an elected Palestinian leadership, and the formal formula drafted by Baker in his five-point plan concerning the Palestinian delegation and the agenda. Second, Baker was an active mediator who did not wait for the parties to accept his proposal. He presented himself as acting in the name of the president of the United States and applied pressure to all the relevant parties. Baker took advantage of the collapse of the Soviet Union, and of America's position as leader of the victorious Gulf War coalition in order to create a situation in which the sides could not reject his plan. The fact is that the major participants in the conference – Israel, the Palestinians, and Syria – dragged their feet all the way to Madrid, but in the end they got there.

Third, Baker succeeded in redefining the questions of principle as procedural problems. Baker's goal was to encourage all the parties to make procedural and symbolic concessions and to leave the fundamental issues for the negotiations. He knew that there was an issue of substance behind every minor and symbolic procedural concession, but with regard to the procedural issues Baker suggested compromises that were difficult to reject. The same was true of the issue of Jerusalem. Unlike Shultz, Baker understood that it was impossible to ignore Jerusalem entirely. He imposed a compromise between Israel's desire to remove Jerusalem from the Madrid conference and the Palestinian desire to link it inexorably to the fate of the rest of the 1967 territories. Fourth, Baker pulled the parties into the process by promising compensation if the move succeeded, and by continually increasing the price of failure. Baker also knew that the further the process progressed and the involvement of the different sides increased, it would be harder for them to free themselves, to shake off responsibility for the failure of the talks and to accuse their opponents of being the reason for the breakdown. At times of crisis he thus repeated to each party that they could not allow themselves to be accused of responsibility for leaving the process to die. When there seemed to be no will to succeed and the collapse of the whole enterprise seemed imminent, Baker knew how to get each person he spoke to to react to American anger. These each then tried to prove that the failure of the talks was not their fault. He was not a well-liked mediator but he was efficient, aloof, and shrewd. Those who sat across from him feared him and were afraid to disappoint him. Don't let the cat die on your doorstep, he would repeatedly warn the different parties, each one in turn. At the same time, Baker knew how to arouse expectations and deepen trust and confidence in his word.

He first dealt with Shamir, whom he estimated to be the toughest customer. Baker did not want to begin from ground zero, but instead from the agreements that had been achieved between Shamir and Shultz in the Israeli plan of May 14, 1991. One of these agreements had to do with the international opening, Shamir's term for an international conference of a single session, after which there would be direct bilateral talks between Israel and each of its neighbors. The second agreement was that each of the negotiating channels would be independent of the others. The third agreement was that no official representative of the PLO would participate in the conference. On April 19, 1991, Baker told Shamir that if the Palestinian representatives on the joint delegation declared that they represented the PLO, Israel could leave the talks, and the United States would follow. But this promise was not sufficient for Shamir, and he demanded that the Palestinians participating in the conference not mention the PLO at all; he also demanded that they provide written statements that they did not represent Arafat.

Baker was not willing to go that far. He made it clear to Shamir that no Palestinian would be able to attend the conference without an explicit or secret green light from the PLO, because otherwise his or her life would be forfeited. The representatives of the West Bank and Gaza Strip would be required to declare that the PLO did not oppose their inclusion in the delegation, the secretary of state claimed. This could lead to an agreement between him and the Palestinians on maintaining contact. In order to promote this possibility, Baker asked Shamir not to speak out against the PLO. The West Bank and Gaza Strip representatives would, for their part, not sing the PLO's praises and claim to be its proxies. Under Baker's overbearing, intimidating, and blunt pressure, Shamir was forced to agree grudgingly to a Palestinian delegation that was in practice linked to the PLO but which denied this, or at least did not explicitly confirm it. This was an opening that had never before been available to the PLO, and through which it could worm its way into the negotiations. Baker also knew how to extend Shamir a bag of carrots – on April 19, 1991, he agreed with Shamir that if the initiative failed because of Palestinian inflexibility, they would both blame the PLO. In exchange for Shamir's procedural concessions, Baker moved towards him on other procedural matters: the conference would have no power to compel, it would not take votes, and it would not make decisions. It would be a ceremonial conference and no more, Baker and Shamir agreed. On May 22, 1991, Baker put his understandings with Shamir into writing. The U.S. understood that Israel would not agree to sit down with people unacceptable to it, but neither would the Palestinians of the West Bank and Gaza Strip come if the PLO actively opposed it. They required personal, individual permission, a kind of tacit sanction, to participate in the conference. Shamir was not enthusiastic and tried to change Baker's position, but to no avail. The debate now proceeded to other issues. On May 28, 1991, there was a discussion about how the Palestinian representatives to the conference would be chosen and how the PLO leadership would give its covert green light. At this point two of Shamir's aides tried to turn the clock back and reject any link of the delegation to PLO headquarters in Tunis or to the PLO at all. Baker reacted sharply, demanding that Shamir keep his commitments. Having obtained guarded consent from the Israeli side, Baker had to go to the PLO and show it why it would be persuaded to accept Shamir's preferred framework.

Baker took care of the PLO on several channels. First, the PLO had to approve the meeting between the "internal" leadership and Baker so that the talks on convening the Madrid conference could get underway. In the light of the PLO's low international status, it could not refuse, and in this regard Baker was in a better position than Shultz had been. Moreover, since Shultz's initiative, the PLO's authority over the Palestinian political leadership in the territories had increased, and thus its ability to prevent them from becoming an alternative to the leadership in Tunis. The leaders in the territories seemed, to the U.S., to be appropriate partners for dialogue, not only because they had been so portrayed in past diplomatic initiatives, but also because they had expressed reservations about the PLO's unambiguous support for Saddam Hussein during the Gulf War. Under the circumstances created after the war, negotiations through the leadership in the territories looked to Israel like a way of getting around the PLO, and to the PLO as the high road into the international arena. Even the negotiations about the negotiations gave political prestige to the Palestinians and to the PLO. The Palestinians' positive response was given on March 10, 1991, and two days later a Palestinian delegation met with Baker at the American Consulate in west Jerusalem (the delegation had 11 members; five came to the next meeting, and thereafter three: Hanan Ashrawi and Faisal Husseini from Jerusalem and Zakariya al-Agha from Gaza). At the first meeting Baker notified the Palestinians that it was none of his business who their leader was and from whom they were receiving instructions. He was looking for leaders from the territories who were not officially members of the PLO, who were prepared to conduct direct negotiations with Israel on a two-stage solution based on UN resolutions 242 and 338, who rejected terrorism and who supported the principle of territory for peace. The Palestinian representatives clearly needed the PLO's blessing, and Baker allowed them to consult with Tunis. In this way the PLO became an "absent presence" in the negotiations.

Second, since Baker lacked an official negotiating channel between the PLO and the U.S., he enlisted King Fahd of Saudi

Arabia and President Mubarak of Egypt, his partners in the war coalition against Iraq, in order to extract the PLO's consent to refrain from taking an official role in the lead-up to and at the Madrid conference. The PLO would still, however, be tied to the process so that it could not run away from or torpedo it. Third, Baker had a relatively easy time closing a deal with King Hussein. Jordan agreed in principle to a joint delegation with the PLO because it wanted to improve its relations with the U.S., damaged by its failure to join the anti-Iraq coalition. On May 14, Hussein and Baker agreed that the delegation of "insiders" would work openly with Hussein, but would covertly mediate between him and Arafat to set up a joint delegation. Hussein even agreed, for appearance's sake, not to invite Arafat to visit Amman so long as the deal had not been closed. Above all, Hussein also agreed to exploit his direct negotiating lines with Israeli leaders in order to pass on to Shamir a promise that there would be no "bad surprises" in the joint delegation. In other words, Arafat and his people would not suddenly materialize as members. This was a smart move by Baker and Hussein. Even though Shamir did not have Hussein's confidence (Shultz, 1993: 942–4), Hussein had Shamir's confidence after having kept the promises he had made to the prime minister at their meeting on the eve of the Gulf War. At that time Hussein had asked Shamir for an Israeli commitment that Israeli air or ground forces would not pass through his kingdom if Israel decided to retaliate against an Iraqi attack. Hussein did not want his country to turn into a battlefield. Shamir prevented any action by Israeli forces against Iraq, justifying this, among other reasons, by stating that he could not violate Jordanian sovereignty (Zak, 1996: 21, 35, 48, 51). Thanks to this pact with Hussein, Shamir was able to stand firm against the pressures from his cabinet and from the Israeli military to retaliate against the Iraqi missile attacks against Israel. He thus avoided endangering the American–Arab coalition against Iraq. In short, the PLO accepted Baker's line that Shamir should be given the procedural commitments he demanded, while standing firm only on purely substantive issues that would be brought up at the conference itself.

As was his habit, Shamir engaged in procedural politics with the goal of gaining time and benefiting from the complications being encountered by his Palestinian partner. Baker proposed a formula to Shamir that the latter thought would allow him to continue to conduct his procedural politics. At the same time, Baker succeeded in persuading the Palestinians to be considerably more flexible about procedural questions in exchange for parallel concessions on the Israeli side, and in exchange for a letter of assurance from the U.S. that was closer in its content to the Palestinian position than that of the Israeli's.

The problem of Jerusalem came up at the beginning of Baker's contacts and accompanied them as they progressed, although not always with the same intensity. At times the issue was only mentioned, at others it was discussed at length. In April and May 1991 a solution took form and in later contacts it was accepted by the parties because the deal as a whole satisfied each of them. The question of Jerusalem had two elements: first, the participation of representatives from East Jerusalem in the Palestinian delegation; second, the inclusion of the Jerusalem question on the conference's agenda. On April 10 Shamir demanded that Jerusalem be completely eliminated from the framework of negotiations at the conference, hoping to thus obtain *de facto* recognition of the facts that Israel had created in the city after 1967. From Shamir's point of view, the very fact that the issue of Jerusalem was on the conference's agenda called the annexation into question, so he demanded that the East Jerusalem representatives be forbidden to participate in the delegation. Baker refused to promise this to Shamir, and agreed only to try to persuade the Palestinians to give their assent. In order to help gain the Palestinians' consent, Baker asked Shamir to refrain from publicly declaring his ultimatum. Baker made it clear that he did not agree with the Israeli position that categorically rejected, in every way and all times, the participation of East Jerusalem representatives in the negotiations. The U.S. would work to achieve this, but it could not promise that they would not participate in the future, Baker explained to Israel in his diplomatic way. Between April 10 and 18, 1991, Baker proposed that the Palestinian delegation include Faisal Husseini from Jerusalem, who had met Shamir previously in other circumstances. As for the agenda, Baker proposed that the Jerusalem question not be discussed during the first stage of the conference, which would be devoted to the interim arrangement. Jerusalem would be raised for discussion only in the context of the permanent settlement; the U.S. was willing to commit itself to this in writing. This being the case, Baker argued, the East Jerusalem representatives could participate in the joint Jordanian–Palestinian delegation during the talks on the interim agreement. If Israel were to continue to reject the participation of East Jerusalem representatives at all times and at all stages, if it refused to allow discussion of the eastern city, and if it made both these preconditions to the conference, there would be no peace process, Baker warned. In this way Baker sought to mediate between Shamir's position and that of the Palestinians, towards whom Baker was using similar language. The Palestinian demands were, of course, the opposite of Shamir's, and were meant to reject the facts that Israel had unilaterally established. First, the Palestinians demanded the inclusion of East Jerusalem representatives in their delegation; second, they demanded that East Jerusalem be included in the self-governing area during the period of the interim agreement; and finally, their position was that the conference was meant to ensure the full implementation of Resolution 242, including Israeli withdrawal from East Jerusalem.

On April 26, 1991 there was progress in the wide-ranging contacts Baker was conducting, and he informed Shamir that his procedural conditions had been accepted – the East Jerusalem representatives would not participate in the Palestinian delegation, and Jerusalem would not be put on the agenda of the conference, which would be discussing the interim agreement. In exchange, Baker extracted Shamir's consent that the joint Jordanian–Palestinian delegation would include one or two members who bore Jordanian passports and who had been born in East Jerusalem, or who lived there. However, on May 17, 1991, Shamir reneged and wrote to Baker that he was not prepared to accept participation by any representatives of East Jerusalem, and Baker accepted this. After accord was reached on the composition of the Palestinian delegation, the discussions concentrated on the question of how the composition of the delegation would be assured – who would choose the Palestinian representatives, and could Israel veto them?

During the course of their contacts with Baker, it had been difficult for the Palestinians to assimilate the Baker–Shamir understanding that neither the subject of Jerusalem nor the representatives of the city's Palestinians would be allowed into the conference. From their point of view this was tantamount to recognition of the annexation of East Jerusalem to Israel. At one of their meetings Faisal Husseini even told Baker that the secretary of state was speaking with a dead man. Despite all this, Baker managed to persuade the Palestinians to be more flexible on procedural matters and to defer obduracy to the discussions on substance. He argued that in the substantive talks the solution that would take shape would be closer to their model than to Israel's. Baker even promised Faisal Husseini and Hanan Ashrawi, residents of Jerusalem with Israeli identity cards, that while they would not be members of the Palestinian delegation to the conference, he would continue to meet with them and to coordinate his actions with them. Baker reiterated that these restrictions were temporary and applied only to the first stage of the talks and accords. He pledged that the letter of guarantees would unambiguously state the American position on the issue of East Jerusalem. The final argument in this series was conducted around the Palestinian demand to be the sole determinants of the membership of their delegation. Shamir would not consent to this because he suspected that PLO members or East Jerusalem representatives would be named to the delegation at the last minute. The compromise stated that the names of the members of the Palestinian delegation would be delivered to Baker and he would certify that they did indeed meet the Israeli conditions. Baker pledged to the Palestinians that he would not show the list to Israel so that Israel would not be in the position of certifying it or determining whom the Palestinian representatives would be. Baker notified Shamir that the Palestinian delegation met Israel's conditions, and that Israel should thus confirm its participation. Israel gave its consent on August 2, 1991.

On the eve of the Madrid conference, on October 3, 1991, all that remained to be determined were the rules of the game between the PLO and Jordan, regarding the joint delegation. The Palestinians wanted to reach an advance agreement with Jordan on a delegation that was joint in name but separate in practice. Baker encouraged the leaders from the territories to travel to Jordan in order to prove to Shamir that the PLO was indeed not participating in the Madrid conference. Ashrawi, Husseini, and al-Agha went to Amman, and at the same time a PLO delegation, headed by Abu-Mazin, also arrived. The U.S. saw to it that the two visits were coordinated in such a way that Shamir and his government could not object to anyone. According to the American staging, the delegation from the territories was in the media spotlight while the PLO delegation remained in the shade. The "internals" went with the media to the office of Jordan's prime minister, and at the end of the meeting announced that agreement in principle had been reached on the structure of the joint Jordanian–Palestinian delegation. After the "internal" group and its party had left, the PLO delegation strode in. At this meeting it was agreed that each of the two components of the joint delegation would discuss the issues germane to it. With U.S. acquiescence, it was agreed that the delegation would have two co-chairmen of equal status, and that both of them would address the Madrid conference at its opening session (Abas, 1995: 86–7).

Thus, denial by both sides of the PLO's activity in Jerusalem was a consensual falsehood. The media made fun of Israel's prohibition of contact with the PLO. The operational leadership of the Intifada took advantage of Israeli law in Jerusalem to direct the Intifada and organize it in accordance with instructions that arrived from Tunis by telephone and fax. The political leadership of the territories was, after the Intifada, subordinate to the "external" leadership, and turned East Jerusalem into the focus of its activities. This was an unelected political elite that worked on a voluntary basis, but it had an elevated status in the PLO organizations "inside," and decided at the beginning of the Intifada to coordinate public relations and political activity. These leaders lived in the Jerusalem metropolitan region and acted inside it. From the beginning of the Intifada they initiated public relations activities for the world's media and for the representatives of foreign consulates in the territories who were attracted to the fire of the popular uprising in the territories, and who even exchanged ideas with the PLO leadership in Tunis (Ashrawi, 1995: 50–7).

Palestinian political activity in East Jerusalem moved up one level when Baker began to shuttle between the region's leaders. While his Palestinian contacts met with him in the American consulate in the west side of the city, most of the preparations for these meetings took place in Jerusalem at Orient House. This building belonged to the Husseini family, and Faisal Husseini used it as the offices of his Arab Studies Society. The preparations for the meetings with Baker included ongoing contacts with PLO headquarters in Tunis, and this established a political fact that was

very difficult to challenge thereafter. Moreover, Baker was negotiating on the composition of the delegation and on the inclusion of
Jerusalem on the peace conference's agenda with East Jerusalem
leaders and with the PLO, with the full knowledge of the Israeli
government.

The local Palestinian panel had 18 meetings with Baker, most
of them in Jerusalem. These consultations with the PLO and with
Baker were conducted under the watchful eyes of the media. Several foreign consulates also took an interest. By far the greater part
of this feverish activity took place in Jerusalem, with the knowledge, but also the denial, of the Israeli government. The Israelis
hoped that denials would preserve something of its symbols of
sovereignty in the city, while it waited, teeth gritted, for an alternative, non-PLO Palestinian leadership to appear. Baker's argument against Shamir had been that if Israel did not provide the
local leadership with the means to take the PLO's place, it would
not be able to get off the ground. Shamir and his colleagues were
waiting for the moment at which the ostensibly more amenable
"internal" leadership would disassociate itself from the "external"
leadership and the PLO establishment would itself unwittingly
authorize those who would take its place. They did not guess that
the opposite would happen and that the "internals" would be the
official means by which the PLO would establish its foothold in
the territories and at the Madrid conference. The Israeli government of the time believed that the PLO's extremism was a matter
of principle and that its representatives would not demonstrate
political flexibility, whereas the internal leadership would be different. As will be seen, this perspective was not born out in practice. The "external" PLO was flexible and shrewd and imposed
political concessions on the "internals" (Abas, 1995: 87; Ashrawi,
1995: 50–7).

The nature of the links between the "internals" and Tunis did
not remain as they had been in March 1991 when Baker began to
shuttle among the Middle East's capitals on his way to the Madrid
conference. The Palestinian delegation to the talks with Baker
astutely and gradually notched up its level of activity in Jerusalem
and its links with the PLO leadership, taking care not to make any
move that would sever the contact with Baker. Initially, the presence of Baker and Arafat in Amman in September 1991 was used
to discuss the issue of the joint Jordanian–Palestinian delegation

to the Madrid conference. First there was a secret meeting between Ashrawi and Arafat, and the latter's position was later conveyed to Baker at an open meeting between him and Ashrawi. Since Ashrawi did not want to deny her ties with the PLO, she and Baker agreed to remain silent until the media left the room. This plan was upset when a CNN correspondent asked Ashrawi whether she had a message from Arafat to Baker and she responded in the affirmative. This was not the only fact established by the Palestinians during this visit. The PLO arranged an official car with a Palestinian flag to take Ashrawi from the Allenby Bridge to Amman; after her meeting with Baker, she conducted a press conference at the PLO embassy in Jordan, where a Palestinian flag stood by her side and a portrait of Arafat gazed out from above her (Ashrawi, 1995: 95–100).

A further promotion of their status occurred when Husseini and Ashrawi appeared before the Palestinian National Council (PNC). The PNC convened its 20 session in 1991 for the purpose of approving participation of a Palestinian delegation in the Madrid conference. Baker was involved in this as well – he coordinated the trip with the PLO and with Israel. He warned the Palestinians against leaking news of the story. They did so anyway, though they refused to confirm it officially. Israel was furious about the leak, and threatened to take legal action under the law that forbade meetings with PLO officials. Baker once again went into action and obtained the Palestinian delegation's consent not to return to Israel until the matter had been cleared up with Shamir. Once the scenario had been written the Palestinian actors played their roles to the hilt. Ashrawi and Husseini returned to Israel and told the press and the police that they had not violated Israeli law. Two days later, on October 10, 1991, they flew to meet Baker in Washington, a meeting that had been scheduled before their return from Tunis to Israel, and which was meant to prevent their arrest (Ashrawi, 1995: 101–15).

From Jerusalem to Tunis, Madrid, Washington, Oslo, and back

The 20 session of the Palestinian National Council authorized the PLO's Executive Committee to "respond favorably" to the proposal to convene the Madrid conference after two conditions had been met (*Al-Quds*, 29 Sept. 1991). These two points were emphasized in the PNC's political program. First, the conference was to ensure Israel's compliance with resolutions 242 and 338, meaning a full withdrawal from the occupied lands, including Jerusalem. Second, that a Jerusalem representative had to be included in the Palestinian delegation (Ayalon, 1993: 241).

The PLO chairman decided to confirm the participation of the Palestinian delegation despite the absence of any mention of Jerusalem in the invitation and without the PNC's conditions having been met. Arafat, who had always maneuvered beyond the restrictions imposed on him, gave his consent because of the achievements the PLO had obtained up until then. He was also counting on the letter of assurances from the U.S. to the Palestinians of October 18, 1991, in which the U.S. had expressed its substantive position on the issue of Jerusalem. The U.S. did not recognize the annexation of East Jerusalem and believed that its inhabitants had the right to vote for the self-governing authority during the interim period and to be included in the delegation that would negotiate the final settlement (Laqueur & Rubin, 1995: 573–6).

In general, everything that Israel saw as a gain in shaping the Madrid conference was not accepted by the U.S. Moreover, the U.S. refrained from making its position clear to Israel. At the earliest stages of the discussions between the U.S. and the "internal" leadership on the letter of assurances that was to be sent to the Palestinians, Baker asked the Palestinians not to leak even a draft of the letter on the grounds that Israel would object sharply and block it. Things reached the point that Baker asked the local Palestinian delegation not to disseminate the letter of assurances even among the delegates of the PNC. The Palestinians acceded to his request and made do with giving the PNC a reworked summary of the U.S. commitments (Ashrawi, 1995: 100). Since Jerusalem was not mentioned in the U.S. letter of assurances to Israel, the Israeli leadership assumed that the issue had not been mentioned in the letter to the Palestinians, either. The letter to Israel emphasized that Israel would not be required to talk to any interlocutors it did not accept at the Madrid conference, during the initial stage of the talks, and beyond (Bentzur, 1997: 135). But the U.S. did not obligate itself to support the Israeli position if Israel did not agree to sit down with representatives of East Jerusalem, or if Israel refused to discuss the future of this part of the city during the final status talks. It is not hard to imagine how the Israeli leadership would have felt if they had seen the American letter to the Palestinians.

The PLO elegantly circumvented the procedural roadblock that Israel placed in the way of the East Jerusalem representatives by creating special titles for them. A negotiations steering committee was set up, including Faisal Husseini, Hanan Ashrawi, and two other representatives of parties that were not represented at Madrid – FIDA and the People's Party. Alongside them were three "externals," which strengthened the hand of the leaders from Jerusalem and their identification with the PLO establishment in Tunis. Moreover, Faisal Husseini was appointed to head the delegation to the Madrid conference and Hanan Ashrawi became its spokesperson (Ashrawi, 1995: 124–30). While they themselves did not participate in the talks, they were present and involved in the diplomatic process, which was conducted in the media no less than in the conference room, and the media extravaganza was conducted as much around the conference room as inside it. Thus, thanks to Israel's procedural restrictions, Faisal Husseini and Hanan Ashrawi from Jerusalem were the focus of special attention and stood out in their roles as delegation head and spokesperson.

The Palestinian delegation went even further by making a night-time trip from Madrid to Tunis to meet with Arafat (Ashrawi, 1995: 150). At this stage the meeting was secret and was not leaked to the media. Later, in June 1992, Ashrawi and Husseini, who were by then heading the Palestinian delegation to the bilateral talks with Israel in Washington, went to visit Arafat at the hospital in Amman where he was undergoing an operation. Two months earlier, when an airplane Arafat was flying in crashed, Ashrawi had stated publicly that if he had indeed been killed (as was at first supposed), it would be necessary to organize elections for his replacement. This had angered Arafat and in June 1992 Ashrawi understood that she needed to meet with the PLO chairman. Ashrawi apparently sought, by publicizing the trip, to atone for her outspokenness, to clear her name, and to re-establish her loyalty to Arafat. Israel announced that Ashrawi and Husseini would be arrested upon their return to Israel in accordance with the law forbidding meetings with the PLO. This was a week before the elections in Israel and the Americans, who as usual rushed in to resolve the crisis, recommended to Ashrawi and Husseini that they remain in Jordan until after the poll. A week later the Israeli government changed and the matter lost its importance (Ashrawi, 1995: 209–13).

In parallel with the Madrid talks, and with the subsequent talks in Washington, activity in Orient House began to burgeon. The Palestinian delegation used it as a base to prepare for the talks, and Dr. Sari Nusseibeh convened groups of local experts there to advise the delegation and prepare position, working, and background papers on various subjects. The Palestinian media closely followed the extensive activity and gave great emphasis to East Jerusalem as the political center for the Palestinians in the West Bank and Gaza Strip.

After the opening session, the Madrid Conference broke up into multilateral and bilateral negotiating groups, with the talks between Israel and the Palestinian delegation taking place in Washington beginning in December 1991. In accordance with the prior agreement between the PLO and Jordan, at the very first stage of these discussions the Palestinians, through a series of unilateral actions, separated themselves from the Jordanian delegation. The Palestinian delegation arrived separately at the hotel and the conference room, conducted its own briefings and press conferences, and demanded that Israel conduct separate negotiations with the Palestinian and the Jordanian delegations. The Palestinian demand roused the ire of Israel, which refused to commence negotiations with the Palestinian delegation. The Palestinian provocation was effective. In Washington, as in Madrid, they succeeded in portraying the Palestinian problem as separate from the Jordanian issues, and in directing the spotlight at Hanan Ashrawi and Faisal Husseini as representatives of Jerusalem (Ashrawi, 1995: 158–68). Until a compromise was reached in January 1992, the talks between Israel and the joint delegation were conducted in a corridor of the State Department building in Washington, and were limited to talks between the two delegation heads. The compromise achieved in January stated that the joint delegation would split into two parts, each of which would include two representatives from its sister delegation. Furthermore, the U.S. agreed to grant a visa to Nabil Sha'th, a PLO official from Tunis who bore an American passport, who was sent by the PLO to coordinate between Tunis and the team in Washington. Sha'th was sent for symbolic–political, not practical, reasons. His very presence was a political statement. In fact, it complicated the functioning of the Palestinian delegation and its channel of communication with Tunis (Abas, 1995: 88; Ashrawi, 1995: 168–73).

Of course, the entire course of the talks in Washington was accompanied by a wide-ranging web of discussions and consultations between the Palestinian delegation and PLO headquarters. The Palestinians in the territories also followed events closely. The consultations between Washington and Tunis were ongoing, and they became public at times of crisis. As might have been expected, there was no shortage of such crises. The disagreements surrounding the issues under discussion were only one cause. A second cause was the interest that each side had in initiating crises in order to gain support at home. The Palestinians were particularly persistent in this. At the end of each round of talks and before the opening of the next round, they announced consultations about their participation in the coming round. This calculated crisis made it possible for the members of the delegation to reiterate the PLO's position as the guiding hand behind the Palestinian delegation. It also answered an internal political imperative – the involvement of a large number of representatives, streams, and organizations in the process, and the release of ideological and political pressures on the part of PLO elements in Tunis. The East Jerusalem representatives played a special role in these consultations. The senior status of the Jerusalem representatives in the delegation was recognized not only by the Palestinians, but also, at a certain stage, by the U.S. and Israel. At the fourth round of talks, in February 1992, Baker sent an official letter to Faisal Husseini in his role as head of the Palestinian delegation (Abas, 1995: 89, 239–50; Ashrawi, 1995: 171–3). On the eve of the ninth round, in May 1993, Israel agreed to allow Husseini to participate officially in the talks.

The problem of Jerusalem was not raised in Washington until the ninth round. In preparation, the Palestinian delegation drew up what it considered an appropriate model for Palestinian self-government (PISGA – Palestinian Interim Self-Governing Authority) during the transition period. The Palestinian document noted over and over again that the arrangements applying to the "occupied Palestinian territories" during the transition period should also apply to Jerusalem. It stated that the inhabitants of East Jerusalem and their descendants, those listed in the population registry on June 4, 1967 as residents of the city, should be allowed to be elected to the PISGA legislative council. The Palestinians viewed the enlargement of Jerusalem's municipal borders and its annexation to Israel as illegal unilateral actions that were void by their very nature. Jerusalem, the members of the delegation noted, was the heart of Palestinian national identity, and as such they were determined to make it the capital of their independent state when it was established (Abdul Hadi, 1997, Vol. II: 133–4). In fact, the Palestinian position regarding the application of the interim administration's legal authority to Jerusalem had been formulated prior to this, in the period leading up to the seventh round of talks in November 1992, but it had not yet been raised in the discussions (Abas, 1995: 94).

After the Labor Party's return to power in 1992, Israel agreed that Faisal Husseini, a resident of East Jerusalem, could officially participate in the Palestinian delegation beginning with the ninth round of talks. According to the new Israeli position, when the time came, the inhabitants of East Jerusalem would vote – but could not be candidates – in the elections to the Palestinian interim self-governing authority. Israel's flexibility led the Palestinians to take a less rigid position in the statement of principles they submitted during the ninth round than they had taken in the PISGA document. The draft said that the Palestinians listed in the population registry as residents of the city on June 4, 1967, and their descendants, would "participate in the elections," without specifying whether this was just as voters or also as candidates. The draft also stated that the 1967 territories were for the Palestinians a single unit, implicitly including Jerusalem. "The authority of PISGA will extend to all the Palestinian territories occupied since June 1967, which is an integral whole and constitutes a single territorial unit under one system of law" (Abdul Hadi, 1997, Vol. II: 134). Even though this declaration was a reiteration of the Palestinian position on Jerusalem, they did not emphasize it as they had in the past. They thus hoped to satisfy Israel. This was the maximum concession the Palestinian delegation, headed by residents of East Jerusalem, felt it could make, especially given that the PLO leadership in Tunis was spurring the delegation in Washington to take a tough position on the issue. In order to cover for the progress that had been achieved behind the scenes in Oslo, Arafat called Washington several times a day, personally instructing his delegation to stand firm. The result was that in the ninth round the Jerusalem issue again became a focus of disagreement. Under pressure from the PLO leadership and from Arafat personally, the Palestinian delegation in Washington demanded that all Palestinian legislation apply to Jerusalem. Israel, of course, refused (*Al-Sharq al-Awsat*, 10 Aug. 1993; *Al-Watan al-Arabi*, 20 Aug. 1993; Ashrawi, 1995: 183–4, 218; Naufal, 1995: 67).

In the tenth round of talks, in June 1993, the U.S. submitted its own proposal for a statement of principles between Israel and the Palestinians. In contrast with the position of the PLO and of the Palestinian delegation in Washington, which maintained that East Jerusalem had to be a part of the Palestinian authority and that the elected Palestinian council's legislative authority would also apply to it, the American proposal was that both sides agree to postpone discussion of the question of Jerusalem until the final agreement, and to remove it from the interim arrangements. The Palestinians fiercely opposed the American proposal, both because of the instructions Arafat had given (intended to bring the talks to a dead end) and because of the fact that several members of the delegation lived in East Jerusalem. A sharp memorandum handed by Faisal Husseini to Dennis Ross, the American coordinator of the peace talks, on July 1, 1993, stated that there was a large gap between the letter of assurances that the U.S. had given the Palestinians on the eve of the Madrid conference and the American proposal to postpone the discussion of the Jerusalem question (Abdul Hadi, 1997, Vol. II: 135–7). While the Palestinians in Washington were raining down fire and brimstone on the U.S., the PLO had already agreed in its secret contacts with Israel in Oslo to put off discussion of Jerusalem to the talks on the permanent settlement. The U.S. did not have detailed and up-to-date information about the talks in Oslo and it did not attribute any importance to what was happening there. The U.S. worked in June and August 1993 to issue a joint Israeli–Palestinian statement of principles from Washington. In order to get around the sharp opposition of the Palestinians in Washington to the postponement of the Jerusalem issue to the permanent settlement, the U.S. proposed ignoring the subject entirely. The leaders of the delegation in Washington rejected this proposal as well. As will be shown below, the PLO leadership in Tunis "suffered" from having been all too successful in stiffening the position of their representatives in Washington.

In August, the PLO responded to the U.S. proposal with its own document, which also omitted mention of Jerusalem. The leaders of the Palestinian delegation in Washington declined to convey the document to Secretary of State Warren Christopher on the grounds that it was a capitulation to the American position. Instead of the paper prepared in Tunis, they wanted to give Christopher a document of their own that would state that the legal and legislative power of the Palestinian Authority would apply to East Jerusalem as well. The Revolutionary Council of the Fatah, the PLO's main faction, affirmed this position at the end of July 1993 (*Filastin al-Thawra*, 30 July 1993). An editorial in the PLO weekly also stated that "without recognition of the rights of the Palestinians in Jerusalem there will be no peace agreement" (*Filastin al-Thawra*, 11 July 1993).

The instructions from Tunis were, however, unambiguous. The document was to be submitted to Christopher. The delegation tried to maneuver and to bargain with Tunis and with the Americans. During the course of the crisis it even learned that the draft PLO response had already been handed over to the Americans, after Nabil Shath, President Mubarak, Egyptian Foreign Minister Amr Musa, and the Egyptian president's political adviser Uthama al-Baz had worked on it in Cairo; the members of the delegation were being asked simply to repeat the act and officially hand Secretary of State Christopher the PLO's response. At the time that the delegation was formulating a counter-response of its own, Faisal Husseini went to Cairo to see the proposed document. He notified his colleagues in Jerusalem that without written instructions from Arafat they dared not submit such a far-reaching document to Christopher. At the request of the delegation, the document prepared in Cairo and Tunis was forwarded to Jerusalem, with an unambiguous order in Arafat's own handwriting attached. It instructed them to submit the document as it was. The delegation was faced with a dilemma. Should it submit a document that in its opinion contained unwarranted concessions, including those on the matter of Jerusalem? Should it agree to such a blatant blow to their status and authority, or should they meekly accept Arafat's dictate? Should they dispute the position of the PLO leaders in Tunis and set up an alternative leadership, or adhere to their previous policy that maintained that only the "external" leaders of the PLO determined Palestinian policy? Christopher met with the members of the delegation on August 3, expecting to receive the response that had been promised to him, but the delegation claimed that it had not yet completed its work on the document. In the meantime, the delegation gained a few hours of debate with Tunis before officially handing over the PLO response to Christopher at their next meeting. In parallel, the delegation's leaders submitted their resignations to Arafat. Arafat invited the resigning delegates to Tunis to discuss the entire issue in the PLO Executive Committee, where he succeeded in resolving it in his own way (Ashrawi, 1995: 250–64).

As became clear at the end of August 1993, the real negotiations were not taking place in Washington, but behind the scenes, between Israel and the PLO, in Oslo. The Oslo channel was not the only one in operation behind the official talks in Washington, but it was the most successful of them. The first back channel was Egyptian, which had taken form even before the Norwegian channel began to function. In October 1992 Egyptian foreign minister, Amr Musa, visited Israel and tried to advance the negotiations in all areas in which no progress had been made, including the issue of Jerusalem. These contacts centered on the question of how elections would be held in Jerusalem for the interim period legislative council. Musa proposed involving the Jerusalem Committee of the OIC and conducting elections in Al-Haram Al-Sharif and in the Church of the Holy Sepulcher. Musa hoped thus to bridge the desire of the Palestinians to conduct elections in Jerusalem and Israel's reluctance to discuss it on the grounds that it would lead to the government's fall. Musa also proposed establishing two working groups for discussions with the Palestinians, one on the elections in Jerusalem and the other on the powers of the elected council. Rabin's approach was to put off any discussion of Jerusalem because of the issue's sensitivity in Israel public opinion and because the Palestinians had not yet proved to him the seriousness of their intentions. Rabin complained to Musa that the Palestinian delegation in Washington was chasing after the media and argued that the public nature of the talks was destroying any chance of producing results. If the Palestinians would consent to accept his approach about the need for secret talks, he, Rabin, would be willing to discuss with them Egypt's proposal for conducting elections in East Jerusalem (Abas, 1995: 67–9).

Two months later, in a meeting between Afif Safia, the PLO's representative in Britain, Abu-Ala, and Dr. Yair Hirschfeld in London in December 1992, the Oslo channel was born as a secret, unofficial, semi-academic channel. (On the circumstances by which it came into being, see: Abas, 1994: 112; Beilin, 1997: 63–80.) From the moment it became clear that the Oslo channel was promising and might produce results, both sides mobilized for it. They halted their other attempts to establish a secret channel and concentrated solely on this one. When other channels opened in parallel it was as assistance to the Oslo channel rather than as alternatives to it. The Oslo talks encompassed the entire range of issues that were at stake between Israel and the Palestinians. In these talks, Jerusalem was not perceived to be a special issue; it was not taboo, untouchable or set aside for separate treatment. Furthermore, not finding a comprehensive and immediate solution to the Jerusalem issue did not prevent progress on other subjects. On the contrary, once there was significant progress it was possible to arrive at arrangements for bargaining and compromise on the issue of Jerusalem precisely because the city was not discussed as a separate issue. While the Palestinian delegation was composed of important political figures and senior commanders such as its head, Abu Ala (Ahmad Qri'a), was the Fatah's financial affairs chief; Maher Al-Kurd, Arafat's economic adviser; and Hassan Asfur, secretary of the committee for negotiations with Israel and assistant to Abu Mazen, who held the Israel portfolio in the PLO Executive Committee. The Israeli delegation was composed of two scholars who did not hold official posts. Dr. Yair Hirschfeld and Dr. Ron Pundik drew their unofficial authority from Yossi Beilin, Israel's deputy foreign minister, who, at his own initiative, assumed responsibility for instructing them. The Israelis' impression was that the Palestinians assumed that Peres and Rabin were behind the envoys from Israel and that the channel should therefore be taken very seriously (Beilin, 1997: 82).

Two issues relating to the subject of Jerusalem stood out during the talks. The first was how the inhabitants of East Jerusalem would participate in the elections, and whether they would only be allowed to vote, or whether they would also be allowed to be elected. The second was whether the city would be removed from the framework and be left for the final agreement, and if so, whether the fact that it was being removed would be stated in the document. The major part of the debate did not focus on these subjects at every round of talks. As will be shown, in some rounds the lack of agreement between the parties was noted and the major effort to bridge the gaps was devoted to other questions.

At the first round of talks in Oslo in January 1993, and during the second round of talks in February 1993, the Palestinians presented their traditional position. The Arab inhabitants of East Jerusalem would participate in the elections to the legislative council of the interim arrangement just like their Palestinians brethren in the territories, and the interim agreement would have to apply fully to all the 1967 territories, including East Jerusalem. Against the Palestinian's maximalist opening position, the Israeli approach at the second round was pragmatic. The Israeli representatives, Hirschfeld and Pundik, made an interesting proposal at this stage, and many of its elements were included in the Oslo agreements at the end of the convoluted bargaining. They arrived at the meeting with an organized, written draft of a declaration of principles between Israel and the Palestinians that took into consideration the positions of both sides and attempted to find a way between them.

The talks had, however, rules of their own, and they were not the same as those that Israel dictated. At the second meeting in Oslo, Hirschfeld and Pundik proposed separating the discussion of East Jerusalem from the discussion of the rest of the territories and postponing the decision on its future to the permanent arrangements. In the meantime, the city would be given a special status under the interim agreement while preserving its physical unity. The special status, according to Hirschfeld, would include recognition of Orient House as a political headquarters, recognition of official Palestinian institutions operating in Jerusalem, and even the construction of public housing projects for the Palestinian inhabitants of the city. According to Abu Mazen, Hirschfeld argued that Jerusalem should remain under Israeli sovereignty, but that its Palestinian inhabitants could be linked politically to the Palestinian Authority through elections to the legislative council. At this stage, Hirschfeld did not distinguish between voting and candidacy, but rather focused on the placement of the polling stations – whether they would be inside or outside the city. Israel would not agree to have the polling stations for the elections to the legislative council inside the city itself, and it also opposed allowing the city's inhabitants to run for elective office. Ron Pundik complemented Hirschfeld's suggestions by proposing that the representatives of East Jerusalem be elected by running in the adjacent Ramallah district (Abas, 1995: 120–6; Beilin, 1997: 84). But according to one of the Israeli representatives, the subject of voting by the Palestinians of East Jerusalem was not even mentioned in the document submitted by Hirschfeld. The subject was raised only later in an appendix to that document.

Between the second and the third round Beilin briefed Peres on the secret talks, and showed him the minutes of the discussions. Peres updated Rabin, who listened and did not veto continuation of the contacts. From this point onward Peres was at the apex of the pyramid guiding the Israeli delegation. The delegation was not, however, authorized to tell the Palestinians that Peres was in the picture; this information was conveyed, however, by the Norwegian intermediary, Terje Larsen. At the third round, in March 1993, the Israelis sought to insert changes into the model of how the inhabitants of East Jerusalem would vote, and they encountered pragmatism on the Palestinian side. Abu Ala proposed that the Jerusalem polling places be located in the Al-Aqsa mosque and in the Church of the Holy Sepulcher, in accordance with the Egyptian proposal of October 1992. With this proposal, the Palestinians created an opening for granting a special status to Jerusalem during the period of the interim accord, a principle that the Israeli delegation had demanded to implement since the first round at Oslo. In the meantime, however, Israel's position had become more rigid. Between the third and fourth rounds, Peres sought to amend the appendix to the paper submitted by the Israeli team and to distinguish between voting in the elections and running for and being elected to office, in keeping with the Labor Party platform (Beilin, 1997: 90). According to this approach, the act of voting linked the voter politically to an outlying elected institution, while the act of being elected to the body applied the authority of the elected institution, the legislative council, to the voter. In other words, allowing inhabitants of East Jerusalem to be elected to a Palestinian institution would bring the West Bank to Jerusalem and it was therefore rejected by Peres, as opposed to the act of voting, which preserved the distance between the two regions.

Jerusalem did not come up in the fourth round of talks, from the end of April to the beginning of May 1993, even though the Israeli delegation had, in its preparatory talks, agreed that it would request to reopen the question of the way in which the inhabitants of East Jerusalem would vote. In this round it was the Palestinians who pushed forward, while the Israelis sought to hold back progress because Peres and Rabin had not yet completed discussing the statement of principles (Beilin, 1997: 99). Under Palestinian pressure a joint draft statement of principles was formulated at the fifth round of talks, in May 1993. This draft put into writing only those issues agreed upon by the parties. It was not merely a technical step, but rather a signal that agreement had been reached on a series of questions. The draft noted that the resolution of the Jerusalem issue would be left for the discussions on the permanent agreement; the jurisdiction of the legislation of the elected Palestinian council would include all of the West Bank and Gaza Strip. With regard to the elections, it said, "Palestinians of Jerusalem have the right to participate in the election process as candidates and as voters. Voters in Jerusalem will cast their ballots at the Al-Aqsa Mosque and the Church of the Holy Sepulcher" (Abas, 1995: 146–7). Would the Palestinians act on their right to be elected to office? No answer to this was formulated. This question remained controversial and was passed on to the next stage of the talks, in which the senior professional level would take the place of the academic delegates. With regard to the election process, the parties agreed to adopt the Egyptian compromise proposal. Instead of taking the polling stations outside the city entirely, it was agreed that they would be placed in the holy sites, thus giving the elections in Jerusalem a special flavor. The draft was built on an additional compromise about Jerusalem – in exchange for the Palestinians' willingness to put off discussion of the Jerusalem question to the permanent arrangements, the Israelis were willing to grant Jerusalem special status. Furthermore, for the first time since 1967 they would agree to discuss the annexation of East Jerusalem, placing an official question mark over the continuation of Israeli sovereignty in the city.

Progress in the secret Oslo channel had a good effect on the open channel in Washington. Faisal Husseini arrived in Washington as an official member of the delegation on the eve of the ninth round of talks in May 1993. This move was part of an effort to shore up the Fatah in the West Bank and Gaza Strip in preparation for Israel allowing the return of some 400 Hamas activists who had been deported the previous December. The deportation had held up the diplomatic process and hurt Israel. With the mediation of the U.S., Egypt, and Jordan, a compromise was reached under which Israel would allow the phased return of the Hamas deportees, but not before allowing the Fatah activists it had deported in the late 1960s and early 1970s to return (Klein, 1996a). The Palestinians in Oslo saw this move as compensation for their consent to postpone the discussion of Jerusalem to the permanent status talks. That same month, in the fifth round, the status of the Oslo talks was reinforced when it became clear to the PLO that it was talking with an authorized Israeli representative. An official representative of the Israeli government, Director-General of the Foreign Ministry Uri Savir, was put at the head of the delegation, above the two academic experts. In this round and the subsequent one the question of Jerusalem came up in full force and the discussion was conducted around two aspects on which the Oslo talks had focused in the past, citing the issue as being among those that would be left to the permanent agreement, and the participation of the inhabitants of East Jerusalem in the elections.

In the meantime there was drama in Jerusalem as well. Attorney Yoel Zinger joined the Israeli team in Oslo and proposed mutual recognition of Israel and the PLO. Peres had reservations about this but not about the development of the negotiations in Oslo, whereas Rabin had reached the mistaken conclusion that the Palestinian representatives in Oslo were not faithfully representing the PLO's position and were, perhaps, even trying to mislead Israel and prevent an agreement with the moderate "internal" leaders. Rabin did not understand why the Palestinian delegation in Washington was becoming more rigid in its positions, in accordance with instructions from PLO headquarters in Tunis. Rabin saw the PLO leaders in Tunis as being more rigid and hawkish than the leaders from the territories with whom Israel was conducting the official negotiations, and when Tunis instructed the delegation to be less flexible, Rabin understood this to be a true expression of the PLO position; the moderate position taken by the PLO leaders in Oslo seemed to him to be a deception. Therefore, at the beginning of June 1993 Rabin expressed his reservations about the list of agreed points composed in Oslo in May 1993. It was Peres who showed Rabin his error, and in order to satisfy Rabin it was decided to re-examine the understandings formulated in Oslo. On June 10, 1993, Rabin gave a green light to continue with the talks. He even allowed Yoel Zinger, who became his personal representative in the negotiations, to propose mutual recognition, as a personal suggestion (Beilin, 1997: 107–12).

Rabin's entry into the negotiations as the main decision maker for Israel formally institutionalized the negotiations and reinforced Israel's commitment to the talks. Furthermore, there was a change in Israel's style, emphases, and in some of its positions. Rabin adopted Hirschfeld and Pundik's idea of putting off the discussion of Jerusalem, and sought Palestinian reaffirmation of this understanding. Rabin was concerned that the Palestinians might have had second thoughts about this, especially because Israel was taking a somewhat tougher position.

The seventh round of talks, which began on June 13, 1993, provided an opportunity to test whether the understanding was still in force. This was the first round in which Yoel Zinger participated, and he made frequent references to Rabin as a way of hinting to the opposite party that the negotiations had taken another step forward, and that he had been sent by the Israeli prime minister. Zinger presented the PLO with 40 questions, which had been composed in consultation with Rabin after they had read the draft of the joint declaration. Rabin was particularly troubled by two issues concerning Jerusalem. First, Rabin, naturally suspicious, wanted to be certain that the PLO really did stand behind putting off discussion of Jerusalem to the permanent status talks; second, Rabin wanted to know whether the Palestinian Authority would operate in Jerusalem, and whether its offices would be established in Jerusalem or in Jericho. "If your answer is Jerusalem this will create a problem" (Abas, 1995: 154), Zinger told the Palestinians, who thought that they had arrived for a concluding discussion, after which the document would be passed on to Washington to be signed by the two delegations. Now they realized that the negotiations were continuing and going in new directions. Zinger mentioned his personal ideas about mutual recognition, amendment of the Palestinian Covenant (the PLO's foundation document, expressing its ideology of destroying Israel), and the cessation of the Intifada. The Palestinian delegation had not prepared itself for this and so had to pass the matter on to Tunis for clarification. Zinger's impression was that the Palestinians stood behind the agreement to put off discussion of Jerusalem to the permanent status talks and he conveyed this to Rabin. As a result, Zinger could, at his next meeting with the Palestinian team, concentrate on other questions relating to Jerusalem (Abas, 1995: 153; Beilin, 1997: 112–6; Savir, 1998: 49–55).

The removal of Jerusalem from the interim agreements raised a series of subsidiary questions that affected the subsequent negotiations. First, as already noted, would Palestinian institutions be removed from the city, and if so, would this apply to the existing institutions or just to the new ones established by the Palestinian Authority? Second, was the city not to be included only in practice or also in the wording of the framework agreement? In other words, should Jerusalem be mentioned in the document, even though the document did not apply to it? Perhaps the fact that the interim agreement did not apply to the city should be stated explicitly? Third, should the framework agreement state that the elections to the Palestinian Authority Council would be held in Jerusalem as well? And if so, would that be merely a general reference or would the special election arrangements for the city be spelled out?

In the eighth round of talks, at the end of June 1993, Zinger expressed Israel's desire to have Jerusalem mentioned in the statement of principles only in the context of the elections, without mention of the postponement of the Jerusalem issue to the permanent status talks. Israel sought in this way to play down the discussion of sovereignty in East Jerusalem. In addition, Israel demanded that the elections in the city not be run as they would be run in the rest of the 1967 territories, while also refusing to locate polling stations at the holy sites, as previously agreed. Israel also opposed granting the elected council legislative authority in East Jerusalem, and stated explicitly that the inhabitants of East Jerusalem would be allowed to vote but not be elected to office. Israel believed that elections that didn't give the elected officials legislative authority over the voters in Jerusalem would minimize the political link between East Jerusalem and the Palestinian institutions and would do only minor injury to Israel's rule over the eastern city. Abu-Ala did not focus on the new issues raised by Zinger, and instead addressed issues that Israel had presented in the previous round. In Arafat's name he demanded to know what the fate of the Palestinian institutions functioning in East Jerusalem would be if the Palestinian Authority did not operate in the city. Who would look after the needs of the residents of East Jeru-salem? Zinger's reply was that no agency of the Palestinian Authority would be allowed to operate in the city, and that the existing institutions could continue to operate as before (Beilin, 1997: 119–20; Hirschfeld, 1998).

The matter of mutual recognition by the PLO and Israel came up for discussion when Abu-Ala accepted Zinger's private idea (Savir, 1998: 69–71; Zinger, 18 Sept. 1998), and this step enlarged both delegations' room for maneuver. It is important to note that the Palestinians' agreement to postpone the question of Jerusalem to the permanent status talks preceded the tabling of the proposal for mutual recognition. The Palestinians had consented in May to put off the issue of Jerusalem while the proposal about mutual recognition had come in June 1993. In other words, it was not the discussion of mutual recognition that brought about the PLO's agreement to postpone the issue of Jerusalem, but rather its understanding that it had to make more concessions on Jerusalem than Israel did. The leadership in Tunis seems to have realized that without this there would be no interim agreement and the basis for a Palestinian state would be lost. Furthermore, at the first meeting Pundik and Hirschfeld had presented the far end of the Israeli consensus on Jerusalem, as they understood it. From the very beginning of the contacts they had made it clear that making Jerusalem part of the Palestinian autonomy would be accepted neither by the Israeli government nor by Israeli public opinion. Nevertheless, it is nearly certain that the June discussion on mutual recognition spurred the PLO to move forward in this direction. Israeli recognition of the PLO promised the organiza-tion benefit, even if it conceded on the Jerusalem issue in the interim period, and gave it a better opening position in the perma-nent status talks.

The negotiations received a facelift in the next round of talks, the ninth, which ended on July 6, 1993. Israel refused to mention Jerusalem at all in the joint document. This position had been dis-cussed by the oversight team in Jerusalem some time before and was now placed before the Palestinians. Israel's position gained the support of Foreign Minister Johan Jorgen Holst of Norway, who tried, during a visit to Tunis, to persuade Arafat to accept it. Arafat refused. In Tunis and Oslo the Palestinians demanded that the statement of principles mention the elections in Jerusalem

only as a subject that would be raised for discussion in the framework of the negotiations on the election arrangements, but that it
be stated that the Arabs of East Jerusalem would participate in the
elections. At this stage the Palestinians revised the position they
had presented in the Oslo talks. They preferred that East Jerusalem's inhabitants participate in the elections as candidates but not
necessarily as voters (Abas, 1995: 160–1), even though prior to this
they had wanted both. The Palestinians presented, as a bargaining
position, a mirror image of Israel's position. They wanted to get
East Jerusalem's inhabitants the right to be elected and, in
exchange, to give up the right to vote entirely, including the special arrangement for polling stations. By making a concession in a
direction that was uncomfortable for Israel, they hoped to maneuver Israel into a compromise, even though this involved giving up
one of their two original demands. All in all, the Palestinian
approach in this round was characterized by rigidity deriving from
tactical considerations. Abu-Ala arrived with a list of 26 demands
for changes in Zinger's draft declaration from the previous round
(Beilin, 1997: 121–3).

The Palestinians arrived at the tenth round of talks on July 21,
1993 with a new idea. Instead of the tit-for-tat compromise (yes to
candidacy, no to voting) that they had previously insisted on, they
now proposed meeting in the middle on each of the disputed
questions. Arafat agreed that the statement of principles would be
somewhat vague about Jerusalem. Instead of mentioning Jerusalem as a city, the document would refer to the holy places, and this
change made it possible to locate polling stations on the Temple
Mount and in the Church of the Holy Sepulcher. Arafat's representatives in Oslo also demanded that Jerusalem not be left out of
the document entirely, and that there be some reference to the
issue of the city being raised in the permanent status talks. There
was also a debate over the question of what kind of link there
would be between the elected institutions and Jerusalem. Israel
demanded that all connection between the Palestinian Authority
and Jerusalem be severed, while the Palestinians demanded a
compromise on this issue, as well as on the problem of how the
elections in Jerusalem would be conducted (Abas, 1995: 107–8;
Beilin, 1997: 128, 162).

On July 20, a day before this round of talks began, a new Israel–
PLO channel was opened. In light of the sharp disagreements and

polarized positions at the ninth round of the Oslo talks, Rabin sought to check out, once more, a series of issues, among them whether Arafat still accepted the postponement of the Jerusalem issue to the permanent status talks. For his part, Rabin gave reassurances on his commitment to recognizing the PLO. Minister of health, Haim Ramon, met with Arafat's adviser, Dr. Ahmad Tibi, in Jerusalem, and proposed a tradeoff on the issues of greatest concern to the two sides – a postponement of the Jerusalem issue in exchange for solid, meaningful Israeli recognition of the PLO. Ramon told Tibi that removal of Jerusalem from the interim arrangement was a condition for progress in other areas. In exchange, Ramon promised, in Rabin's name, that if a joint statement of principles was reached the PLO would sign it in the name of the Palestinians, which would be tantamount to mutual recognition of two enemies. Israel even promised that the recognition would have practical consequences. If 99 per cent of the subjects under discussion were resolved, there would be a public meeting between the PLO chairman and the prime minister of Israel. Ramon acted, and was used, as a channel secondary to and different from the Oslo agreement. In Oslo recognition had not been made dependent on the Jerusalem issue; Ramon linked them. While it is not clear whether he did so at his personal initiative or under instructions from Rabin, he seems to have had two reasons. First, Rabin, or Ramon, had to give the PLO something in exchange for its consent to postpone the Jerusalem issue – this is how negotiations work. Second, Ramon was not negotiating details, but rather inquiring about a specific point. He did not have the room for maneuver and the options that the Israeli team in Oslo had. He could not maneuver between the range of issues connected to Jerusalem, making a concession here to make a gain there. He sought to clarify a matter of principle and he had to offer a concession of principle in exchange. In short, Ramon's offer was the exception that proved the rule that was taking shape in Oslo.

Tibi's response was candid. He expressed the PLO's fear that removing East Jerusalem from the interim arrangements would give Israel a free hand to establish facts on the way to the permanent agreement – in other words, to change the status of the Palestinians and their existing institutions in Jerusalem. Despite this, Tibi said, the Palestinians were prepared to negotiate a special arrangement. Using plain white letter paper rather than official

Israeli letterhead, Ramon submitted to the PLO, via Tibi, four questions from Yitzhak Rabin. One of these addressed Jerusalem: "Does the PLO accept in principle the concept of a phased solution involving an interim arrangement to precede a permanent settlement?" (Abas, 1995: 81).

The PLO's response was conveyed to Ramon on July 26, the day the eleventh round of talks in Oslo began. It stated, "We agree that its [Jerusalem's] permanent status is to be discussed within the framework of a permanent settlement. Position at present: there should be full participation in the elections by candidates and voters. There should be linkage between Jerusalem institutions and the interim authority which will oversee them" (Abas, 1995: 81). The PLO reiterated the position it had presented in Oslo: postponement of discussion of Jerusalem in exchange for full participation in the elections and a link between the institutions of the PLO and of the Palestinian Authority. It should be emphasized that the compromise offered by the PLO was in line with the Oslo approach of give-and-take on the Jerusalem issues, rather than concessions in exchange for recognition of the PLO. At the same time, the PLO returned to its maximalist opening position and demanded that East Jerusalem's Arabs be allowed both to vote and to be elected, and that there be a clear link between the institutions of the Palestinian Authority outside Jerusalem and those that functioned in the city. Taking this position was a tactical measure in order to get itself into a good bargaining position, just as it did at this stage in Oslo. According to Abu-Mazin, Rabin's reply on August 1, after reading the PLO's response, was positive. Rabin was prepared to move in the PLO's direction on all the points in dispute, except with regard to the application of Palestinian legal authority on East Jerusalem. If Jerusalem was not included in the framework of the interim agreement, the Palestinian Authority had no jurisdiction there, Rabin maintained, and it was thus important to state this in the Declaration of Principles. The Palestinian position was, naturally, the opposite (Abas, 1995: 76–81).

In the eleventh round of talks, on July 26, the points of agreement and disagreement were put into writing, as were the compromise formulations that they were proposing. With regard to Jerusalem, the Palestinians demanded that the city be cited among the issues to be discussed in the permanent status talks, while

Israel demanded that the formulation be that in the permanent status talks each side would be allowed to bring up any issue of concern to them, without stating explicitly what those issues would be. Both sides agreed that, when the joint Declaration of Principles was signed, talks on mutual recognition of Israel and the PLO would commence. In other words, mutual recognition remained on the table. It was not dependent on the Declaration of Principles, which would be signed even without official recognition, and it was not linked to Jerusalem nor to the Palestinians' willingness to put off discussion of the city's future to the permanent status talks. Moreover, the Palestinians accepted Israel's position that the Palestinian Authority's offices would be in Jericho and not in Jerusalem. In exchange, the PLO demanded a letter from Israel's foreign minister to Norway's foreign minister and the Oslo mediator, Holst, in which Israel would commit itself to preserving the status of the Palestinian institutions in East Jerusalem (Abas, 1995: 171–3). Israel refused to issue such a letter.

At the twelfth round of talks, on August 14, the issues in dispute regarding Jerusalem were again cited, but they were not debated in detail. This debate occurred on August 17, when Peres arrived in Stockholm. There, on the night of August 18, he conducted an eight-hour conference call with Israel and Tunis, in which the specifics of the joint Declaration of Principles were resolved (Abas, 1995: 177). The debate focused on the questions of where the offices of the Palestinian Authority would be located and what would be the fate of the Palestinian institutions in Jerusalem. Arafat proposed that the Palestinian Authority operate within a defined area within East Jerusalem or, alternatively, that its location not be mentioned at all in the Declaration of Principles. Arafat, of course, wanted to advance not only the cause of a Palestinian state but also Israeli recognition of East Jerusalem as its capital, whether explicitly or tacitly. But Peres stood firm in his position that the Palestinian Authority's offices could not be located in or operate within the city. Rabin and Peres demanded an explicit statement that the Palestinian Authority would be run from Jericho and Gaza, so as to leave the question of Jerusalem open. But Arafat was not willing to leave the matter open because he feared that Israel would try to prejudice the status of the PLO's institutions in the city with the intention of weakening the Palestinian position in the final status negotiations. Only after long

wrangling did Peres promise not to hurt existing Palestinian institutions in East Jerusalem, including the Orient House, in
exchange for Arafat giving in to his demand to remove the city
from the jurisdiction of the Palestinian Authority. In other words,
Arafat was prepared to postpone discussion of the planned capital
of the Palestinian state in order to advance the establishment of a
Palestinian state. For the PLO, Israel's recognition and its agreement to the establishment of a Palestinian Authority for a limited
period was a jumping-off point for the establishment of a Palestinian state in the 1967 territories. Thus, while the Palestinian delegation in Washington was, with the encouragement of the PLO
leadership, presenting tough positions on the Jerusalem question,
the same leadership was making its position more flexible in the
secret Oslo channel. The Palestinians would not take an oral
promise and demanded that Israel provide a written commitment
to take no action against its existing institutions in East Jerusalem.
At first Peres agreed, but he then retracted his consent under
instructions from Rabin. Peres made the argument that Israel's
representatives had made throughout the Oslo talks – fear of
Israeli public outrage that would topple the government. After
additional negotiations, the Israelis agreed to send the letter the
PLO demanded. There was then a debate among Israel's representatives about whether the letter should be made public. The
opponents of publication had the upper hand and the Palestinian
side agreed that it would be kept absolutely secret and would not
be brought to the knowledge of the PLO's supreme institutions,
which would be called on to ratify the Palestinian decisions
(Beilin, 1997: 135; *Ha'aretz*, 6 June 1994, 9 June 1994; Makovsky,
1996: 71–3; Naufal, 1995: 123–6).

It should be noted that when the Jerusalem issue was agreed on,
there was still no agreement on mutual Israel–PLO recognition.
The issue of recognition came up in the talks and advanced understanding by Israel and the PLO about a series of subjects that were
in dispute. But since both delegations related to Jerusalem as one
of the issues to be decided and not as a special issue that stood on
its own, there was no longer any reason to condition it on recognition. In the big picture, the compromise on Jerusalem was
achieved through give-and-take on questions relating to Jerusalem itself. Jerusalem was one of several issues under discussion,
and unlike the Camp David model, the discussion of Jerusalem

began in parallel with discussion of the rest of the issues. Putting off a final decision did not prevent the negotiators from breaking down the Jerusalem issue into its constituent parts, and from reaching give-and-take agreements. Jerusalem had lost its mytho-logical status and become a political issue.

While Peres's letter to Holst bears the date September 9, 1993 (that is, four days before the signing of the declaration of principles on the White House lawn), it was not conveyed to the PLO on that date and was not signed that day, but rather on October 10 or 11, after the Knesset had approved the declaration of principles and Rabin had declared that there were no secret commitments supple-mentary to it (Makovsky, 1996: 71–3; Musallam, 1996: 37–48). Peres wrote in his letter:

I wish to confirm that the Palestinian institutions of East Jerusalem and the interest and well-being of the Palestinians of East Jerusalem are of great importance and will be preserved. Therefore, all the Palestinian institutions of East Jerusalem, including the economic, social, educational, and cultural, and the holy Christian and Moslem places, are performing an essential task for the Palestinian population. Needless to say, we will not hamper their activity; on the contrary, the fulfillment of this important mission is to be encouraged.

(Abdul Hadi, 1997, Vol. II: 154; according to *Ha'aretz*, 7 June 1994, this letter was dated Sept. 11)

Israel's commitment in the letter is consistent with the general direction of the Oslo agreements – bargaining and compromise on Jerusalem – but in some ways goes beyond it. This was the first time that Israel had used the term "East Jerusalem" to designate the Palestinian character of this area. It named not simply a geo-graphic area, but also a demographic and social region, and politi-cal meaning could also be derived from it. Furthermore, this was the first time that Israel recognized not only Muslim and Chris-tian religious institutions, but also the Palestinian institutions in the eastern part of the city and their importance to the population. Israel promised not only to preserve the *status quo* with regard to these institutions but also to encourage their activity. While Arafat did not obtain Israeli recognition of East Jerusalem as the capital of his country, he did manage to get a commitment to preserve the Palestinian character of the eastern city. From Arafat's point of view this was a significant step towards disconnecting sovereignty over East Jerusalem from sovereignty over West Jerusalem and

from turning the east into his capital. Later Israeli attempts to por-
tray the commitments in the letter as touching solely on the continued operation of institutions that are not governing institutions
(such as those that offer health, education, charity, and welfare
services) were forced, not to say pathetic (letter from Foreign
Minister Peres to the Peace Watch organization, Appendix 3 to
Peace Watch Report 1995, "What are the Palestinian Authority
institutions in Jerusalem"). It is no wonder, then, that Israel tried
to keep the existence of the letter secret. It became public only in
the wake of remarks made by Arafat during a visit to a mosque in
Johannesburg.

The Israel–Palestinian Declaration of Principles

The Declaration of Principles signed by Israel and the Palestinians
in September 1993 stated that talks on the permanent agreement
would include the issue of Jerusalem, and that in the interim
period Palestinian self-government would not apply there. "Jurisdiction of the Council [the Palestinian Authority Council, the
Palestinian governing authority in the interim period] will cover
West Bank and Gaza Strip territory, except for issues that will be
negotiated in the permanent status negotiations: Jerusalem, the
settlements, military and Israeli areas" (State of Israel, 1993). The
permanent status talks were to commence no later than the beginning of the third year of the interim period. Both sides also agreed
that the results of the permanent status talks would have no effect
on the interim period, and that the postponement of the discussion of these issues would not affect the negotiations on the permanent status. In other words, postponement of the discussion of
the Jerusalem question should not be taken to mean that the Palestinians accepted the *status quo*, and Israel could not use the Palestinians' consent to this as a debating point in the future
negotiations. The differences of opinion, and the common desire
to arrive at an agreed-upon declaration of principles, required that
another issue be postponed. This was whether and how the Palestinian inhabitants of East Jerusalem would participate in the elections to the Palestinian Authority Council. Special talks would be
devoted to this question. "Palestinians of Jerusalem who live there
will have the right to participate in the election process according
to an agreement between the two sides," the Declaration of

Principles stated without mentioning whether they would participate just as voters or also as candidates (State of Israel, 1993). Resolution of this issue remained open to the general negotiations on
the conditions of the elections. It should be noted that the declaration of principles differed from the invitation to the Madrid conference. There Jerusalem was not mentioned at all, whereas in the
Declaration of Principles, Jerusalem is cited as one of the issues in
dispute whose solution would be put off to the permanent status
talks. The disagreement on the issue now received the official
imprimatur of both parties, who agreed that the dispute over Jerusalem should not prevent agreement on other subjects. This
meant that the Jerusalem question was not a total one, nor was it a
litmus test for the intentions of the other side. It was not a world-
shaking question on which the entire agreement would stand or
fall, even in the interim period. It was an important problem, but
only one of several, and it was addressed as fundamentally political
in nature. Jerusalem would be brought up in political negotiations, and both sides would be able to bargain and to compromise.

The Declaration of Principles produced a new PLO approach
to the permanent arrangement in Jerusalem. In the past, the official Palestinian position had been that sovereignty in Jerusalem
should be divided, and nothing PLO leaders said in public devi-
ated from this. In September 1993, however, the official approach
changed. In an interview with *Der Spiegel* on September 20, 1993,
Arafat replied to Rabin's declaration that Jerusalem would forever
remain Israel's capital:

> If he meant all of Jerusalem he is wrong. ... East Jerusalem is the capital
> of the State of Palestine and Jewish West Jerusalem is and remains the
> capital of Israel and will remain such, and against which there are no
> objections. ... When the time comes, the human brain, that is, we, will
> certainly find a model that fits Jerusalem. I know one thing for certain:
> Palestinians and Israelis will live peacefully side by side in the city.
>
> (FBIS, Daily Report: 21 Sept. 1993)

Arafat made similar remarks in an interview with the BBC on
September 15, 1993, and in an interview with CNN on September 14, 1993, as well as in an interview with Radio Monte Carlo on
December 30, 1993. Faisal Husseini took a similar position on the
city's future: "As a resident of Jerusalem I do not want the city to be
divided. ... We want Jerusalem to be an open city, the seat of two
capitals with joint arrangements for both sides" (*Ha'aretz*, 8 June

1994; *Kol Ha-Ir*, 6 May 1994). The PLO's ambassador in Cairo reiterated this position in an interview with Egyptian television on December 24, 1993 (Albin, 1992: 24–5). What is clear is that since the Oslo agreements, PLO leaders do not refrain from stating that different rules apply to Jerusalem and to the West Bank and Gaza Strip. The principles that guided President Sadat have become the property of the PLO leadership – sovereignty in the city will be divided in the permanent arrangement but the city will not be divided physically, and unlike in the rest of the 1967 territories, there will be special arrangements to enable Palestinians and Israelis to live together.

The September 1993 signing of the Declaration of Principles and Peres's letter to Holst did not allay the Palestinians' fears about what Israel might do in Jerusalem during the interim period, before the future of the city came up for discussion. Their fears derived from the reality that Israel controlled the city. The Palestinians were concerned that Israel would operate in opposition to its commitments in Peres's secret letter to Holst, and that Israel would even claim that the Palestinians' public willingness to put off discussion of Jerusalem's future was to be taken as its acquiescence in the *status quo* that allowed Israel to gain a firm hold in East Jerusalem. The Palestinians expressed their fears both in word and deed. The political manifesto of the Palestinian Authority expressed the traditional PLO position on Jerusalem – UN resolutions 242 and 338 required Israel to retreat from all the territories, and the establishment of an independent Palestinian state with its capital in Jerusalem. The PLO itself declared:

We will also reject any interpretation of the postponement of the final status of Jerusalem that would allow the occupation authorities to change the physical or demographic status through illegal settlement activities or the continuing development and isolation of the Arab city of Jerusalem. We emphasize the Arab and Palestinian character of Jerusalem and its people. ... The Palestinian Authority will work to realize that principle in all its work plans.

(*Daily Report*, 31 May 1994)

The Palestinians did not interpret Peres's letter to Holst, even though it went far beyond previous Israeli statements of policy as a long-range change in Israeli policy. In their evaluation, there was no difference between Likud and Labor governments in Israel, since both claimed that Jerusalem was entirely Israeli. Israel was not prepared to compromise on the issue of Jerusalem and there-fore the Palestinians felt that they needed to initiate and establish unilateral facts on the municipal level and with regard to daily life. They did not feel obligated at this point to spar with Israel over the question of sovereignty over East Jerusalem, but they had to estab-lish a realistic foundation for this demand in the future. Palestin-ian academics in Jerusalem developed this approach, and it has been accepted as PLO and Palestinian Authority policy since the signing of the Declaration of Principles (Albin, 1992: 32–5).

Arafat's speech in the Johannesburg mosque in May 1994 was exceptional in the sharpness of the language he used. It was also exceptionally inaccurate – to say the least – in explaining why he had participated in the Madrid conference, and why he had, in view of the whole world, refused to sign a part of the Cairo accords (the agreements that arranged for Israel's withdrawal from the Gaza Strip and the Jericho area, May 1994). In his speech, Arafat emphasized that:

The *jihad* will continue and Jerusalem is not for the Palestinian people, it is for all the Muslim *umma* [nation]. … There is a continuous conspiracy against Jerusalem. … They will try to demolish and to change the demographic of Jerusalem. … "

(Musallam, 1996: 26, 28)

Arafat's words angered Israel, which demanded an unambiguous retraction of his reference to a *jihad* – holy war. This, Israel main-tained, contradicted the Oslo accords. Palestinian officials explained Arafat's statement in a variety of contradictory ways – his words had been taken out of context and had not been prop-erly understood, because all Arafat wanted to do was to explain why he supported the Oslo and Cairo agreements. Or Arafat had indeed erred and used terms that he should not have used. Or the error was not Arafat's but rather that of the Palestinian public rela-tions operation, which did not explain to the world media the real meaning of Arafat's speech. Then there was the explanation that the word *jihad* was not a political term but rather a religious one, and that it did not mean physical battle as Islamic extremists say, but any great effort, including a peaceful one. The *jihad* that Arafat spoke of was the unflagging effort to establish peace and build up the Palestinian Authority's institutions and economy (Musallam, 1996: 21–4, 32–5).

Beyond the debate over the meaning of the word *jihad*, it would seem that Arafat's need to present the Jerusalem issue so sharply and to distort the events of Madrid and Cairo derived not only from the audience he was addressing – pious Muslims at a Friday prayer service – but also from the subject at hand: Jerusalem. Arafat was expressing his fears as a result of Israel's actions in Jerusalem during the interim period, and his concern that the Palestinians did not intend to do anything about it.

Sa'ib Ariqat, a member of the Palestinian delegation to the bilateral talks with Israel, sketched out the Palestinian line of action after the agreement with Israel: "With or without an agreement we must do our utmost to create facts on the ground on a daily basis and do so fast to safeguard Jerusalem's holy places and Arab character" (Sawt al-Arab, Cairo Radio, 8 Oct. 1993, quoted by BBC, SWB, 11 Oct. 1993).

As a rule, the tendency of the political leaders on both sides to put off the decision on Jerusalem's future to the end of the diplomatic process did not freeze reality. In practice, both sides have been acting to establish facts in preparation for the decision on the future of East Jerusalem. This will be discussed in chapters 5 and 7.

Peres's letter to Holst, as far as it went in Israel's promise to preserve the Palestinian character of East Jerusalem and to assist the operation of the Palestinian institutions there, did not serve as a basis for creating a new consensual reality, but was rather an incentive for both sides to intensify the competition between them over the fate of East Jerusalem. Israel wanted to make up for its promises through deeds, while the Palestinians aspired to strengthen the Palestinian character of East Jerusalem and perhaps only thereafter to demand that Israel abide by its commitments. And in fact, ever since the Oslo agreements, there has been a race between Israel and the Palestinians to determine the future face of East Jerusalem. Clearly, the Declaration of Principles put off discussion of the Jerusalem question but did not put off the attempts by both sides to establish facts in anticipation of the permanent status talks. It should be emphasized, however, that the contest is not an equal one. Israel controls the city and its policy is directed by a central government, even though the Jerusalem municipal council, in Likud hands since 1993, would have liked to have seen a broader and more strenuous policy. In contrast, the Palestinian Authority cannot, according to the Oslo agreements, operate within Jerusalem, and the governing center in Gaza has no interest in building up Jerusalem's status as an independent and free Palestinian center. The Palestinians' actions have thus been lesser in their extent and in their force than those of Israel, as will be shown below. Nevertheless, the Palestinians have created a critical mass that cannot be ignored.

4

THE CHORUSES

THE ARAB LEAGUE AND THE O.I.C.

While the major part of the negotiations on Jerusalem were conducted between Israel and the Palestinians, two collective organizations also played a role – the Arab League, through the vehicle of the summit of Arab heads of state, and the OIC (the Organization of the Islamic Conference). The "Palestine question" has been one of the central preoccupations of the Arab League since it was established in 1945, and has been the focus of its gatherings since the first summit conference of Arab leaders in 1964. Over the years these summits have become one of the most important political institutions in the Arab world. The first summit of heads of Islamic states, convened in Rabat, Morocco, in 1969, was directly linked to events in Jerusalem – specifically, an arson attack on Al-Aqsa Mosque – and these events have since been the major subjects of its deliberations. The forum was formally constituted as the OIC in 1972. It in turn formed a Jerusalem Committee headed, until his death, by King Hassan II of Morocco.

The role played by the Arab and Islamic states in the negotiation of a solution to the Jerusalem problem is a secondary one. It can be compared to the role of the chorus in a play. The Arab and Muslim states grant existing norms legitimacy but do not create them; they chant "amen" or sing a refrain of routine formulations, but do not initiate new melodies or improvise lyrics.

As collective organizations, the Arab League and OIC do not conduct negotiations with Israel, nor do they set policy. The negotiations on Jerusalem are conducted in bilateral talks, with the multilateral framework established by the Madrid Conference remaining in the background. In characterizing the roles of collective organizations in the negotiations, it should be remembered that the decisions of the Arab and Islamic summits are always made unanimously, by consensus. Only when a new consensus crystallizes is it ratified *ex post facto* in a collective decision. So when negotiations require concessions and compromises and make extraordinary breakthroughs, the collective institutions, by their very structure, cannot participate in them. Their role is limited to lending support to the prevailing norm. This is part of the Arab starting position and a background factor that must be taken into account during the diplomatic give-and-take between the parties. It goes without saying that the decisions of summit conferences are toothless. True, conferences declare that they will take action, but they have no ability to actually do anything. In declaring political and economic measures, the Arab summits seek to establish the authority of the collective Arab will, but they can do no more than make declarations. Nevertheless, the collective organizations do carry a certain intra-Arab weight. Via the pan-Arab and pan-Islamic frameworks, one central player can neutralize an exceptional initiative by an opponent. This is what the PLO did when Jordan signed a peace treaty in which Israel promised to grant it, in the permanent settlement to the Israel–Arab conflict, a preferred position in the Islamic holy places in Jerusalem.

The Arab summit conferences

An old refrain in a new song

The official Arab collective position is that East Jerusalem is an inseparable part of the territories occupied in 1967; therefore, the large-scale construction of Jewish neighborhoods on the eastern side of the city is illegal settlement activity in the full sense of the term. This has been reiterated in all concluding resolutions and decisions passed by Arab summit conferences since 1967, for example in the decisions of the Amman Conference on November 11, 1987 (*Filastin al-Thawra*, 1 Dec. 1987) and of the Algiers Summit of June 9, 1988 (*Filastin al-Thawra*, 19 June 1988). This approach was also expressed in the peace initiative approved by the summit conference of Arab heads of state in Fez at the beginning of September 1982. The Fez decisions demanded that Israel withdraw from East Jerusalem, which had the same status as the rest of the 1967 territories. The Arab leaders demanded that Israel dismantle all the settlements it had built in the 1967 territories, and indicated that this included the Jewish neighborhoods in East Jerusalem. Instead of being under Israeli sovereignty, the eastern side of the city would be under Palestinian sovereignty, and East Jerusalem would be the capital of an independent Palestinian state (Sela, 1983: 259).

The only innovation in the plan is recognition of the Jewish right to freedom of religious worship in their holy places. It is reasonable to assume that the Arab states meant the Western Wall and not the Temple Mount, and that they wanted to make a commitment similar to the one Israel has made since 1967 – that is, granting freedom of worship to all religions at holy sites under Arab sovereignty. The Fez program did not, however, address the regime or administration that would oversee the Islamic holy sites after Israel's ejection from them. Saudi Arabia, Jordan, Morocco, and even Egypt see themselves as taking part in the control and management of the Islamic holy sites in Jerusalem, alongside the Palestinians. The sites holy to Islam in Jerusalem are sources of legitimacy for the rulers of those countries. The Arab states united only in determining that political sovereignty in East Jerusalem must be given to the Palestinians.

Despite the clear continuity in the collective Arab position on Jerusalem, it has evolved in keeping with its context. The first step came when Egypt was invited to the Casablanca conference of 1989, after having been excluded since it signed the Camp David agreements. It was allowed to participate, it should be emphasized, without having to repudiate its peace treaty with Israel. In returning to the body that was the agent of the Arab consensus, it contributed to a moderation of the collective position (Sela, 1983). Second, during the 1980s there was a change in the collective approach to an accommodation with Israel. The Fez program of 1982 does not deal with direct negotiations with Israel or with the granting of direct Arab guarantees of enforcing a peace agreement with it. The Casablanca decisions of 1989, however, confirmed the PLO's acceptance of UN resolution 242 and thus the PLO's *de facto* recognition of Israel. The decisions of the 19 Palestinian National Council in November 1988 were considered a breakthrough at the time, and a year later, at the Casablanca summit of 1989, they were already part of a new Arab consensus (*Filastin al-Thawra*, 4 June 1989).

The focuses of friction between the Palestinians and Israel in Jerusalem provided the leaders of the Arab states with many opportunities to strengthen the Palestinian hand in its contest for Jerusalem. So, for example, the question of Jerusalem was cited in the concluding statement of the Baghdad conference of May 30, 1990, in the context of two developments of this period that were of concern to the Arab states: the establishment of a Jewish settlement in the Old City's Christian Quarter in 1990, and the settlement of new immigrants from the Soviet Union in parts of the city that were not under Israeli control in 1967 (FBIS, 31 May 1990). The same is true of the Cairo summit of June 1996, which was convened after the publication of the program of the new Israeli government of Prime Minister Binyamin Netanyahu.

Even though there was no great difference on the Jerusalem issue between the Netanyahu government's program and that of the previous Rabin and Peres governments of 1992–1996 (*Ha'aretz*, 17 June 1996), the Palestinians and Arabs were worried about what the new Israeli government was likely to do. The reason was that the Likud's leaders had, during the election campaign, made extensive promises about Jerusalem, including committing themselves to the closure of the Orient House and to removing the Jerusalem question from the permanent status talks. The Cairo summit, the first summit since the Arab world split over Iraq's invasion of Kuwait in August 1990, was meant to be pre-emptive. The Israeli government's statement of its intentions helped the Arab world unite, if only for a brief moment, around the Jerusalem problem (*Al-Quds*, 24 June 1996).

Ultimately, collective organizations support successful negotiations and thus create a new consensus. The Casablanca conference of 1989 gave its imprimatur to the PLO's recognition of Israel one year previously, and the Cairo summit of 1996 gave its seal of approval to the Oslo accords, even though they were far from the Arab consensus. The negotiations over Jerusalem are not conducted between a pan-Arab or pan-Islamic organization and Israel, but rather between Israel and each of the parties directly involved. Negotiations that produce an agreement acceptable to the countries involved, and which are acceptable to the international community, will receive the retroactive blessing of the collective organizations.

The Organization of the Islamic Conference (OIC)

The Washington Declaration and the peace agreement between Jordan and Israel

The peace talks between Israel and Jordan produced the Washington Declaration signed by Rabin and Hussein on July 25, 1994. One of the Declaration's sections relates to Jerusalem's holy places. This section, later copied in substantially similar language into the Israeli–Jordanian peace treaty of September 1994, confirmed Palestinian apprehensions about Israeli activities in Jerusalem, and rekindled discord between the PLO and Jordan. The Washington Declaration states that:

Israel respects the present special role of the Hashemite Kingdom of Jordan in Muslim holy shrines in Jerusalem. When negotiations on the permanent status will take place, Israel will give high priority to the Jordanian historic role in these shrines. In addition the two sides have agreed to act together to promote interfaith relations among the three monotheistic religions.

(Laqueur & Rubin, 1995: 655)

This clause did not appear in the Declaration of Principles that King Hussein and Israeli Foreign Minister Shimon Peres were to sign on November 2, 1993, although that agreement is generally similar to the Washington Declaration (*Ha'aretz*, 23 Nov. 1994). Rabin and Hussein drafted this clause themselves (Ad. M. Kokhanovski, Legal Adviser of the Ministry of Defense, in *Ha'aretz*, 27 Oct. 1995), with the purpose of separating the discussion of political sovereignty over Jerusalem from the issue of the religious status of the holy places. In fact, until the signing of the Washington Declaration, there were disputes within the Israeli establishment between the heads of the Foreign Ministry, the Ministry of Defense and the prime minister as to whether Israel needed a stronger Jordan for the formulation of the permanent agreements. The Foreign Ministry saw in the proposed clause a needless provocation and an insult to the Palestinians. They believed that a Palestinian state was inevitable, and that Israel should therefore not try to prevent it from developing by placing a Jordanian protectorate over the Palestinian Authority. Neither, they maintained, should Israel assist Jordan in becoming the dominant partner in a Jordanian–Palestinian confederation. In any case, Foreign Ministry officials maintained, the Hashemite kingdom was likely to disappear after Hussein's departure. Giving precedence to Jordan would only infuriate the Saudis and Moroc-cans, who would do their best to frustrate any such plan. The Ministry of Defense and the prime minister believed, however, that it would be possible to overcome Arab opposition to a special role for Jordan. They maintained that Hashemite Jordan would not disappear, and it was in Israel's interest to supply it with the means to oversee the Palestinian neighbor that both established states considered suspect and had an interest in keeping small and weak. They also claimed that this approach was acceptable to Jordan, which would, at the time of the permanent settlement, establish an alliance with Israel (Galili, 5 Aug. 1996).

In fact, Jordan went along with the new direction set by Prime Minister Rabin when he forced his opinion on the Foreign Minis-try and Peres. In his speech before the United States Congress, King Hussein stated:

My religious faith demands that sovereignty over the holy places in Jerusalem resides with God and God alone. Dialogue between the faiths should be strengthened; religious sovereignty should be accorded to all believers of the three Abrahamic faiths, in accordance with their religions. In this way, Jerusalem will become the symbol of peace and its embodiment, as it must be for both Palestinians and Israelis when their negotiations determine the final status of Arab Eastern Jerusalem.

(140 *Congr. Rec.* H6204, H6205, daily ed. 26 July 1994; *Ha'aretz* 27 July 1994; *FBIS* 27 July 1994)

Crown Prince Hassan of Jordan was more open and direct. He stated that Jordan had never, and would never, relinquish its responsibility over the Islamic holy places in East Jerusalem. In his view, it was necessary to do everything to separate the religious and political issues in East Jerusalem, not only in the interim period but also in the permanent settlement. This might even involve dividing Jerusalem in different ways for religious and political purposes. In the permanent agreement, he suggested, political sovereignty would be in Palestinian hands, should they attain it, but religious sovereignty would be in the hands of a pan-Islamic Council in which both Palestinians and Jordanians would participate (*Ha'aretz*, 20 July 1994).

In the Washington Declaration, Israel undertook an initial commitment about the permanent status of Jerusalem. For all practical purposes it relinquished any claim to sovereignty over the Islamic holy places in Jerusalem and to the Temple Mount as a religious site. Israel claimed that its paramount interest was to guarantee its political sovereignty over the eastern city, and that management of the Islamic holy places and their religious status was not part of political sovereignty. Furthermore, in the Washington Declaration, Israel officially recognized for the first time Jordan's special status in regard to the Islamic holy shrines in Jerusalem. Historically and traditionally, the *Waqf* (religious endowment administration) has been responsible for these holy shrines. After the annexation of the West Bank to Jordan in 1951, the Waqf was subordinated to the Jordanian authorities. The Hashemites developed a special attachment to the Islamic holy places in Jerusalem, deriving from the shrines much of the legitimacy for their rule and a good part of their political resilience. The Jerusalem Waqf remained subordinate to Jordan even after the Israeli conquest of 1967, and even the severance of Jordan's legal and administrative ties to the West Bank in July 1988 did not alter this. But until the Israeli–Jordanian treaty, Jordan maintained this role because it was the *status quo*, rather than by force of any decision regarding the future of the sites. The Washington Declaration established the possibility of a future expropriation of Jerusalem's Islamic holy places from any political sovereignty.

In 1992, Adnan Abu Odeh, the former Jordanian prime minister and King Hussein's confidant, suggested – possibly with the king's knowledge – that the Old City of Jerusalem (inside the walls) should not be under the political sovereignty of any state but rather be designated a holy place. A joint Jewish–Muslim–Christian council would administer the site, and each religion would have custody of its own shrines (Abu Odeh 1992: 183, 185; see also *Ha'aretz*, 23 April 1992). It should be emphasized that in the Washington Declaration, Israel and Jordan adopted only one of Abu Odeh's guiding principles: the separation of political from religious sovereignty. The Washington Declaration went further than his plan. Abu Odeh did not advocate a preferential position for Jordan in the administration of the holy places, nor did he intend to accord even indirect legitimacy to Israel's political hold over Eastern Jerusalem. On the contrary, he sought to oust Israel. This makes it clear that he considered the new Israeli neighborhoods in East Jerusalem to be illegal settlements.

Although Abu Odeh's statement did not elicit any response from Israel at the time, after the Oslo agreements the Jordanian inclination to separate the political future of Jerusalem from the future of the holy places became an Israeli inclination as well. Since 1967, Israel has aspired to retain political sovereignty over East Jerusalem and to accord its actions a pan-Arab, pan-Islamic, and international legitimacy. In return for Jordan's agreement to separate political and religious questions regarding Jerusalem, Rabin was willing to endorse Jordan's special religious status in the Islamic holy places in Jerusalem, although he stated informally that he wished to discuss their future with more than one partner (*Ha'aretz*, 27 July 1994). Jordan claimed to have received from Israel a foothold in the Islamic holy places in Jerusalem by excluding Israel from them. Thus, it argued, Israel had moved closer to acceptance of expropriating the holy places from all political sovereignty, including its own. While Israel claimed to have gained support for its view that the mere existence of Islamic holy places in East Jerusalem does not in itself eviscerate Israel's political sovereignty over the city, Jordanian–Israeli cooperation weakened the Palestinian position in their struggle to establish East Jerusalem as their capital.

As expected, the Palestinians did not accept the Washington Declaration. The Palestinian Authority organized a popular campaign against it, and protested to the president of the OIC and the secretariat of the Arab League (Musallam, 1996: 93–103). In response to Israel's invitation to King Hussein to come and pray in Jerusalem and the rumors in the West Bank that this invitation would soon be acted upon, Chairman Arafat declared that he alone had the right to issue invitations to prayer in Jerusalem. Arafat mobilized the Supreme Muslim Council headed by Hassan Tahboub, who declared that the Council was the sole body responsible for the Islamic holy places in Jerusalem. Arafat also accused Israel of violating the Israeli–Palestinian Declaration of Principles, and added that the Palestinians therefore demanded the accelerated commencement of negotiations over the future of Jerusalem (Musallam, 1996: 93–104; *Ha'aretz*, 27 July 1994).

Did Israel indeed violate its agreement with the PLO? Two briefs by Israeli jurists state four reasons why Israel did not. First, Jordan was not a partner in the negotiations for the permanent settlement, and the agreement with Jordan contained nothing that would have a substantive effect on the results of the negotiations over the permanent status of Jerusalem. All that had been determined was that Israel would consider assigning a higher priority to Jordan's role in the holy places in all future negotiations. Second, the agreement with Jordan did not obligate the PLO and did not compromise Palestinian rights; it simply testified to what Israel's priorities would be when it sat down to talk with the PLO. Third, the agreement with Jordan addressed the permanent status, whereas Israel's commitment to the PLO promised preservation of the *status quo* during the interim period. Fourth, Israel's agreement with the organization set out only the timetable for discussing the question of Jerusalem. At the most, Israel's agreement with Jordan went beyond Palestinian expectations (*Ha'aretz*, 4 Aug. 1994). Rabin and Hussein formulated the clause in the Washington Declaration in such a way that the Palestinians would not be able make a legal claim that it contradicted Israel's undertakings to the Palestinians, while at the same time seeing it as an indirect confirmation by Jordan of Israeli political sovereignty in East Jerusalem (*Ha'aretz*, 23 Nov. 1994).

From a legal and verbal point of view Israel may not have violated its agreement with the PLO, but this is certainly not the case from a political point of view. Israel wanted to exploit its contacts with Jordan in order to influence the permanent status of Jerusalem and to weaken the Palestinian claim to sovereignty in East Jerusalem.

The Washington declaration quite naturally raised the PLO's hackles because the Palestinians understood it to be an Israeli and Jordanian attempt to narrow the Palestinian Authority's range of options and push it into a corner. According to the Palestinian position, Israel was not an owner with rights to hand out the Temple Mount – al-Haram al-Sharif – to whomever it sought to favor. Israel was an occupier. Political ownership had to be in Palestinian hands, and they would make the decisions about the future of the Islamic holy places in Jerusalem. In their opinion it was not possible to separate political sovereignty over the holy places from their religious status, especially given that a great part of the Palestinian claim to political sovereignty in East Jerusalem was based on the religious status of al-Haram al-Sharif in Islam. The PLO thus saw the agreement between Israel and Jordan as an attempt to pull the rug out from under it in Jerusalem and to leave it without any special religious standing. The PLO read the agreement as a deal under which Jordan was willing to accept Israeli political sovereignty in East Jerusalem in exchange for getting exclusive (in the interim agreement) or dominant (in the permanent settlement) responsibility for the Islamic holy sites. In this way Israel created a prior fact in relation to a subject that was supposed to be discussed in the framework of the permanent status talks and in opposition to Peres's commitments in his letter to Holst. Finally, the agreement between Israel and Jordan left the Christian holy sites under Israeli sovereignty, whereas the Palestinian Authority maintained that it should receive responsibility for them because they were located on territory occupied by Israel in 1967. Christian freedom of worship was to be granted by Arafat, the legal claimant to political sovereignty there, and not by the Israeli occupier (Musallam, 1996: 75–89). "No Arab or Israeli leader rules over the holy places in East Jerusalem. That right lies solely with the Palestinians," a statement of Arafat's declared (*Ha'aretz*, 27 July 1994).

In response, King Hussein suggested that the debate being stirred by the PLO over Jerusalem's holy places was aimed at covering up the organization's failures – its inability to wrest from Israel either al-Haram al-Sharif or a sovereign Palestinian state with Jerusalem as its capital. Hussein pledged that Jordan had no interest in competing with the PLO on the political level. Jordan may well have caught the PLO by surprise in its agreement with Israel but, Hussein noted, the PLO had given Jordan no less of a surprise by not coordinating policy with it while it was negotiating with Israel and secretly concluding the Oslo agreements (interview with *Der Spiegel*, printed in *Ha'aretz*, 22 Aug. 1994). Trying to conciliate the PLO, Hussein stated that the separation of the political question of Jerusalem's future from the religious problem did not interfere with the PLO's political negotiations with Israel, nor with the PLO's political status as the sole legitimate representative of the Palestinians.

The debate between Jordan and the PLO over the preferred status on al-Haram al-Sharif was no more than an extension of the mutual suspicion that had long characterized the relations between Arafat and Hussein and between the two political entities. So, for example, on the eve of the signing of the Declaration of Principles between Israel and the Palestinians on August 23,

1993, Arafat visited Amman and told King Hussein that there had been secret contacts between him and Israel that had involved formulating a Declaration of Principles, but the matter was still unfinished. Furthermore, he did not present the details or show Hussein a draft of the agreement, even though he had showed it to Mubarak. Despite the efforts of his aides and advisors, Arafat was not persuaded that signing the Oslo accord had laid the "Jordanian option" to rest once and for all; in his view there was still a danger that it would be realized and leave the Palestinians without independence. Arafat feared this, and so demanded of Israel that, in addition to its redeployment in the Gaza Strip, it also withdraw from Jericho, the city that had in 1948 served as Jordan's portal to the West Bank. It was in Jericho, after all, that the "Jericho Congress" had been convened – that is, the conference in which Palestinian public figures petitioned King Abdallah to take the West Bank under his protection. In 1974 Israel and Jordan discussed the future of Jericho in the context of Jordan's entry into the diplomatic process and into the West Bank. Israel then offered Jordan a "Jericho corridor," a plan under which Jordan would receive a corridor linking Jericho to the heights near Ramallah as a first step towards the implementation of the Allon Plan, a proposal for territorial compromise in the West Bank put forward by Israeli minister of labor, Yigal Allon. But Jordan wanted a complete Israeli withdrawal from the West Bank, and as a first step demanded a separation of forces along the length of the Jordan Valley, just as Israel had withdrawn its forces on the Egyptian and Syrian fronts, (Zak, 1996: 163–6). The signing of the Declaration of Principles just a few days after Arafat's visit with him angered Hussein. He viewed Arafat's failure to report to him on the impending agreement as an expression of lack of confidence and ungratefulness, for the significant assistance that Jordan had granted to the PLO from the time of the contacts that preceded the convening of the Madrid Conference (Naufel, 1995: 143–4).

Hamas was also critical of the Washington Declaration, even though it had been inclined, since its inception, to benefit from Jordanian support against the Palestinian Authority and the PLO. The agreement laid the foundation for peace and normalization between the two states, which Hamas was resolutely opposed to. Hamas argued that Jordan's agreement with Israel harmed the PLO and made it easier for Israel to negotiate with the Palestinians on the permanent settlement, and that Jordan had also conceded political sovereignty in Jerusalem to Israel. Furthermore, Hamas claimed, Jordan's action had increased the friction between Jordan and Saudi Arabia, and the sole beneficiary of this division – as of the division between the PLO and Jordan – was Israel. True, Hamas abstained from raining fire and brimstone on the Washington Declaration as it had on the Oslo accords, but it considered the declaration to be a total capitulation and a betrayal of all sacred values. In its desire to diminish Arafat's standing, Hamas voiced agreement with the idea of divine sovereignty in Jerusalem. Nevertheless, it attacked the Washington Declaration for what it viewed as a grant to Israel of political sovereignty on al-Haram al-Sharif and in Jerusalem (*Al-Biyyan*, 22 July 1994, 29 July 1994; *Al-Istiqlal*, 28 Oct. 1994; *Al-Maqadameh* (undated); *Filastin al-Muslima*, Sept. and Nov. 1994, quoted in Shabbat, 1997).

In the meantime, there were attempts to bridge the differences between Jordan and the PLO and to moderate the dispute. Prince Hassan, Jordan's heir apparent, tried, at the beginning of November 1994, to persuade the Palestinians that Jordan was acting as no more than an agent of the Arab and Islamic worlds for the purposes of getting the Islamic holy places out of Israel's hands, and that in the final account this also served the Palestinian interest (FBIS, 3 Nov. 1994). Previously, Jordanian Prime Minister al-Majali had spoken more bluntly (FBIS, 31 Oct. 1994). Unlike Prince Hassan, who had conditioned transferring authority over the Islamic holy sites in Jerusalem to the Palestinians on them receiving this responsibility from the Israelis, al-Majali conditioned it on obtaining political sovereignty. It was clear to everyone that al-Majali's standard was higher than Hassan's, and whoever perceived profound doubts about whether the Palestinians could remove Israel politically from East Jerusalem in al-Majali's statement was not mistaken.

At the beginning of December 1994, Faisal Husseini, who held the Jerusalem portfolio in the PLO Executive Committee, went to Jordan in an attempt to bridge the differences on Jerusalem and prepare the ground for an official visit by Arafat in Jordan. At the end of his trip he declared:

These holy places are being deposited with Jordan, which will hand them over the Palestinians when we reach a position that will allow us to assume this responsibility. We have agreed that the situation remain as it is, with greater coordination between the Jordanian and Palestinian parties. In the absence of coordination even measures taken with good intent are liable to produce results that will be misinterpreted by one side or the other.

(*Al-Quds*, 5 Dec. 1994; *Ha'aretz*, 5 Dec. 1994)

In other words, both parties agreed that the Palestinian Authority would recognize the *status quo* prevailing in Jerusalem since 1967, granting Jordan responsibility for the Islamic holy places in the city. In exchange, the Jordanian authorities agreed to view this guardianship as a trust to be handed over to the Palestinians when they could assume responsibility. It is not clear whether or to what extent Arafat had given Husseini a mandate to reach such a compact, which was closer to Jordan's position than to the Palestinians'. In any case, Arafat was not prepared to approve the agreement, and his planned December 1994 visit to Jordan was called off. As an alternative, Arafat brought the dispute between him and King Hussein for resolution into a new arena – the OIC.

The OIC: December 1994–January 1995

The OIC, which convened in Casablanca in December 1994, blazed its way straight into the dispute between the Palestinian Authority and Jordan over the Islamic holy places in Jerusalem. Jordan was supported by Qatar, Yemen, and Oman, and demanded that the conference's concluding statement commend Jordan's role as guardian of the holy places and that it applaud King Hussein for his concern. In his attempt to enlist the support of the Islamic heads of state, King Hussein claimed that immediately upon the conclusion of a Palestinian–Israeli agreement on the permanent status of Jerusalem, Jordan would hand over the guardianship of the city's holy places. But the PLO, supported by Saudi Arabia, Egypt, and Morocco, discerned Jordan's political purposes and adamantly refused to agree to this. The Palestinians claimed that the section of the Jordanian–Israeli agreement dealing with this subject was an obstacle to achieving sovereignty in East Jerusalem and in effectuating Israeli withdrawal. Morocco, Saudi Arabia, Egypt, and the PLO even tried to persuade the conference to establish a committee that would take over guardianship of the holy places from Jordan until the Palestinian Authority received full authority in East Jerusalem. When he was unable to convince a majority of the delegates to recognize Jordan's role as guardian of the holy places until a permanent settlement was reached, King Hussein left the conference. For the first time since the organization's establishment in 1970 there was no consensus for its decisions, which were, for all intents and purposes, imposed on Jordan (*Al-Quds*, 15 Dec. 1994; *Al-Wasat*, 19 Dec. 1994).

The concluding statement noted that the Conference "stresses once again that the problem of Palestine and the sublime Jerusalem is a fundamental problem for all Muslims and that they express their identification with the Palestine Liberation Organization in its just struggle to remove every remnant of Israeli occupation and to build the Palestinian national institutions on the land of Palestine" (*Al-Quds*, 16 Dec. 1994). The statement declared that the members of the OIC should "assist the PLO in future negotiations so that all the powers and areas of responsibility in the occupied lands, including sublime Jerusalem, will be transferred to the Palestinian National Authority and in order to ensure the return of Jerusalem to Palestinian sovereignty" (*Al-Quds*, 16 Dec. 1994). The statement emphasized that "sublime Jerusalem is an inseparable part of the Palestinian territories occupied by Israel in 1967 and all rules that apply to the occupied territories apply to it" (*Al-Quds*, 16 Dec. 1994). Moreover, the announcement maintained that, during the interim period, authority in Jerusalem should be transferred to the Palestinian Authority; it completely ignored Jordan's role in the holy places (*Al-Quds*, 16 Dec. 1994; *Ha'aretz*, 22 Dec. 1994, 2 Jan. 1995).

As can be seen, this statement emphasized the political aspects. It was not Jordan's preferred religious status that caused the antagonism of the strong Middle Eastern Islamic states, but rather the political significance implicit in the Washington Declaration, the indirect recognition that Jordan had given to Israel's annexation of East Jerusalem. The debate among the Islamic states on the holy places was not about the religious issue, but rather about political sovereignty. Saudi Arabia, Egypt, Morocco, and the PLO reasoned that the status of the holy places in Jerusalem was derived from political sovereignty over the city, and therefore that if political sovereignty remained in Israel's hands, the holy places were not liberated from occupation as Jordan claimed. Saudi Arabia added to this the argument that a separation of religion and politics of the type Hussein had sought to accomplish in Jerusalem was alien to Islam. On January 16, 1995, the OIC's Jerusalem Committee convened in Morocco in its new configuration, one that had been initiated by Morocco, Saudi Arabia, Egypt, and the PLO. In this framework the dominant members of the organization completed what they had begun at the Conference's plenary session a month before. The Jerusalem Committee refused to recognize the preferred status that Jordan was to receive from Israel, and did not agree with the claims favorable to Jordan (*Al-Quds*, 18 Jan. 1995).

The agreement between the Palestinian Authority and Jordan

After the issue of the holy places was decided in the Palestinians' favor, the way was clear for Arafat to visit Jordan. On January 25, 1995, Arafat arrived in Amman to sign a memorandum of understanding and cooperation between the Palestinian Authority and the Hashemite Kingdom of Jordan in the areas of communications, the movement of goods and people, banking, mail, culture, education, and local administration. The signing of these agreements had been delayed since the establishment of the Palestinian Authority, and in 1994 Jordan signed separate economic agreements with the Palestinian Authority and with Israel. The agreements between Jordan and the Palestinian Authority were meant to put their bilateral relations in order, and in their wake Jordan also decided to open a liaison office in Gaza. As a preamble to this series of agreements, Jordan and the Palestinian Authority also signed a political document drafted as a treaty between two political entities of the same diplomatic standing. This document did not mention Jordan's special status in Jerusalem and did not directly address the Islamic holy places in the city. At the same time, however, it did note the political sovereignty of the Palestinian people in Jerusalem. The Palestinian side viewed with favor the peace treaty between Jordan and Israel and stated, in opposition to the Syrian position, that this treaty did not interfere with the other channels of negotiation between Israel and its neighbors – in other words, Syria's efforts to return the Golan Heights to its sovereignty. Jordan's peace treaty with Israel was presented in the document as assuring Jordan's right "to its land, water, and borders, and an act to ensure the rights of the displaced persons and refugees" – that is, it did not violate Palestinian rights (*Al-Hiyat*, 24 Jan. 1995; *Al-Sharq al-Awsat*, 27 Jan. 1995; *Ha'aretz*, 27 Jan. 1995).

Jordan thus committed itself to help the Palestinians and the PLO realize their right to self-determination and to a state with Jerusalem as its capital. This meant that the Jordanians would not be permitted to place an obstacle in the Palestinians' way in the form of separating political sovereignty in Jerusalem from religious sovereignty in the holy places. The same thing is implied in the section in which Jordan committed itself to cooperate with the Palestinian Authority and to assist it in the establishment of its national institutions. In fact the agreement between Jordan and the Palestinians contains no mention of Jordan's preferred status in the Jerusalem holy places, and one of the prominent sections in the peace treaty between Jordan and Israel was dealt with in the Palestinian Authority–Jordan treaty as if it did not exist.

The new situation created by the OIC in the wake of the agreement with the Palestinian Authority was imposed on Hussein. He found it difficult to make his peace with it. Knowing that the question of Jerusalem had not been decided yet and that it would be discussed at length as part of the establishment of the permanent arrangements between Israel and the Palestinians, he hoped that in time he would be able to turn the clock back. In his remarks at the signing ceremony for his agreement with the Palestinian Authority, King Hussein said that his country would continue to do its duty and to extend its protection to the holy places in Jerusalem "as in the past." Jordan would do so "on the basis of its efforts to foster these holy places and as fulfillment of its duty to preserve Jerusalem and foster its Arab and Islamic identity" (*Al-Hayat*, 27 Jan. 1995; *Al-Sharq al-Awsat*, 27 Jan. 1995). The extent to which the issue of Jerusalem was convoluted and complicated for King Hussein can be seen in an interview he granted to Ibrahim Nafa, editor of the Egyptian daily newspaper *Al-Ahram*, about a month after the signing of the agreement with the Palestinian Authority (FBIS, 21 Feb. 1995). It was hard for anyone to get an unambiguous answer about Jordan's policy because of the contradictions that emerge from each of Hussein's sentences and the awkwardness apparent in them. Jordan, according to the king, was responsible for East Jerusalem, but the Hashemite Kingdom of Jordan had no aspirations in Jerusalem. The permanent status talks between Israel and the Palestinians would determine who would be sovereign in Jerusalem, but at the same time Jordan believed that national–political sovereignty in the Holy City should not be given to one of the contending parties; he hoped that Jordan would be a partner in shaping the permanent arrangements, but said also that the Palestinians were the ones who would make the agreements with Israel, and that the goal of the peace process was to establish Palestinian rule on Palestinian land. Even though he stated that Jordan had no goals in Jerusalem, the kingdom would continue to supervise the holy places in the period of the interim agreement, because this was its obligation. Even though the general direction of his remarks was a retreat from the Washington Declaration in the direction of Adnan Abu Odeh's plan, Hussein did not say this explicitly. In practical terms, the OIC had shuffled the deck for Hussein. He was squirming in a situation that had been forced on him, had a difficult time accepting it, and since East Jerusalem's final status had not yet been determined in the framework of the dispute between Israel and the Palestinians, he still hoped that in the future the Islamic states would accept his position.

The Islamic holy places – a political problem

Israel may have thought it could deal the PLO a political blow by playing the religious card, but the Islamic countries finessed it. Just as in 1974, when the summit conference of Arab heads of states demoted Jordan from being a legitimate representative of the Palestinian people alongside the PLO, so 20 years later the Islamic heads of state demoted it from its preferred status in the Islamic holy places in Jerusalem. At base, the debate among the Islamic states was between two political alternatives. Jordan maintained that it was doubtful whether the Palestinians would succeed in getting Israel to agree to turn the Palestinian Authority into a state, and it was even more doubtful whether Israel would agree to concede its sovereignty in East Jerusalem. Therefore, Jordan argued, at the very least, action should be taken to end Israel's religious grip on the Islamic holy sites in the city by separating political sovereignty from religious sovereignty. Of course, Jordan maintained that this could best be done by buttressing Jordan's religious standing in Jerusalem. The great majority of Arab and Islamic states, however, considered this to be tantamount to recognition of the political annexation of East Jerusalem to Israel. In their opinion, ending Israel's religious grip on the Islamic holy sites in Jerusalem was inseparably tied up in ending the occupation.

They believed that the Palestinians should be strengthened and they did not believe that they should consent to a preferential religious status for Jordan, because that would clearly weaken the Palestinian claim to full sovereignty and independence. The Arab and Islamic states were certain that they would be able to get Israel to agree to turn the Palestinian Authority into a state with its capital in Jerusalem.

The dispute between Jordan and the Islamic states was a fundamentally political one, and this has significance for the administration of the Islamic holy places in the future. It is not at all certain that the Islamic states will consent to exclusive Palestinian administration of the holy places themselves; at the very least, this is not required by their decisions thus far. The Islamic states, in the view presented here, have sought a way to end Israel's occupation of East Jerusalem, and this led them to support the Palestinian demand. They have still not decided how the holy places will be run after Israel transfers East Jerusalem to Palestinian sovereignty. The option of the Islamic holy places in Jerusalem being under the religious administration of several states under a Palestinian political roof has not yet been stricken from the agenda.

With the Islamic states joining his ranks, Arafat was in a better position for his next dispute with Hussein. The establishment of the Palestinian Authority in mid-1994 brought up the question of who would control the Waqf in Jerusalem – the Palestinian Ministry of Religious Endowments, which was responsible for the Waqf in the West Bank, or the Jordanian Waqf, as in the past, since the Palestinian ministry was prohibited from operating in Jerusalem. In August 1994, Arafat decided to set up a Palestinian Waqf in Jerusalem that would replace the Jordanian body. He conducted a series of contacts in order to obtain Jordan's consent to this, but failed (*Ha'aretz*, 8 Aug. 1994). As a result, Arafat decided that, from the beginning of October 1994, the Palestinian Waqf ministry would be responsible for the Waqf in both the West Bank and in Jerusalem. Realizing that being removed from the Waqf administration would end its senior status on al-Haram al-Sharif, Jordan quickly appointed loyalists to the Waqf administration in Jerusalem and increased its financial aid to the Jerusalem institutions it supported through the Waqf, such as Al-Maqased Hospital. Jordan took advantage of the prohibition against the Palestinian Authority operating in Jerusalem in order to argue that its removal from the city would leave a vacuum that Israel would fill. Jordan could not ignore the fact that the Palestinian Authority enjoyed legitimacy and full authority in the areas under its control. Therefore, on September 29, 1994, the Jordanian government decided to disassociate itself from the Waqf administration in the West Bank and to transfer it to Palestinian minister of religious endowments, Hassan Tahboub, who also headed the Supreme Muslim Council, whose seat was in al-Haram al-Sharif. Jordan transferred to Tahboub all documents relevant to administering the Waqf in the West Bank, but not those dealing with the Jerusalem district (Musallam, 1996: 105–9).

From this point onward, the dispute between Jordan and the Palestinian Authority was limited to Jerusalem and encompassed three issues. The first was the right to appoint the mufti of Jerusalem. In mid-October 1994, Mufti Suleiman al-Ja'bri, scion of a well-known pro-Jordanian family, died. Jordan quickly appointed a replacement, Sheikh Abd el-Qadr Abadin. That same day Arafat, as head of the Palestinian Authority, appointed his own candidate to the post. Arafat's appointee was no other than Akaramah Sabari, whom Jordan had fired in June 1987 from his post as chief imam of Al-Aqsa. Sabari had angered Jordan by supporting the PLO in a dispute with Jordan in 1985. The dispute over filling the post of mufti of Jerusalem, a post of extremely high Palestinian–religious rank ever since it had been held by Haj Amin al-Husseini, leader of the Palestinian national movement in the time of the British Mandate, was also a dispute over the powers of the head of the Palestinian Authority. Did Arafat's authority extend to Jerusalem and to the religious administration there that Jordan controlled? No less so, the debate reflected an attempt by the two competing sides to enhance their hold on the Islamic holy places in Jerusalem. In time, the dispute was decided in Sheikh Sabari's favor, thanks to the Palestinian Authority's means of control and oversight. The Palestinian Authority's security apparatus saw to it that people who came to call on the mufti of Jerusalem were sent to Sabari's chambers, and Sheikh Abadin was thus left with no more than his title. When Sheikh Abadin retired in 1998 Jordan did not appoint a replacement and made do with appointing a young sheikh, Abd al-A'zim Silhab, to be responsible for the two Sharia' courts in Jerusalem that had been under Abadin's supervision (*Kol Ha-Ir*, 27 Feb. 1998).

The second issue under dispute between Jordan and the Palestinians had to do with the permanent status talks. In May 1996, on the eve of Israel's national elections, King Hussein, President Mubarak, and Arafat met in Cairo to coordinate their moves. The opening of the permanent status talks that month, talks in which the question of Jerusalem was to be discussed, made Arafat apprehensive. He worried about possible collusion between Jordan and Israel aimed at weakening his hold in Jerusalem in general and on al-Haram al-Sharif in particular. Arafat's fears were not unjustified, because it had been a Labor government that had signed the agreement giving the Hashemite Kingdom preferred status in Jerusalem. This could repeat itself if the Labor Party candidate, Shimon Peres, won the prime ministerial elections. While the summit's participants were hardly hoping for a victory by Peres's opponent, Binyamin Netanyahu, they were apprehensive about that possibility as well, since Israeli public opinion polls were predicting a close race.

Of the three leaders, Arafat was the most worried, for the reason that King Hussein had refrained from making critical remarks about Netanyahu and had even received him for a conversation during his campaign. Arafat enlisted Mubarak in order to tie Jordan's hands no matter what the outcome of the election. In the summit talks Hussein promised not to conduct negotiations over the permanent status of Jerusalem behind Arafat's back and, at Arafat's request, to forbid Hamas leaders in Jordan to act against the Palestinian Authority or conduct a campaign of incitement against it. Arafat saw a connection between the two: in his opinion, Jordan permitted Hamas to operate on its territory and to attack him personally as preparation for usurping his place in Jerusalem with Hamas backing. For his part, Arafat promised to coordinate his positions and moves with Jordan, and accepted Jordan's contention that the kingdom would be affected by the results of the negotiations between Israel and Palestinians on the issues of refugees, permanent borders, and Jerusalem. Regarding Jerusalem, Arafat agreed to leave responsibility for the Islamic holy places in Jordanian hands and accepted Jordan's claims that its abdication would only serve Israeli interests. In exchange, Jordan reiterated its previous promise to be the first state to recognize Palestinian sovereignty over East Jerusalem, if and when the Palestinians achieved this (*Al-Quds*, 13 May 1996, 14 May 1996,

15 May 1996). At the opening session of Jordan's parliament, he declared: "We have announced with full clarity to the Arabs and the Muslims on our duty to the holy places ... we will hand them over to the Palestinians after the end of the permanent status talks and the establishment of a Palestinian state with Al-Quds as its capital" (*Al-Quds*, 20 Nov. 1996).

In the framework of this mini-summit, Arafat brought up the idea of declaring a Jordanian–Palestinian confederation, even at this early stage. This, he suggested, would give him a stronger position at the negotiating table, since it would demonstrate that he had Jordanian recognition of a Palestinian state in his pocket. Such recognition, Arafat thought, would pre-empt any possibility of an Israel–Jordan combination against Palestine. In this, Arafat was changing the tactics that had characterized him from the mid-1980s to the mid-1990s. Then he had feared a confederation between the senior and established Hashemite Kingdom and a weak Palestinian entity. He thus aspired to establish such a confederation only after achieving Palestinian independence. Now Arafat sought to exploit the confederation idea as a tactical move, a political tool, a seal of approval with which it would be possible to achieve full Palestinian independence. According to Arafat's plan, the confederation would have real significance only after Palestinian independence was achieved. Jordan rejected the proposal just as it had rejected it at the end of 1995 and the beginning of 1996, on the grounds that it was premature. The Palestinians first needed to make an agreement with Israel that would define their legal and political status and determine whether they would get a state and within what borders. Only afterwards would it be possible to agree on a confederation between Jordan and the Palestinians. Jordan was concerned that the Palestinians would not succeed in obtaining Israeli recognition of their independent state. In such a case the Palestinians would derive recognition only from their membership in a Jordanian–Palestinian confederation in which the Jordanian side was dominant, and the Palestinians, Jordan feared, would blame Jordan for their failure (*Al-Wasat*, 25 Dec. 1995; *Al-Quds*, 7 Feb. 1996, 14 May 1996).

From the time when the idea of a Jordanian–Palestinian federation was suggested, during the talks on the Amman agreement (Klein, 1988), Jordanian policy on the Palestinian problem vacillated. It wavered between cooperation with Israel, or at least

standing to one side and waiting for the outcome of the Palestinian negotiations with Israel, and assisting the PLO so that it could
achieve independence. The first approach was taken during the
period of Israel's Labor government, while the second was taken
when Israel was headed by a Likud-led coalition. Jordan estimated
that the Likud's traditional policy, which advocated widespread
Israeli settlement in the West Bank, endangered the existence of
the Hashemite Kingdom east of the Jordan. This policy, the Jordanians believed, would push many Palestinians over the river
into the East Bank and upset the demographic balance between
Palestinians and native Jordanians. The Hashemite character of
the East Bank had been achieved with great pains, during which
Jordanians of Palestinian origin had become central supporters of
the Hashemite regime. These were largely Palestinians who had
been absorbed into the country when it annexed the West Bank in
1949, and the refugees of 1967. Many members of the merchant
class, the families of government employees, the middle class, and
a large part of Jordan's economic sector were of Palestinian origin
and had contributed greatly to the country's stability and development. The Jordanians of Palestinian origin had made a political
alliance with the palace and supported King Hussein in identifying the state with the Hashemite descent of its ruler. They had
influenced Hussein to stand firmly behind the PLO and to create
a link between the political establishments of both sides of the
Jordan. The Likud's policy even aided this by narrowing support
for Jordanians of the opposite viewpoint – members of the bour-
geoisie, intelligence and army chiefs, and senior government officials who advocated developing an exclusively East Bank identity
and close cooperation with Israel (al-Tal, 1996; Susser, 1995).

   In the 1980s the Jordanians worked hand in hand with the PLO
in order to help the Palestinians remain tied to their land. On the
eve of the Madrid conference they even provided the PLO with
the necessary cover to establish a joint delegation, and with
Netanyahu's accession to power they stood at Arafat's side in his
bargaining with Israel. It had been King Hussein who, in January
1997, brought Netanyahu a compromise Palestinian, Jordanian,
and Egyptian proposal on the redeployment agreement in Hebron
and the rest of the West Bank. Moreover, Hussein was the first
Arab head of state to visit, in October 1996, the Palestinian
Authority in Jericho, against the background of the "Al-Aqsa

incident" (the violent Palestinian response to the opening of the Western Wall Tunnel by the Netanyahu government). The visit was meant to express the fact that Jordan had completely removed itself from the negotiations on the West Bank, and it stood shoulder to shoulder with the Palestinians against the Israeli government (Jordanian minister of propaganda, Marwan Mu'ashar, *Ha'aretz*, 4 Nov. 1996).

The third issue was control of the Waqf in Jerusalem as a whole and on al-Haram al-Sharif in particular. In October 1996 a fight broke out between the Jordanian Waqf officials and their Palestinian colleagues. Against a background of rumors about financial corruption, the Palestinian minister of religious endowments and the governor of the Jerusalem district demanded that the Waqf's treasurer (a Jordanian appointee) hand over his authority to a Fatah activist that Arafat had appointed to replace him. Their demands were accompanied by a display of force by the presidential security apparatus (Force 17), one of the Palestinian Authority's security forces. The Jordanian Waqf administration referred the matter to its offices in Amman, and the heads of the Jordanian Ministry of Religious Endowments invited their colleagues from across the river to talk. It was agreed that Jordanian sponsorship of the Waqf within al-Haram al-Sharif would continue, and that the Jordanian-appointed treasurer would remain in his post. Until such time as a permanent status accord was reached, "the Palestinian Authority has high regard for Jordan's role and its sponsorship of the Islamic holy places and religious endowments in Jerusalem," declared a member of the Palestinian delegation, Tayib Abd al-Rahim, secretary-general of the presidential office in the Palestinian Authority (*Al-Quds*, 5 Nov. 1996).

Outside the city in its Israeli borders, in the Palestinian Authority's Jerusalem district (identical to the former Jordanian Jerusalem district), responsibility for Waqf properties and administration would be handed over to the Palestinian Authority. This included 150 people out of the 700 who worked in the city and district, officials responsible for schools, mosques, and other Waqf properties in the urban suburbs of Jerusalem such as Abu-Dis and Al-Azaria, where the Palestinian Authority ruled (*Al-Quds*, 5 Nov. 1996, 6 Nov. 1996, 11 Nov. 1996). Jordan now recognized the Palestinian Authority's status in the Jerusalem municipal space, recognition it had not granted previously.

Jordan's interest in the Waqf was now reduced to al-Haram al-Sharif, the only site in Jerusalem on which Jordan's eyes were set and where it was determined not to lose its role in the permanent settlement. A first symbolic expression of this appeared in the Jordanian government's announcement, during the talks with the Palestinian delegation, that King Hussein had decided to personally assume the renovation of the Al-Aqsa Mosque, as he had with the renovation of the Dome of the Rock in 1994. Second, at the same time the pro-Jordanian East Jerusalem daily newspaper *Al-Nahar* was closed. (It had been founded in the summer of 1986 because of the shift in the editorial policy of the largest circulation East Jerusalem daily, *Al-Quds*, which passed into new, pro-PLO ownership.) By this time *Al-Nahar* had neither a readership nor political and economic backing. Jordan's interest in al-Haram al-Sharif did not justify its maintenance of a daily newspaper (Rubinstein, 6 Jan. 1997).

In practice, from early 1997 onward, Jordan's effective authority in al-Haram al-Sharif was very limited. Jordan's sponsorship of the Islamic holy places in Jerusalem is, in practice, window dressing, behind which Palestinian elements operate (*Ha'aretz*, 9 Sept. 1998). The story of the Supreme Muslim Council is a good illustration of this process of Palestinization in al-Haram al-Sharif. The Supreme Muslim Council was established during the British Mandate and renewed its activity in the city after the 1967 war. The Council was not recognized by Jordan's governments in the 1948–1967 period, nor by Israel (from 1967 onward), and Israel even deported the man who headed it in 1967, Sheikh Abd al-Hamid Sa'ih, later speaker of the Palestinian National Council. Most of the Supreme Muslim Council's business was closely supervising events in al-Haram al-Sharif and in the Waqf institutions. On the eve of the establishment of the Palestinian Authority in 1994, the Waqf's director, Hassan Tahboub, later to be the Palestinian minister of religious endowments, was chosen to head the council; Faisal Husseini, who holds the Jerusalem portfolio in the PLO executive committee, was chosen to be his deputy. In this way the Council became a body whose leaders were top local national political figures, and this aided the Palestinian Authority in the conduct of its struggle for control of al-Haram al-Sharif. The next stage in the struggle took place in January 1997, when Arafat decided to appoint 18 representatives of the West Bank and

Gaza Strip to the council, among them former Palestinian minister Dr. Abd al-Aziz al-Haj Ahmed and the Palestinian Authority's
governor of the Jerusalem district, Jamil Othman Nasser, whose
office is located in Abu-Dis (Rubinstein, 26 Jan. 1997). In this way
the entire council, not just its leaders, became a body whose principal members were Palestinian government officials who could,
in practice, manage the affairs of al-Haram al-Sharif and oversee
the Waqf, which remained under Jordanian sovereignty.

5

THE P.L.O. AND THE PALESTINIAN IDENTITY OF EAST JERUSALEM

Patterns of political organization in Palestinian society have changed since 1967. Under Jordanian rule, as during the British Mandate period, political power in the West Bank lay in the hands of a traditional elite, which had land, capital, high social status, and family connections. Political organizations were established around these elites, and the extended family (the *hamula*) played a major political role, particularly in the area of recruitment and organization. The veteran elite's power extended not only to political life, but also to religion – it controlled the Muslim endowments and properties, from which the elite could allocate resources to its followers as compensation for their political loyalty. This congruence of political power and control of the religious establishment provided the veteran leadership with the highly effective legitimacy of tradition and religion.

Under Israeli rule, however, the political elite in the West Bank and Gaza Strip became more heterogeneous in its status, education, and social composition, and it came to be organized around ideology and political institutions. Beginning in the mid-1970s, the leading political role played by the hamulas weakened as Palestinian political organizations, the PLO chief among them, gained strength. The PLO penetrated from the "outside" to the "inside" via three processes. First, from 1974 onward it gained a firmer position in the Arab world and the recognition of the international community. Second, it gained control of or founded its own welfare, youth, sport, and health organizations (called "popular organizations" by the Palestinians), professional associations and unions, and placed its own activists in top municipal positions in the territories. Third, it benefited from the aspirations of young Palestinians, especially middle- and lower-class students, to take a leading role in politics and society and to eject the veteran pro-Jordanian elite that had been part of the Jordanian regime's ruling apparatus before the 1967 war. Instead of an exclusive club based on kinship and traditional deference, the PLO offered ideology and organization to those seeking to break into politics. Instead of tradition, it offered a politics of protest and revolution. The PLO realigned the axis around which political life in the 1967 territories had been organized and broadened the social composition of the political elite. By co-opting the members of the veteran elite, it brought them into PLO frameworks and assigned them a defined place. It refused to accept the existence of any non-PLO leadership, thus preventing the growth of an "internal" establishment that might develop into an alternative to its own authority.

The PLO knew how to buy the political fealty of the veteran elite, allowing it to serve as an intermediary between the organization and the local population, or between it and Israel and the U.S. It should be noted, however, that the PLO did not change the patron–client mode of the relationship between the elite on the one hand and both the rank-and-file and the masses on the other. While loyalty to the PLO political establishment replaced loyalty to the hamula, this was not abstract or general loyalty to the organization or the national idea, nor did it mean becoming part of an organization in which all leaders were equal. The PLO has been characterized by vertical political alliances, from top to bottom, by echelon. These alliances have encouraged personal loyalties and animosities and turned the organization's hierarchy of ranks into a hierarchy of patrons that use the PLO power vested in them to gain their own personal supporters. Alongside these vertical ties, there have also been, from time to time, horizontal political alliances, between patrons, generally between those who have held senior positions at the organization's top levels (Klein, 1997; Robinson, 1997; Sayigh, 1997).

These changes occurred in Jerusalem as well, but they were manifested in a different way for a variety of reasons. A part of the veteran Jerusalem elite had emigrated in the wake of the 1948 war, and there was a wave of immigration into the city from Hebron. A young, college-educated generation, graduates of the West Bank universities that had opened their doors in the mid-1970s, matured and entered the labor market and political arena. The same period saw the rise of a new class of Palestinians who earned comfortable incomes from work in Israel. They had money and political ambitions but no connections to high-placed families. Furthermore, Israel emasculated the veteran elite with its annexation of East Jerusalem and by transferring prerogatives and positions of power from the traditional elite to Israeli bodies. The elite no longer supplied municipal services and did not deal out favors to its loyalists. Israel left it only a small part its former role of mediator between the state and the populace. The focus of decision-making on the local level moved from the east side of the city to the west, or to PLO headquarters. Moreover, the powers of the elite in Jerusalem were even fewer than those of the elite groups in the rest of the cities of the West Bank and Gaza Strip. These groups retained the municipalities and local councils, while in Jerusalem the powers of the East Jerusalem municipality were transferred to Israel. The weak Jerusalem elite did not govern within the city, much less on a national level. As a rule, Israel prevented local leaders from turning into national leaders and the Jerusalem elite from establishing centers of influence in other cities. Finally, some members of the veteran Jerusalem elite were deported and some of their institutions were closed. Prominent in the heterogeneous elite of post-1967 Jerusalem were immigrants who had moved to Jerusalem from Hebron and become well established in the city. The traditional and religious background of the former Hebronites and their major role in commerce helped them capture key positions in the Waqf and in commercial organizations. Since 1967, many members of the Jerusalem elite moved gradually from identification with Jordan to adoption of Palestinian identity and support for one or another of the PLO's constituent factions. Elite groups in the rest of the 1967 territories underwent the same metamorphosis, but the pace of change in Jerusalem was slower than in the West Bank and Gaza Strip and to a more limited extent. As a result, there was a higher level of friction between the Jerusalem elite and the PLO's leadership than there was between the overall "internal" and "external" leaderships. East Jerusalem preserved its unique character (Sabella, 1997a). In the final analysis, the PLO's entry from Tunis and Beirut into the West Bank and from the West Bank into Jerusalem, and its actions to intensify the Palestinian identity of East Jerusalem, has been conducted along two parallel paths: confrontation with Israel and its actions, and confrontation with the local elite and the local political establishment.

Boycotts of institutions and political processes

After the annexation of East Jerusalem in 1967, Israel granted its Arab inhabitants the right to vote in municipal elections, but the vast majority preferred to boycott the elections as a way of protesting about Israeli rule. The Palestinians in Jerusalem did not accept Israel's contention that their participation in elections was a municipal act with only local implications. In the 1969 elections, 21.5 per cent of eligible Arabs voted; in 1973, only 7.3 per cent; in 1978, 14.4 per cent; and in 1983, 18.4 per cent. During the Intifada, in 1989, this fell to 2.75 per cent, and in 1993, after the PLO's agreement with Israel and despite an attempt to enlist massive East Jerusalem Arab support for the candidacy of Mayor Teddy Kollek against his right-wing challenger, Ehud Olmert, only 7 per cent of the eligible East Jerusalem Arabs voted (Halabi, 1993: 35; Romman & Weingrod, 1991: 207). This meant that the Declaration of Principles signed in 1993 had but a negligible affect on the political behavior of East Jerusalem's Arabs. Politically, the East Jerusalem Arabs see themselves as part of the Palestinian political system. This also found expression in the 1998 elections, when only 6.5 per cent of Arabs voted (*Ha'aretz*, 12 Nov. 1998).

On the eve of the 1989 elections, at the height of the Intifada, Hana Sinyora, a well-off East Jerusalem political activist and newspaper editor who identified with the PLO but voiced independent opinions, floated the idea of running for the city council as a candidate of the residents of East Jerusalem. Sinyora argued that these were local elections whose significance was limited to the administration of day-to-day life in the city. East Jerusalem representation in the city council, he maintained, would act to reduce inequality between the two sides of the city in the allocation of resources and in positions of power, especially if it became part of the governing coalition. The idea aroused great opposition in East Jerusalem and in the PLO headquarters in Tunis. Sinyora's two cars were set on fire and he received death threats until he withdrew his proposal (al-Qaq, 1997). The idea of participation in local elections came up again in November 1993, after the signing of the Declaration of

Principles between Israel and the PLO. This time the idea was considered seriously and did not arouse the antagonism that Sinyora's proposal had, but it was again rejected.

In this case the proposal was to run a joint Arab–Jewish slate for the city council on a platform of granting political rights to East Jerusalem Palestinians, cessation of Jewish construction in East Jerusalem, and making East Jerusalem the capital of Palestine without physically dividing Jerusalem. Naturally, most of the slate's support was expected to come from East Jerusalem, and bringing Palestinian voters to the polls would have required the intervention of both the local leadership and the PLO "outside." The PLO leadership in Tunis took into account the possibility that massive Palestinian support for the slate was likely to change the political map of the city council, but the price would be *de facto* recognition of the annexation of East Jerusalem to Israel. For this reason, the PLO leadership preferred to let the local leadership decide; they rejected the initiative on September 24, 1993. Aside from the matter of principle, the local leadership gave other, practical reasons for not participating in the elections. At a time when Israel was continuing to pursue its policy of making East Jerusalem Jewish, the local leadership argued, it would be inappropriate to establish a joint city council. The city council, they maintained, was not the arena where decisions were being made about Jewish construction in East Jerusalem and about the purchase of Arab houses by Jews. The national arena was the only place to influence Israel's actions in East Jerusalem and only diplomatic contacts between the PLO leadership and the Israeli government would solve the problem. If the slate would have no influence on an issue so painful to the Palestinians, why should they participate in the elections? The local leadership also argued that there was room for suspicion that some of the members of the slate – apparently, the slate's Jewish candidates – would support, after being elected, Teddy Kollek's "One Jerusalem" policy. Moreover, even if the slate managed to gain seven to ten seats on the 31-seat city council, they would still be a minority facing a majority that advocated the entire city remaining under Israeli sovereignty. The local Palestinian leadership preferred not to recognize the annexation *de facto*, even if doing so would promote redivision of the city and turn East Jerusalem into the capital of the state of Palestine. In the 1993 elections, right-wing candidate Ehud Olmert beat Teddy Kollek (*Ha'aretz*, 29 Sept. 1993; 3 June 1994; Halabi, 1993: 38–43).

In the summer of 1998 there were exploratory talks between Uzi Baram of the Labor Party, who was then considering running for mayor that coming November, and the Palestinian leadership in Jerusalem about calling on the Palestinian public to participate in the elections for mayor and help oust Olmert. Despite Olmert's actions in Jerusalem, the response was adamantly negative. It should be noted, however, that the Palestinians had not sat on their hands since the Intifada; the boycott of the elections did not indicate a passive response to the annexation of East Jerusalem. Faisal Husseini chose to define Palestinian actions in this way: "We do not establish facts in the field. We are the facts in the field" (*Ha'aretz*, 1 June 1994).

Building counter-institutions

Even before the Oslo agreements, the Palestinians began operating a variety of institutions in Jerusalem. There were professional associations for engineers, economists, journalists, lawyers, nurses, doctors, pharmacists, artists, writers, laborers, and farmers; there were trade unions, chambers of commerce, and an industrialists' association; there were charitable, welfare, and health organizations, children's and youth groups, sports associations, councils for education, housing, tourism, health, culture and public relations, industry, and agriculture; there were women's organizations and an office of statistics and demographics.

In the educational area, East Jerusalem had al-Quds University and the Palestinian Open University, junior colleges and vocational institutes. The city is not a center of industry, but it is home to institutions for economic development, credit companies, and the electric company. The Islamic holy places gave Jerusalem great religious importance and it is thus home to the most important Palestinian religious institutions, such as the Supreme Muslim Council, the Waqf, and the religious court. Jerusalem is also a center of Palestinian culture and media; it houses the most important Palestinian museums and several theaters, among them the Palestinian national theater, Al-Hakwati (*Ha'aretz*, 20 May 1994, 8 June 1994, 26 June 1994; Passia, 1994). Obviously, not all these institutions are large, national, well-functioning institutions, and not all were founded after the signing of the Declaration of Principles. For our purposes, the level of institutionalization, organization, and functioning is not important, but rather the fact that they are located in Jerusalem. For the Palestinians, Jerusalem is the capital-designate and they are trying to locate all their national, social, religious, scientific, cultural, media, employment, and economic institutions in the city, especially those whose field of activity is not municipal but national and covers the entire West Bank.

The jewel in the crown of the Palestinian institutions in Jerusalem is Orient House. The building belongs to the Husseini family, and there, in 1979, Faisal Husseini opened the offices of the Arab Studies Society, which documents Palestinian activity and roots in Jerusalem. The building served as the headquarters for the Palestinian delegation to the peace talks from March 1991 until the signing of the Declaration of Principles in September 1993, and it was also the place of work for the "technical committees," the expert panels whose job was to prepare working papers for the delegations engaging in the bilateral and multilateral talks with Israel. They also prepared the scholarly and professional infrastructure for the Palestinian self-government that was discussed in the talks with Israel. Until Arafat and the Palestinian Authority's offices established themselves in Gaza in June 1994, Orient House functioned as an unofficial political arm of PLO headquarters in Tunis with regard to the local population. In the field of foreign policy, Orient House became the focus of the PLO's public and official contacts with the Palestinian delegation between 1991 and 1993.

After the signing of the Declaration of Principles there was a change in the building's function, and Orient House began to represent East Jerusalem's Arabs to the Israeli government and to the Palestinian Authority. It also served as an unofficial arm of the Palestinian Authority. Most of the Authority's meetings and the principal diplomatic work of the Palestinian leadership is accomplished in Gaza, with a smaller portion being conducted in Ramallah, Nablus, and Hebron. Jerusalem hosts only ceremonial and symbolic meetings meant to demonstrate the Arab and Palestinian identity of East Jerusalem. For this reason a Palestinian flag flies on the building's roof and security guards protect it. As with all Orient House's activity, the Palestinian guards in the building also began to operate with Israel's approval. This was at the beginning of the contacts on the participation of a Palestinian delegation in the Madrid conference, at a time when threats were being made against the Palestinian representatives, in particular Faisal Husseini. When the Palestinian threats on Hussein's life dissipated and his activity received the PLO's blessing, threats began coming from the Israeli extreme right. It was thus necessary to continue to provide guards for him and for the institution he heads, in addition to Israel's peripheral protection. The Palestinian security guards are seen as not only having security roles but also as symbols of sovereignty. Israel has not allowed them to bear arms nor to operate outside the building, and in response the Palestinian security staff has refused to allow the Israeli bodyguards assigned to the Egyptian foreign minister and the Turkish prime minister to accompany them into Orient House when they visited, and in both cases the Palestinian and Israeli guards tussled with each other (Mussallam, 1996: 51–4, 59, 63–4).

Orient House does not function only as a political center. It is also an address for resolving problems that Jerusalem Palestinians have with the Israeli authorities – obtaining licenses, identification cards, and work permits, receiving discounts on the payment of property taxes and water rates, expedition of requests for family reunification and permits to visit relatives in Arab countries. It also functions in municipal arenas such as in the construction and renovation of schools, tourist and economic development, and in legal areas such as mediating civil disputes, approving property transactions, mediating and deciding land disputes and financial claims between spouses, all this circumventing the Israeli court system. (Rulings are enforced by the preventative security apparatus in the West Bank, headed by Jibril Rajoub.) Orient House also coordinates requests for allocations of financial assistance from the Palestinian Authority's institutions and from private donors to schools, clubs, non-profit organizations, and Palestinian charitable organizations in East Jerusalem, and mediates between them and the Palestinian Authority. In the past it even granted office services to Palestinian Authority officials such as the chief of municipal affairs, to PECDAR (Palestinian Economic Council for Development and Reconstruction) and to the Palestinian Center for Statistics (*Ha'aretz*, 16 Nov. 1994, 20 Dec. 1994, 7 July 1996; *Peace Watch*, 1995; Shragai, 9 July 1996). But from the beginning of 1997 there has clearly been a decline in the range of activities at the building and in its status, together with a rise in the status of the central Palestinian regime. From 1997 the governor of the Jerusalem district has successfully competed with Orient House.

Beyond this, members of the Palestinian Preventative Security Force in the West Bank, under the command of Jibril Rajoub, filled the police vacuum that had been created in East Jerusalem after the Intifada. The Intifada disturbances, and the resignation of Arab policemen during the course of the uprising, left the Israeli police in East Jerusalem overworked. Their limited resources were directed at crime prevention and at keeping the drug trade from spreading from the Arab to the Jewish sector; little man-power was left to enforce law and order in the streets of East Jeru-salem. Rajoub's men stepped into this opening. They began to carry out policing activities, to accept complaints from the public, to take action against drug and sex offenders and against prostitu-tion, often with much violence. They conducted police investiga-tions in East Jerusalem and functioned as an enforcement agency, carrying out the rulings of the voluntary court system sponored by Orient House and returning stolen property (*Ha'aretz*, 16 Nov. 1994, 20 Dec. 1994; Shragai, 9 July 1996).

The Israel police force also generally refrained from patrolling non-Jewish holy places in the Old City. When pickpockets and thieves around the Church of the Holy Sepulcher and other Christian shrines became such a nuisance that tourists began avoiding them, church income declined. Church leaders applied to Arafat, and he ordered Rajoub's men to function as a tourist police force as well. Rajoub professionally instructs his men on this assignment and the churches pay their salaries of approxi-mately $525 a month, which is some 50 per cent higher than the average salary of a Palestinian policeman in the Palestinian Authority. This is an incentive given to them to encourage them to work in Jerusalem (*Kol Ha-Ir*, 7 March 1997; Temkin, 9 April 1999; *Ha'aretz*, 2 Aug. 1999). Rajoub's men operate in the political arena as well. At times of tension between the Palestinian Author-ity and Jordan, Jibril Rajoub's forces have supervised the sermons in Al-Aqsa, have prepared lists of East Jerusalem residents going on the pilgrimage to Mecca via Jordan, and have recorded the names of people visiting the office of the Jordan-appointed mufti of Jerusalem. Moreover, Palestinian intelligence agents have operated against opposition elements and have worked to lower the tones of Arafat's critics. Such actions have included the arrest of civil rights activist Basem Eid, threats against the editorial offices of East Jerusalem newspapers, and the arrest of journalist Daoud Kutab for having conducted a live broadcast, on the al-Quds University television station, of deliberations of the Palestinian Legislative Council in which delegates were sharply critical of financial and personal corruption among senior Palestinian Authority officials. The corruption charges reverberated among the Palestinians and the Preventative Security Service used force to silence the criticism (*Ha'aretz*, 26 May 1997).

The Palestinian Preventative Security Force began to operate in Jerusalem in mid-1994 with the blessing of Israel's General Security Service (GSS), the country's covert security agency. The GSS, which had difficulty collecting intelligence in Palestinian Authority territory as it had done in these areas before the Oslo agreements, received assistance from its Palestinian colleagues. The GSS's interest was that there should be no vacuum when Israel evacuated these areas and that there should be an authoritative address to which Israel's security services could apply. Providing a firm foundation for the authority of the Palestinian Preventative Security apparatus was also important to the GSS because it wanted the Palestinian force to be able to gather intelligence and prevent terrorism. In exchange, the GSS permitted Rajoub to expand his field of activity in the West Bank, including the Jerusalem area. In late 1994 the GSS's policy aroused the ire of the Israel police, whose interest was the enforcement of law and order in Israel. The Israel police and the minister of police claimed that the activity of Rajoub's forces called into question Israel's sovereignty in East Jerusalem. Rabin took the side of the police, but in practice Israel had little capability to prevent the Palestinian activity. From the beginning of 1996 through to mid-1997, Israel arrested 76 Palestinian security agents on charges of illegal activity in Jerusalem. Of these, 66 were arrested for abducting residents of Jerusalem and taking them for interrogation in the territory of the Palestinian Authority, six were arrested for assault, and four for carrying illegal weapons (*Ha'aretz*, 26 May 1997; 16 Feb. 1998). During the course of 1995 other Palestinian security forces also began to operate in Jerusalem – General Intelligence, under the command of Amin al-Hindi; the Presidential Security Guard (the former

Force 17), and Jerusalem District Security, an organization established by the Palestinian governor of the Jerusalem district, Jamil Othman Nasser. The range of activity of the Palestinian security agencies grew over time, and to the functions already noted, the protection of public figures and facilities was added (*Ha'aretz*, 26 May 1997, 16 Feb. 1998). The activity of the Palestinian intelligence organisations in Jerusalem takes place under camouflage within civilian sites and is possible because their authority is accepted by the Palestinian inhabitants of the city. These see the forces as legitimate national organizations and, for this reason, do not quickly make complaints to the Israeli authorities (*Ha'aretz*, 26 Dec. 1994, 22 Feb. 1997, 28 Feb. 1997, former GSS deputy director Gideon Ezra to Melman, 29 Aug. 1995).

The Oslo agreements prevent inhabitants of East Jerusalem from operating in the framework of the Palestinian Authority, so Husseini stated that Palestinians should "act in such a way that it would not be possible to prevent the activity as a violation of the law" (*Ha'aretz*, 9 Feb. 1996; *Kol Ha-Ir*, 9 Feb. 1996). Husseini himself served as a personal example of the policy he had recommended – he did not run in the elections for the Palestinian Authority's Legislative Council in January 1996, since, had he been elected, he would have had to disassociate himself from Orient House or shut it down. After his election to the PLO Executive Committee by the Palestinian National Council, which convened for its 21 session in Gaza in May 1996, and the reports in the Palestinian press on his appointment to the Palestinian cabinet, Husseini quickly convened a press conference and declared that he had never been a member of the executive branch of the Palestinian Authority. His post, he said, was that of being responsible for Jerusalem affairs on the PLO Executive Committee (*Al-Quds*, 13 May 1996; *Ha'aretz*, 14 May 1996). Husseini's official omission from the list of Palestinian cabinet ministers does not interfere with his functioning as the official responsible for Jerusalem affairs. Since the 21 Palestinian National Council was convened, meetings of the Palestinian cabinet have been held jointly with meetings of the PLO Executive Committee, under the rubric "meetings of the Palestinian leadership." From Israel's point of view there is no legal reason to prevent Husseini from being a member of the PLO leadership, since it no longer defines the PLO as a terrorist organization. In the same way, the

Palestinian minister of religious endowments, Hassan Tahboub, has operated officially in Jerusalem under his title of chief of the Supreme Muslim Council, but not as a member of the Palestinian cabinet.

Jerusalem versus Gaza

The "internal" leaders based in Orient House have always led Palestinian activity in East Jerusalem. Their approach has been more activist than that of the PLO leaders "outside," in Tunis, until mid-1994. The leaders of the public "inside" felt the problem of Jerusalem in full force, unlike the leaders in Tunis. The organizational and personal priorities were different – the heads of the organization in Tunis wanted to obtain broad international recognition of the organization, while squelching the growth of an alternative leadership from the "internal" Palestinian public. They believed that recognition of the right to self-determination and of the right to establish an independent state took precedence over all else, even buttressing the status of Jerusalem as the Palestinian capital. The PLO leadership in Tunis managed to maneuver the internal leadership into complete political dependence on them, and cut short the internal leadership's attempts to put Jerusalem at the top of the PLO agenda. Such an attempt was made in May 1992, when a discussion of the Jerusalem question was held in the framework of the expert committees who assisted the Palestinian delegation to the peace talks. Three approaches emerged from the discussion. The first advocated unilateral Palestinian action in Jerusalem. This was unconnected to the negotiations with Israel, apparently on the assumption that Israel would not be prepared to concede its sovereignty in East Jerusalem. The second approach advocated bringing the issue up for negotiation with Israel, not by the PLO alone, but rather in cooperation with the Arab and Islamic states, which would serve as a counterweight to Israel. The third approach was that there was no point in raising the issue of Jerusalem, at least not for the present. But, unlike the first approach, which maintained that the "internal" Palestinians should bear the sole burden of establishing unilateral facts in Jerusalem, the supporters of the third approach believed that the "internals" should collect the necessary information and use it to prepare a plan of action. In their opinion, however, the actual execution of the plan should be in coordination with the "external" PLO leadership, with its support and approval (Halabi, 1993: 49). This was the majority approach and the "internals" intended to operate in accord with it.

The Palestinian Academic Society for the Study of International Affairs (PASSIA) was the first Palestinian institution to prepare working papers on Jerusalem, among them papers on making East Jerusalem the capital of Palestinian state; the establishment of an Arab municipality in East Jerusalem for the management of day-to-day affairs; the creation of public awareness of the Palestinian apparatus managing daily life in East Jerusalem; the question of Palestinian political sovereignty in Jerusalem; the geographic reality in the city; and the status of al-Haram al-Sharif, the Jewish Quarter, and Jewish settlements and settlers in the Old City and outside it (Halabi, 1993: 50). PASSIA's director, Dr. Mahdi Abdul Hadi, presented a summary of the deliberations to the PLO leadership on September 12, 1992. Abdul Hadi remarked on the lack of coordination between the different arms of the Palestinian establishment responsible for Jerusalem. Even worse, he maintained, the different branches of the PLO working on the Jerusalem issue were at times fighting each other. He proposed that the PLO create an apparatus for coordinating between these different bodies, and for rousing Palestinian public opinion in Jerusalem and in the 1967 territories about the importance of the struggle for the city. According to Abdul Hadi, it was important to achieve coordination not only within the PLO establishment, but also between it and the Arab and Islamic states. He also noted the importance of establishing a database on East Jerusalem and of methodically and periodically issuing working papers on issues relating to the status of Jerusalem in the interim period, and on how to turn it into the capital of the Palestinian state in the permanent settlement. He proposed that, in its negotiations with Israel, the PLO stress Jerusalem as the focal point of the 1967 territories. Abdul Hadi's assumption was that a single rule would apply to Jerusalem and the rest of the 1967 territories in the interim settlement, and that both national and municipal elections would be held there. On the basis of this assumption, Dr. Abdul Hadi expressed his disappointment that the PLO had no position on and was making no demand to conduct elections to an Arab municipality in East Jerusalem in parallel with the elections that were supposed to be held in the 1967 territories, under the framework agreement of the Madrid Conference.

Dr. Abdul Hadi recommended that the PLO leadership plan for the establishment of an Arab municipality in East Jerusalem, including a city council, bureaucracy, municipal institutions, and a department for cooperation with other municipalities around the world. He proposed enlisting between 100 and 150 public figures to establish a 15-member National Organization for Arab Jerusalem (*al-Haya al-Wataniya li-Al-Quds al-Arabiya*). This body would function as an East Jerusalem municipality alongside the Israeli municipality (Halabi, 1993: 50–3). However, the PLO leadership did not adopt the program, preferring to negotiate with Israel. The way in which the Oslo accords were produced indicates that the "external" PLO preferred to progress towards obtaining a Palestinian state in preference to buttressing the status of East Jerusalem as the Palestinian capital. In opposition to the "internal" leadership, which was largely ensconced in the Jerusalem area, the PLO leadership reasoned that a Palestinian state would guarantee obtaining Jerusalem as a capital, rather than the other way around. There were both political and personal motives for this stand. The PLO leadership had wanted in the past to prevent the growth of an alternative leadership among the "internals," and had taken no steps to establish a Palestinian institutional presence in Jerusalem as Faisal Husseini had suggested. From the beginning of the implementation of the Oslo accords, the Palestinian Authority's leaders had thus preferred to operate the institutions in Jerusalem as arms of the Gaza regime, rather than risking the creation of a parallel, independent local establishment.

For this reason, the "internal" leadership decided to implement on its own some of the proposals the PASSIA experts had made, while adapting them to the new reality created by the signing of the Declaration of Principles. This meant, for most part, the establishment of representative institutions from the top down.

The first step in this direction was taken on November 1, 1993, when Faisal Husseini called on Palestinian public leaders to establish a Jerusalem National Organization – Palestine (*Hayat Al-Quds al-Wataniya*) as a source of national Palestinian authority for managing local Jerusalem matters. His assumption was that alongside management of the Palestinian Authority from Gaza, there was room during the interim period to create a parallel system on the local level. If it went well, it would provide a dimension of sovereignty to the Palestinians in the city, ensure their presence there and the Palestinian character of East Jerusalem, so when the question of Jerusalem came up for discussion in the permanent status talks the Palestinians would be in a better position than they had been in previously. Hussein's proposal spoke of the establishment of a 21-member body that would operate out of Orient House in: municipal planning, economics, law and justice, basic services, religion, finance, external relations, development of public institutions, and public security and order. Faisal Husseini took it upon himself to head the body that would prepare for the establishment of this institution, and he chose Hassan Tahboub, head of the Supreme Muslim Council, as his deputy (*Ha'aretz*, 20 May 1994, 3 June 1994, 7 June 1994, 15 June 1994; Halabi, 1993: 53–6).

This initiative was, however, unsuccessful, so Husseini tried a new tack – re-establishing the municipal government of Arab Jerusalem. On June 27, 1967, the Israeli military government had disbanded to the city council of Arab Jerusalem, a body of 16 members headed by Mayor Ruhi al-Khatib. Thereafter, the Arab city council existed on paper only, and in 1994 Israel deported al-Khatib, who died later that year. Now, in mid-1995, Husseini notified Dr. Amin Majaj, a member of the defunct city council and a former member of the Jordanian parliament, that the Palestinian Authority's cabinet had decided to re-establish the Arab city council and to appoint him mayor.

When Husseini declared the re-establishment of the city council, only six of the original 16 members were still alive. Replacements had to be chosen. Furthermore, the re-established city council had an economic problem. Financing of the council's activities had been placed on the shoulders of the Palestinian Authority – Jordan had, in severing its constitutional and administrative connections with the West Bank in 1988, ceased to transfer funds to the Arab Jerusalem city council (*Ha'aretz*, 12 June 1995, 13 June 1995, 14 June 1995; *Kol Ha-Ir*, 16 June 1995). No funding was, however, forthcoming, and the fate of the Palestinian city council was the same as that of the Jordanian one. Like its predecessor, it remained on paper (*Ha'aretz*, 9 Feb. 1996). Neither did the shadow city council's status change when al-Majaj died at the end of 1998. At the beginning of 1999 a new mayor was appointed, Zaki al-Ghul, along with 12 council members. Al-Ghul himself,

like several members of the council, lives in Jordan. Most of the
council's members are well-off, elderly notables and do not constitute a representative cross-section of the city's population (*Al-
Quds*, 21 Feb. 1999; *Ha'aretz*, 22 Feb. 1999).

Husseini's plan did not focus only on the area of municipal services; it also sought to establish an institution parallel to the Palestinian Authority in Jerusalem, one that would operate in a large
variety of areas. The Palestinian Authority leaders in Gaza seem to
have been concerned precisely about this, since their agreement
with Israel forbade them officially to operate Palestinian Authority institutions out of Jerusalem. They did not want to see a parallel, competing apparatus come into being, so they did not take any
real action to implement Husseini's program. The Palestinian
Authority leadership preferred to compete with Israel in Jerusalem by operating local institutions and leaders by remote control
or as arms of the central establishment in Gaza. Gaza was the seat
of most of the Palestinian Authority's institutions, including
Arafat's office, Palestinian police headquarters, and most of the
ministries. The Palestinian Authority was not concerned that its
operations in Jerusalem remained weak and inefficient. Since the
Palestinian Authority could not operate in East Jerusalem it was
wary that any body operating there might slip out of its control.
Moreover, the traditional power base of the "internals" lay in
Jerusalem and its environs. From this point of view, it was not
coincidental that Jibril Rajoub's force operated in Jerusalem. Via
the Preventative Security apparatus, one of the pillars of the Fatah
in West Bank and Gaza Strip, Arafat apparently hoped not only to
strengthen East Jerusalem's Palestinian identity, but also to keep
tabs on the activity of the Jerusalem political elite and to prevent
Faisal Husseini from becoming a national leader (Klein, 1997).

In the summer of 1995 Husseini tried to go in a different direction. Instead of incessantly trying to establish new bodies,
Husseini understood that it was necessary to improve the functioning of the existing bodies and to coordinate between them.
Likewise, Husseini sought to increase the sums of money sent
from outside the country – specifically, from the oil emirates – to
Orient House in order to enhance the status of the local institutions as against the national system in Gaza.

When this did not succeed, either, Husseini had a new idea – no
more top-down institutions and no more attempts to enlist

masses and governments outside Palestine; he now sought to mobilize the Jerusalem public to build institutions from the grassroots. He proposed establishing an East Jerusalem development authority, which would be a corporation in which every Palestinian inhabitant could buy a share for one Israeli shekel. The shareholders would choose a management that would also serve as a political–municipal representative of the Arab neighborhoods in East Jerusalem. In this way Husseini hoped to achieve several goals. First, he sought to establish a company with capital that could develop East Jerusalem and serve as a strong counterweight to the Israeli Jerusalem Development Corporation, which invested its resources in developing the Jewish part of Jerusalem. Second, Husseini wished to mobilize the larger Palestinian public to be active and involved in the fate of East Jerusalem. Third, Husseini hoped to turn the East Jerusalem development authority into a broad-based political representation. These hopes would not be achieved without mass Palestinian response (*Ha'aretz*, 9 Feb. 1996; *Kol Ha-Ir*, 9 Feb. 1996; Musallam, 1993: 17–18), which was not forthcoming. It was easier to mobilize the Palestinian masses for brief political protests against the Israeli occupation than to get them to participate in ongoing constructive action.

In parallel with his attempt to organize the East Jerusalem population from the grassroots, Husseini worked to consolidate a united front of political leadership in the city. He understood that Jerusalem is a frontier city, so he did not want to exacerbate the political differences within the Palestinian camp. Rather, he sought to rise above them. To this end he put together a representative panel with members from all Palestinian political groups. In addition to Husseini himself, the group included Hanan Ashrawi, Ziyad Abu-Zayad, and Dr. Sari Nusseibeh, all Fatah supporters; Dr. Muhammad Jadallah of the Democratic Front; Dr. Riad al-Malki, now independent but formerly a member of the Popular Front; Ghassan al-Khatib of the People's Party (the former Communist Party); and Sheikh Jamil Hamami of Hamas (*Ha'aretz*, 11 Feb. 1996). In practical terms, this was not the establishment of a new institution but rather cooperation between prominent political figures in the Jerusalem area who represented a spectrum of positions. The timing of the initiative was not a coincidence – it was close to the elections for the Palestinian Legislative Council. Husseini hoped that the panel would run as a consensus slate in the elections, but the Popular Front and Hamas objected and the initiative failed. The failure did not prevent Husseini from turning the panel into a permanent group that met with high-level foreign visitors in Orient House (*Ha'aretz*, 8 Sept. 1996; 28 Jan. 1997; *Kol Ha-Ir*, 29 March 1996). In practice, this group became, along with the members of the Palestinian Legislative Council elected from the Jerusalem area, including the Council's speaker, Abu-Ala, the political leadership of East Jerusalem.

Most of the attempts by the Palestinian establishment in Jerusalem to compete with the national leadership by establishing local institutions with "outside" or mass support were failures. Dr. Mahdi Abdul Hadi understood this as early as 1995, when he analyzed the shortcomings of Palestinian policy on Jerusalem and argued that there were contradictions between the different lines of policy that Palestinian leaders were declaring. Often, he said, leaders made commitments and statements that were not implemented, or declarations that harmed the Palestinian interest in Jerusalem. There was no coordination between the different arms of the Palestinian administration dealing with Jerusalem; on the local level there were no properly functioning planning and executive frameworks operating the Palestinian institutions in the city; the activities of Jordan and Saudi Arabia were not coordinated; the national administration in Gaza did not coordinate its actions with the local establishment in Orient House and with local officials; the Palestinian institutions in the city suffered from a lack of financial support from the central administration in Gaza, and planned institutions remained on paper. Dr. Abdul Hadi's conclusion was that without bodies to mobilize the Palestinian population in East Jerusalem, and without a framework to coordinate between the institutions operating in Jerusalem and between the establishment in Jerusalem and external elements – the central administration, the population of the West Bank and Gaza Strip, and the Arab and Islamic states – there was no point in going into the permanent status talks, since the Palestinians would suffer from a doubly inferior position (Abdul Hadi, 1996: 213–22).

During 1997, after its confrontations with the Netanyahu government, the national leadership gained support in Jerusalem at the expense of the local establishment. Since politics is often personal as well, the national and local leaderships soon developed low opinions of each other's ability to defend the Arab character of

East Jerusalem (Rubinstein, 23 June 1997). Politically, Arafat took Husseini's place as the director of protest and as the main address for negotiations on resolving the dispute. Arafat established a Jerusalem Committee under his chairmanship to serve as a national task force. It included ministers and the directors of national and municipal bodies operating in the Jerusalem area (*Al-Iyam*, Jan. and Feb. 1988). Arafat co-opted the local establishment into the committee, making it part of a larger framework under his direct control. While it is not the most efficient of groups, it has given Arafat a mechanism for controlling and supervising the local Jerusalem establishment and a way of circumventing the local leadership via national bodies. The national security, intelligence, and police forces have established themselves in the areas around Jerusalem that are under their control, and use those areas as bases for intensive activity within Jerusalem itself. The governor of the Jerusalem district in the Palestinian Ministry of the Interior, Jamal Othman Nasser, and the chief of the district police, Colonel Khalid Tantash, now played roles that had previously been played exclusively by Orient House. These included investigation of complaints and resolution of civil conflicts via compromise and arbitration, housing assistance for the indigent, issuing permits, project planning and budgeting, organizing ceremonies and public gatherings on Jerusalem, organizing protest activities against Israel (while interfering with similar initiatives from Orient House), encouraging illegal construction in unsettled areas of the city and its environs, investing in infrastructure, urban planning aimed at creating a contiguous Palestinian built-up area from East Jerusalem to the north, criminal investigations, information collection on real estate up for sale (in particular real estate on offer to Jews), and guarding public figures and facilities (*Ha'aretz*, 1 Feb. 1998, 9 Sept. 1998; Qashu'a and Cohen, 19 June 1998).

During the first half of 1997, Arafat also tried to gain control of Orient House's budget, demanding that all or most of it be funneled through the Palestinian Authority. Husseini refused, claiming that the money had been contributed specifically for Jerusalem and had been deposited with him personally. According to Husseini, the operating costs of the Palestinian institutions in East Jerusalem were some $5 million a month. A part of this sum came from the Palestinian Authority's budget (*Ha'aretz*, 9

Feb. 1996) and part from the World Islamic Association in Saudi
Arabia and from contributions raised personally by Husseini in
the oil states – for example, the $8 million collected in a fundrais-
ing campaign conducted by the Saudi television station MBC
(*Ha'aretz*, 17 June 1998). In his struggle to preserve freedom of
action and budgetary independence, Husseini made use of the
prohibition that Israel had made against the Palestinian Authority
operating in Jerusalem. Husseini was fearful that the Palestinian
Authority would skim a "commission" off his funds or at least use
control of the money as a way of applying political pressure on
him and restricting the freedom of action of the leadership in
Jerusalem. In response, Arafat delayed the transfer of funds to
Orient House, including for East Jerusalem projects funded by
Husseini's institution, creating a deficit for Orient House that
caused it difficulty in meeting its payroll (*Kol Ha-Ir*, 7 March
1997). Despite this, the local institution was able, at the beginning
of 1997, to receive a contribution of $19 million from Saudi
Arabia, earmarked for the construction and renovation of homes
in East Jerusalem, and another $5 million to cover Orient House's
running expenses (Rubinstein, 23 June 1997). The tension
between the local establishment and the national leadership frequently turned into personal tension between Arafat and
Husseini. This often came out in meetings of the Palestinian leadership, when the two traded harsh language and accusations about
who was responsible for the failure to allocate funds for various
East Jerusalem projects, or for Palestinian negligence in the struggle with Israel over control of East Jerusalem (Rubinstein, 20 July
1998).

As noted, the Jerusalem leadership had limited room for
maneuver compared with the Palestinian leadership in Gaza. The
only efficient way for the local political establishment to buttress
its position against Gaza was to receive grassroots public support
via the elections to the Palestinian Authority's Legislative Council
in January 1996. As elected officials, deriving their legitimacy
from personal, regional elections, and as members of the Legislative Council, the delegates from the Jerusalem area could present
themselves as a local leadership with a popular base of support
(the elections in Jerusalem are discussed in chapter 6).

An internal confrontation between the two Palestinian establishments, the local and the national, broke out at the beginning of

August 1996, when a member of the Legislative Council, Khatim Abd al-Qadir Eid, opened a parliamentary office in his home in Jerusalem's Bait Hanina neighborhood. Jerusalem viewed Eid's action as a violation of the Oslo accords, and Prime Minister Netanyahu's staff requested of Arafat that he order the office to close. Arafat complied and even ordered the Voice of Palestine not to cover Eid's activities. Eid, for his part, ignored Arafat's command and even refused to report to the Palestinian police station in Jericho for the purpose of signing a commitment to close the office. The Israel police served Eid with a warning demanding that he provide, within 24 hours, an explanation for his actions. If no satisfactory explanation was forthcoming, the minister of internal security would shut down his office immediately, the warning stated. Under pressure from the Palestinian administration in Gaza, Eid declared in writing that the office in his home was a private one and had no connection to the Palestinian Authority or Legislative Council, and that he had no intention of violating the law (*Ha'aretz*, 2 Aug. 1996, 5 Aug. 1996, 8 Aug. 1996, 11 Aug. 1996, 12 Aug. 1996).

This was more of an internal Palestinian conflict between the parliamentary group in Jerusalem and the central administration in Gaza than a conflict between Eid and Israel. It was but one link in a series of confrontations between the national and local leaderships that took place in the spring and summer of 1996 and at the beginning of 1998 against the background of attempts by Fatah activists and the Jerusalem representatives in the Legislative Council to turn up the heat on Israel in Jerusalem, in opposition to the policy of the central Palestinian regime and its executive arm (Cohen, 29 April 1998). By the time the Eid affair came to an end the Palestinian political system realized that it was very difficult for a local element to act against the central regime on a long-term basis, especially if the independent activity puts the national leadership in conflict with Israel. In other words, the conflict between Israel and the Palestinians in Jerusalem broke out when the two central establishments faced off against each other alongside the local institutions, as happened later when the Western Wall Tunnel was opened and during the protests against Israel's construction of a new Jewish neighborhood, Har Homa, on land claimed by Palestinians in southern Jerusalem. In contrast, during the Ras al-Amud crisis of the summer of 1997, the central

administration was apathetic about the demonstrations, commercial and school strikes, and other protest activity organized by
Orient House. Despite the local establishment's attempts to esca-
late the protest, it remained small in scope, decentralized, and
without direction and coordination. This was the result of actions
taken by the central leadership in Gaza, which preferred to deal
with the issue through diplomatic channels with the U.S. (*Al-
Quds*, 10 Sept. 1997, 29 Sept. 1997, 30 Sept. 1997, 26 Oct. 1997;
Rubinstein, 18 Sept. 1997, 22 Sept. 1997).

Palestinian competition with Israel in Jerusalem is accompanied by an ever-present fear of unilateral Israeli actions that will
tilt the balance against the Palestinians. The opening position of
the local leadership was that, so long as no permanent settlement
had been signed, Israel would certainly try to modify the situation
in Jerusalem in its failure. The Palestinian leadership in Jerusalem
saw evidence of this in the restrictions that have been placed on
the activities of Palestinian institutions in the city since 1993. Even
the occasional closure that Israel has imposed on the West Bank
since 1995 in response to increased Hamas terrorism within Israel
has been seen by the Palestinians as being motivated more by
political rather than security requirements. Israel, they believe,
wishes to cut Jerusalem off from its social and economic hinterland and detract from its status as the capital of the West Bank and
as the lynchpin linking the southern and northern West Bank
(*Ha'aretz*, 1 June 1994). When a Likud-led right-wing religious–
nationalist government came to power in Israel in 1996 there were
additional Israeli actions such as the construction of new Jewish
neighborhoods, Jewish settlers entering homes in Arab neighborhoods, and the withdrawal of residence status from some Palestinians living in Jerusalem (Abu-Arafa, 1985; *Al-Hayat*, 14 June
1994; al-Nakhal, 1993, 1994; *Al-Quds*, 18 Jan. 1995; Faisal
Husseini on the Voice of Palestine, 18 Jan. 1994, 19 Jan. 1994,
FBIS). The Palestinians maintained that the arena should not be
left vacant for Israel. The Palestinians were indeed the weaker
party in the field and at the negotiating table, but just as they had
brought Israel to recognize the PLO and to discuss Jerusalem with
it, so they would succeed in obtaining sovereignty in East Jerusalem, thanks to a well-managed and assertive struggle that would
impose outcomes on Israel (Husseini, 1996).

6

AN EAST JERUSALEM POLITICAL PROFILE

Public opinion

Public opinion polls have been conducted on a regular basis in the West Bank and Gaza Strip since September 1993 and provide a political profile of the inhabitants of East Jerusalem.

At the beginning of the 1980s, as PLO officials began to focus on the diplomatic process as a means of achieving a Palestinian state, they became interested in the opinions of the Palestinians in the territories. This interest was further spurred by the Intifada, the popular and spontaneous uprising that broke out at the end of 1987, during which the PLO found itself competing with Hamas for the hearts and minds of the territories' inhabitants. The inhabitants themselves became familiar with polls through their long-standing and close acquaintance with Israeli democracy and public opinion, as well as with representatives of international diplomacy and the media. Furthermore, there was the PLO's transformation from an organization representing the Palestinians into an organization that headed a regime, a process that opened an ongoing dialogue between the Palestinian public in the territories and its political leadership. As in all political systems, the Palestinian leadership aspires to enlist public support and respond to public expectations, while the public seeks to maximize its influence over decision makers.

This interest produced something unique in the Arab world – a series of regular opinion polls, conducted monthly in the West Bank and Gaza Strip since September 1993 by the Center for Palestinian Research and Studies (CPRS). The polls survey a representative sample of the population of the territories, including Jerusalem.

At the end of 1993 the population of the territories, according to Israel's Central Bureau of Statistics, was 1.084 million, not including East Jerusalem, while the Palestinian Central Bureau of Statistics counted 2.19 million Palestinians in the territories, including East Jerusalem (*Ha'aretz*, 8 March 1995). The sample taken for the polls is not of a fixed size, but it is large relative to the population, averaging 1,223 adults over the age of 18 in the polls conducted from 1994 to 1996. All the polls were conducted via personal interviews in the homes of the subjects. The CPRS polls are national rather than municipal. I have isolated the data for Jerusalem for the years 1994 and 1995, which I have compared with the national findings. The margins of error for Jerusalem are much wider than the margins of error for all the territories, since the sample in Jerusalem is small. However, since the discussion below is a comparative one and covers two years, and since the intent is to sketch a political profile of the Palestinian inhabitants of Jerusalem rather than to aim for percentage point precision, the surveys paint a valuable general picture.

The discussion below is based first and foremost on CPRS's findings, but they will be placed alongside polls conducted by the Jerusalem Media and Communication Centre (JMCC). While there are differences in both the methodology and results of the polls conducted by these two institutes, the overall picture they provide is similar. Elections can be seen as active political behavior and are in fact the most reliable and comprehensive of public opinion polls. For this reason, I will also examine to what extent the results of the elections in Jerusalem manifest the trends that appeared in the public opinion polls of the preceding two years.

Political support: organizations and parties

In general, the CPRS polls of 1994–5 show that Fatah, the central faction in the PLO, was weaker in East Jerusalem than in the rest of the territories; however, it was never supported by less than one-third of the public. This means that Fatah had a solid base of support in Jerusalem during this period, albeit a smaller one than elsewhere. In comparison with the movement's other branches, the local Fatah leadership in Jerusalem is more independent – it has its own international standing and financial resources. Furthermore, since Israeli law applies to East Jerusalem, the institutions of the Palestinian state-in-the-making have had trouble functioning in the city. On the eve of the elections for the Palestinian Authority's Legislative Council and presidency, Fatah made an effort to enlarge its support, and in fact at the end of 1995 support for Fatah in Jerusalem passed the 40 per cent mark.

During 1994–95, support in East Jerusalem for the coalition that had voted in favor of the Oslo accords in PLO forums (Fatah, FIDA, and the People's Party) was solid and ranged from 35 to 40 per cent. From July 1995 onward the People's Party and FIDA ceased to have any statistically significant existence in the city, leaving Fatah as the sole standard-bearers for the pro-Oslo camp.

In contrast with the solid support for Fatah in East Jerusalem, support for the opposition (Hamas, Palestinian Islamic Jihad, the Popular Front for the Liberation of Palestine, and the Democratic Front for the Liberation of Palestine) was smaller, variable, changeable, and was largely a protest vote against the ruling elite. Furthermore, while the coalition fully exploited its base of support in Jerusalem, the opposition was unable to mobilize additional support from among those who backed independents or "none of the above" (these categories are discussed below). The opposition has ceaselessly criticized the Oslo accords, emphasizing in particular that the PLO leadership has not stood firm on Jerusalem. Yet this has not resonated with Jerusalem's inhabitants. On the contrary, the Palestinians of Jerusalem have been skeptical of the opposition.

The opposition's core support in Jerusalem does not come from Hamas partisans. With the exception of October 1995, during the entire two-year period under discussion here, Hamas was weaker in East Jerusalem than in the rest of the country. Support for Hamas was concentrated in the rural areas around Hebron, Bethlehem, and Jerusalem. The central West Bank cities (Bethlehem, Jerusalem, and Ramallah) have the greatest support for the independent nationalists, a category that is discussed below (Ross & Sa'id, 1995). East Jerusalem is a Palestinian frontier city under Israeli control, and also Islam's third-holiest city. But in the large picture, Hamas has no solid, consistent base of support among the Palestinian public in Jerusalem.

Support for unaffiliated opponents of the current political establishment is measured by these surveys under the category "independents." These are organizations or persons with either Islamicist or nationalist ideology who do not belong to a political organization such as Hamas or Fatah. Support for this category may well reflect aversion to, reservations about, and apparently also repugnance for the establishment rather than positive support for these candidates. The level of support for "independents" in Jerusalem in 1994–95 was high, but it was not solid support – these were clearly protest votes. In contrast, support for "independents" on the national level was more or less fixed, at a lower level – generally a much lower level – than in Jerusalem. As the elections for the Palestinian Authority Legislative Council approached, voters became more concerned with finding effective representatives. Support for the politics of protest declined. Some of the protestors switched their support to Fatah, while those who did not wish to participate in the elections or who rejected them switched from the independents to the organized opposition.

Support for "none of the above" denotes distaste for all the political forces on the Palestinian map. Support for "none of the above" in Jerusalem is highly variable on a monthly basis. On a national level, support for "none of the above" is lower. This provides further confirmation of the previous conclusion that there is a floating protest vote that leans towards the opposition whose potential has not been fully exploited and institutionalized in Jerusalem. The solid base of support for "none of the above" is based on distaste and repugnance for everything on offer in the political market, while the peripheral support for "none of the above" has tended to indicate voters floating between the opposition and the independents.

Support for presidential candidates

The polls also measured support for the Palestinian Authority's president, Arafat, and for his chief critics, who were seen as potential rival candidates in the elections. The most prominent figure in the Islamic opposition was Sheikh Ahmad Yassin, leader of the Hamas. A prominent leader of the secular–Marxist left was Dr. George Habash, the chairman of the Popular Front for the Liberation of Palestine. Habash advocated the staged plan of 1974 (founding a Palestinian state in the 1967 territories as the first stage in "liberating" all of Palestine) and a Greater Palestine ideology. Another potential presidential candidate was Dr. Haidar Abd al-Shafi, chairman of the Palestinian delegation to the Madrid conference and to the bilateral talks with Israel in Washington. He supports reaching an accommodation with Israel but not Arafat's concessions. Abd al-Shafi is also a sharp critic of Arafat's methods. At the end of 1994 he founded the Movement for Democratic Construction, which enlisted support for the independents.

According to CPRS surveys, Arafat's support in Jerusalem rose from 25 per cent in November 1994 to 48.1 per cent in December 1995. On the national level, however, support for Arafat was much higher, 44.2 per cent in November 1994, reaching 68.5 per cent on the eve of the December 1995 elections. In contrast, support for Sheikh Yassin in Jerusalem was lower, ranging between 20.8 per cent in November 1994 and 14.3 per cent in October 1995. Yassin's backers did not succeed in broadening his circle of support in any significant way or for any length of time, while Arafat's support grew significantly. It should be stressed, however, that Arafat improved his standing much more on the national level than he did in Jerusalem.

In general, the Popular Front's Habash has enjoyed greater support in Jerusalem than in the rest of the territories, as has Abd al-Shafi. There was more support for Abd al-Shafi, however, both on the local and on the national level, because Abd al-Shafi was perceived as a constructive critic. Nevertheless, the candidacy of Abd al-Shafi, who lives in Gaza, did not captivate the Palestinians in Jerusalem. The major pattern of protest in Jerusalem was a large measure of support for "other" or "none of the above." In other words, the protest vote in Jerusalem is not Islamic–extremist but rather, for the most part, nationalist.

While full data on the educational level of the inhabitants of East Jerusalem has not yet been published, one cannot ignore the link between education and political criticism that appears time and again in the polls. According to CPRS surveys, support for nationalist independents is widespread in the Jerusalem area and higher among the educated and professionals, whereas support for Islamicist independents is concentrated in the villages in the central and southern West Bank and comes from people who are less educated and younger (Ross & Sa'id, 1995). Furthermore, the level of post-secondary education in the Jerusalem district was particularly high among those who participated in the exit polls in the 1996 elections: 31.8 per cent as opposed to 20 per cent (or less) in the other districts. In contrast, the percentage of those with a complete or partial elementary school education was 15.2 per cent in Jerusalem, but twice that in the other electoral districts (Awartani, 1997: 65).

The national figures in the CPRS surveys point to a close link between educational level and criticism of the Palestinian Authority and Arafat. The higher their education, the more critical the Palestinians in the territories are of Arafat and his movement, Fatah. So, for example, in November 1994, a full 49 per cent of voters who had not finished high school supported Arafat, but only 34 per cent of those with undergraduate degrees and 33.3 per cent of those with advanced degrees supported him. Support of Sheikh Yassin also varies with education – among voters who had not finished high school he garnered 18.7 per cent, as opposed to 6.75 per cent among those with advanced degrees. The college-educated showed relatively high levels of support for Abd al-Shafi, 13.3 per cent, whereas only 6 per cent of voters who had not finished high school supported him. This same survey showed correlation between low educational level and support for Fatah – 44.5 per cent of the voters who had not completed high school supported Fatah, as opposed to 31.3 per cent of those with undergraduate degrees. It is interesting to note that, among Palestinians in the territories, the lower the educational level the higher the optimism. Higher education makes Palestinians in the territories more pessimistic. Naturally, support for the continuation of the negotiations with Israel was higher among the poorly educated optimistic supporters of the establishment than among the more educated and alienated pessimists, who leaned towards the opposition.

Support for Arafat among the employed was no higher than among the unemployed. The long closure imposed on the West Bank and Gaza Strip from the end of January 1995 worsened the economic condition of the Palestinians in the territories and increased the rate of unemployment. According to CPRS surveys, the unemployment rate in the refugee camps, villages, and towns was higher than in the large cities, and lower among those with academic degrees than among those with only an elementary education. Unemployment was lower in the central West Bank than elsewhere, apparently because many Palestinians from the Jerusalem metropolitan area, unlike their compatriots in other parts of the West Bank, were able to continue to work in the Jewish sector. The generally higher educational level of the inhabitants of East

Jerusalem was undoubtedly a factor as well. Even so, the city's Palestinians were highly critical of the Palestinian Authority. This
was not a result of the economic situation. The Palestinian
Authority's and Arafat's most consistent supporters were the
poorly educated residents of the refugee camps, villages, and
towns, where unemployment was most severe. Nationally, the
statement that the economic situation had improved since the
Oslo agreements was supported by relatively large percentages in
the Gaza Strip, and this means that people answered the question
not in accordance with their economic situation, but rather in
accordance with their political situation. Since the Oslo accords,
the economic position of the residents of the Gaza Strip has gotten
worse and their standard of living has declined, but they feel better
about their lives and are more confident politically.

Candidates for vice-president

The post of vice-president of the Palestinian Authority is an ima-
ginary one, since no such position exists in either the PLO or the
Palestinian Authority. Arafat has consistently refused to delegate
even a part of his authority. The conductors of the CPRS survey
invented the job in order to examine who the Palestinians in the
territories see as being second in rank to Arafat. At the end of 1994
and beginning of 1995 no one person was seen by Palestinian
public opinion to be Arafat's deputy. His image overshadowed the
entire Palestinian political system and dwarfed all the other political figures, even when people were asked to choose Arafat's
deputy and not his replacement. The protest vote in East Jerusalem led to more than 50 per cent support for "other" or for "no
opinion."

Political positions on ongoing issues

As might have been expected, support for the Oslo agreements
was lower in Jerusalem than in the rest of the Palestinian territories. East Jerusalem's removal from the jurisdiction of the Palestinian Authority lowered the expectations of the residents of East
Jerusalem as to the likelihood of finding a satisfactory solution to
their problem. The Palestinians in Jerusalem, more than those
living elsewhere, rejected the assumption that the historic
achievements of the Palestinian national movement in the

negotiations with Israel demonstrated that it would in the future be able to achieve an acceptable solution in Jerusalem as well. Even in December 1995, on the eve of Israel's withdrawal from the West Bank and at the height of the preparations for the elections, the Palestinians in Jerusalem were less optimistic about the future, felt relatively less secure, and were more concerned and skeptical than the Palestinians of the territories as a whole about the present and future.

Evaluating the Palestinian Authority

The residents of East Jerusalem gave the Palestinian Authority a lower grade than did the Palestinians of the territories as a whole in all categories, or answered "don't know" more than their countrymen did. At first, the negative view of the accomplishments of the Palestinian Authority was firmer and less forgiving than in the rest of the country, but at the beginning of 1995 there was a notable drop in the assertiveness and critical attitude of the Palestinians of East Jerusalem, and positive attitudes to the Palestinian Authority's accomplishments increased.

Armed actions by the Islamic organizations

In the period between January 1995 and March 1996, Hamas and Islamic Jihad launched a series of terrorist attacks against Israeli civilian targets. In January 1995 suicide bombers attacked the bus station at the Beit Lid junction between Tel Aviv and Haifa, and in July and August there were similar attacks on buses in the Tel Aviv suburb, Ramat Gan, and in Jerusalem. In February and March 1996 there was a series of four horrible attacks. Some 100 people were killed and 200 injured; 47 of the dead and 162 of the wounded were in Jerusalem. Israel's major responses were the imposition of a total closure on the territories of the Palestinian Authority and pressure on Arafat to take aggressive steps against extremist Islamic organizations.

At the beginning of 1995 there was a great deal of ambivalence among the Palestinians of East Jerusalem about Islamic terrorism, much more so than in the rest of the Palestinian territories. From the summer of 1995 onwards, however, the East Jerusalem public stood firmly against terrorist attacks, more so than Palestinians nationwide. The change in opinion was apparently due to the fact that the extremist Islamic organizations had no firm hold in East

Jerusalem, and because Palestinians from East Jerusalem had been among the victims of the terrorist attacks (al-Shikaki, 1997a: 149; Shikaki, 1996: 9–15).

"Soft" protest in Jerusalem

The people of East Jerusalem were very conscious of two things – that discussion of their future had been suspended, and that the Palestinian Authority was officially absent from the city. The Palestinian Authority's successes on the national level did not seem particularly relevant to the residents of East Jerusalem, and they demanded that the Palestinian Authority produce gains on the local level. More than in the rest of the country, the Palestinian residents of East Jerusalem were firm in their negative attitude towards the Palestinian Authority's achievements. The people of East Jerusalem were not seeking to protest for its own sake – they wanted a real change in their status. In other words, the contest for the floating and protest vote in East Jerusalem was fought on the issue of who could work most effectively to improve the lot of the city's residents. Even though many of these did not think much of the Palestinian Authority's accomplishments, its prospects for persuading the floating and protest voters to join its camp improved as the elections approached. The Palestinian Authority's gains in its dispute with Israel over the election arrangements in Jerusalem strengthened its position in the city and made the people of East Jerusalem more willing to participate in the elections. The consistent gains in support for Arafat and Fatah on the national level at the end of 1994 and beginning of 1995 also led many people in East Jerusalem to the conclusion that, despite their reservations, there was no alternative to Arafat and his associates, and that it would be better to produce the desired change via the existing Palestinian establishment.

East Jerusalem is a capital-in-waiting for the Palestinians, and every capital loses some of its significance when its nation's entire political establishment lives and works outside it. For this reason, the Palestinian Authority has sought to penetrate and operate in East Jerusalem. Israel has tried, for its part, to frustrate these initiatives or keep them to a minimum. Beyond the national aspect, the ruling coalition in the Palestinian Authority, and Fatah in particular, had political–organizational interests in penetrating East

Jerusalem and establishing a foothold there. The weakness of the opposition in Jerusalem tempted them because they knew that broadening the Palestinian Authority's power and legitimacy in Jerusalem would reinforce their regime on the national level. Up until mid-1995 they had only limited success at this, but this grew after their gains on the subject of the polling in East Jerusalem, and as the elections themselves approached.

Political behavior: the elections to the Palestinian Authority's Legislative Council and presidency

The elections to the Palestinian Authority's Legislative Council and presidency, held in January 1996, were the most important political event since the signing of the Declaration of Principles between Israel and the Palestinians in 1993. For the first time in the history of the Palestinian national movement Palestinians chose their own political leaders (elections in the West Bank and Gaza Strip had, since 1967, been limited to municipal governments, student governments at the universities and to labor and professional organizations). This was a grant of legitimacy both to the Palestinian Authority and the PLO. The elections were a constitutive event for other reasons as well – they changed the basis of legitimacy for the Palestinian national movement and the division of powers in the political institutions, and marked the arrival of a new political order. The PLO's institutions were never elected; instead, they were based on an intra-Arab, international, and Palestinian consensus, and on the material resources that the organization oversaw and allocated. Membership in political institutions was determined via consensual quotas for political–ideological groups that were members of the PLO's ruling coalition, or via political appointments by the ruling PLO establishment. Until the establishment of the Palestinian Authority, the institutions of the PLO, the national umbrella organization, enjoyed preeminence over all the local institutions that developed in the West Bank and Gaza Strip and in the smaller Palestinian diasporas. Since Israel prevented the PLO's official entry into Palestine, the outside had to run the "inside" by remote control.

The 1996 elections opened a new stage in the politicization of the Palestinian public. For the first time ever, elections gave the Palestinian political system the legitimacy that comes from representatives being directly elected by the public. It is important to note that the previous basis of legitimacy did not completely disappear – it was only weakened. The dual foundation of legitimacy was reflected in an official duality of institutions – the PLO and the Palestinian Authority. This raised the question of priority – did the high legitimacy of elections place the Palestinian Authority above the PLO, at least in value terms? But the political platform of the Palestinian Authority and decisions of the PLO Executive Committee explicitly stated that "the Authority draws its legitimacy from the PLO, which is to be the source of political and constitutional power" (*Davar*, 31 May 1994).

The entry of "outside" PLO officials into the "inside" and their contesting of the elections dulled the urgency of the question and created a certain amount of congruency between the PLO and the Palestinian Authority. The weekly meetings of the "Palestinian Leadership" were demonstrations of this new reality. This forum is composed of the members of the PLO Executive Committee, the members of the executive branch of the Palestinian Authority, the chiefs of the security and police forces, and the negotiators with Israel. It was established in order to circumvent the problem that could have arisen if either the PLO's Executive Committee or the Palestinian Authority's cabinet functioned as the main decision-making forum.

The Palestinian agenda also underwent considerable change. In the past, ideological–political debates took up most of the Palestinians' attention, and the military and political confrontation with Israel served as a tool for nation-building (Sayigh, 1997). The establishment of the Palestinian Authority put more prosaic matters on the agenda, such as the operation of political institutions and the use of the organs of government as the means to build the nation. The issues that had preoccupied the Palestinian establishment in the past and which nevertheless remained on the agenda took on a new cast. The debate within the Palestinian establishment, and the debate between it and Israel, has focused less on overarching questions such as the permanent borders of the Palestinian state and the relation between national goals and the means used to achieve them, and more on a series of very well-defined issues such as arrangements for the elections, the placement of Israeli policemen at the border crossings leading from the Palestinian Authority to Egypt and Jordan, entry permits to Israel, and the operation of cooperative security arrangements with Israel. Even the definition of the nation-state has changed. In the past there was identity between the national movement – the PLO as an organization – and the definition of the nation and nationalism; according to the PLO charter, every Palestinian was a natural member of the organization. Since 1994 the definition of the nation and the state has come to correspond more and more to the population living in the West Bank and Gaza Strip. An opening has been created for distinguishing between the nation-state and Palestinian citizenship therein and a Palestinian national identity that is ethnic–cultural and historical at base, while at the same time maintaining a strong link to a defined territory, Palestine (*al-Bilad*, 25 March 1996).

The agreement between Israel and the PLO in September 1993 opened the door to the PLO and allowed it to make an official entry into a land in which it aspired to establish Palestinian self-government. In practice, the PLO institutions that remained "outside" evaporated, and the same happened to political figures who refused to enter the Palestinian Authority territory under the aegis of the Oslo accords. In the transition period between the signing of the Declaration of Principles in September 1993 and the elections in January 1996, the period in which the PLO establishment moved from "outside" to "inside," the PLO enjoyed an advantage in the contest for leadership with local forces. The PLO assigned to itself the glory of the historic achievement, and the agreements with Israel allowed it to establish a provisional regime for the transition period. This regime (the Palestinian Authority) was constructed on the superiority of the "outsiders" who had recently arrived, and on the exploitation of contention between different social and political groups on the "inside." This allowed it to place the local forces in the places that the ruling elite assigned it. The Palestinian Authority's ruling elite enjoyed no small advantage when the election campaign began (al-Shikaki and Qasis, 1997; Klein, 1997).

Willingness to participate in elections

The elections to the Palestinian Authority Legislative Council were held even before the Israeli army had retreated entirely from the West Bank and Gaza Strip, yet the Palestinians were still very keen on participating in them. Most of the population understood

the historic importance of the elections, and participation was perceived as a national duty and a part of the struggle for independence. Beyond national and historical consciousness there was also
lively democratic consciousness, a product of the population's
painful contact with Israeli democracy. From the very first, the
elections were perceived as a national event and not a matter of
concern only to the ruling elite, and the same was true of voter
registration. Registering was a prerequisite for voting and, had
there not been widespread participation, the elections would have
lost some of their national value. This was precisely the intention
of various opposition groups who viewed the elections as a stage-
managed show by the ruling elite aimed at legitimizing the "capitulation," as they termed it, inherent in the Oslo accords. These
opposition groups failed, however, to win broad support for their
boycott of registration. In the CPRS poll of December 1995, the
percentage of those intending to participate in the elections passed
the 70 per cent mark, in Jerusalem and in the territories as a whole.
Moreover, a full 75 per cent of Hamas supporters viewed elections as the proper way of choosing a Palestinian leadership
(Shikaki, 1996: 27). The Palestinian Authority was not blamed for
the special election procedures in Jerusalem and the arrangements
had no effect on the willingness of the inhabitants of East Jerusalem to participate in the poll. Furthermore, the inhabitants of East
Jerusalem seem to have expected that they would be able to
change the city's status with their votes.

East Jerusalem was part of general Palestinian trends in other
ways as well. The people of East Jerusalem responded much like
Palestinians in the rest of the territories in citing the factors that
would determine their choice of candidates. According to CPRS
surveys conducted in October 1995, willingness to vote for
women was about the same in Jerusalem as throughout the territories (74.7 per cent on average – 78.1 per cent in Bethlehem, 80.8
per cent in Tulkarem, 80 per cent in Jericho, and 60.7 per cent in
the north and central Gaza Strip). As in the rest of the territories,
political affiliation and holding an academic appointment did not
play an important role in the choice of candidates in Jerusalem.
Residents of East Jerusalem placed less weight on family connections. There was no clear picture of the religious factor – the
extreme Islamic groups were relatively weak in Jerusalem, and
Christians were allotted two of the Jerusalem District's seats.

The positions taken by the residents of East Jerusalem were affected by the city's status as a frontier city. In a CPRS survey conducted in December 1995, the residents of East Jerusalem cited participation in the struggle as a criterion that would help determine their choice of candidate. This was higher than in the rest of the territories (39.7 per cent as opposed to 26.6 per cent). Furthermore, in Jerusalem the percentage support for candidates who favored the Oslo agreements was one of the lowest in the country, even though it stood at 79 per cent. In the Gaza Strip, for example, support for this criterion reached 94.4 per cent. It should not be concluded from this, however, that support for candidates who opposed the Oslo agreements was higher in Jerusalem than elsewhere. In Jerusalem only 10 per cent of respondents to the survey said that they would vote only for opponents of the Oslo accords, the same percentage as in Jenin, a Fatah stronghold and the first West Bank city that the Israeli army evacuated in the period just before the elections.

Election procedures, slates of candidates, preparations, and propaganda

The electoral system was determined after a debate between those who supported a first-past-the-post constituency system in which votes would be for individual candidates and those who supported nationwide proportional representation in which votes would be cast for a party slate. The supporters of the first method pointed out that the largest political organization would sweep the poll and would gain a decisive majority in the Palestinian institutions. According to the advocates of the second system, granting representation to the maximum number of political streams was a more important principle than the regime's ability to make decisions, and more appropriate to the heterogeneity of Palestinian society. The debate was not between factions, but rather crossed political boundaries, especially within the Fatah organization (al-Shikaki and Qasis, 1997).

In the end, a system of personal voting was adopted. The vote for president was personal and first-past-the-post, with each voter required to choose one of the two candidates. The elections for the Legislative Council, held simultaneously, had a regional element. The West Bank and Gaza Strip were divided into 16 electoral districts, with each district assigned several seats. The number of polling stations was set at 1,696, of which 165 were in the Jerusalem district; only five were placed in territory that Israel had annexed. Voters were required to mark the names of a number of candidates equal to the number of seats allocated to their district. The Jerusalem District received seven seats, with two being reserved for Christian candidates. This system reduced the importance of political movements and turned attention to the individual competing candidates, in contrast with the system of political and appointment quotas practiced in the PLO. Further-more, the PLO was run by consensus (consociational) politics, and in general there was no open competition between the differ-ent organizations, but rather negotiations between their leader-ships for the achievement of an accommodation.

The Palestinian Authority elections instead created competi-tion, and this innovation was accepted because, from the point of view of the PLO's constituent movements, the system chosen solved the problem they had been struggling with since 1993 – whether to dissolve themselves and turn into political parties in every sense of the term, or to preserve their existing structures and allow their members to run in the elections. The personal–regional system also solved the problem of the inhabitants of the West Bank and Gaza Strip who had not taken an active role in the PLO establishment and who were unsure how they would be able to contest elections in which only political parties participated. While the system made it possible for several candidates to orga-nize as a slate in which candidates lent each other mutual support, the elections were nevertheless personal and this made the phe-nomenon a marginal one. The system did not have antagonism built into it, nor was it amenable to a campaign by one camp to defeat another, mostly because the large number of candidates dissipated tension and competition. Furthermore, the system opened the door to independent candidates. From the point of view of the "internals," who had little acquaintance with the estab-lishment "outside," this was, of course, an advantage, but from the point of view of the established movements it was the salient dis-advantage of the method. The Popular Front for the Liberation of Palestine, the Democratic Front for the Liberation of Palestine, and Hamas opposed participating in the elections and were thus forced to decide what their attitude would be to candidates who shared their ideologies but who had disassociated themselves from these movements and entered the race on an independent–

opposition platform. In contrast, Fatah had to cope with hundreds of independent candidates who did not accept their non-inclusion in the official Fatah slate.

The 16 voting districts were drawn as the election approached. The Jerusalem district was defined not only as an electoral district, but also as an administrative district in the Palestinian Authority's Ministry of the Interior. The administrative district was headed by Attorney Jamil Othman Nasser, a member of Fatah and an Arafat loyalist. The district offices were located in Abu-Dis, a suburb that is not within Jerusalem's municipal boundaries. The district was in practice composed of those areas that had been part of the Jordanian Jerusalem district, except for the part that had been annexed to Israel. The district stretches from the outskirts of Ramallah in the north to the edge of Bethlehem in the south, and from the northwestern corner of the Dead Sea to the Green Line (the border with the State of Israel) in the West (*Ha'aretz*, 19 Jan. 1996). Defining the Jerusalem electoral district to be the same as the Palestinian administrative district, rather than using the municipal boundary established by Israel in 1967, made it possible to hold elections in East Jerusalem and find pragmatic and functional solutions to the demands of Israel and the Palestinians. The territory of the electoral district was much larger than the municipal area of Jerusalem and included the city. Israel wanted the major part of the elections to be held outside its territory, while the Palestinian Authority planned for them to be held in the city, despite the annexation. This arrangement had internal Palestinian significance as well, because including Jerusalem in a larger district made it easier for the Palestinian Authority to cope with East Jerusalem criticism of the national regime. In this way Jerusalem and Gaza became closer to each other.

The negotiations with Israel on the right of the residents of East Jerusalem to vote and be elected produced a new order: Palestinians who were citizens of Israel were not allowed to participate in the elections, but residents of East Jerusalem were allowed to vote and to be elected as well. Those who wanted to be candidates had to have a dual address, in Jerusalem and outside it. The second address did not have to be a residence. The candidate was required to prove a link to some location outside Jerusalem, for the purpose of residence, work, or business (*Ha'aretz*, 16 July 1995).

According to the Palestinian election law, approved in December 1995, the number of seats in the Legislative Council up for election was 89, including the president of the Palestinian Authority. At first, the Palestinians demanded that Israel agree to a council of between 130 members (the number of members that had been proposed for the Palestine National Council, the PLO's representative body, after a structural reform in the mid-1980s) and 180 (the number of seats allotted to the "internals" on the Palestine National Council, but which had never been filled and which were not included in the quorum of members, which reached 486 at its last session). Israel proposed between 30 and 40 members, so as to give the Legislative Council a local character, rather than the parliamentary character that the PLO wished it to have. In the end the Palestinians agreed to make do with 89 members. The Israeli achievement was disconnecting the number of members in the Legislative Council from the number of members in the Palestine National Council, while the Palestinians gained a council that had more members than was customary for the legislative bodies of cities or districts.

At first Jerusalem was allotted six seats, one of them reserved for a Christian. At the beginning of January 1996 this was increased to seven, with two seats for Christians. Christians were reserved five seats on a nationwide basis – two in Jerusalem, two in Bethlehem, and one in Ramallah. Since the Christians made up approximately two per cent of the Palestinian population in the territories, their representation in the Legislative Council was about three times what strict proportionality would have provided. For political reasons, and in order to demonstrate the multicultural character of the Palestinian Authority, one seat in the Nablus district was reserved for a member of the miniscule Samaritan community. In contrast, no seats were reserved for women. There were five women candidates each in the Jerusalem and Han Yunis (Gaza Strip) districts, while in the rest of the districts there were between one and three women (*Al-Quds*, 16 Dec. 1995, 6 Jan. 1996; Ukal and al-Surani, 19 Jan. 1996). The assignment of seats to the electoral districts was not in accordance with population or eligible voters. In the Jerusalem district each seat represented 11,309 eligible voters, whereas in North Gaza, each seat represented 8,949 eligible voters; in Gaza City each seat represented 10,414 voters and in Tubas, in the northern West Bank,

16,349 voters (*Al-Nas Wa-al Intikhabat, Al-Quds*, 20 Jan. 1996;
Ganim, 1996; Shikaki and Kasis, 1997).

About 40 per cent of the total population of Jerusalem registered to vote, the same as in Ramallah and Rafiah, and the same as
the national average (Ukal and al-Surani, 19 Jan. 1996). The division of seats among the electoral districts was determined by a set
of factors that was not sufficiently transparent. These were the
size of the population in each district (so that the elected council
would have the same regional cross-section as the population),
the number of registered voters in each district, and "other criteria," as Sa'ib Ariqat, the Palestinian Authority minister in charge
of the elections, put it (*Ha'aretz*, 4 Dec. 1995). It is reasonable to
assume that among these unstated considerations was the strength
of Fatah in each district, and each region's status and national
importance.

Fatah candidates were selected in a two-stage process. Primaries were conducted in the district branches of the movement,
after which a placement committee was convened, composed of
members chosen by Fatah's two leading "inside" institutions, its
Central Committee and Revolutionary Council. This committee
decided which seat each candidate would contest, meaning that
the primary results were in reality merely advisory.

The placement committee was set up in order to balance
between the various elements that Arafat wanted to see represented in the Council. First, Arafat was anxious to bring in the
young leadership that had born the burden of running the Intifada. This group had gained the public's sympathy when it fought
Israel, and when some of its members spent time in Israeli jails or
were deported. This group was not closely linked to national politics, and its close ties to the common man and its collective, clean
image stood in sharp contrast to the corrupt image of the members of the PLO establishment, who were perceived as conde-
scending and distant from the public. Second, Arafat and the
Fatah leadership wanted to construct a slate that would represent a
range of social strata and political classes. This was aimed at
enhancing their own representative power and legitimacy, so that
they could maneuver politically between different and opposing
elements. He wanted to place activists from the field alongside
known political figures, members of the establishment, representatives of ethnic communities and minorities, and the heads of

notable families (Rubinstein, 25 Dec. 1995). Third, by doing this, Arafat sought to retain control of the institutions of the Fatah movement during its transition into a political party, and to influence the composition of the parliament. Arafat knew that by controlling who Fatah's candidates were he could minimize the party's and the parliament's oversight of the executive organizations that he headed. Nevertheless, it was important to him to give the elections a democratic and representative appearance, and this led to the decision on the two-stage process of putting together the movement's recommended slate.

Eighteen candidates ran in the Jerusalem primaries, competing for the votes of the city's approximately 400 Fatah activists (members of the Fatah party apparatus, popularly called *al-tanzim* – "the organization"). The top five spots were won by: Khatim Abd al-Qadir Eid, one of the prominent Intifada commanders in the city; Ahmad Ghanim, a member of Jabril Rajoub's Preventative Security force in Jerusalem; and three minor local activists: Muhammad Suan, Muhammad Khalid, and Salwa Hudieb, chairman of Fatah's local welfare organization (*Kol Ha-Ir*, 15 Dec. 1995). The movement's better-known figures did not compete. They had no need for such an entry ticket, nor did they need to catch the attention of Arafat or the placement committee. To compete against a group of youngsters would have been undignified.

The placement committee was headed by one of the top figures in the Fatah organization, Sakhr Habash. Fatah also appointed a political committee headed by Abu-Mazin (who also served as chairman of the Central Election Commission on behalf of the Palestinian Authority), and a communications committee headed by Nabil Sha'ath. The West Bank organization committee was headed by Faisal Husseini, and the parallel committee in the Gaza Strip was chaired by Zakariya al-Agha, both of them leaders of the movement in their respective areas. Abu-Ala ran the finance committee, and Um-Jihad the women's committee (*Al-Quds*, 21 Nov. 1995).

Many Fatah activists, those unhappy with the decisions of the placement committee and losers in the primaries, did not accept the movement's verdict and Arafat's decision. They decided to run as independents. The direct, first-past-the-post multi-member constituency system created a negative dynamic for Fatah. The more candidates there were in a district, the fewer votes were needed to win a seat in the Council. Even before the independents rebelled against their movement's central authority, the number of candidates was large, and this spurred Fatah activists who did not agree with the placement committee's decision to run against the representatives of the establishment and the political organizations, hoping to be elected on the basis of their personal accomplishments and reputations in their home districts. Fatah did not look kindly on this political rebellion, and ruled that anyone who ran as an independent would be expelled from the movement. But there were so many Fatah members running as independents, and their standing in the movement was so high, that it was impossible to kick them out without dealing a mortal blow to the organization. So the Fatah leadership could do no more than hope that its official candidates would beat the independents.

Unlike in the rest of the country, the placement committee was not authorized to compose the Fatah list in Jerusalem district (*Al-Quds*, 27 Dec. 1995). Arafat assigned this job to Faisal Husseini. In doing this, Arafat enhanced Husseini's power and that of the local Jerusalem leadership at the expense of the Fatah organization (*al-tanzim*) on the national level – Sakhr Habash, Marwan Barghuthi, Abas Zaki, and Muhammad Ghanim. Husseini's strengthened position also came at the expense of Rajoub. Rajoub had a great deal of influence in the Fatah organization. Many of its operatives were agents of his Preventative Security Service. Despite Rajoub's rivalry with the national civilian branch of Fatah, the two had a common interest in restricting the power of the local establishment in Jerusalem. The source of the rivalry between the political establishment in Jerusalem – Husseini's Orient House – and the leaders of the national Fatah organization had its base in the relations between the "outside" and the "inside." Husseini, it should be recalled, is one of the leading figures of what was formerly the "inside," while Sakher Habash, Muhammad Ghanim, and Abas Zaki were Fatah officials from "outside." Hussein's appointment as Fatah chief in the West Bank, in September 1993, and the entry of the "outside" officials to the "inside", in mid-1994, turned the prior rivalry into one that was now between a center of power that had once been national and was now local in Jerusalem, and a national center of power that now wanted to subjugate the different local branches to its command and which was unwilling to accept the independence of the Jerusalem organization. The struggle between the Fatah apparatus and Husseini's Jerusalem political elite was also a generational one. The Fatah organization opposed Husseini's political and social Orient House elite with young field operatives who had won glory in the Intifada.

In order to maneuver between the constraints he faced, Husseini tried to operate the Jerusalem district differently to the other districts and to draw up a united consensus slate of candidates that would represent all political factions. However, two opposition organizations, Hamas and the Popular Front for the Liberation of Palestine, forbade their representatives, Sheikh Jamil Hamami and Dr. Riad al-Malki, from participating in the elections. Negotiations between Husseini and the opposition groups ended without issue just before the deadline for registering candidacies. At this point the Jerusalem district had been assigned six seats, one of which was reserved for a Christian, leaving four places for which more than 20 prominent activists were competing. There was no way to decide among them in the few hours that remained to register candidates on December 12, 1995 (*Ha'aretz*, 24 Dec. 1995).

In addition to these difficulties, Husseini had to cope with the problems that the placement committee and the national Fatah leadership had already faced – the young Intifada leadership's demand for representation. The local Fatah activists who had been successful in the movement's primaries in Jerusalem also demanded recognition. Prominent among these two groups were the young candidates whom the national Fatah organization supported. They hoped to exploit their reputations as fighters against the Israeli occupation to win out over what they called "the salon and media leadership" (the veteran politicians) and the newcomers from outside who had never suffered the vicissitudes of the occupation (members of the PLO establishment). This group refused to join a united slate with veteran candidates because they knew that they would be poorly represented. The people, they argued, should be allowed to have their say. The inability to decide who would be on the slate led to a situation in which the official Fatah slate in the Jerusalem district originally only included two names – Abu-Ala, about whose candidacy there was general consensus, and Faisal Husseini (*Al-Quds*, 22 Dec. 1995, 25 Dec. 1995; *Ha'aretz*, 24 Dec. 1995).

A few days later a new list containing four names was issued. In the other electoral districts Fatah ran slates with a number of candidates equal to the number of seats allocated to the district, but in the Jerusalem district the Fatah list left two spaces open, granting tacit legitimacy to other candidates to run as independents and ask the judgment of the voters. This time Faisal Husseini was not included in the list, because participating in the elections would have required him to disassociate himself from Orient House (as explained in chapter 5). The slate now included Abu-Ala, one of the architects of the Oslo accords; Ahmad Hashim al-Zughayir, a fruit and vegetable dealer originally from Hebron, Fatah activist, and member of the United National Command (the body that had coordinated the Intifada); Khatim Abd al-Qadr Eid, who had come in first in the Fatah primary elections in Jerusalem; and Emil Jarjuʻi, a pediatrician who had never been politically active – he was adopted as a Christian representative by the Fatah organization in Jerusalem because they thought he would be loyal. It is interesting that the Fatah list included only one Christian candidate even though two places were reserved for Christians. Dr. Hanan Ashrawi was too independent for the national Fatah leadership, so she ran on her own. Other prominent Jerusalem area figures also ran as independents – Hana Sinyora, a well-off pharmacist who was also editor of the daily newspaper *Al-Fajr* and who had opposed Arafat during the 1980s; Ziyad Abu-Zayad, lawyer, journalist, and Fatah activist; and Jonathan Kutab, lawyer and political activist. Abu-Zayad and Kutab tried to organize a block of five prominent independent candidates, including the popular Abu-Ala, but they were unable to reach an agreement and in the end each ran on his own (*Al-Quds*, 22 Dec. 1995, 25 Dec. 1995; *Haʼaretz*, 26 Dec. 1995). In addition to the independents, FIDA (a political party formed by ex-DFLP members in 1991) ran one candidate (Zuhira Kamal), and the People's Party, the former Communists, ran four candidates. There were also two blocs of relatively anonymous candidates – the Independent Bloc, with four candidates, identified with Fatah, and the National–Palestinian Union, with three candidates (*Al-Ayam*, 6 Jan. 1996). The major race, however, was between the Fatah slate and the most prominent independents, who had bucked Fatah discipline while remaining loyal to its ideology.

In general, the candidates could be categorized in several over-lapping and intersecting ways. There were Fatah representatives versus independents identified with Fatah; Fatah members versus members of other organizations and parties; members of political organizations versus completely independent candidates; well-off candidates (such as Hana Sinyora or Rajah Abu-Asab, who sells electric appliances) versus members of the middle and lower classes; young Intifada fighters and commanders versus public figures and political activists such as Haj Abu-Diab, chairman of the union at the East Jerusalem Electric Company; or Dr. Anis al-Qaq, a doctor and secretary-general of the Palestinian Council for Medical Services; and attorney Ali Jozlan, chairman of the Committee of Arab Attorneys. There were people with exposure in the international media versus people known only to the Palestinian public, or only to the people in his or her electoral district; people from notable families with social or economic position versus people with no family connections; recently arrived operatives from "outside" versus people from "inside." In Jerusalem there were also candidates from the city's Hebron immigrants versus those whose families had been in Jerusalem for generations. For example Sheikh Nabil al-Ja'bari, director of Hebron University, who lives in Jerusalem, belongs to one of the most socially promi-nent families in Hebron and, until the 1970s, also the most impor-tant political family in the Hebron area (Rubinstein, 2 Nov. 1995; JMCC, 1996: 187–216).

The Central Election Commission began registering candi-dates a month before the election, on December 19, 1995, and was meant to complete this task two weeks later. In districts where no problems rose, registration was indeed completed by the target date, but this was not the case in Jerusalem, Hebron, Khan Yunis, and Gaza City, so in these locations the deadline was put off for another week. In total, there were 676 candidates for 88 seats. These included 76 official Fatah candidates and about 50 who ran on the slates of other parties and organizations. In Jerusalem the declared Fatah candidates were 7.6 per cent of the total number of candidates; opponents of the Oslo accords were 7.4 per cent; and Islamic independents were 3.7 per cent. The great majority (81.3 per cent) were independent candidates, similar to the percentage of independent candidates on the national level, 82.6 per cent (Ukal & al-Surani, 19 Jan. 1996). Fatah was the largest of the parties that competed in the elections, followed by the People's Party, which ran 25 candidates. The great majority of the candidates, however – 550 of them – defined themselves as independents. These included 23 women, 300–350 Fatah members who ran without the support of their party, and some 200 independents who either did not belong to a political organization, or whose political organization had forbidden them to run. Finally, there were 15 candidates identified with extremist Islamic organizations who decided to participate in the elections despite the veto imposed by their factions (Shikaki, 1996: 34–7).

The number of candidates in each district, in relation to the number of seats apportioned to it, provides a picture of the level of competition. In Jerusalem there were 7.4 candidates per seat, as opposed to 8.6 nationwide (Ganim, 1996: 11), that is, there was a bit less competition in Jerusalem than there was nationally, but not much less. It should be recalled that the campaign was a short one, and this also moderated competition and rivalry.

The candidates invested about $2.5 million in their campaigns. About 90 per cent of the candidates were members of the middle class (college-educated technocrats and professionals), or former blue-collar workers who had risen into the upper economic class. These two groups make up, however, only about five per cent of the Palestinian population in the West Bank and Gaza Strip. The lower classes were not represented among the candidates in numbers anywhere near their proportion in the population. In the Jerusalem district they were only 6.7 per cent of the candidates. In comparison with other districts, this was low – in the Northern Gaza Strip they were 10.4 per cent of the candidates, in Nablus 12.9 per cent, in Jericho 16.6 per cent, and in Ramallah 9 per cent. Jerusalem had, however, a higher percentage of lower-class candidates than did Hebron (4 per cent) and Khan Yunis (4.5 per cent) (Ukal & al-Surani, 19 Jan. 1996).

Only 359 candidates (55 per cent) placed advertisements in the daily newspapers as part of their campaigns. Sixty per cent of these did so once or twice; only 40 per cent published three or more advertisements. These were the candidates who had financial support from their movements (Fatah gave each of its candidates $10,000 in campaign funds) (Hilal, 1997: 118), or had the independent financial means to pay for advertisements. The use of the newspapers was influenced by the candidates' level of education and their target audience. In Jerusalem independent candidates Hanan Ashrawi, Jonathan Kutab, and Hana Sinyora stood out. They were vying for the Christian seats and targeted the educated population. The fact that a relatively large number of Jerusalem candidates used the daily press as a campaign forum is an indication of the economic and educational level of the candidates and their target population. In Jerusalem, 41 out of 54 (77 per cent) of the candidates used the press, in contrast with other districts, in which the candidates preferred to contact the voting public face to face, in small gatherings over coffee and to print their own campaign material. In Jerusalem candidates were forbidden to hold outdoor election rallies, but even in other places rallies were not used to reach the voters. Candidates and voters preferred personal contact to mass gatherings (*Al-Nas Wa-l-Intihabat*, *Al-Quds*, 20 Jan. 1996). Except for a few incidents in which the Israel police prevented Hanan Ashrawi from conducting prohibited outdoor campaign rallies, there were no confrontations between the candidates and Israeli security forces. Ashrawi had wanted to make use of the Israel police in order to reinforce her image as a fighter for Palestinian rights, but she did not succeed, and the several incidents she arranged had little effect. The voters did not want to shout, demonstrate, or confront the Israeli authorities, but rather to talk to the candidates and hear what they had to say. After doing so and hearing the high-sounding nationalist declarations they expected to hear, the voters wanted to be given solutions to their day-to-day problems and to know more about the elections and how to vote (*Ha'aretz*, 14 Jan. 1996, 18 Jan. 1996; Nir, 15 Jan. 1996).

The negotiations about the elections began in May 1995, and the detailed talks about the arrangements in Jerusalem were conducted from September 1995 onward. In May it was agreed that the Palestinians would be allowed to conduct a census of voters in Jerusalem, under the rubric of a "population and housing survey." The debate focused on the question of where the polling stations would be located – at the city limits, in UN facilities, or in churches and mosques. At this point Israel opposed having polling stations in the city, and also opposed allowing the city's inhabitants to be elected to the Palestinian Authority's Legislative Council. In June 1995 it was agreed that the polling stations would be placed on the municipal boundaries and that the right to be a candidate would be granted only to people with a double address, one in Jerusalem and one outside it (*Ha'aretz*, 9 May 1995, 7 July 1995, 20 July 1995, 8 Aug. 1995, 19 Sept. 1995). Agreement on the conduct of the elections in East Jerusalem was achieved in September 1995, two months before the agreement on the Israeli redeployment in Hebron. In other words, the compromise on Jerusalem was easier than the compromise on the Jewish settlement in Hebron.

Initially, the Palestinians wanted the post offices in East Jerusalem to serve as fully-fledged polling stations. In the working paper they submitted at the beginning of the talks they demanded that the voting procedures at these stations be the same as at all other stations, with the exception that there would be no redeployment of Israeli forces. They therefore demanded that the preparations for the elections – registration of candidates and voters, campaigning, the opening of an office of the Central Elections Commission, security for polling places and international oversight of the elections – take place in Jerusalem just as they were to take place in the rest of the 1967 territories (*Al-Quds*, 20 May 1995). Israel rejected the Palestinian position on the grounds that the voting in Jerusalem was being done by mail, and that every detail of the voting procedures had to be in keeping with that definition. Israel wanted the mail services to function as usual, with the vote being only a part of those services; the Palestinians demanded that normal post office services be suspended while the vote was taking place; Israel opposed this. Israel demanded that the ballots be placed in double envelopes that would be sent as pieces of mail rather than inserted into a ballot box; the Palestinians, of course, opposed this. Then there was the question of who would transfer the ballot boxes for counting outside the city – the staff of the Central Elections Commission, as the Palestinians demanded, or post office workers, as Israel demanded? The dispute extended even to the design of the ballot boxes – Israel demanded that the slit be on the side of the box, as in mail boxes. The Palestinians demanded that the slit be in the middle of the top of the box, as is customary with ballot boxes. There was even a semantic problem – what would the boxes be called in the agreement: ballot boxes or mail boxes?

All these issues were resolved through mutual concessions and compromises. According to the Oslo II agreement of September 1995, which laid out the procedures for Israeli troop redeployments and the Palestinian elections, not all inhabitants of East Jerusalem would vote in the five post offices: the central post office on Salah al-Din Street, the Jaffa Gate post office, the post offices in Sho`afat and Bait Hanina in the northern part of the city, and the Mount of Olives post office in the east. The number of voters assigned to these post offices would be limited in accordance with their capacities. Each voter would receive, from the Central Election Commission, notification of where he would vote. Upon arriving, the voter would be asked to identify himself to a post office worker and present his voting certificate. Only this, rather than an Israeli identification card, would be used for identification, as in the rest of the territories. Elsewhere, however, the elections were conducted by people appointed for that purpose, while in Jerusalem post office workers performed this task. Post office employees would hand the voters the ballots and envelopes, would receive the sealed envelopes in return, and insert them into the ballot boxes. The compromise found for the design of the boxes was that the slit was placed at one of the edges of the top of the box. This way it did not make it too much like a ballot box for the Israelis and not too much like a mail box for the Palestinians. As for the terminology, the two sides agreed to use the neutral term "receptacles," although the voting documents would be called "ballots." Likewise, the post office staff would be responsible for transferring the sealed ballot boxes to Palestinian officials outside the city for counting. According to the agreement, the international observers who were to oversee the elections would be allowed to function in East Jerusalem as well. The Palestinians saw this as an achievement that, to a certain extent, put the elections in East Jerusalem under international supervision and outside the range of Israeli law, but Israel claimed that the observers were meant to ensure a fair election and did not symbolize the end of Israel's annexation (*Ha'aretz*, 16 July 1995, 4 Sept. 1995, 5 Jan. 1996, 15 Jan. 1996; State of Israel, 1995: 119–20).

According to the Oslo agreement, public election campaigning in Jerusalem was restricted. At a cost, posters could be pasted up only on 35 billboards that the Jerusalem municipality erected for this purpose in central locations. The candidates who wished to use the billboards had to apply to the Central Elections Commission, which in turn applied to the Israeli–Palestinian Committee on Civilian Affairs, a committee set up in 1993 in the wake of the

Oslo agreement. This cumbersome procedure was meant to provide an indirect way for Palestinians to receive a permit from the
Jerusalem municipality for the use of the billboards. Israel viewed
this procedure as recognition of its sovereignty in East Jerusalem
because the permit was issued by the Israeli municipality, while in
the Palestinian view they were applying to a special body of their
own that dealt with the elections, rather than to the Jerusalem
municipality. The Central Election Commission did not occupy
itself only with obtaining permits for public advertising. It also
vetted content, making sure that there were no racist slogans or
anti-Israeli incitement. This arrangement grew out of Israel's fear
that the election campaign, especially in Jerusalem's public places,
would turn into a protest against the annexation. For this reason it
agreed to grant the Central Elections Commission the authority
to inspect campaign material. This was not explicitly stated in the
Oslo agreement, which spoke instead about examining whether
the campaign material was in contravention of the Palestinian
election law and the agreement. In practice not all the provisions
were observed, and many posters were pasted up on store doors,
walks, and electric poles, and not just on the municipal billboards.
In no case, however, did the campaign material contain anti-
Israeli statements (*Ha'aretz*, 5 Jan. 1996; State of Israel, 1995: 119).

Unlike the rest of the electoral districts, the voter rolls in Jerusalem had, according to the Oslo II agreement, to receive the
approval of the Israeli Ministry of the Interior. The ministry
checked to ensure that the rolls included no Israeli citizens. Aside
from the practicality of this arrangement (which enabled the Palestinians to make use of Israeli records and the Israelis to ensure
that no Palestinians who were Israeli citizens voted in the Palestinian Authority elections), Israel considered this a symbolic
expression of its sovereignty in East Jerusalem, while the Palestinians saw it as a technical step meant to ensure that its lists were
precise. Since the Palestinians had no population registry of their
own and had no time to conduct a population and housing census,
the Palestinian Authority used the records and data of Israel's
Civil Administration and Ministry of the Interior, the Israeli
administrative organ in the territories (*Ha'aretz*, 1 Jan. 1996).

Employees of the school system carried out voter registration,
and in East Jerusalem the registration stations were manned by
teachers and students from Al-Ibrahamieh College, who also

went from door to door in East Jerusalem's neighborhoods (*Ha'aretz*, 22 Nov. 1995). Registration began in mid-November 1995 and was supposed to last for two weeks. The number of registrants reached 1.01 million. During the registration period Israeli right-wing groups launched a psychological campaign against East Jerusalem voters, pasting up notices and spreading rumors that those who registered would prejudice their status as residents of Israel, leading to the loss of their Israeli identification cards, social security payments, and other social benefits that residence qualified them for (*Ha'aretz*, 7 Dec. 1995, 16 Jan. 1996). These activities had their effect on the Palestinians, even though top Palestinian political figures in Jerusalem and Gaza repeatedly promised that nothing bad would happen to those who registered, and that "registration for the elections is a national duty … and counters the attempts to change the Arab–Palestinian identity of Jerusalem" (*Ha'aretz*, 22 Nov. 1995).

When the official deadline for registration arrived, at the beginning of December 1995, it turned out that only 35,000 people had registered in East Jerusalem. In Hebron, in comparison, 135,000 people had registered, and in Nablus 100,000. The Palestinians estimated that there were 280,000 inhabitants of the Jerusalem district, 40 per cent of whom were eligible voters – a total of 110,000. The combination of the psychological campaign and Jerusalem's marginal position in the Palestinian political system had led to a low response. The low level of registration was diametrically opposed to the expectations of the local Palestinian leadership, which had hoped for 90 per cent registration. The Jerusalem leadership understood that with such a response the Jerusalem district would be among the smallest, and the Palestinians would lose their claim on the national identity of East Jerusalem. It was thus decided to extend the registration period in Jerusalem, as well as the opening hours of the registration offices, and to launch a public relations campaign. The number of registrants in the district soon grew to 80,051 (40 per cent of them women), approximately 65 per cent of eligible voters. However, only 40 per cent of these were from East Jerusalem (Ganim, 1996: 21–4; *Ha'aretz*, 3 Dec. 1995, 4 Dec. 1995, 7 Dec. 1995; Markaz al-Quds Li-al-Nisa, 1996: 11). The number of voters in the city itself was 32,316, making up 40.37 per cent of the total number of voters in the district (*Al-Quds*, 23 Jan. 1996). Accordingly, each parliamentary seat in Jerusalem represented 27,000 residents and 11,000 eligible voters (Ukal and al-Surani, 19 Jan. 1996).

A breakdown of Jerusalem's voter rolls by age shows that Jerusalem is not much different from the rest of the territories – in Jerusalem, as there, half the population is under voting age, so it is clear that the political process is relevant to only half the population. Eight per cent of the voting population was made up of young people between the ages of 18–49 (Ukal and al-Surani, 19 Jan. 1996). Most of them had been born after Israel occupied the territories; none of them had been a part of the political process under Jordanian rule. Ten years after the Intifada, the "children of the stones" had turned into voters and their commanders into candidates. The only political arena they identified with and considered themselves part of was the Palestinian one.

Jerusalem's distance, as a frontier city, from the political center was expressed in the elections not only by the low level of registration and low number of participants, but also by a lack of order, bad organization, and no information on the election procedures. Even in Silwan, which became part of the front line against the annexation in the 1980s, when Israeli settlers bought houses there and moved in, only 40 per cent of eligible voters registered (Cohen, 19 Jan. 1996). The elections emphasized Jerusalem's remoteness from the political center rather than the front line of the confrontation with Israel.

The elections

As befits a historic event, the Palestinians turned out for the election in high numbers – 75.3 per cent of those registered on the national level. The turnout in the West Bank was 69.5 per cent, in the Gaza Strip 86.2 per cent (*Al-Quds*, 23 Jan. 1996; al-Shikaki, 1997: 304). It is interesting to note that there was a high turnout, 60 per cent, even among supporters of Hamas, which was officially boycotting the elections. In contrast, however, the turnout in East Jerusalem was only about 30 per cent, with 40.3 per cent voting in the Jerusalem District as a whole – 32,316 voters out of 80,051 eligible voters (*Al-Quds*, 23 Jan. 1996; JMCC, 1996: 17; Shikaki, 1996: 34). Of the 4,500 Palestinians eligible to vote at the post offices in East Jerusalem, only 500 actually voted (*Kol Ha-Ir*, 26 Jan. 1996). According to a survey conducted on election day, more men than women voted in the Jerusalem area, presumably because they were more willing to confront the obstacles Israel placed in the way of voters (as is related below). Age and education were also linked to participation – in Jerusalem, young educated people were more likely to vote (Awartani, 1997: 63).

The Jerusalem District had the lowest voter participation by far of all districts, the next lowest being the Hebron District with 66.4 per cent (Ganim, 1996: 16–17). Jerusalem and Hebron are on the front lines of the political confrontation with Israel, and both the elections were conducted under the presence of Israeli forces. Participation in the Palestinian elections on the national level was high compared to that in most Western democratic regimes. It was almost as high as the voter turnout in the 1996 general elections in Israel (78 per cent), where citizens are very involved politically and election campaigns "hot" and long. Nevertheless, the Palestinian voter turnout was about 10 per cent less than what was generally seen in the first-time democratic elections held in Eastern Europe in the 1990s. It should be kept in mind, however, that the elections in the former Soviet bloc were held after the previous regimes collapsed, whereas in the West Bank and Gaza Strip the Israeli occupation was reduced and withdrawn, but had not disappeared entirely.

Concern about a possible low voter turnout led the Palestinian leadership in Jerusalem to call on the public to come to the polls despite the psychological and physical obstacles that Israel police placed in their way. The arguments were openly nationalistic, reminding the Palestinian public that the struggle for sovereignty in East Jerusalem and the terms of the permanent settlement would be affected by the turnout and political involvement they displayed (*Ha'aretz*, 16 Jan. 1996, 19 Jan. 1996). Despite this, the turnout in Jerusalem was very low. Israel made it difficult for voters to reach the polls by placing large contingents of policemen around the five polling places in East Jerusalem, claiming that large forces were necessary to protect the Palestinians from right-wing Israeli elements who were threatening to disrupt the voting. The forces were much larger than the threats justified, and the policemen were overly active, setting up roadblocks and closing off the roads around the polling stations, photographing people who came to vote, and checking Palestinians' identification and voting documents. At the entry points into the city Israeli soldiers held up buses organized by the Central Elections Commission and those organized by candidates, and also refused to allow private vehicles to take voters to their polling places outside the city. Furthermore, just before the elections, activists belonging to Israel's right-wing Likud party spread false rumors and threats about punishments that would be meted out to voters, including the revocation of their right to live in the city. On election day, extreme right-wing Israeli activists clashed with Palestinian voters, aiming to keep turnout low. These elements believed that a low turnout would serve their interests, enabling them to claim that Jerusalem's Palestinians did not feel connected to the Palestinian political system. These deliberate disruptions caused Israel a loss on the symbolic level, for they kept the post offices from continuing to supply regular postal services during the vote, as Israel had originally intended (*Ha'aretz*, 19 Jan. 1996, 21 Jan. 1996; Markaz al-Quds Li-al-Nisa, 1996: 8–9).

The obstacles created by Israel were not the only causes of the low turnout. The organizers of the poll themselves created technical difficulties and confusion about the polling places. The Central Election Commission did not divide the voters up among the polling stations in advance and did not establish far in advance who would be allowed to vote in the post offices and who would vote outside the city limits. For purely technical reasons it was impossible to have the tens of thousands of eligible voters in East Jerusalem vote in the post offices. It was obvious that only 4,500 voters would be able to vote within the city, and that the other 28,000 would have to go to polling stations outside the city boundaries. This required good organization – notices had to be sent out and transportation arranged. But it was only at a relatively late stage, after the candidates had begun to organize transportation of their own, that the Central Elections Commission made 150 buses and 80 vans available to the voters (*Ha'aretz*, 12 Jan. 1996, 14 Jan. 1996, 19 Jan. 1996; Markaz al-Quds Li-al-Nisa, 1996: 8–9; Nir, 15 Jan. 1996). Additionally, many voters did not participate in the election because of their reservations about the Palestinian political system, and the fact that they lived in a frontier city, relatively far from the political center.

The winners

Arafat won the presidential elections, receiving an official 88.1 per cent of the vote nationwide (*Ha'aretz*, 21 Jan. 1996, 23 Jan. 1996), almost the same level of support he received in Jerusalem, where he won 88.8 per cent of the vote (JMCC, 1996: 172). The official results did not, however, include blank ballots – ones in which the voter declined to choose either of the two candidates. According to CPRS, about 22 per cent of the ballots were left blank, about four per cent of them as a result of technical problems, with 18 per cent being intended as protest votes. Thus, according to CPRS, Arafat was really supported by only 70 per cent of the voters, with 12 per cent of the vote going to the alternative candidate, Samiha Khalil (Shikaki, 1996: 28).

The Legislative Council representatives in Jerusalem make up 7.9 per cent of that body's membership. The Jerusalem district returned four official Fatah candidates and three independents identified with the organization. The winners were: Abu-Ala, a national establishment figure and member of Fatah, who received 18,839 votes, 58.3 per cent; Dr. Hanan Ashrawi, an independent Christian, 17,944 votes, 55.5 per cent; Ahmed al-Batsh, a young independent who had been a field commander in northern Jerusalem during the Intifada, 9,846 votes, 30.4 per cent; Ziyad Abu-Zayad, attorney, independent, and a member of the veteran political leadership in Jerusalem, 8,434 votes, 26.1 per cent; Khatim Abd al-Qadir Eid, 8,307 votes, 25 per cent; Ahmad Hashim al-Zughayir, 7,613 votes, 23.5 per cent; Dr. Emil Jarju'i, a Christian pediatrician, Fatah member, and Husseini loyalist, who won 5,334 votes, 16.5 per cent (*Al-Quds*, 23 Jan 1996; Cohen, 26 Jan. 1996; JMCC, 1996:166). Two who came close to being elected were Zuhira Kamal of FIDA, who had Fatah's support in the framework of a deal struck between the two movements, and Rana Nashashibi of the People's Party. On Election day, the Fatah campaign worked only to elect al-Zughayir and Eid.

The Fatah organization did not support al-Batsh despite the fact that his age and Intifada record put him in the same group as al-Zughayir and Eid and most of the Fatah organization's apparatus in Jerusalem. Batsh was too independent for the machine. Nor did it mobilize itself to support Abu-Ala, a member of the central establishment who was older than most of the activists who had recently arrived from Tunis. Neither did it go all out for Dr. Jarjuʻi , who was seen as a loyalist of the Jerusalem political establishment rather than of the city's Fatah organization. By mobilizing to elect only two candidates, the organization also took into account the political assertiveness of the East Jerusalem voting public. The organization allowed voters to choose other candidates as well, thus increasing the chances for success of its preferred candidates. This consideration was proven correct by the election results.

More than elsewhere, voters in Jerusalem did not vote blindly for the Fatah slate. While the level of support for independent candidates in Jerusalem, 43.4 per cent, was very similar to the support that winning independent candidates received nationally, 45.5 per cent, the support for the independents in Jerusalem was more notable. On the national level, the average support per candidate was about 24 per cent. Notable candidates on the national level, such as Hanan Ashrawi in Jerusalem, Abd al-Jawad Salah in Ramallah, and Haidar Abd al-Shafi in Gaza were able to garner broad support exceeding 50 per cent (Shikaki, 1996: 38). Ashrawi received nearly as many votes in Jerusalem as the candidate for the PLO organization, Abu-Ala, and three independent candidates were among the seven representatives the district sent to the Legislative Council. It should be noted that these three received more votes than three of the four official Fatah candidates.

Only one of the seven victors in Jerusalem – meaning 14.2 per cent of them – lacked an academic degree (al-Batsh). The proportion of those with degrees (85.8 per cent) is similar to the proportion of college graduates in the Legislative Council as a whole (82.9 per cent). Women are better represented in the Jerusalem delegation than on average nationally: 14.2 per cent as against 5.6 per cent.

Most members of the Legislative Council are experienced politicians; blue-collar workers and businessmen are underrepresented. This characteristic becomes sharper when one looks at the composition of the Jerusalem delegation – only one of the representatives was a businessman before he was elected, and none of them are blue-collar workers (JMCC, 1996: annex vi).

Fatah ran 75 candidates and 50 were elected; 11 national–independents and seven Hamas supporters won. Fatah's victory was almost absolute. Thirteen other organizations and political parties ran their own candidates, receiving 10 per cent of the vote, but only two of these parties succeeded in getting represented in the Legislative Council, one representative each: Azmi al-Shu'ybi of FIDA in Ramallah, and Haidar Abd al-Shafi of the National Democratic Alliance in Gaza (Shikaki, 1996: 37). The system was skewed in Fatah's favor; the large number and disorganization of the independent candidates, in contrast with the strong district organization of Fatah, swung the election to Fatah. While 505 independent candidates received 60 per cent of the votes, they received only 39.8 per cent of the seats in the Legislative Council. In contrast, Fatah candidates received only 30 per cent of the votes, but won 58 per cent of the seats (Ganim, 1996: 18). The 21 members of Fatah who ran and were elected as independent candidates should be added to the 47 victorious official Fatah candidates, bringing the Fatah representation in the Legislative Council to 68 out of 88, or 77.3 per cent of the total (Hilal, 1997: 116).

It is important to note that family connections played no role in the elections. The attenuation of the extended family's importance was predicted by pre-election polls, in which respondents did not cite family as one of the factors in their choice of candidates. Furthermore, in no insignificant number of cases, several candidates from the same extended family ran against each other.

This detailed survey of the election shows that Jerusalem differed from the rest of the Palestinian territories in almost every criteria – election procedures, voting arrangements, polling places, slates of candidates, campaigning, the right to vote and to be a candidate, voter registration, average campaign expenses, voter turnout, and Israeli activity aimed at limiting voter turnout. It is important to note that these were not artificial differences, even though one of the ways in which they were enshrined was through negotiations with Israel. Yet these negotiations did not lead to results that were fundamentally different from the political reality of East Jerusalem. The aggressive actions Israel took in order to limit voter turnout in East Jerusalem, it turns out, are not what made the elections in the city unique. Israel's unilateral actions certainly added some special elements to the vote in East Jerusalem, but they were not what set these elections apart. At base, their effect on the political character of East Jerusalem was marginal. More important was a correspondence between the political profile of East Jerusalem's Palestinians and the results of the negotiations with Israel on the arrangement, conduct, and participation in the elections. Furthermore, a comparison of the delegation that East Jerusalem elected to the Legislative Council to those elected in the other districts – by social background, educational level, economic status, age, affiliation, and political position – also testifies to Jerusalem's unique place on the Palestinian political map. In other words, not only was the process different in Jerusalem, but the results were also different, in keeping with the political profile of East Jerusalem.

Eight per cent of the members of the Legislative Council are former deportees, 59.1 per cent are original inhabitants of the West Bank and Gaza Strip, and 33 per cent are "returnees," PLO activists who came to the territories in the wake of the agreements with Israel. But none of the Jerusalem representatives is a former deportee, and only one, Abu-Ala, is a "returnee" (JMCC, 1996: annex vi). The election results confirmed that Jerusalem is the political stronghold of the leaders of the former "inside" (JMCC, 1996: annex vi; Ode, 1997: 122). In contrast, there is no difference between Jerusalem and the rest of the territories with regard to the representation of 1948 refugees. Two of Jerusalem's delegates (28.6 per cent) are from families who became refugees in 1948; on the national level 28.3 per cent are. But unlike some of their colleagues from adjoining districts, the Jerusalem representatives who come from 1948 refugee families do not live in the refugee camps on Jerusalem's outskirts.

Geographically, 60.2 per cent of the Legislative Council's members live in the cities, 22.7 per cent in towns and villages, and 17.0 per cent in refugee camps. In the Jerusalem district, however, all the representatives live in the city (JMCC, 1996: annex vi). In Jerusalem the link between place of residence and political activity, including ties to the political establishment, is stronger than elsewhere, although it is impossible to say what came first – whether place of residence drew people to politics and the establishment, or whether the opposite is the case.

Before their election, five of the seven Jerusalem representatives were active on the national level, in the West Bank or in the PLO, and only one (Jarju'i) has no background of political or Intifada anti-Israel activity. Three of the other six have impressive records of diplomatic activity (Ziyad Abu-Zayad, Ashrawi, and Abu-Ala) and three other were prominent commanders in the

Intifada. On the whole, the proportion of Intifada commanders in the Jerusalem delegation was high, 42.6 per cent (Hilal, 1997; JMCC, 1996: 219–25).

Professionally, a majority of the members of the Jerusalem delegation are technocrat-professionals, PLO organization figures, or Intifada activists. There are no blue-collar workers, which make up 8 per cent of the membership of the Legislative Council as a whole, and none are private-sector wage earners, although these make up 5.8 per cent of the Legislative Council's members (Hilal, 1997: 120). The Jerusalem voters placed representation of the West Bank's most political city into the hands of experienced politicians. Jerusalem stands out in this regard in comparison to the national average. Only one of Jerusalem's representatives is neither an experienced politician nor a member of the political establishment (14.2 per cent), whereas 25 per cent are politicians on the national level (Hilal, 1997: 119–27). The political prominence of the East Jerusalem delegation is expressed in the posts they hold in the Legislative Council (Abu-Ala is the speaker) and in each of the two compositions of the executive Council. Hassan Tahbub and Hanan Ashrawi were both members in 1996, the former as minister of religious endowments and the second as minister of higher education, while Ziyad Abu-Zayad served as minister without portfolio in 1998.

In terms of economic status, most of the Jerusalem representatives are of high economic position, relative to the national average. True, two of the Jerusalem representatives (28.5 per cent) have low incomes (up to 600 Jordanian dinars a month), compared to 22.4 per cent of national representatives. The Jerusalem delegation, however, has no members of middle income (up to 1,000 dinars a month), while this group makes up 24.7 per cent of the Legislative Council's members as a whole. Five (71.4 per cent), have high incomes (more than 1,000 dinars a month); this group makes up 51.8 per cent of the Council's members on the national level (Ode, 1997: 122).

The age of the Jerusalem delegation is greater than in the Legislative Council as a whole. In Jerusalem, 56.8 per cent of the delegation are between the ages of 51 and 60, as compared to 30.6 per cent on the national level. In the 41–50 age group the picture is almost identical. In Jerusalem 43.2 per cent of the delegation fits into this group, as does 42.4 per cent on the national level. The

Jerusalem delegation contains no young people under the age of 40, nor does it include anyone over the age of 60, when on the national level these figures are 17.4 per cent and 10.2 per cent respectively (Hilal, 1997: 123; Ode, 1997: 164–6). In this context it should be noted that there is a correspondence between the representatives' ages and their previous political and organizational positions, and that this itself corresponds to their income level.

The Palestinian Authority elections marked the end of a chapter in the history of the Palestinian national movement. Unlike the general identification with the PLO, which stood "outside" as an object of identity and symbol of national aspirations, the Palestinian public in the West Bank and Gaza Strip organized into grassroots political frameworks, from the neighborhoods, villages, and streets. This process accelerated during the 1980s, when PLO organizations penetrated "inside" and established chapters and local focuses of activity, women's and youth organizations, professional associations and student organizations (Hess, 1996: 57–70; Robinson, 1997). When the Palestinian Authority was established "inside" in the middle of 1994, it completed this process. It established representative institutions from above and "swallowed up" local bodies. The elections strengthened the status of the "returnees," the people from "outside," and effaced the previous geographical distinction between "outside" and "inside," which had existed since the mid-1970s. Prominent figures from the Palestinian establishment "outside" were elected with broad support: Tayib Abd al-Rahim, who had been secretary-general of the PLO Executive Committee; Nabil Sha'ath, minister of the economy and international cooperation; Abas Zaki, one of the top figures in the Fatah organization "outside;" Hakim Bal'awi, formerly the PLO's ambassador to Tunis and one of the chiefs of Fatah's internal security apparatus; Um Jihad (Intisar al-Wazir), who had headed Fatah's welfare institutions in Tunis and who was the widow of Abu-Jihad, who had been killed by Israel commandos there; and Ahmad Qria' (Abu-Ala), Fatah's economic chief.

The contours of Palestinian political organization

There are five research approaches explaining the contours of Palestinian political organization (Brynen, 1995a, 1995b). The first approach believes that the Palestinian political elite is affected by primordial ties, blood ties between members of the extended family (*hamula*). As we have already seen, the results of the Palestinian elections invalidate this explanation. It is true that the *hamula* was a decisive element in the political map during the British Mandate period, but in the wake of the wars of 1948 and 1967, and of Jordanian and Israeli rule in the West Bank, the veteran political and social elite that had been based on family affiliation was destroyed. New groups took their place and the political power of the extended family diminished considerably. In addition, PLO organizations were constructed on an entirely different social base than the Palestinian national movement during the British period had been; the link to the organization, its worldview, and its policies were more important than primordial ties and affiliation to a given social class.

The second approach states that Palestinian political organization is based on affiliation to a counter-elite, a new social stratum that has come out against its predecessor, the veteran elite with its high social status and its property. The veteran elite had controlled the political institutions in the major Palestinian cities during the British Mandate period and under Jordanian and Israeli rule. The new elite appeared as a result of the processes of modernization and development, in particular the acquisition of higher education by the middle class and the process of urbanization. The Fatah leadership sprouted from this stratum during the late 1950s and the 1960s, and the leadership of the Intifada, which broke out in 1987, grew up in this same environment during the decade 1975–85 (Kimmerling & Migdal, 1994: 205–8, 246–75; Quandt, Jabber & Lesch, 1973; Robinson, 1997). This characterization is correct with regard to the founding fathers and the central members of the various component factions of the PLO, and valid until 1968, at which time the new elite replaced the veteran leadership of the PLO. Furthermore, the explanation is valid with regard to infighting within the ruling establishment elite, but is of doubtful value when it comes to the relations of the PLO elite with the Palestinian public. In this case the elite has grown up outside the territory that it aims to rule and in which it aims to establish its authority. The PLO "outside" was a political organization without sovereignty and without a monopoly on making the rules in the region it sought to govern. In practice, it was a political establishment without a nationwide economic and social infrastructure. Given this data, it is difficult to accept the explanation that the salient element in shaping Palestinian political and executive institutions has been social–economic interest. The elections of January 1996 also challenge this thesis, at least as a primary explanation, since they proved that the Palestinians' socio–political portrait is very complex, at least in some of the districts. Even in the Jerusalem District the local elite is not cut from a single cloth.

The third approach suggests that the tension between "outside" and "inside" is by far the most important factor in the Palestinian political map. The source of this tension is, in one version, the tension between the traditional elite and the counter-elite, a division congruent with the split between the leadership "inside" and the PLO establishment "outside" (Robinson, 1997); in a different version, the source is the difference in geographical location. These two groups are geographically distinct and wage a struggle for political control and social authority. As we have seen above, the elections blurred the difference between the two leadership groups. As has been proven in the previous chapters, the elections brought to its conclusion a process that began a long time previously. As early as the late 1970s the left-wing factions in the PLO began operating on the civilian level in the West Bank and Gaza Strip as a way of gaining a political and social foothold. The PLO's evacuation of Lebanon in 1982 and the enforced transfer of its political headquarters to Tunis motivated the PLO to use the 1967 territories as its rear and major stronghold. The Intifada did not break out in a vacuum in 1987, and it was institutionalized and directed into political and diplomatic channels by the PLO in Tunis. This process strengthened the seniority of the PLO establishment "outside," which, little by little, also became an organization with a firm hold "inside" (Klein, 1997). Again, the 1996 elections erased the final traces of the difference between "outside" and "inside."

The fourth approach argues that the organizing principle of Palestinian politics is neo-patrimonialism. This refers to a kind of modern paternal authority that expands on the rule of the *hamula* chief in traditional Arab society. As a result of modernization, this authority has been transferred from the extended family or tribe to the political–institutional realm. The system is headed by a father figure whose authority is sanctioned by political structures and bureaucratic institutions. Additionally, the leader reinforces his strength through patronage. He grants his protection to his political "clients," so buying their loyalty. On the political level the entire system is characterized by a series of patron–client, command–comply relations. The authority of those on the lower rungs of the ladder is drawn from and depends on the authority and power of the patrons above them, up to the leader himself. The advocates of this explanation do not restrict it to the Palestinians alone, but claim that it is typical of the entire Arab political–social system (Sharabi, 1988). Even, however, if there are political systems in the Arab world for which this explanation is valid and useful, there would seem to be some serious questions about whether it is fully appropriate to the Palestinian case. The Palestinian political system, and specifically the PLO and Fatah systems, are characterized by a well-developed culture of debate. The PLO has, since it was founded, conducted many lengthy discussions and its leaders have developed a politics of consensus, not a politics of decision-making, as would be the case in the dependent, hierarchical system described by this theory. In the framework of these discussions, Arafat's subordinates have frequently differed with him, criticized him, and even interrupted him (Rubinstein, 1995). As we have already seen, in the 1996 elections the father–leader had a hard time controlling his sons, and many Fatah partisans ran as independents. If there was ever a neo-patrimonial Palestinian system, it collapsed on the eve of the elections.

The fifth approach is the organizational approach. Its supporters argue that the Palestinian political system is an organizational one, and that this determines membership in the political and organizational elite. This approach also has two different explanations: one argues that the organizations differ from one another on the basis of their orientation to one or another of the Arab countries or superpowers. It would seem, however, that the PLO's increasing strength as an independent organization, whose determining orientation is towards the Palestinians, and the fact that it has set as its goal the establishment of an independent Palestinian state, disproves this explanation with regard to the largest and most important PLO organizations. The abortive 1982–3 pro-Syrian rebellion in Fatah and in the PLO led by Abu-Musa, removed the pro-Syrian PLO factions from the organization and marginalized them. The collapse of the Soviet bloc destroyed the world of the leftist Palestinian factions, who watched anxiously and incredulously as Hamas became firmly rooted in Palestinian society. The second explanation emphasizes organizational affiliation in the Palestinian arena. Since the PLO turned, in 1968, into a coalition of organizations, the organizational principle did indeed turn into the key according to which representational quotas, jobs, and budgets were handed out. But this explanation is not sufficient, because in most political debates the dividing lines were not just between organizations, but were also conducted within Fatah itself, especially since the organization stepped up its diplomatic efforts in the decade beginning in 1983. Furthermore, as the major organization, Fatah, grew stronger and the infrastructure it established for a Palestinian state broadened, so Fatah became the ruling establishment. Aside from the other changes, the establishment of the Palestinian Authority created a fundamental change in the PLO's political contours. This requires a new explanation that will take the nature of this change into account.

All this indicates that the principal contours of the Palestinian political establishment are no longer inter-organizational, Fatah versus the PLO's small factions, but are rather of those inside the establishment and those outside it. It is not official membership in Fatah that counts, but rather affiliation to the ruling establishment or standing independent of it. Moreover, location on the establishment ladder is also a decisive element because a high position increases the control of material resources and enlarges effective authority. The obvious conclusion is thus that power struggles in the Palestinian political system are conducted between different branches of the ruling establishment, with each branch seeking to increase its power, or between the holders of power and the seekers of power knocking at the gates of the political system (Klein, 1997). The elections of 1996 were an important milestone in the politicization of the PLO and of turning it from an organization focused on armed struggle into a "normal" political establishment.

7

ISRAELI POLICY IN EAST JERUSALEM

Keeping Palestinians in line

The Oslo II agreements, signed in June 1994, established the Palestinian Authority, an autonomous regime with full powers over areas designated as Zone A (mostly Palestinian urban centers) and civil, but not security, powers over areas designated as Zone B. The agreements explicitly excluded it from having any authority or right to act in East Jerusalem. Neither the Palestinian Authority administration nor any of its agencies was to operate there. To ensure compliance with these previsions, the Israeli Ministry of Justice drafted legislation enabling Israel to close Palestinian institutions operating in East Jerusalem in contravention of the agreement. The law was passed by the Knesset on December 26, 1994 (*Laws of the State of Israel* 1497, 28 Dec. 1994; *Ha'aretz*, 15 June 1994, 26 June 1994, 13 July 1994).

Since independent Palestinian political and public affairs activities were permitted in East Jerusalem so long as they were not connected with the Palestinian Authority, the Israeli security establishment formulated criteria defining what Palestinian operations in East Jerusalem were forbidden and what were permitted. Prohibited activity included the kind typically carried out by a government ministry, operations funded by and bureaucratically subordinate to the Palestinian Authority and the operation of offices that associated themselves with the Palestinian Authority in a symbolic way (such as by using a logo containing symbols or elements used by the Palestinian Authority, or by giving their senior officials titles that indicated a connection to the Palestinian Authority) (Shragai, 9 July 1996).

Israel took action along several lines. The first was closing in on the Preventative Security Service, which had turned the larger Jerusalem metropolitan area into a staging ground for operations in East Jerusalem. Its men collected protection money from storeowners, summoned suspects to interrogations in Abu-Dis and Anata, bought land in East Jerusalem to counter land purchases by Israel, resolved civil disputes, and fought the drug trade. While the Palestinian policemen did not carry weapons, they were effective because they acted in the name of the security system. It was precisely this that roused the Israel police and the Jerusalem municipality against them (*Ha'aretz*, 21 July 1995; 8 May 1996). In September 1994 the Israeli government ordered that Jibril Rajoub's Preventative Security Service operations in East Jerusalem be halted. By the beginning of 1995 the Israel police had dealt with 23 incidents involving Palestinian security agents, arresting 22 suspects, of whom 13 were brought to trial (*Ha'aretz*, 20 Sept. 1995). Israel did not succeed, however, in hampering the Palestinian force's operations.

The Likud government that came to power in 1996 decided to fight the presence of Rajoub's agents by establishing new police stations in Arab neighborhoods and manning them with 400 policemen who would be assigned "to enforce Israeli sovereignty in East Jerusalem" (*Ha'aretz*, 3 June 1997). However, budgetary difficulties prevented the implementation of this decision (*Kol Ha-Ir*, 9 May 1997, 15 Aug. 1997; *Ha'aretz*, 3 June 1997, 5 June 1997). At the beginning of 1998 the police force tried to overcome these difficulties by reorganizing its manpower, moving policemen's residences to the Old City, and by installing close-circuit televisions for surveillance on the central roads in the Old City (*Ha'aretz*, 24 June 1998; *Kol Ha-Ir*, 30 Jan. 1998). However, Israel had but a limited capability to restrict the Palestinian force's room for maneuver, for two reasons. First, the Palestinian security systems camouflage their activities. They use some 100 apartments lying outside the city limits as bases for operations in the city, as interrogation rooms, and as headquarters (*Ha'aretz*, 2 Sept. 1996, 1 Aug. 1997). Second, the Palestinian population in Jerusalem grants these agents legitimacy and authority that it does not grant to the Israel police. So, in fact, Israel took action only in exceptional cases, such as the abduction of an Israeli Arab citizen in East Jerusalem by Rajoub's agents (*Ha'aretz*, 21 July 1996).

The second line of action was launched in mid-1994, when Rabin decided to prevent the establishment of new political institutions in East Jerusalem and to restrict the activity of the existing institutions to their range of activities before the signing of the Declaration of Principles with the Palestinians. According to Israel's security agencies, at that time there were 13 Palestinian national or governmental institutions operating in East Jerusalem (*Ha'aretz*, 10 Feb. 1995). However, according to a report by the Peace Watch organization, there were only seven institutions with clear links to the Palestinian Authority, and two more whose link to the Palestinian Authority was doubtful (Peace Watch, 1995). The Israeli government took action against only a few of these institutions. This generally involved collecting evidence and presenting it to the officials of the institution that was slated for closure. They were then allowed to respond. The Palestinian side was presented with the choice of severing all links with the Palestinian Authority, as was done in August 1995 by the Palestinian Council on Health and the Palestinian Broadcast Corporation (*Ha'aretz*, 18 Aug. 1995, 28 Aug. 1995, 3 Sept. 1995, 14 March 1997), as well as the National Institutions Office, the National Islamic Committee for the Struggle against Settlements, the Palestinian Institute for the Wounded; and the Jerusalem Association for Welfare and Development, all on March 4 (*Ha'aretz*, 12 Feb. 1997, 14 Feb. 1997, 18 Feb. 1997, 20 Feb. 1997, 23 Feb. 1997, 5 March 1997, 6 March 1997, 11 March 1997, 14 March 1997, 26 March 1997). Another option was to move the institutions to a location outside the municipal border, as was done in mid-1994 by the Palestinian Central Bureau of Statistics, the Housing Council (*Ha'aretz*, 1 June 1994, 8 June 1994), and PEDCAR (Palestinian Economic Council for Development and Reconstruction) – an organization that coordinates planning and oversight of economic and social projects in the Palestinian Authority, as well as infrastructure reconstruction. PEDCAR's headquarters were transferred to the al-Ram neighborhood, just a few meters outside the Jerusalem city limits. Under Israeli pressure the word "Jerusalem" was also eliminated from the organization's logo (*Ha'aretz*, 31 May 1994; Peace Watch, 1995: 23–4). The Jerusalem branches of the Palestinian Prisoner's Club and the office of the deputy minister for Christian affairs were closed in April 1999 (*Ha'aretz*, 9 April 1999; 14 April 1999).

Israel's activities against the Palestinian Authority institutions in East Jerusalem were affected first by its ability to prove its claims in court. Second, the government had to take other factors into account, such as whether it would be able to shut down offices and institutions without rousing Palestinian or international ire. These considerations prompted Israel not to take action against the mufti of Jerusalem and the Waqf, even though there was sufficient evidence against their operations in East Jerusalem. Israel did not want to ignite a religious conflagration whose outcome was impossible to predict. Third, Israel could shut down Palestinian offices, but it was very difficult to prevent activity by Palestinian Authority institutions that sent personnel into Jerusalem without having a bureaucratic base of operations in the city. A financial pipeline connects the Palestinian Authority with al-Maqasid Hospital and the Palestinian Authority participates in determining policy in the areas of welfare, health, housing, tourism, building and neighborhood reconstruction, transportation, management of holy places, and the school system (*Ha'aretz*, 24 March 1999). Fourth, Israel cannot efficiently control entry into the city. True, at the end of 1995 the Israel police prevented the Palestinian minister of education, Yasir Amar, and the deputy minister for planning and international cooperation, Dr. Anis al-Qaq (a resident of Jerusalem) from participating in a conference held at the al-Hakawati Theater to mark Palestinian Teachers' Day (*Ha'aretz*, 15 Dec. 1995). On four occasions during the first half of 1996, Israel also prevented Palestinian Authority officials from participating in conferences held by non-governmental Palestinian institutions (*Ha'aretz*, 7 March 1996, 3 April 1996). In the summer of 1997 Israel went so far as to prevent the appearance of a ballet company from Chile at al-Hakawati on the grounds that the event, as publicized in the Palestinian press, was under the sponsorship of the Palestinian Ministry of Information as part of the company's tour in Palestinian Authority cities (*Ha'aretz*, 4 Aug. 1997). But the Palestinian Authority's minister for Jerusalem Affairs, Ziyad Abu-Zayad, regularly entered the city, even when the Israel government revoked his entry permit between March and August 1999, and the minister of tourism and archaeology and the minister of labor and welfare has held business meetings with local bodies operating in their areas of responsibility (*Ha'aretz*, 19 March 1999; 18 April 1999; 1 Aug. 1999; 5 Nov. 1999).

The most prominent Palestinian institution in East Jerusalem is Orient House. In the period between the talks about going to Madrid and the signing of the Israeli–Palestinian Declaration of Principles (1991–3), Israel did not prevent foreign diplomatic delegations from visiting Orient House. The Israeli government hoped that these visits would encourage the local Palestinian leadership to present itself as an alternative to the PLO (Musallam, 1996: 60). After Jerusalem was excluded from the territory of the Palestinian Authority, the diplomatic visits to Orient House began to disturb Israel, whereas the Palestinians did not want to give up the diplomatic gain that these visits constituted. From September 1993 to March 1995, at least 47 diplomatic meetings took place at Orient House. During this period issues relating to the Palestinian autonomous regime were conducted and aid and cooperation agreements were signed (*Ha'aretz*, 13 July 1994; Peace Watch, 1995). From the signing of the Cairo agreements in May 1994 through to the summer of 1999, representatives of 29 countries visited Orient House at some 50 diplomatic meetings. These representatives included one prime minister, two deputy prime ministers, five foreign ministers, two deputy foreign ministers, nine other ministers, and a large number of ambassadors and consuls (*Ha'aretz*, 15 Aug. 1995). Since the establishment of the Palestinian Authority in mid-1994, the diplomatic meetings at Orient House have become symbolic ceremonies or have been given a local character, as opposed to the meetings that are devoted to national issues, which are conducted in Gaza.

In June 1995 the deputy prime minister of Sweden stormed home from Israel in anger after not being allowed to make an official visit to Orient House, and the Irish foreign minister demanded to visit the institution the following August. Rabin responded by declaring, "I will not station policemen to prevent a foreign minister's visit [to Orient House]." However, Rabin added, "We have determined for ourselves that we will not accept personal meetings higher than the ministerial level if [the visitor] visits Orient House" (*Ha'aretz*, 1 Nov. 1995). The Labor–Meretz government decided that visits by ministers to Orient House would have to be on a private basis, and that the guests would have to declare this publicly. The foreign minister of Ireland and the British minister of housing conformed to this requirement in August 1995, as did the French foreign minister in December

1995 (*Ha'aretz*, 19 June 1995, 15 Aug. 1995, 29 Oct. 1995, 24 Dec. 1995, 29 Dec. 1995). This arrangement continued under the Netanyahu government. In January 1997, the Belgian secretary of state for international cooperation visited Orient House while his foreign minister met with a Palestinian delegation at the American Colony Hotel, next door to Orient House (*Ha'aretz*, 28 Jan 1997). And in January 1999 the Greek deputy foreign minister paid an official visit to Orient House.

With the approach of Israeli elections in 1999, the Likud government issued closure orders to three offices operating in Orient House: Husseini's office, the International Affairs Department, and the Mapping and Geographical Department. (Israel had no legal foundation for closing the entire building, as the government would have preferred.) Israel made this move after Husseini and three Legislative Council members met at Orient House with 30 foreign consuls and diplomatic representatives in a counter-event to Israel's Independence Day. This meeting was held after the director-general of the Israeli Foreign Ministry had written to the foreign diplomatic corps in Israel requesting that they not attend diplomatic briefings in Orient House because this was in violation of the Oslo accords and constituted intervention in the Israeli election campaign. In response, the European Union sent an official letter to Israel stating that the EU's member states reaffirmed Jerusalem's status as a *corpus separatum* in accordance with the UN resolution of 29 November 1947. According to this decision, the city was to be administered by a special international regime run by the UN. The European countries did not simply send the letter, which itself was a slap in the face for Israeli policy, but also permitted their representatives to participate in the Orient House event. The Israeli government's capacity to absorb such blows on the eve of the elections was exhausted and the closure orders were delivered to an Orient House representative, despite warnings from Israeli defense figures that carrying them out was liable to lead to bloodshed (*Ha'aretz*, 19 March 1999, 11 March 1999, 15 March 1999, 27 April 1999, 10 May 1999, 11 May 1999; Eldar, 11 March 1999). The crisis had the potential of becoming international because the European consuls decided that they would appear at the building if Israel were to try to enter by force to carry out the closure orders (*Ha'aretz*, 11 May 1999).

Israel's minister of internal security, Avigdor Kahalani, and Husseini met to try to find a compromise but failed. Kahalani suggested that the Mapping and Geographical Department and the International Affairs Department close their Orient House offices and be transferred to Abu-Dis, whereas Husseini's office would continue to function normally. Orient House, for its part, proposed that only certain functions of the offices be transferred outside Jerusalem but that the offices themselves remain open. Furthermore, Orient House's top officials would declare in writing that they had no link with the Palestinian Authority. While these discussions were in progress it became clear that the two national leaders were finding it difficult to accept a compromise. Arafat wanted to demonstrate that he and not Faisal Husseini was making the decisions about Jerusalem, so he refused to endorse the compromise proposals formulated by Orient House. In parallel, Netanyahu contributed his share by drafting the Israeli proposal in a form that invited Palestinian rejection – he demanded that the Palestinians declare publicly that the offices were being transferred out of Israel and promise that Orient House's activities would be based on Israeli law (Benziman, 14 May 1999; *Ha'aretz*, 10 May 1999; Eldar, 10 May 1999, 11 May 1999).

The crisis was resolved when Israel's Supreme Court issued an interim order forbidding the Israeli government to carry out the closure orders. The court accepted a petition by nine Israeli intellectuals who argued that a decision of this type should not be affected or motivated by electoral considerations (*Ha'aretz*, 12 May 1999). With the accession of the Barak government, tacit agreement was reached on the continued operation of Orient House within the lines set by the Rabin government. Faisal Husseini met with the British foreign secretary at the American Colony Hotel in October 1999, and with the French and Dutch foreign ministers in East Jerusalem hospitals (*Ha'aretz*, 4 Nov. 1999). On this level, only Zimbabwe's foreign minister had the privilege of meeting Husseini in Orient House (*Ha'aretz*, 4 Nov. 1999). There were, however, Orient House meetings with lower-level delegations, such as members of parliament from Morocco and Jordan (*Kol Ha-Ir*, 5 Nov. 1999). Israel and the Palestinians walked a fine line distinguishing between diplomatic meetings held at Orient House, and those held in neutral places such as hospitals or in health and welfare institutions, and between high- and low-level meetings.

Israel's actions regarding the Palestinian institutions in Jerusalem received the Supreme Court's approval at the end of January 1996 (Rulings, High Court of Justice, 2142/95, Vol. 49, 1995: 363–5; *Ha'aretz*, 30 Jan. 1996). The court ruling clearly indicates that the Israeli government had reached arrangements with the various Palestinian institutions regarding the form of their operations, including those against which evidence justifying their closure had not been obtained. These arrangements were opposed by Jerusalem Mayor, Ehud Olmert, (Rulings, High Court of Justice, 1995, 365). Olmert and the Likud's hawks made no distinction between official operations of the Palestinian Authority and unofficial operations, nor between the activity of a person in one of the Palestinian Authority institutions and his activity in a local Jerusalem institution. Nor did they distinguish, on the one hand, between an institution operating in Jerusalem as an arm of the Palestinian Authority or a religious or community institution that the Palestinian Authority had decided to recognize and, on the other hand, an institution over which the Palestinian Authority exerted influence to ensure the appointment of its own loyalists to the governing board. An example of the first kind of institution is al-Quds University, which operates in East Jerusalem under the accreditation of the Palestinian rather than the Israeli Council for Higher Education. Examples of the second are the al-Maqasid and Augusta Victoria hospitals. Likewise, the hawks made no distinction between an institution located in Jerusalem and a body located outside the area in which Israeli law applies, but whose workers frequently enter Jerusalem (*Ha'aretz*, 12 Feb. 1997, 14 Feb. 1997, 9 Sept. 1998). These arrangements indeed blurred the boundary between local and national institutions, and helped the Palestinian Authority cover its tracks in Jerusalem. While for the Israeli government the distinction between the two, narrow as it was, had political significance, it is hard to demonstrate from a legal point of view that these institutions broke the law. The Israeli government did not seek to weed out every single national aspect of these local bodies and people, but rather made do with granting a special, Jerusalem flavor to the operations.

The Jerusalem municipality versus the Israeli government

In keeping with its traditional policy, the Labor government invested considerable resources in what was defined as "Greater Jerusalem" – the area stretching from north of Ramallah to south of the Etzion Bloc, and from east of Ma'aleh Adumim to west of Beit Shemesh (Shragai, 20 Jan. 1995). At the end of 1994, the general of the Central Command enlarged Ma'aleh Adumim's jurisdiction westward in the direction of Jerusalem, so that legally the two municipalities share a border. Various government forums secretly discussed applying Israeli regulations and bylaws to this area (Shragai, 20 Jan. 1995).

Municipal policy changed in November 1993, when the Likud's Ehud Olmert defeated the Labor candidate, Mayor Teddy Kollek. Instead of a quiet, creeping annexation of East Jerusalem and its surroundings, Olmert believed that the annexation should proceed openly and dramatically. The Labor–Meretz national government wished to adjust Mayor Kollek's classic Labor Party policy to the new political reality created by the Oslo accords. Olmert's goal was, however, diametrically opposed. He viewed the talks with the Palestinians as a threat to exclusive Israeli sovereignty in the city, and wished to use his authority as mayor to resist the Oslo accords' implications for Jerusalem. To this end he wielded his construction and planning powers, as well as the law enforcement system in these areas, to a twofold purpose: to demonstrate who was sovereign in Jerusalem and to create cracks in the political structure that the Oslo agreements had established. So long as a Labor government was in power, Olmert was a belligerent oppositionist who, together with the leaders of his party, put Jerusalem at the top of the political agenda. After the change of government in Israel, in May 1996, Olmert played a central role in the government's decision-making on Jerusalem, even when he found himself at odds with Prime Minister Netanyahu. When his position was not accepted or when he acted alone, he functioned as an internal opposition (*Ha'aretz*, 2 Jan. 1997).

In mid-1994, when the Palestinian Authority was established, Olmert announced his support for the construction of new Jewish neighborhoods. One of these was located on the south side of the city and was meant to serve as a buffer between Jerusalem and the Palestinian cities of Bethlehem and Bait Sahur, which were under the full control of the Palestinian Authority. Their purpose was to separate them from the al-Azariya–Abu-Dis region. These Palestinian suburbs of Jerusalem, outside the municipal borders, were classified as Zone B (Map 4). In the Beilin/Abu-Mazin plan (p. 301) they were proposed as a possible seat for the Palestinian capital. Abu-Dis now houses the offices of the Palestinian governor of the Jerusalem District, and other Palestinian government offices also operate there and provide services to other areas, including East Jerusalem. At the beginning of 2000, the Palestinians completed the construction of a compound in Abu-Dis that could serve as a parliament building (*Al-Ayam*, 13 Feb. 2000; *Ha'aretz*, 9 Jan. 2000). Al-Azariya and Abu-Dis are closed off on the east by Ma'aleh Adumim, which in 1997 had 25,000 inhabitants. On the north, the area was to be cut off, according to plan, by three new neighborhoods: Jewish Abu-Dis, Sha'ar Mizrach, and Plan 1E. In this way the principal Palestinian region in the Jerusalem area would become an isolated enclave, like the small Zone B regions to the city's north.

Execution and planning did not happen fast enough to keep up with political aspirations. By the end of 1997 not much had been done to further these plans, despite the Likud's national victory a year earlier. At the beginning of January 1997, the Jerusalem city council appropriated funds for the planning of a Jewish neighborhood of 250 apartments on 180 dunams of Abu-Dis at the edge of the municipal territory, on land that was privately owned by Jews. The slow pace of planning led the Ministry of Agriculture to examine the possibility of building greenhouses on the land in order to establish a presence, and thus achieve at least some of the plan's political goals (*Ha'aretz*, 29 Sept. 1997; *Kol Ha-Ir*, 19 Sept. 1997). Planning of the neighborhood was resumed at the beginning of 2000, when the Israeli government considered the possibility of turning Abu Dis from Zone B to Zone A (*Ha'aretz*, 17 Jan. 2000).

In contrast, the area designated for Plan 1E was not owned by Jews. The concept was to build 1,500 housing units (to be expanded in the future to 20,000 units), 3,000 hotel rooms, as well as additional tourist attractions, on 12,000 dunams on and around which live 44,000 Palestinians. The vacant land was the available expansion space for the Palestinian inhabitants (*Ha'aretz*, 18 Feb. 1997). To advance this project, it was proposed to expand Ma'aleh Adumim's jurisdiction by more than 12,000 dunams (*Ha'aretz*, 21

May 1998). The plan was approved by minister of defense Moshe Arens in May 1999, and Ma'aleh Adumim now encompasses more territory than Tel Aviv (*Ha'aretz*, 3 March 1997, 28 March 1997, 28 May 1999, 30 May 1999).

The Sha'ar Mizrach plan is for the construction of 8,000 housing units on a total area of 2,400 dunams lying between French Hill and Pisgat Ze'ev. It also includes commercial centers, industry, and public institutions (*Kol Ha-Ir*, 27 March 1998). The plan was first put forward in 1991, before the Oslo accords, but the Labor government froze it after September 1993. Olmert decided that Israel should implement it quickly and unilaterally, before a permanent settlement on Jerusalem was reached, and this despite the fact that it required the expropriation of private land (*Ha'aretz*, 23 Jan. 1995, 7 April 1995, 4 Jan. 1996; Rubinstein, 10 Jan. 1995). Moreover, Olmert demanded that the government carry on with its traditional policy of using administrative measures to restrict the demographic presence of Arabs in Jerusalem (Benvenisti, 22 Aug. 1996; *Ha'aretz*, 6 May 1994, 3 June 1994, 4 July 1997; Hess, 2 July 1997; *Kol Ha-Ir*, 6 Dec. 1996). Together with Eliyahu (Eli) Suissa, then chairman of the District Planning and Construction Commission of the Ministry of the Interior, and from mid-1996 minister of the interior, he launched an initiative of demolishing East Jerusalem buildings that had been constructed without permits. The Rabin government, however, opposed Olmert's initiative (*Ha'aretz*, 14 June 1995, 5 July 1995, 23 July 1995, 2 June 1997). In 1993, the Interior Ministry issued 56 demolition orders, of which only 48 were carried out; in 1994 a full 65 orders were issued but only 29 were carried out; in 1995 the number of orders issued rose to 117, but only 25 were carried out; and in 1996, a total of 66 orders were issued, of which only 17 were carried out (data supplied by Ir Shalem). Israel also demolished buildings in the area outside the Jerusalem municipal boundaries. In 1993, 47.7 per cent of all the demolitions carried out in the West Bank were in the Jerusalem region; in 1994 they were 34.8 per cent; in 1995 they were 58.1 per cent, and in 1996 they were only 23.8 per cent (B'tselem, 1997). The 1996 figures can be attributed to the Western Wall Tunnel incident of September 1996, in the wake of which Netanyahu refused to approve the implementation of dozens of demolition orders that the Interior Ministry and

Jerusalem municipality had issued (*Ha'aretz*, 29 May 1997, 13 July 1997, 16 July 1997; *Kol Ha-Ir*, 28 March 1997).

The institution that most infuriated Israeli right-wing groups was Orient House. In September 1993 they began demanding that the building be shut down. Rabin refused (*Ha'aretz*, 17 Jan 1995), but Olmert insisted and, in mid-1995, in parallel with a sit-down strike staged by Israeli right-wing groups opposite the Palestinian institution, the Jerusalem municipality's Local Planning and Construction Commission launched procedures aimed at shutting down Orient House on the grounds that the building was zoned for use as a hotel and not as an office building, and because the staff there had declared that it did not recognize the authority of the Jerusalem municipality and the Israeli government (*Ha'aretz*, 25 June 1995, 30 June 1995).

Olmert wished to take advantage of the illegal construction that had been carried out at Orient House and use it as an excuse for shutting down the institution. However, the government refused to grant Olmert a proxy to act in the name of the state. Unlike Olmert, the minister of police, Moshe Shahal, and the minister of justice, David Libai, did not want to halt Orient House's public affairs work – they sought only to end its diplomatic activity. The attorney general ruled that the mayor could take action against building violations or additions built without a permit, but had no authority to shut down an institution on the grounds that it had changed its use (*Ha'aretz*, 12 July 1995, 24 Aug. 1995). Olmert was compelled to make do with a limited administrative measure. In July 1995 he served the Orient House staff with an order forbidding activity in the northern part of the building, which had been built without a license (*Ha'aretz*, 13 July 1995). The Orient House staff asked to be allowed to carry out renovations, and permission was granted. The municipality viewed this as an acknowledgement by Orient House that it was subject to Israeli law and to the Jerusalem municipality. Orient House was willing to pay this price in order to continue its operations. By doing so, it showed the municipality's demand for a total shut-down of the site to be unrealistic. But the Israeli opposition did not give up, and at the beginning of 1996 it succeeded in getting the Knesset to send to committee legislation mandating the closure of Orient House (*Ha'aretz*, 8 March 1996).

The battle waged by the Likud and the Jerusalem municipality against the Labor government had reverberations in the U.S. as well. The Republican opposition, led by Senate Majority Leader Robert Dole, a supporter of a hawkish Israeli policy, came out against the Democratic president, Bill Clinton. Dole and Netanyahu had a close working relationship, just as President Clinton did with King Hussein, President Mubarak, Chairman Arafat, and even more so with Prime Minister Yitzhak Rabin. With the encouragement of Likud leaders in Israel and their supporters in the American Jewish community, Senator Dole introduced legislation declaring that Jerusalem had been Israel's capital since 1950 and that United States policy was that the city should remain undivided and that the rights of ethnic and religious groups would be guaranteed within it. The law stated that the U.S. should recognize Jerusalem as the capital of Israel and that the American embassy should be moved from Tel Aviv to Jerusalem by mid-1999, that is, by the time of the permanent status agreement between Israel and the Palestinian Authority. Finally, the law appropriated money for this purpose (Halberstam, 1998).

The legislative initiative was opposed by the Democratic administration, which announced that President Clinton would veto the bill if it did not include a section granting the president the power to suspend its implementation. Administration representatives also demanded the elimination of the binding target date; the requirement to report to the House of Representatives on the allocation of the necessary funds for the project and on progress towards its implementation; and a section that imposed sanctions if the project did not progress as expected. The administration, in short, wanted declarative legislation, whereas the bill's sponsors were aiming for operative legislation. In the end, the only amendment made was the addition of a section that allowed the president not to allocate funds for the embassy's move if he proved to Congress every six months that this was necessary to protect the national security of the United States. The law was passed by the House of Representatives and the Senate on October 24, 1995, and went into force on November 8, 1995 (Eldar, 27 Oct. 1995; *Ha'aretz*, 26 Oct. 1995). Since then, President Clinton has suspended implementation of the law on the grounds that it would hinder the peace process and harm the American national interest. Even the apartment that the U.S. embassy leased in March 1999 in a Jerusalem hotel for the personal use of the ambassador was not used for official meetings, as some members of Congress suggested it should be (*Ha'aretz*, 6 May 1999, 14 May 1999, 20 June 1999, 17 Dec. 1999).

Jerusalem: escape hatches from the Oslo accords

The government that the Likud established with the religious parties at the end of May 1996 put Jerusalem at the top of the Israeli and Palestinian agendas. At first, the new government toyed with the idea of changing the rules of the game at the most fundamental level. Specifically, it proposed closing the offices of the Palestinian minister of religious endowments, Hassan Tahboub; the holder of the Jerusalem portfolio in the PLO Executive Committee, Faisal Husseini; and of the mufti of Jerusalem appointed by Arafat, Sheikh Akaramah Sabri. Similarly, it would have revoked Palestinian responsibility for the public education system in the city and closed al-Quds University (*Ha'aretz*, 4 March 1996, 12 June 1996, 12 July 1996; Rubinstein, 15 July 1996).

The Netanyahu government soon realized, however, that not everything they had advocated from the opposition benches was actually feasible. So it initially stayed within the lines laid down by the Rabin and Peres governments (*Ha'aretz*, 30 June 1996, 5 July 1996; Shragai, 9 July 1996), and made do with taking action against a few offices that were demonstrably linked to the Palestinian Authority. The government also demanded an end to the preventative intelligence activity of Rajoub's agents in Jerusalem (*Ha'aretz*, 28 July 1996, 9 Aug. 1996, 21 Aug. 1996). As a result, the Mapping and Geographical Department returned to its original location in Orient House, and the offices of the Youth and Sport Division and the Vocational Training Institute were transferred to Ramallah (*Ha'aretz*, 14 March 1997). The new government did not, however, manage to halt the activity of the Palestinian security organizations in Jerusalem (*Ha'aretz*, 22 Aug. 1996).

Israel's inability to do this led to frustration, which caused efforts to be diverted from preventative measures to increased positive action in the capital.

The contest for the Arab space

In contrast with the policies pursued by all previous Israeli governments, which limited themselves to building Jewish neighborhoods on the heights around East Jerusalem, at the end of 1996 the minister of the interior, Suissa, and Mayor Olmert sought to promote a plan to build a Jewish enclave of 132 housing units in the heart of the Arab neighborhood of Ras al-Amud, in which some 11,000 Arabs live. At the beginning of the 1980s, while Teddy Kollek was mayor, a smaller, 75-unit building plan had been prepared, spurring a sharp debate in the municipality and the government. One of that plans' supporters was Suissa, who was then chief of the Ministry of the Interior's Jerusalem district office. Over a five-year period, he conditioned his approval of a plan for the construction of 560 Arab housing units in the neighborhood on approval of the Jewish enclave. In May 1992, under pressure from Kollek, the Jerusalem city council approved the program, but Rabin ordered it halted. In December 1996, after the national change of government, the Local Planning and Construction Committee in the Jerusalem Municipality approved a plan of double the size and sent it to Eli Suissa. True, this was not construction on confiscated land but rather on land owned by Jews, but the intention and identity of the purchasers were clear. They wanted to change the character of East Jerusalem and settle as many Jews as possible in the Arab neighborhoods in order to carry out their religious Zionist program, and in order to frustrate a permanent agreement that would link the East Jerusalem Arab neighborhoods to a Palestinian state and create a Palestinian corridor to the Temple Mount (*Ha'aretz*, 23 Dec. 1996, 2 Jan. 1997; Shragai). The construction plans prepared for the neighborhood reflect this – the Jews were granted construction density of 115 per cent, while the Arabs were granted only 50 per cent. The Arabs were required to preserve a distance of six meters between one home and another, and were limited to two stories, while the Jews were not restricted on the distance between houses and were allowed to built four stories (*Ha'aretz*, 5 Dec. 1996; Rubinstein, 13 Dec. 1996; Shragai, 23 Dec. 1996, 1 Aug. 1997). Under pressure from Jordan and the Palestinians, in the summer of 1997 Netanyahu froze implementation of the program and, in September 1998, even promised the U.S. in writing that no Jewish neighborhood would rise on the site in the near future (Benvenisti, 12 Dec. 1996; *Ha'aretz*, 5 Dec. 1996, 26 May 1997, 2 Sept. 1999; *Kol Ha-Ir*, 23 May 1997).

For this reason the Jerusalem city council approved, on July 24, 1997, implementation of the smaller plan (*Ha'aretz*, 27 July 1997). It also permitted three families to settle on the site in a house purchased by Erwin Moskowitz, the financial patron of the Jewish settler organizations in the Arab areas of East Jerusalem (*Ha'aretz*, 15 Sept. 1997, 16 Sept. 1997, 17 Sept. 1997, 18 Sept. 1997, 19 Sept. 1997). To Olmert's displeasure, the Israeli government believed that this was not the appropriate time for the construction of a settlement in Ras al-Amud. The national government was able to prevent construction by means of an opinion composed by the attorney general, which stated that, because of the near certainty that implementation of the project would lead to a disturbance of public order and endanger the public peace, the owners of the property should be prevented from actualizing their rights (*Ha'aretz*, 28 July 1997, 29 Sept. 1997, 11 June 1998; Hareuveni and Dayan, 1 Aug. 1997). At Netanyahu's initiative, the settler families were evacuated and ten people took their place "for the purposes of protection and upkeep of the properties" (*Ha'aretz*, 19 Sept. 1997). At the beginning of February 1998 the minister of the interior approved, with Netanyahu's support, the large plan, and in August 1998 the first two families moved into the compound (*Ha'aretz*, 11 June 1998, 4 Sept. 1998). Israel's move was made by taking advantage of the fact that several Arab residents of Ras al-Amud had petitioned the Israeli Supreme Court against the linkage between their building plan and that of the Jewish settlers, and against holding their plan hostage until the Jewish plan was approved (*Ha'aretz*, 4 Feb. 1998). Even before the petition was heard, the Ministry of the Interior announced that it was severing the linkage, and the petition was revoked. After this, the ministry decided to approve the Jewish construction plan. Israel's move was made while the U.S. was involved in making military and political preparations by the United States for its attack on Iraq. The construction work began in May 1999, without the Labor government finding any legal means to stop it. At the end of 1999, four families were living in the compound (*Ha'aretz*, 19 May 1999; 6 July 1999; *Kol Ha-Ir*, 5 Feb. 1999, 20 Aug. 1999).

Israel's effort to revise the municipal geography of East Jerusalem was also conducted, at specific locations, by the purchase of individual houses in the heart of Arab neighborhoods. In the mid-1980s, settler organizations began receiving control of homes in Silwan and in the Muslim Quarter. They had the assistance of the government organizations that provided some $20 million, as well as information and legal backing. "No tenders were issued for granting rights to the properties. The political level decided which organizations [Ateret Kohanim and Elad, two settler groups] would win." These deals "were planned in advance" and the Custodian of Abandoned Properties "did not apply the minimal level of judgment required from the person holding this position (The Klugman Report, B'tselem archive; Cheshin et al., 1999: 215–17; *Ha'aretz*, 25 Sept. 1996; Rubinstein, 24 Sept. 1996). The rise of the Labor Party in 1992 led to the unofficial elimination of government aid to settler organizations and their straw men. Since then, most purchases have been made by a private person, Erwin Moskowitz. In this way, by June 1998, some 62 housing units had been purchased in the Muslim Quarter, in which about 1,000 Jews lived, among them 400 yeshiva students. At a conservative estimate, about half of the homes in the Muslim Quarter belong to the Waqf and are thus not for sale, so it is clear that the Jewish purchasing potential is limited. Seventeen houses were purchased in Silwan, and in March 1997 about 100 Jews lived there, including 30 yeshiva students. According to the settlers there, about half the houses in Silwan have been transferred to Jewish ownership, but only about 30 per cent of them are occupied; occupation of the others has been delayed for tactical or legal reasons (*Ha'aretz*, 21 March 1997, 11 June 1998, 27 July 1998, 20 Sept. 1998). Individual houses have also been purchased in the Christian Quarter and in Sheikh Jarah, and a small number of families live there (*Ha'aretz*, 22 March 1999; 28 April 1999, 12 July 1999). From the beginning, these purchases by Jews have led to a series of legal battles between the purchasing organizations and the Palestinian owners, and in most of the cases the purchasers have won (*Ha'aretz*, 29 Sept. 1996, 27 Dec. 1996). The evacuation of the Arab tenants has produced not only legal and political questions, but also moral dilemmas and human tragedies. The Jozlan family, with 28 members, had lived in Silwan for 32 years. The court ruled in favor of the Jewish purchaser, the Elad organization, and the family was required to evacuate the house so that the new owners could take possession. The fact that the Jozlan family possessed an official certificate from the Jewish National Fund testifying to their having saved Jews during the 1929 riots was of no avail. Elad activists explained their attitude towards the Jozlans: "The most important thing in this place is its location and importance ... to leave and not evacuate them is to miss the most important thing, which is that the City of David is ours" (Shragai, 27 July 1998).

Under Olmert's leadership, the municipality switched from restraining settlers who were penetrating the Muslim neighborhoods, as Teddy Kollek advocated, to using the city's planning and construction powers, in coordination with the national infrastructure minister, Ariel Sharon, to assist them. Sharon had been the driving force behind this activity during his tenure as housing minister in the Likud government prior to 1992. In December 1996 the District Planning and Construction Committee approved the building of four homes for Jews in the Arab neighborhood of Sheikh Jarah (*Ha'aretz*, 22 Dec. 1996), and Sharon authorized Elad, the organization that promoted Jewish settlement in Silwan, to plan a Jewish neighborhood of 200 housing units there (*Ha'aretz*, 25 Sept. 1996; *Kol Ha-Ir*, 13 Dec. 1996). In June 1996 the Jerusalem municipality approved the publication of a plan for building 48 housing units for Jews in the Arab neighborhood Al-Tur, along with the approval of the construction of 100 housing units for the area's Arab inhabitants. The city's mode of action was similar to that in Ras al-Amud – linking a Jewish building plan to existing Arab building plans; approval of the Arab building plan by changing the designation of the area from "green" to residential housing; and raising the construction density proposed to Al-Tur in the original plan from 50 per cent to 70 per cent (*Ha'aretz*, 10 June 1998). Finally, during the second half of 1998, discussion began on the plan of the Ateret Kohanim organization to build 200 housing units for Jews in the Muslim Quarter, near Herod's Gate, on land that the Israel Lands Administration had appropriated a year before (*Ha'aretz*, 26 May 1998, 27 May 1998, 28 May 1998, 29 May 1998, 3 June 1998, 5 June 1998, 8 June 1998; *Kol Ha-Ir*, 5 June 1998).

In response, the Palestinian Authority made several moves. First, the local Palestinian authorities in Orient House sought to establish bodies that would compete with the Israeli organizations and purchase Palestinian properties that were up for sale. In July 1995 the establishment of a Palestinian Investment Company was announced, and a year later an Association for the Development of the Old City, headed by Faiz Daqaiq. These two organizations did not succeed in preventing the sale of Arab real estate to Jews. After the failure of attempts to establish local bodies, the local authorities turned to wealthy Palestinians overseas. At the end of March 1997, Munib al-Masri, Abd al-Majid, and Hasib Sabagh, wealthy Palestinians with experience in national institutions, established the Jerusalem Fund for Development and Investment with initial capital of $100 million. It was decided that its profits would be assigned to fund the purchase of land and properties put up for sale in East Jerusalem, the goal being to prevent their sale to Jews. The Palestinian Housing Council tried to draw up a plan to encourage Palestinian construction, and at the end of 1996 it adopted a proposal to provide long-range loans on easy terms to Palestinians who wished to build houses or housing projects in Jerusalem (*Al-Quds*, 2 March 1998; *Ha'aretz*, 11 July 1995, 27 Dec. 1996, 28 July 1997, 17 Aug. 1997; *Kol Ha-Ir*, 4 Nov. 1997). In mid-1997, the Islamic Development Bank in Saudi Arabia established a $19 million fund for private construction in Jerusalem, to be administered by Orient House (*Ha'aretz*, 23 June 1997). According to Husseini, during 1997 about $9 million of this was allocated in housing loans (*Ha'aretz*, 23 June 1998). In 1999 the Palestinian Housing Council granted several home loans of up to $45,000 per family for renovations (*Kol Ha-Ir*, 29 Oct. 1999). It was only at the end of 1997 and the beginning of 1998 that Israeli authorities became aware of the Palestinians' initial successes in real estate purchases. Palestinian General Intelligence located potential sellers, Arabs and Jews, and persuaded them to sell lots in Ras al-Amud, Jabel Mukabar, the Old City, Sheikh Jarah, and Wadi Joz to representatives of the Palestinian Authority or Orient House. In some of these places the extent of Palestinian purchases was greater than those of the Israeli settlers (*Ha'aretz*, 8 Feb. 1998, 9 Feb. 1998; *Kol Ha-Ir*, 30 Jan. 1998; 10 Dec. 1999).

The competition between the Palestinians and Israel over the purchase of real estate in East Jerusalem was not between two equal sides. The Arab organizations and states who promised to help the Palestinians in this area talked more than they acted. For example, the Jerusalem Treasury Fund, founded by the King of Morocco in January 1995, began operating only in April 1997, and by December 1997 had raised only $5 million out of the $500 million that the king wanted to devote to "saving Jerusalem" (*Al-Quds*, 3 Dec. 1997). Even though the pace and extent of Israeli purchases is not especially high, and their demographic effect nearly nil, they have been very visible, given the Palestinian establishment's impotence in preventing the sale of Arab property to Jews.

This state of affairs led the Legislative Council to pass a law in May 1997 forbidding Palestinians to sell houses and land in East Jerusalem to Jews; religious leaders concurred and issued a ban against the dealers. The Palestinian cabinet announced that violators of the law would receive the death penalty. It ordered General Intelligence to block such transactions and to hunt down and punish the sellers. General Intelligence identifed 16 dealers who had been active during the five previous years. In May 1997 three land dealers were murdered and about 12 arrested, with the Israel police succeeding in preventing, at the last minute, the murder of another. In Israel's view, these actions infringed on its sovereignty because the victims were residents of East Jerusalem who held Israeli identity cards and who had been murdered by the Palestinian Authority for doing business with Israelis. Consequently, Israel equipped the dealers with alarms and pistols, conducted a propaganda campaign against the Palestinian Authority for carrying out death sentences without trial, and appealed to the U.S. to pressure the Palestinian Authority to desist from this activity immediately. The U.S. acceded to Israel's request on humanitarian grounds, and Arafat acceded to the American request out of political expediency (*Ha'aretz*, 2 May 1997, 6 May 1997, 25 May 1997, 2 June 1997, 5 June 1997, 6 June 1997, 8 June 1997, 10 June 1997; Kol Yisrael, 1 July 1997).

Israel challenges the demographic balance

As has been noted, Israel was concerned about the changing demographic balance between Jews and Arabs in Jerusalem. Israel estimated that between 50,000 and 80,000 of East Jerusalem's 180,000 inhabitants had moved to the suburbs outside the Jerusalem city limits, although their lives continued to be centered on Jerusalem (*Ha'aretz*, 26 Jan. 1997, 17 March 1997). By law, as

upheld by the Supreme Court, permanent residence status term-
inates automatically if the holder of the document remains outside
Israel for seven years, even if he makes brief visits. It is also void if
he receives a permit to reside permanently in a foreign country, or
becomes a citizen there. Unlike Israeli citizenship, permanent
residence can be transferred from parents to offspring only under
certain restricted conditions. "Mixed" couples – those in which
one spouse has resident status and the other does not – must
submit requests for family unification to gain the non-resident
spouse the right to live in East Jerusalem. Such a request must also
be submitted by residents of East Jerusalem who for any reason
were not present in the city at the time of the 1967 census. All this
makes it much easier for the minister of the interior to revoke permanent resident status than to revoke citizenship (B'tselem and
Center for the Defense of the Individual, April 1997).

Up until the beginning of 1996 there had been only random
action against those whose permanent resident license was no
longer valid. In 1993, resident status was revoked from 32 people;
in 1994 from 45 people; and in 1995, from 96 people (B'tselem,
1998: 9). The increase in 1995 may be attributed to the activity of
the investigations branch of the Social Security Institute, which
began methodically checking homes in the Jerusalem suburbs and
recording who lived in them. The purpose was to identify all registered residents of East Jerusalem. Since Israeli regulations did not
lay out what circumstances prove that a person has settled outside
Israel, the regulations were adjusted to the new policy. First, in
December 1995 it was decided that the Jerusalem suburbs and
West Bank would be considered to be outside Israel for the purpose of the invalidation of permanent resident permits. For Israeli
settlers, the West Bank was part of the State of Israel, but for Palestinians it was considered a foreign country. Second, the term
"center of life," mentioned in the law, was interpreted to apply to
the past as well as to the present. If in the past the center of a Palestinian's life had moved outside Jerusalem, his residence rights
were revoked even if he had, in the meantime, returned to live in
the city. Third, the burden of proof was transferred from the
Israeli authorities to the Arab residents. They were required to
present receipts for the payment of Jerusalem property taxes,
apartment rental contracts from their day of marriage onward,
receipts for the payment of electricity and water from previous

years, and proof that they had medical insurance in the city and that their children studied in Jerusalem schools. In the past these demands were made only of people who had sought to receive a residence permit in the framework of family unification, or in the case of registering a child on the identity card of his Jerusalem resident mother when his father was not a resident of the city. This proof now became extremely difficult to provide, since the criteria were more rigorous and more people were required to meet them. Those who did not qualify were required to return their identity and transit documents and to leave Jerusalem and live in the West Bank (*Ha'aretz*, 17 March 1997; B'tselem and the Center for the Defense of the Individual, April 1997). A Palestinian whose identity card was revoked lost his right to live in and visit Jerusalem; to move freely within Israel (an extremely important benefit held by East Jerusalem residents, who were able to travel through and work in Israel during the closure that prevailed in the West Bank during the 1990s, when many West Bank residents could not); to receive welfare payments that Israel provided to residents; and the right to register his children and spouse as residents of Jerusalem.

The Ministry of the Interior took advantage of every application for service (birth registration, replacement of a damaged or lost identification card) and border crossing to examine the eligibility of the applicant for permanent resident status in Jerusalem according to the new criteria (B'tselem and the Center for the Defense of the Individual, April 1997; *Ha'aretz*, 22 Aug. 1996, 27 Nov. 1996). The ministry also revised its treatment of East Jerusalem residents who held two passports; these were required to choose between Jerusalem residency and their foreign citizenship. Some 70 Palestinians who also held American citizenship were required to choose between Israeli identity cards and their American passports, a move which brought an official protest from the U.S. Consul-General in Jerusalem (*Ha'aretz*, 17 March 1997; Rubinstein, 23 Aug. 1996, 26 Jan. 1997, 3 Feb. 1997). Finally, the Ministry of the Interior also revoked most temporary Jerusalem resident permits, including those of people whose family reunification requests had been approved. According to the ministry, this was done because in the years 1974–7 it was flooded with 7,202 family unification requests (HCJ 474/97; 2227/98; Algazi, 9 Sept. 1998). Instead of supplying an Israeli identity card promptly, the ministry began granting the documents only five years after the request was approved. In the meantime the couple was given a temporary permit, and once a year their eligibility for continuing to live in Israel was re-examined (B'tselem and the Center for the Defense of the Individual, April 1997).

The Social Security Institute operated alongside the Ministry of the Interior in its area of authority, and at the beginning of 1998 transfer payments to East Jerusalem residents who had moved to the West Bank were halted. In addition, in January 1998 the Israeli press revealed that Jerusalem hospitals were requiring Palestinian mothers to pay hospitalization costs when they gave birth. Social Security, it turned out, would not promise to cover hospitalization costs without first checking to see whether the mother or her husband had moved outside the city. This took a long time, since the Social Security office in East Jerusalem employs only five investigators and the process is generally conducted after the birth. In the wake of a petition to the Supreme Court, Social Security restricted the application of this practice only to mothers whose spouses were not residents of Jerusalem (B'tselem, 1998: 22–30; *Ha'aretz*, 13 Jan. 1998, 1 Feb. 1998; *Kol Ha-Ir*, 9 Jan. 1998).

According to the Palestinians, Israel used these measures to confiscate some 4,000 identity cards (www.pna.net, 25 Nov. 1997). Israel reported that between 1967 and 1996 the residence status of 3,874 people had expired, including those who had moved from Jerusalem to other countries (*Ha'aretz*, 9 Sept. 1998). In the period from the beginning of 1996 to the summer of 1999 the residence status of another 2,711 people was revoked (*Ha'aretz*, 16 June 1999, 21 July 1999), of which only about 200 were Jerusalem residents who had moved into the suburbs; most of them lived outside the West Bank (*Kol Ha-Ir*, 22 Aug. 1997). Even though the information on people whom Israel alleged had left Jerusalem was gathered methodically, Israel's new policy was not implemented in a similar way. According to the Social Security Institute, the permanent resident permits of tens of thousands of Arabs had expired – but these people never received notice of the fact. A few thousand of them found out only when they applied to one or another government service and their ID cards were confiscated. Others continued to hold their cards, unaware that their status had changed (State Controller, Annual Report, 1996, 47:576).

In the final analysis, Israel's policy accomplished little, since it brought about no change in Jerusalem's demographic balance. On the contrary, even though its implementation was spotty, the new policy alarmed 50,000–80,000 Palestinians who were concerned that they might become its victims (*Ha'aretz*, 2 June 1997, 3 June 1997; *Kol Ha-Ir*, 6 June 1997). Between 20,000 and 30,000 residents of the suburbs returned to live in Jerusalem in harsh housing conditions so as not to lose their Israeli identity cards and their residence rights. The demand for housing rose and prices spiraled upwards, housing density increased, and housing and living conditions worsened (*Ha'aretz*, 2 June 1997, 10 June 1997, 17 June 1998; *Kol Ha-Ir*, 22 Aug. 1998). The result was that at the end of 1997 the ministry decided to slow down implementation (Rubinstein, 12 Feb. 1998), and in October 1999 it announced that it would no longer check to see if a person had been absent from Jerusalem for seven years, on condition that he or she demonstrated a "suitable connection" to the city (*Ha'aretz*, 18 Oct. 1999). It is doubtful, however, if the policy has really been changed (*Al-Quds*, 11 Nov. 1999). Both Social Security and the health plans have continued with their policies, and East Jerusalem residents who have sought health services in the hospitals or who have applied to Social Security to cover health costs were required to prove that they bore Israeli identity cards. A Social Security investigation took several months, during which the right to receive medical care was suspended. This policy was criticized by the ombudsman for the national health law, who ordered that medical care could not be denied to babies and to those whose lives were in danger during the course of a Social Security investigation (B'tselem, 1998: 20–37; *Ha'aretz*, 14 May 1998; Hess, 25 March 1998). It took a Supreme Court appeal to get the state to agree not to revoke rights under the national health law before all the bureaucratic steps had been taken to determine that the person in question was not eligible (*Ha'aretz*, 26 Nov. 1999). The myriad problems these policies caused led the Israeli authorities to use the planning and construction laws to tip the demographic balance in Jerusalem in Israel's favor.

Construction against Oslo

Demographic growth and the shortage of housing and land for the residents of East Jerusalem led to large-scale illegal construction in the Jerusalem area (*Ha'aretz*, 10 June 1996, 3 July 1997, 4 July 1997, 16 July 1997), especially in the city's north and northeast, on vacant land separating the Palestinian neighborhoods. Arab construction tends to be spontaneous and private, not planned from above by the local or national leaderships (Cohen, 1993: 4; *Ha'aretz*, 9 July 1997, 10 July 1997), although both welcomed this method of building. Since 1997, the Palestinian Authority has attempted to encourage it by issuing its own building permits in the Zone B areas of the Jerusalem District. A total of 1,777 such permits have been issued thus far, in response to 2,977 official requests. It is reasonable to assume that the actual number of Palestinians seeking permits is even larger (data provided by Orient House and the Palestinian Ministry of Local Government). Such construction created contiguity between the Arab neighborhoods in the city's north, preventing them from remaining isolated islands surrounded by Jewish neighborhoods and connecting them with Ramallah. Palestinian construction tightens East Jerusalem's links to the Palestinian Authority, blurs Israel's annexation lines, and even threatens to surround and isolate some of the Jewish neighborhoods in the city's east. The Jerusalem municipality treats this phenomenon as a challenge to Israeli sovereignty in the city. Furthermore, illegal Palestinian construction in northeast Jerusalem can frustrate Plan 1E, which was meant to link Ma'aleh Adumim with Jerusalem. It could also prevent the creation of Jewish contiguity from Neve Ya'akov to the center of town. "It is a cancer that is a clear and present danger to Israel's sovereignty in Jerusalem," Olmert has stated (*Ha'aretz*, 2 June 1997).

To battle against illegal construction, the Ministry of the Interior and the Jerusalem municipality adopted a policy of demolishing illegal buildings at various stages of construction, such as skeleton, foundations, and during the expansion of existing buildings. According to data collected by Ir Shalem, the municipality issued 245 demolition orders in the years 1992–8, of which 83 were carried out. According to the Jerusalem municipality, 97 orders out of 272 were carried out (*Ha'aretz*, 4 June 1998, 2 March 1999, 26 Nov. 1999; *Kol Ha-Ir*, 26 Feb. 1999). In other words, less than a third of the orders were implemented. At the end of 1999 there were 839 demolition orders in force in East Jerusalem, but only 141 (16.8 per cent) had been carried out (Galili, 12 Jan. 2000; *Kol Ha-Ir*, 10 Dec. 1999). The relationship between the implemented demolition orders and the number of building violations identified by the municipality is even smaller – about eight per cent – according to Ir Shalem's data, and about four per cent according to municipal figures (*Ha'aretz*, 21 Aug. 1996, 22 Aug. 1996, 25 Aug. 1996, 26 Aug. 1996, 18 Sept. 1996, 20 Sept. 1996, 29 May 1997, 13 July 1997, 16 July 1997). In addition, Israel's civil administration has carried out demolitions in the West Bank suburbs of Jerusalem. Between July 1997 and July 1998 the Civil Administration demolished 29 structures in the Jerusalem area, about half of the total number of demolitions in the West Bank as a whole (*Al-Quds*, 1 Aug. 1997; B'tselem, 1997; *Ha'aretz*, 4 Aug. 1997, 2 March 1999). During the first half of 1998, five out of 42 orders were carried out (*Ha'aretz*, 4 June 1998), but according to B'tselem's figures, nine orders were carried out, as were another 17 in the metropolitan area. According to the Palestinians, 40 demolitions were carried out during this period (Rubinstein, 22 June 1998). In any case, the pace of Israeli actions did not keep up with the Palestinians. During the second half of 1997, Mayor Olmert urged the demolition of a large number of illegally built buildings and homes, but the Israel's General Security Service opposed this out of fear that it would cause a general conflagration. Prime Minister Netanyahu also requested of Olmert, for diplomatic reasons, that he postpone the implementation of the orders (*Ha'aretz*, 2 June 1997, 23 June 1997, 10 July 1997).

Demolitions had led to large-scale disturbances a year before, on August 27, 1996, when the municipality, in coordination with the prime minister's office, demolished a building belonging to a Palestinian charitable organization in Bourg al-Laqlaq, in the northeastern corner of the Old City's Muslim Quarter. The building had been renovated without a license with the help of a donation from the Canadian government, and was intended to serve as a sports facility for the neighborhood's children (*Ha'aretz*, 28 Aug. 1996). The Palestinian establishment did not view the Netanyahu government's actions in Jerusalem as a local matter, but rather as an expression of a comprehensive policy aimed at sabotaging the Oslo accords (Galili, 30 Aug. 1996; *Ha'aretz*, 25

Aug. 1996, 29 Aug. 1996, 3 Sept. 1996; Rubinstein, 30 Aug. 1996). The Palestinians planned, in response, a series of skirmishes for August 30, which was named al-Quds Day. The first lesson in Palestinian schools that day was devoted to the dispute over Jerusalem (*Al-Quds*, 29 Aug. 1996).

The commercial strike of August 30, 1996 was complete in Jerusalem, but there were no processions, demonstrations, or clashes with Israeli military or police forces. It was a typical warning strike, compliance with which was voluntary. The Palestinians coordinated their actions with the Egyptian and Jordanian leadership. Jordan even went so far as to send its prime minister, Abd al-Karim Kabriti, to Ramallah to meet with Arafat and express his support. This was the first official visit by an Arab leader of this rank in the Palestinian Authority. The businesslike and almost positive position taken by Jordan after Netanyahu came to power was replaced by full support for Arafat (*Al-Quds*, 20 Aug. 1996, 29 Aug. 1996; *Ha'aretz*, 30 Aug. 1996). Despite this, the Palestinian Authority failed both in its attempt to bring the Palestinian masses to al-Haram al-Sharif by breaking through the Israeli roadblocks around Jerusalem, as well as in an attempt to conduct mass prayers next to the Israeli checkpoints. The Palestinian protests were only partially successful (*Ha'aretz*, 1 Sept. 1996), primarily because of the deployment of Israeli forces around the Temple Mount and also because of criticism of the Palestinian administration's corruption, and of the severity and arrogance of the Palestinian police and security services. Two weeks previously, 20,000 Palestinians had demonstrated in Nablus to protest tortures committed by Palestinian naval intelligence, which led to the death of a Fatah supporter in the local jail. Under these conditions, Arafat had a hard time enlisting Palestinian frustration and channeling it into an active confrontation, along the lines of the Intifada. Another reason was that the people who were expert at organizing large-scale protests were out of practice, not having organized such an action for several years. The big protest would come two weeks later, when fire burst forth from Jerusalem and ignited the entire West Bank and Gaza Strip – and an international crisis as well.

On August 22, 1996, evidence first came to light of the Waqf's construction of a mosque in Solomon's Stables, which are subterranean halls dating from Herodian times in the southeastern corner of the Temple Mount, close to Al-Aqsa Mosque. (The name derives from the Crusaders, who attributed the site to King Solomon, and used it as stables. The Muslims call the site the Marwani Mosque, after the Khalif Abd al-Malik ibn Marwan.) On September 4, 1996 the Jerusalem municipality served the Waqf with an order to halt the work, and went to court to enforce it. The court ordered the work halted; in response the Waqf accelerated the project. The mufti of Jerusalem, Sheikh Akaramah Sabri, declared that the mosque lay outside the municipality's jurisdiction. Waqf employees prevented city inspectors from entering the site, forcing the police to photograph it from a distance in order to prove that a violation of the law had taken place. The Ministerial Committee on Jerusalem Affairs discussed the possibility of enforcing the order, but the top police command anticipated that such an action would lead to riots, so Prime Minister Netanyahu rejected that option. He preferred to respond by opening the Western Wall Tunnel (*Ha'aretz*, 8 Sept. 1996, 27 Sept. 1996, 10 Oct. 1996).

On September 24, 1996, the Israeli government broke through the opening of the Western Wall Tunnel, which connects the Western Wall plaza to the Via Dolorosa in the Muslim Quarter. The tunnel is an ancient aqueduct from Hasmonean times, running alongside the Western Wall from south to north, and was uncovered in 1987. As a rule, Waqf (and later Palestinian Authority) officials had, since 1967, opposed Israeli excavations near the Temple Mount and the Western Wall, including archaeological excavations, on both religious and political grounds. Their fear grew when, in 1984, Israeli excavations caused cracks in ancient Mameluke structures in the Muslim Quarter and in the Waqf offices on the Temple Mount; urgent action had to be taken to repair the damage (*Ha'aretz*, 27 Sept. 1996). In the nine intervening years since Israel's Ministry of Religious Affairs had first discovered the Hasmonean aqueduct, the Waqf had stymied two attempts to open it, in July 1981 and in July 1988. In both cases, violent clashes broke out on the site and elsewhere, and Israel backed off (*Ha'aretz*, 27 Sept. 1996).

In January 1996 Peres had intended to open the tunnel in response to the Likud's claim that Peres was planning to divide Jerusalem. On January 16, 1996, aides to the minister of internal security notified Waqf officials that they would be given a permit to use Solomon's Stables as a mosque during the holy month of Ramadan, and that in parallel Israel would open the Western Wall Tunnel. The Waqf's leaders did not respond. Actually, Israel had not expected an explicit response, and was only seeking that they "not make a fuss." Israel took the Waqf's non-answer as tacit agreement, especially after Waqf officials had been taken for a preliminary tour of the tunnel and had seen that it did not lead to the Temple Mount. On January 24, 1996, the Ministerial Committee on Defense approved what seemed to them to be a closed deal. But on February 6, 1996, Waqf officials sent a letter demanding that the tunnel not be opened (*Ha'aretz*, 10 Oct. 1996).

Israel interpreted this letter as having been sent in order to put the Waqf's opposition on the record and so absolve it of responsibility, rather than a demand that the Islamic leadership actually expected Israel to accede to. Only bad weather and the Hamas suicide bombings of February and March prevented Israel from opening the tunnel then. Since the Waqf acted in August 1996 to turn Solomon's Stables into a permanent mosque without an Israeli permit, and because of the difficulty in enforcing planning and construction laws there, Prime Minister Netanyahu decided on September 16, 1996 to treat the matter as a deal in which each side carried out its part unilaterally. The Jerusalem municipality's legal adviser redefined the Waqf's project as an internal change that did not require a license, and ruled that there had not been a substantive violation of the law. A week later the tunnel was opened (*Ha'aretz*, 19 Sept. 1996, 25 Sept. 1996, 26 Sept. 1996, 27 Sept. 1996, 1 Oct. 1996, 10 Oct. 1996, 13 Oct. 1996; HCJ 6403/96, Temple Mount Faithful vs. the mayor of Jerusalem, ruling, N4:241; *Yediot Aharonot*, 4 Oct. 1996).

As later became clear, too late, Israel's decision was an awful one, and the process by which it had been made, faulty. Israel had not anticipated the violent Palestinian response, nor the furious reaction of the Arab countries that had diplomatic relations with Israel. Even though the Palestinians had tried over the previous two weeks to mobilize the masses against Israel, and the organizational infrastructure for this had been created, the Israeli decision makers did not see this as relevant. Similarly, Israel's political leadership did not pick up the voices of protest breaking out of the Temple Mount mosques since the change of power in Israel, voices that had repeatedly warned of the danger posed to the

Islamic holy sites on al-Haram al-Sharif by the Israeli government
and its allies, the extremist Jewish groups seeking to scale the
mountain and change the *status quo* there.

The Palestinians reacted harshly, and that very day declared a general commercial strike in East Jerusalem. Violent demonstrations
broke out in the city. The Palestinian Authority brought mobs out
into the streets and launched a diplomatic campaign against
Israel's move (Shchori, 21 Oct. 1996). There were demonstrations against the opening of the tunnel in Egypt, Jordan, Morocco,
Tunisia, and Turkey, all important Middle Eastern states that had
relations with Israel. Their leaders condemned Israel's actions, as
did Israel's own Palestinian citizens, who staged a day of demonstrations and a general strike (*Ha'aretz*, 13 Sept. 1996, 26 Sept.
1996, 27 Sept. 1996, 29 Sept. 1996). On October 15, 1996 King
Hussein made his first visit to the West Bank since 1967, emphasizing that he was on Palestinian land and supporting the establishment of a Palestinian state (*Ha'aretz*, 26 Sept. 1996, 8 Oct.
1996, 16 Oct. 1996). Hussein made a point of visiting Jericho, the
site of the 1948 Jericho Congress, at which West Bank public figures "requested" that King Abdallah place them under his political
sponsorship. Abdallah entered Jericho on his way to Jerusalem,
and King Hussein visited it on his way home.

The Palestinians turned out en masse to clash with Israeli
forces in what they called the "Al-Aqsa Campaign." Their anger
and frustration were authentic. With the encouragement of the Palestinian Authority leadership, Palestinian policemen and security
personnel joined the demonstrators – not to prevent disturbances,
but as participants. In many places officers and senior commanders stayed behind, increasing the likelihood that the situation
would deteriorate. The demonstrations quickly deteriorated into
a series of bloody battles throughout the West Bank and Gaza
Strip, a "super-Intifada" of mass demonstrations driven by rage,
despair, and frustration. Light weapons were fired by small, half-
organized Palestinian forces operating without coordination and
without a central command. The battles lasted four days and
ended with 16 Israeli soldiers and 74 Palestinians dead, and 58
Israelis and more than 1,000 Palestinians wounded (*Ha'aretz*, 29
Sept. 1996, 2 Oct. 1996, 3 Oct. 1996).

The Solomon's Stables and Western Wall Tunnel incidents
highlighted Israel's short reach and limited authority on the

Temple Mount. The world had now seen that Israel's sovereignty on the Temple Mount was no more than a formal arrangement. Large financial contributions and volunteer labor by Palestinian citizens of Israel helped bring the Solomon's Stables renovation work to completion on October 12, 1996, turning it from a space that was occasionally used for prayers to a permanent mosque in its own right, without a permit from the Jerusalem municipality (*Ha'aretz*, 10 Oct. 1996, 13 Oct. 1996). Similar work was carried out in the basement levels of Al-Aqsa in the years 1998–9, with the Israeli government's tacit consent (*Kol Ha-Ir*, 15 Jan. 1999). This blocked the proposal put forth by several Jewish groups that advocate Jewish prayer on the Temple Mount to turn Solomon's Stables into a Jewish prayer area (*Ha'aretz*, 21 May 1998; Rubinstein, 12 June 1998; Shragai, 8 June 1998).

The Waqf's construction activities were included in the framework of the *status quo* by the end of 1999. In August 1999 the Islamic Movement in Israel, which has evinced great interest in al-Haram al-Sharif and has helped obtain financial resources and provide manpower for the preservation and development of the holy site, cooperated with the Waqf in creating a large ventilation opening in the Al-Aqsa basement, on the southern external wall of the compound. The Israeli government was concerned that this would lead to the opening of a new gate to the Temple Mount and to a radical change in the *status quo*. While willing to accept the Waqf's authority within the compound on a *de facto* basis, the government was not prepared to allow the Waqf to affect the external face of the holy site. At the order of the Barak government, and with the tacit consent of political elements in the Palestinian Authority, the opening was blocked. In exchange, the Barak government approved the creation of an alternative opening to the compound. However, the opening created by the Waqf was wider and deeper than the approved dimensions, and by the beginning of the year 2000 had encompassed five ancient arches over a length of 50 meters (*Ha'aretz*, 1 Dec. 1999, 3 Dec. 1999, 6 Dec. 1999, 3 Jan. 2000).

There were three responses by the Israeli establishment. The Israel Antiquities Authority complained that the archaeology of the site, which dated to the Second Temple period and which had been renovated in the Muslim period, was being damaged (*Ha'aretz*, 7 Dec. 1999). But the Antiquities Authority was unable to evaluate the archaeological damage and did not relate to the place as an active holy site. The Jerusalem municipality, Mayor Olmert in particular, complained of the infringement of Israeli law and sovereignty, since the work was carried out without a city permit. Olmert initiated the process of issuing stop work orders and the municipality threatened to disconnect the Waqf's water supply if the work was not halted (*Ha'aretz*, 3 Dec. 1999, 6 Dec. 1999; *Kol Ha-Ir*, 10 Dec. 1999).

In contrast with these two approaches, which, if implemented, would have led to confrontation, the Barak government preferred talking. Discussions that the minister of internal security, Shlomo Ben-Ami, held with the political leadership of the Palestinian Authority and top Waqf officials led to an agreement that only two of the arches would be left open and that what Israel considered to be archaeological supervision of construction work on the Temple Mount would be renewed. This was, at most, in fact, loose, symbolic supervision from a distance, with discussions between Palestinian and Israeli archaeologists rather than a hierarchical relationship. These government measures were approved by the District Court, which rejected a petition to issue a stop work order against the Waqf because of its damage to Jewish remains and antiquities (*Ha'aretz*, 7 Dec. 1999).

Har Homa: an obstacle to the Oslo accords

Immediately after the 1967 war, Israel declared a hill to the southeast of Jerusalem, called Jabel abu-Ghnim by the Arabs and Har Homa by Israel, as "green" territory, in order to prevent the local Arabs from building there. In April 1991 Israel appropriated 1,850 dunams there for "public use," with the intention of constructing a Jewish neighborhood of 30,000 inhabitants. Only a third of the land was expropriated from local Arabs. The rest was taken from Jewish landowners, half of them private individuals and half public bodies. The change of government in 1992 had no effect on the plan's progress, even though the housing minister tried to push it forward with Rabin's approval and blessing (*Ha'aretz*, 11 Jan. 1995). Israel wanted to use the new residential neighborhood to complete the encirclement of East Jerusalem by controlling all the heights that overlook it. Jerusalem's city engineer said that "Har Homa is not exceptional. Political rather than professional planning considerations dictate the development of the entire city. The greater part of planning and development in the city after unification has been done for political purposes, the principle of which is to establish a Jewish majority in the city and hold the most important strategic positions and establish Jewish neighborhoods on them" (Eldar, 17 March 1997). In the wake of the Oslo accords, the political importance of these neighborhoods increased, because their establishment would create a physical Israeli wedge between Palestinian Authority territory and the Arab neighborhoods of Jerusalem. For the same reasons, the Palestinians had an escalating interest in preventing the establishment of these neighborhoods.

The Israeli government considered the possibility of pushing the program forward, but it generally held back because of the reaction it expected from the Palestinians, as well as from the local and international communities (Shragai, 15 Oct. 1996). Prime Minister Netanyahu did not approve the project for these same reasons, despite efforts by ministers Suissa and Sharon as well as Mayor Olmert (*Ha'aretz*, 19 Dec. 1996, 24 Dec. 1996, 2 Jan. 1997). Netanyahu changed his mind at the end of February 1996. On Feburary 26, 1997 a ministerial committee approved the Har Homa plan, which included 6,400 housing units. The first stage of construction, of 2,450 units, was also approved. Netanyahu was subject to pressures from opposing directions – defense and security officials pressured him, as before, to delay the plan, since carrying it out would bring a harsh Palestinian response (Eldar, 13 Feb. 1997; *Ha'aretz*, 17 Feb. 1997). Against them were ranged political forces that had a more powerful influence on the prime minister – the settler lobby and hawks in the Likud and other coalition parties, including Mayor Olmert. They were prepared to swallow, with difficulty, Israel's redeployment in Hebron on condition that the Har Homa project and the plan to link Ma'aleh Adumim with Jerusalem commence immediately. Netanyahu believed that confrontation with the Palestinians was unavoidable because they would not accept his plan for a permanent settlement, in particular in Jerusalem (*Ha'aretz*, 19 March 1977). Israel's interest, as he saw it, was to begin the confrontation early on and conduct it around the issue of Jerusalem, about which there was a broad consensus in Israel.

At the beginning of his term, the Likud government tried to raise the diplomatic price it was asking the Palestinians to pay, with the intention of blowing up the Oslo talks. The Likud considered the Oslo framework, imposed on it by the previous government, unbearable. Netanyahu's failure to achieve this goal led to the signing of the Hebron agreement. This was the first time that a Likud government had assumed any sort of obligation under the Oslo framework, in contradiction of its previous worldview. The Palestinians and the international community applauded the Israeli government, while the hawks of the Likud and the religious right condemned it. The Netanyahu government had serious difficulties, however, in proceeding along the Oslo path, especially after the Hebron agreement, because that had set dates for the resumption of the permanent status talks and three additional Israeli withdrawals from Zone C areas. The shadow of the permanent settlement, in the framework of which the Palestinians hoped to receive some 90 per cent of the West Bank and establish a Palestinian state, was a threat to Netanyahu's government. He and Olmert wanted to use Jerusalem as a way of getting off the Oslo track, and hoped to drag the Palestinians with them.

The plan to build Har Homa created a threat and presented simultaneous but separate challenges to Israeli and Palestinian sovereignty, demography, and internal politics. For the Palestinians, the most serious threat was Har Homa's challenge to their sovereignty in the Bethlehem and Jerusalem regions. Palestinian sovereignty was called into question by Israel's unilateral decision to build the neighborhood, despite numerous indications from Palestinian figures that they expected to be consulted about the decision (Eldar, 6 April 1998; *Ha'aretz*, 18 March 1997; Segev, 19 Feb. 1997). Beyond this, the construction of the neighborhood was a substantive threat to Palestinian sovereignty. In the permanent settlement, Har Homa would prevent the creation of a link between the al-Azaria/Abu-Dis area, the center of Palestinian administration in the Jerusalem District, and the Bethlehem/Bait Sahur region, over which the Palestinians had complete control (Zone A). Finally, the construction of Har Homa was part of a series of Likud government measures in Jerusalem, all of which the Palestinians saw as attempts to infringe on their limited foothold in the city, and the possibility of enlarging Har Homa in the permanent settlement. The policy of Labor governments and Jerusalem municipal governments under Teddy Kollek had discriminated against East Jerusalem's Arabs on day-to-day issues, in contrast with the momentum given to the Jewish presence in East Jerusalem. At the same time, however, the East Jerusalem Arabs were allowed to compensate for this discrimination by fostering institutions and local and national identity symbols. In contrast, the Likud government and the Olmert administration advocated the full imposition of Israeli sovereignty on the East Jerusalem Arabs, while promising them compensation on the level of municipal services. The Palestinians rejected the Likud–Olmert approach and demanded the continuation of the previous policy, which was consistent with the Oslo accords. But the Likud government realized that Israeli sovereignty in East Jerusalem was being eroded, and feared losing it completely in the permanent settlement.

Demographically, the plan to settle 30,000 Jews in Har Homa, and the Likud government's energetic policy to use administrative measures and legislation to change the demographic balance in Jerusalem, aroused a sharp response from the Palestinian population in Jerusalem and Bethlehem. The protest took on a popular local character, with the public demanding that its political institutions take action. In Israel, in contrast, the demographic threat was the concern of the establishment more than that of the public (Weksler, 15 April 1997).

Arafat's administration faced a challenge when local political establishments in Bethlehem and Jerusalem called on the national administration to oppose the Israeli plan forcefully, and warned it against compromising at the expense of the local residents. The local protest was headed at first by a body called the Emergency Committee for the Defense of Jabel abu-Ghnim, which joined political figures from the Jerusalem and Bethlehem districts with local residents whose land had been expropriated for the construction of the neighborhood (*Al-Quds*, 20 Feb. 1997). At a later stage the protest was led by the Jerusalem and Bethlehem representatives in the Palestinian Authority Legislative Council. The local establishment became the protest group that spurred the national leadership to intensify the struggle and to come out against Israeli settlements in general (*Al-Quds*, 14 Feb. 1997). From the end of February 1997 the national leadership led the protest, turning Har Homa into a symbol of Israel's expansionist activity (*Al-Quds*, 24 Feb. 1997; *Ha'aretz*, 12 March 1997).

A similar challenge developed in Israel when a hawkish pressure group, characterized by manifestly local motives, developed in the Likud, the municipality, and the Knesset. In the absence of communication and mutual trust between Netanyahu and Arafat, the local establishments grew stronger and the national leaderships were unable to control them. The national leadership on both sides of the political divide stood at the head of local forces and created a united front against the other side. Only when the crisis became a regional one, with the involvement of Jordan, Egypt, pan-Arab and pan-Islamic bodies, and the United States, did Israel realize that it had to minimize potential damage and declare some sort of construction for Arabs as well. On February 25, 1997, a ministerial committee decided to order the planning of infrastructure, at a cost of $50 million, for the construction of 3,015 Arab housing units in East Jerusalem over the next ten years (*Ha'aretz*, 25 Feb. 1997). Israel's decision highlighted the gap between the two parts of the city. First, unlike the Har Homa neighborhood, which was to be built with government funding, the decision on Arab housing was only to provide the infrastructure development for private construction (*Ha'aretz*, 25 Feb. 1997, 27 Feb. 1997). Second, full-speed work on Har Homa commenced on March 18, 1997, while the development in East Jerusalem remained on paper, either because the necessary permits had not been issued or because there was no real intention of carrying it out. The harsh international reaction to the ministerial committee's decision led Ölmert and Netanyahu to the conclusion that, without government-assisted housing construction for Arabs, it would be impossible to mitigate the criticism of construction of a Jewish neighborhood. Therefore, when the ministerial committee's decision was brought before the full cabinet for ratification on March 14, 1997, the cabinet instructed Jerusalem's planning institutions to plan for public construction of 400 housing units on state land that had been expropriated in 1968 from the village of Sur Baher, which borders on Har Homa (*Ha'aretz*, 16 March 1997, 18 March 1997). This instruction, however, also remained on paper. The Jerusalem municipality and the Housing Ministry have not yet prepared the necessary plans. Neither has the amount of government assistance for the project been determined (*Kol Ha-Ir*, 28 March 1997), at a time when the Har Homa project has benefited from extensive funds. Israel's decision thus not only called attention to the gap between Jewish and Arab Jerusalem, but also to the fact that East Jerusalem is a disputed area. Israeli construction in East Jerusalem had never before raised so large an international storm.

Faced with construction at Har Homa, Arafat decided to strive to isolate Israel in the international arena and to insert a wedge between it and the U.S. (*Ha'aretz*, 2 March 1997). The Palestinian Authority proceeded along several parallel channels for this purpose. First, the Palestinian Authority staged a series of protests. Its institutions organized a general strike on March 3, 1997, the first step in mobilizing Palestinian society and political forces for ongoing resistance (*Al-Quds*, 3 March 1997, 4 March 1997; *Ha'aretz*, 3 March 1997, 4 March 1997).

The strike's success enabled the Palestinian Authority to switch to a second form of protest, which included demonstrations next to Israeli army and police positions. Disturbances began at Har Homa itself when the decision to build there was made, spreading to the Jerusalem/Bethlehem boundary (*Ha'aretz*, 28 Feb. 1997). When work actually began, on March 18, 1997, Jerusalem's northern border with Ramallah also became a focus of protest. On Land Day, March 30, 1997, the protests encompassed most of the West Bank and Gaza Strip. Land Day, which commemorates the struggle waged by Palestinian citizens of Israel in 1976 against the expropriation of their land in the Galilee, has become an annual day of protest by Israel's Arabs against their government's land confiscations. Twenty-one years later, it turned into a protest against Israeli policy in Jerusalem. Land Day in 1997 was led by Palestinians in the Palestinian Authority rather than by Israeli Arabs. On April 8, 1997 the center of friction moved to Hebron, the only Palestinian city in whose heart lives a small group of Israeli settlers. The settlers and Hebron's Arabs have a long history of antagonism (*Ha'aretz*, 19 March 1997, 8 April 1997, 9 April 1997). The protest was thus expanded from being merely against construction at Har Homa to a protest against the Israeli settlements as a whole. The organization switched from local to national, with Fatah at its head. The movement enlisted young activists in the demonstrations, augmenting them with children and teenagers who were only too happy to throw stones at Israeli forces (*Al-Quds*, 24 March 1997).

The protests were not violent at the start. On the day that work commenced on Har Homa, Arafat spoke on Palestinian radio and appealed to his people not to react violently (*Ha'aretz*, 19 March 1997). The local leadership that led and organized the demonstrations at the construction site also wished to avoid violence (*Ha'aretz*, 18 March 1997, 20 March 1997). As the demonstrations came to encompass more and more people at more and more places in the West Bank, they became more fervent and threw stones and Molotov cocktails at Israeli forces, who responded by firing rubber bullets and tear gas (*Ha'aretz*, 21 March 1997). The first Palestinian was killed on March 29, 1997, ten days after the demonstrations began, and the number of wounded by then was 480 (*Al-Quds*, 31 March 1997). In the first ten days of April the number of Palestinians killed reached six . During the demonstrations, Palestinian police and security forces worked to calm down particularly turbulent focal points of confrontation (*Ha'aretz*, 25 March 1997, 31 March 1997; Segev, 1 April 1997). Violent protest was controlled by preventing physical contact between Israeli soldiers and Palestinian demonstrators, and by placing Palestinian security forces in a dangerous position between the two camps. Rules of the game were established between the sides, preserved thanks to low-level coordination in the field, which continued to take place despite the suspension of political coordination between the Israeli and Palestinian covert security services. In comparison with the Intifada, Israeli soldiers adopted restrained rules of fire, and the tanks that were meant to threaten the Palestinian Authority with the reoccupation of its territory were deployed within army camps rather than on the outskirts of Palestinian cities.

Arafat had the diplomatic arena in mind, and everything he did was meant to further his position there. He decided to cut off all political ties with Israel, looking to the U.S. and hoping to tilt it in the Palestinians' direction (*Al-Quds*, 28 March 1997, 31 March 1997; *Ha'aretz*, 19 March 1997, 20 March 1997, 27 March 1997). On March 16, 1997 he held an international meeting in Gaza "to save the peace process," with the participation of ambassadors from the countries involved in the Oslo accords. The United States was the first country to respond in the affirmative to

Arafat's invitation (*Al-Quds*, 12 March 1997), thereby signaling to the other countries that they should participate. But the U.S. opposed Arafat's intention of turning the meeting from a unilateral event to a permanent forum, and of calling on the participants to intervene directly in the crisis Israel had brought on. As a result, the meeting made no operative decisions (*Ha'aretz*, 16 March 1997).

The Palestinian Authority and the Arab states twice initiated meetings of the UN Security Council, on March 7 and March 21, 1997, in order to propose a resolution condemning Israel for its construction on Har Homa. In the wake of the U.S.'s double veto, the Arab states initiated four sessions of the General Assembly. On March 13, 1997, the General Assembly expressed "serious concern" (*Ha'aretz*, 14 March 1997); on April 24, 1997, a total of 134 countries voted for and three (Israel, the U.S., and Micronesia) opposed a decision condemning the construction at Har Homa, demanding that it be halted forthwith (*Ha'aretz*, 25 April 1997, 27 April 1997). The same pattern repeated itself on July 15 and November 14 of that year (*Ha'aretz*, 9 July 1997, 13 July 1997, 15 July 1997, 16 July 1997, 15 Nov. 1997).

In parallel to its activity at the UN, the Palestinians brought the issue before the heads of state of the Organization of the Islamic Conference (OIC), who met on March 24 in Islamabad. In their final statement, the heads of state, for the first time in the organization's history, expressed support for the Oslo agreements and demanded their full implementation (*Al-Quds*, 24 March 1997).

The Jerusalem Committee of the OIC was convened on March 27, 1997. Behind the scenes there was a struggle between the two approaches. Syria, Saudi Arabia, and Egypt wanted the conference to make an operative decision calling on the organization's member states to freeze their ties with Israel; they were opposed by Morocco and Jordan, with the help of President Clinton's emissary, Dennis Ross, coordinator of the peace talks, who had come to Rabat with the express purpose of preventing an extreme decision. Arafat tacitly joined those seeking a relatively moderate resolution, his purpose being to win U.S. support. The official meeting lasted only 35 minutes, and the final resolution simply repeated the main points of the Islamabad statement (*Al-Quds*, 28 March 1997; *Ha'aretz*, 28 March 1997).

The proposed resolution that was not adopted in Morocco became the recommendation of the foreign ministers of the Arab League, which convened in Cairo a few days later on March 31. They called for halting the normalization process with Israel, including the closure of offices and delegations (*Ha'aretz*, 31 March 1997, 1 April 1997). In order to turn this recommendation into a binding decision of the Arab League, it had to be passed unanimously. An appropriate summit was not called, but despite this, Qatar, Oman, and Tunisia announced that they were freezing the development of their ties with Israel. The Arab states did not want, or perhaps they simply were incapable at this stage, to go so far as to sever relations with Israel, but they marked the path they intended to walk, and waited to see what the U.S. would do.

It was no coincidence that Jordan made a special effort to resolve the crisis. Jordan feared that any worsening of the Palestinian situation in the West Bank would flood Jordan with refugees and migrants (Shamir, 26 Oct. 1997). Unlike Egypt, which favored adopting an aggressive line against the Israeli government, Jordan tried to talk with Netanyahu. Hussein received Netanyahu for an official visit in Amman on February 23, 1997 and entreated him personally, in a last-minute effort, not to build Har Homa. Netanyahu categorically rejected the plea and that same week, on February 24, convened the Ministerial Committee for Jerusalem Affairs to approve the plan. Israel's decision, and Netanyahu's treatment of Hussein, led the king to write a letter to the Israeli prime minister. Its harshness went beyond even Sadat's letter to Menachem Begin after the cessation of the autonomy talks. Hussein trenchantly took Netanyahu to task in a most personal way. Netanyahu's response to Hussein was not long in coming, and was phrased as a cold manifesto on Israeli relations with Jordan. It bordered on hostility to the Palestinians (*Yediot Aharonot* and *Al-Quds*, 12 March 1997).

The United States could not remain indifferent to Israel's decision to build Har Homa. At the beginning of the crisis the Americans tried to obtain bilateral understandings between it and each of the disputant parties with the hope that this would satisfy both sides. Clinton prepared a carrot and a stick. In general, according to the American plan, Arafat was to receive more territory and "more state" and even a discussion of compensation for Israel's damage to the Palestinian identity of East Jerusalem. This

American move expressed the position that the Har Homa construction damaged the Palestinians' status in Jerusalem, and that the U.S. would promote Arafat's preparations for turning the Palestinian Authority into a state. During Arafat's official visit to Washington at the beginning of March 1997, relations between the U.S. and the Palestinian Authority were institutionalized, and in some ways the latter was given the status of a state. This included the establishment of a bilateral committee headed by Secretary of State Albright and Arafat, just like the committees that the U.S. had with Russia, South Africa, and Egypt. Similarly, Clinton promised Arafat that he would exert "his full influence" on Israel to postpone the construction of Har Homa, as opposed to infrastructure work and the preparation of an access road to the site and its connection to the electricity grid, so long as there was no agreement on the subject between Israel and the Palestinian Authority. Furthermore, the U.S. wanted to extract from Israel a series of measures touching on the implementation of the Oslo agreements. Among these were a halt to Israel's confiscation of identity cards from Arab residents of East Jerusalem, the granting of building permits to East Jerusalem Arabs, and a cancellation of demolition orders for illegal structures in East Jerusalem. In exchange, President Clinton asked Arafat not to allow Palestinian extremists to conduct terrorist acts, and to live up to his commitments under the Oslo accords (*Ha'aretz*, 4 March 1997, 7 March 1997). The "carrot" that Clinton offered Israel was a U.S. veto in the Security Council, on March 8, 1997, of the resolution condemning Israel for building Har Homa. The U.S. also accepted Israel's position that its pending withdrawal from Zone C (rural or unpopulated West Bank areas where the Palestinian Authority still had no control) should be limited in scope. Still the U.S. did not accept the miniscule withdrawal that Israel had decided on.

The U.S. hoped that at this stage, after having proved to his party's and his coalition's hawks that he had indeed decided to build Har Homa, Netanyahu would delay the start of the work. Perhaps he would make do with a modest beginning such as a lengthy survey of the site, without bringing in bulldozers and beginning infrastructure work. President Clinton sent a letter to Netanyahu in this spirit on March 13, 1997. Netanyahu categorically rejected the president's appeal. Afterwards, when work had begun, Secretary of State Albright and the president demanded, at a meeting with Netanyahu and minister of defense, Itzchak Mordechay, that the Har Homa construction work be frozen. The Israelis, however, persisted in their refusal (*Ha'aretz*, 30 March 1997, 4 April 1997, 8 April 1997). Clinton even tried to extract a secret promise from Netanyahu that Har Homa was the last Israeli construction project in Jerusalem prior to the permanent settlement, a promise that Netanyahu had previously made to King Hussein. As far as is known, Netanyahu refused to do this as well (*Al-Quds*, 18 March 1997; *Ha'aretz*, 17 Feb. 1997).

The United States, which had not been a partner at Oslo, became responsible for getting Israel back on track, as the Palestinians demanded, and in fact for preventing a complete wreckage of the process that had begun there. Israel's claim that the Palestinian Authority had irreparably damaged the process was not accepted by the U.S. The American efforts did not succeed in calming down either side; both the Israelis and the Palestinians kicked the stick aside and complained that the carrot was too small. Israel was encouraged by the U.S.'s *de facto* acceptance of the decision to build on Har Homa, and was pleased with America's support for the tiny size of the first stage of redeployment in the West Bank. Arafat, for his part, was disappointed with the U.S.'s inability to bring about a suspension of the Har Homa project, and with the planned dimensions of the Israeli withdrawal (*Ha'aretz*, 9 March 1997). The Palestinians had been prepared, at the beginning of the crisis, to reach a deal about the construction at Har Homa. The fact is that their demand for a complete halt to construction there was only an opening position. Yet so long as no compromise was achieved, resentment increased among the Palestinian establishment and frustration grew in the Palestinian street. The entire diplomatic process was on the verge of collapse (*Al-Quds*, 9 March 1997; *Ha'aretz*, 11 March 1997, 18 March 1997).

As a result, the Americans revised their approach and asked Netanyahu to order a halt to the work for a limited period of time. The length of this period varied in the different proposals that were suggested to Israel: (1) a half-year moratorium, after which a decision would be made on whether it should be extended or, alternatively, after the completion of earth and infrastructure work the continuation of the project would be halted until the

completion of work on the construction site that had been promised to the Arabs; (2) the moratorium would last until agreement
was reached on the implementation of parts of the Oslo agreements that had not yet been carried out; (3) Israel would declare
that the neighborhood would not be inhabited until the conclusion of the permanent status talks (*Ha'aretz*, 2 May 1997, 25 May
1997, 26 May 1997). The United States tried to please Netanyahu
by proposing that the project would be stopped only temporarily,
and the Palestinians by getting Israel back on the Oslo track and by
obtaining compensatory construction for Palestinians. But Israel
rejected these proposals, and its supporters in the U.S. applied
counter-pressure (*Ha'aretz*, 2 May 1997, 14 Sept 1997, 19 Sept.
1997, 20 Sept. 1997, 30 Sept. 1997). In June 1997 Congress
passed a resolution stating that united Jerusalem is the capital of
Israel, and in July 1997 a bill was proposed that would require the
government to address all official documents to Israel to "Jerusalem, Israel" (instead of simply "Jerusalem"). Another bill proposed to subordinate the American consulate in East Jerusalem,
which was responsible for contacts with the Palestinian Authority,
to the U.S. embassy in Tel Aviv (the consulate reported directly to
Washington, since the U.S. does not officially recognize East
Jerusalem to be part of Israel) (*Ha'aretz*, 27 July 1997). Beyond
this, Israel's representatives and supporters in Washington tried to
block the improvement of relations between the U.S. and the Palestinian Authority, which it viewed as advancing the Palestinian
Authority's preparations for becoming a full-fledged state. In
practice, the American administration avoided direct confrontation with Israel, out of fear of how its Jewish voters would react.

The discussions about construction for Palestinians in Jerusalem as compensation for the Jewish housing at Har Homa proceeded at a snail's pace. The Americans demanded that
Netanyahu keep his promise to build homes for Arabs in Jerusalem (*Ha'aretz*, 15 April 1997), but discovered that the recommendation to build 3,015 housing units in ten of the city's Arab
neighborhoods could not be carried out, partly because of the
absence of master plans in East Jerusalem and because preparation
of the necessary infrastructure required an investment of NIS 180
million (close to $50 million). Israel thus decided to build housing
for Arabs near Har Homa (*Ha'aretz*, 17 April 1997; *Kol Ha-Ir*, 6
Nov. 1998). But the establishment of an Arab neighborhood of

2,300 housing units alongside Har Homa required the expropriation of land from Arabs, and would turn Har Homa into a Jewish
neighborhood that bordered on three Arab neighborhoods – the
new Arab Har Homa, Bethlehem, and Sur Baher. As a result, on
May 22, 1997, the Jerusalem District Planning and Construction
Committee hastily approved a truncated building plan near Sur
Baher. The plan provided for the first-ever government assistance
for Arab housing in Jerusalem, to enable the construction of 400
housing units on an area of 80 dunams that had been expropriated
from Arabs in 1968. In addition to this, some 3,000 units were to
be built by private initiative in the form of construction on top of
or as an expansion of existing homes, after the construction densi-
ties in Sur Baher were increased from 25 to 70 per cent (*Ha'aretz*,
23 May 1997; *Kol Ha-Ir*, 6 June 1997).

Most of the infrastructure and earthwork at Har Homa was
completed by October 1997. From that date through to the signing of the Wye Plantation agreement on October 23, 1998, tenders
were not issued for the construction of the site. The delay was
ordered by Netanyahu in response to American pressure. Rather
than a trade, then, what emerged was an unofficial suspension of
the construction process (*Ha'aretz*, 10 Dec. 1997, 15 Nov. 1998;
Kol Ha-Ir, 30 Jan. 1998; *Yediot Aharonot*, 8 Jan. 1998). The signing
of the Wye memorandum led to the start of construction and the
marketing of homes to the public. Har Homa can no longer be
stopped, but Israel paid a high diplomatic price for it, a far higher
one than it had ever before paid for building in Jerusalem. Har
Homa is apparently the last Jewish neighborhood that Israel will
build unilaterally in Jerusalem before the permanent settlement.

Israel's Labor government and the Palestinians had an unwritten understanding that breathed life into the Oslo accords. The
PLO and the Palestinian Authority were to pass a series of tests as a
condition of the transformation from a terrorist organization to a
state. This began with the signing of the first Oslo agreement in
September 1993, in which Israel accepted the PLO as a legitimate
negotiating partner. The Labor government maintained that, fundamentally and over time, Arafat had passed the tests. In this view,
the tests imposed by the Oslo accords were bilateral – Israel also
had to pass them. The question of whether the two parties could
live side by side, which was the basis of reaching an interim agreement before a permanent settlement, was a question that applied

to both sides. Quite naturally, Israel took Palestinian violations of the Oslo accords very seriously while minimizing the importance of its own unilateral actions, such as the imposition of a harsh and thorough closure on Palestinian areas, and of its own violations, such as the failure to open the safe passage routes between the West Bank and Gaza Strip and its failure to free Palestinian prisoners. Nevertheless, throughout the service of their governments Rabin and Peres were cognizant of Israel's violations. The Palestinians went along with Israel's violations and unilateral actions because they had received the status of an equal partner, and understood that Israel had difficulty in accepting restrictions on its power and in moving instantly from being an occupier to a situation in which the occupied people had equal status with it. The Oslo process gave both sides hope and enlarged the capacity of each side to accept the other's violations.

The Likud government brought an entirely different outlook to the agreements, acting as if the learning process that the Oslo accords laid out was a one-sided process. The Palestinians were to pass all their tests in full, and only afterwards would they be moved from the status of members of a terrorist organization, or of organizations that encourage terror, to the status of an interlocutor – and even then one of inferior status. The Likud government did not want the permanent settlement to create a Palestinian state with a status equal to that of the State of Israel, but rather to Palestinian autonomy applying to several disconnected territorial enclaves covering just half of the West Bank, leaving broad powers to Israel. To achieve this object, Netanyahu's Likud government launched three parallel paths. The first was to allot half a year to permanent status negotiations, which were to begin immediately, on the assumption that it would succeed in forcing the Palestinians to accept these terms. The Palestinians rejected this absolutely because they wanted to enter the permanent status negotiations while proceeding along the Oslo path and implementing it to its fullest.

Netanyahu's second path was to enter into violent confrontation with the Palestinians, whether it broke out immediately or during the permanent status talks. But the Palestinian Authority acted cautiously and did not want to fall into this trap. The violent reactions to the Har Homa project were discrete, controlled, and supervised. Third, the Likud government acted to expand the

Israeli settlements in general, and Jewish housing in Jerusalem in particular, with the aim of taking control of land that, in its view, had to be under Israeli sovereignty. Unilateral action thus replaced agreements with the Palestinians, and the Likud government stood behind the Oslo agreements only in word. To achieve broad public support for its actions, the Likud government chose to concentrate its efforts in Jerusalem. The capital, it believed, was an area of national consensus, a sacred value that was worth sacrificing and fighting for. However, to achieve even broader support it kept silent about this last argument, and instead formulated its goal negatively: the Labor government, it claimed, had begun the process of handing the city over to the Palestinians (*Ha'aretz*, 19 March 1997, 20 March 1997).

The Likud's policy turned Jerusalem into the essence of the dispute, rather than a separate issue. During the Labor government, which traveled along the Olso path, Israel and the Palestinians reached an understanding of Jerusalem as a problem of its own – not a local and marginal problem, but also not a problem that epitomized the Israel–Palestinian dispute and not the principal dispute between the two sides. The Likud's policy was diametrically opposed because, for the Likud, Jerusalem was at the heart of the confrontation. The way of getting off the Oslo track, or at least of stopping it in its tracks, was to go through Jerusalem, by engaging in intensive unilateral activity there.

The Palestinians viewed Jerusalem as a place they could force the Likud government to continue along the Oslo road (*Ha'aretz*, 24 April 1997). In order to re-isolate the Jerusalem problem from the rest of the pending problems between the Palestinian Authority and Israel, they had to create a controlled diplomatic and violent confrontation with Israel over the opening of the Western Wall Tunnel and Har Homa. From the point of view of the Palestinians, the confrontation over Jerusalem was not meant to blow up or halt the Oslo process, but rather to advance it. When Israel put Jerusalem at the focus of the dispute, the Palestinians also began stiffening their position. Arafat stopped talking publicly about a creative solution to the problem and maintained that Jerusalem was the Palestinians' red line (*Al-Quds*, 8 March 1998). In other words, Jerusalem turned from a different and special issue to the essence of the dispute between Israel and the Palestinians. "The struggle for Jerusalem is for us a question of life or death …

we will mobilize all efforts and abilities to save Jerusalem and against Israel's policy … Israel is a red line" (*Al-Quds*, 2 July 1998).

8

CONCLUSION

BRIDGES OVER A DIVIDED CITY

The beginning of the permanent status negotiations

The permanent status negotiations opened on May 6, 1996, but Israel's change of government that same month quickly put the negotiations into deep freeze, and they were resumed only in October 1999, following the Barak government's accession the previous May. When the talks began in May 1996, Israel was officially promoting the plan that Rabin had presented to the Knesset at the beginning of October 1995, according to which, Jerusalem, in its current borders, would remain united under Israeli sovereignty, with Israel respecting the rights of all the city's religious faiths. Furthermore, Israeli settlements in the "greater Jerusalem" area would be included in its borders: Ma'aleh Adumim, the Etzion Bloc, Efrat, Betar, and Givat Ze'ev (*Ha'aretz*, 6 Oct. 1995).

In mid-1997, Prime Minister Binyamin Netanyahu presented his government with his plan for a permanent settlement, according to which "greater Jerusalem" was much larger than it had been in the Labor Party plan. Netanyahu stretched the "greater Jerusalem" boundary northward to Ramallah in order to include the settlements Pesagot and Beit El, and on the west he significantly broadened the "Jerusalem corridor," the narrow strip of land that had, before 1967, linked Jerusalem to the rest of Israel. The result would have been that the Jerusalem area would stretch from the Dead Sea to Israel's coastal plain, effectively bisecting the West Bank. With regard to the Islamic and Christian holy places, Netanyahu suggested adopting a functional solution that would provide free access along agreed routes, in exchange for parallel passage to those Jewish holy places located in the 40 per cent of the

West Bank that would be under Palestinian rule (*Ha'aretz*, 29 May 1997, 5 June 1997).

Given the limited success of Israel's measures aimed at altering the demographic balance in Jerusalem, and the lack of progress on Mayor Ehud Olmert's construction plans (the exception being the first stage of the Har Homa neighborhood), Israeli planning authorities had no choice but to prepare a significant extension of the city's borders. "Greater Jerusalem" is not understood as a joint, equally divided Jewish and Arab urban space, but rather as an entity with a sharply clear national–ethnic–religious character. As in the past, the boundaries of the urban space were not determined by geographical considerations, but by national ones. On February 12, 1997, the Israeli cabinet decided, secretly, to establish an umbrella municipality for the Jerusalem region. It was clear to the government that it was impossible, from a diplomatic and political point of view, to annex the Jewish West Bank settlements in the Jerusalem region to Israel, so the decision was to grant the umbrella municipality "planning and other powers" in the area "to the east, north, and south" of the city (*Ma'ariv*, 21 June 1998). The cabinet decided to appoint a team of experts to examine how the decision could be implemented. This Commission for the Strengthening of Jerusalem recommended the transfer of powers presently held by the district offices of government ministries to the umbrella municipality and coordination "with representatives of the Ministry of Defense [which is responsible for the West Bank and settlements] about the manner of the integration of the settlements to the east, north, and south, especially regarding planning and construction" (*Ma'ariv*, 21 June 1998).

The commission advised establishing the umbrella municipality via Israeli legislation. Its powers would be divided between it and the municipalities and local councils that would be included within it, and would include areas of authority currently held by Israel's national government. The umbrella municipality would not collect taxes, including property taxes, but would rather address issues of planning and construction, infrastructure, environmental quality, landscaping, economic development, tourism, emergency and security systems, health, immigrant absorption, cemeteries, and all other matters that the minister of the interior would see fit to transfer to it. The umbrella municipality would be headed by the mayor of Jerusalem, and it would receive funding from the national government and enjoy broad powers. A regional planning bureau would be established in the framework of the umbrella municipality, receiving the construction and planning powers that are today invested in the ministries of the interior and defense.

The recommendations do not specify the names of the West Bank settlements that would be included in the umbrella municipality, but they state explicitly that West Bank settlements are to be included. The plan was presented as a "rescue action" against "the demographic threat" presented by Jerusalem's Arabs, who were liable, in the estimate of Israeli authorities, to become a full 40 per cent of the city's population. Even though the plan preserved the autonomy of the small settlements beyond the annexation lines of June 1967, Jerusalem's shadow would fall over them, and the Jerusalem municipality would gain more control of their affairs, in particular in the areas of construction and planning. The documents do not specify which settlements would be included in the umbrella municipality, but it was stated orally that these would be Ma'aleh Adumim, Givat Ze'ev, and Betar. They would not be fully annexed to Jerusalem, unlike the localities that were within the borders of the pre-1967 State of Israel – Ramat Rahel, Beit Zayit, Mevasseret Ziyyon, Ora, Aminadav, Tzur Hadasah, and Mevo-Betar. On June 21, 1998, the cabinet approved the Commission's recommendations and set up a committee of ministry director-generals to formulate recommendations on the structure of the umbrella municipality, the localities to be included in it, its powers, and its operational procedures. The Commission was supposed to complete this task by September 20, 1998, but at the time of writing, it has not done so. Furthermore, the inhabitants of the communities to the west of the city that are slated for annexation have organized themselves to oppose the plan, protesting that they do not want to be forced to become part of a city that many of them deliberately left. As a result, the minister of the interior was charged with drafting recommendations, by August 1, 1998, regarding the jurisdiction of the umbrella municipality (*Ha'aretz*, 11 May 1997, 25 March 1998, 22 April 1998, 20 May 1998, 21 May 1998, 7 June 1998, 19 June 1998, 22 June 1998; *Kol Ha-Ir*, 5 Dec. 1997). These recommendations also have yet to be submitted (*Ha'aretz*, 30 Nov. 1999), apparently because, on second thoughts, he is reluctant to cede a part of his ministry's powers to the Jerusalem municipality (*Kol Ha-Ir*, 20 Oct. 1998). The only body to move towards implementation of the program is the Jerusalem municipality, which on June 23, 1998 approved the establishment of a metropolitan industrial zone near the Al-Za'im intersection in the northern part of the city (*Ha'aretz*, 26 June 1998).

The cabinet's decision has more than the technical–organizational significance that its proponents attributed to it. It involves transferring the above-mentioned West Bank settlements from the oversight of the Ministry of Defense to Israeli civilian authority. The intention is to blur the distinction between Israel and the West Bank in planning and construction, the very areas that were the Likud government's central tool for trying to establish facts in Jerusalem prior to the permanent settlement. Specifically, implementation of the plan will allow Israel to advance Plan 1E and to broaden control in areas of civilian activity that are generally associated with sovereignty. Today, Israeli army regulations allow a Jewish settler in the territories to enjoy, as a private citizen, most of the individual rights of an Israeli citizen. The plan seeks to raise these rights from the particular to the general level. The metropolitan institutions will grant a range of new meanings to the distinction between a Jewish settler and a Palestinian inhabitant, and these will have *de jure* status, as opposed to the *de facto* status of the military orders. Finally, the plan unilaterally divests power from the Palestinians, ignoring the numerical parity between them and Israelis within the boundaries of "greater Jerusalem" (Eldar, 22 June 1998).

The U.S. did not accept Israel's position that the cabinet decision had no diplomatic significance and that there was therefore no reason for intervention in Israel's internal affairs (*Ha'aretz*, 22 June 1998; *Ma'ariv*, 21 June 1998). Not wanting to veto a security council resolution introduced by the Arab states calling on Israel to cancel the plan, the U.S. negotiated with Arab representatives and the two sides agreed that the resolution would be withdrawn in favor of a consensus statement to be issued by the Security Council president to the effect that the Israeli government's decision was "a serious and harmful development" (*Ha'aretz*, 15 July 1998). Israel's unilateral actions in Jerusalem had once again caused King Hussein to place himself at Arafat's side. At a mini-summit convened in Cairo with Mubarak and Arafat, Hussein declared that the plan "requires all of us ... to take a stand against what is happening and to stop any change that takes place in the field. ... We see the establishment of an independent Palestinian state in the Palestinian homeland with Jerusalem as its capital as our major demand and we will not deviate from it" (*Al-Quds*, 6 July 1998).

In parallel with the greater Jerusalem plan, the Ministry of Construction and Housing had published, by the end of 1999, tenders for the construction of 2,506 housing units in the part of the West Bank adjoining Jerusalem. On paper, there is a plan to double the number of housing units in the urban settlements around Jerusalem which, at the beginning of 2000, had about 12,000 housing units and a population of some 66,000 (*Ha'aretz*, 9 Jan. 1998, 6 Dec. 1999; Shragai, 18 Jan. 1998). According to the Israeli government and the Jerusalem municipality, implementation of the construction plans and of the other clauses in the plan to strengthen Jerusalem will create a demographic balance of 70 per cent Jews and 30 per cent Arabs in greater Jerusalem as a whole, and not just within its current borders. This demographic balance has become the guide for Israeli planning authorities, instead of the previous aspiration to reach a 75:25 ratio (*Ha'aretz*, 21 Jan. 1999, 3 May 1999; *Kol Ha-Ir*, 22 Jan. 1999). As noted above in chapter 7, during the years 1997–2000 the number of requests for building permits submitted to the local Palestinian in the Jerusalem district was about 3,000. The demographic balance in the Jerusalem metropolitan area has not changed in Israel's favor.

The Palestinians also commenced preparations for the permanent settlement. At the 21 convention of the Palestinian National Council, held in Gaza in April 1996, it was decided to establish a Jerusalem and Building of the Homeland Committee as a PNC committee, with the goal of influencing the positions to be taken by Arafat in the negotiations over Jerusalem in the permanent status talks.

The committee was headed by Faisal Husseini, whose presence was clearly felt in its decisions. It expressed the positions and concerns of Orient House and the political establishment in Jerusalem. The concluding report laid out the dangers to the Palestinian identity of East Jerusalem as a result of "the lack of a national Palestinian strategy for coping with the measures being taken by Israel" (*Al-Quds*, 26 April 1996). The committee demanded that the Palestinians "prepare with precision their negotiating file on Jerusalem and decide what their red lines are on the subject. This requires enlisting all Palestinian potential, talent, and expertise, as well as the assistance of friends, in order to reinforce the position of the Palestinian negotiator" (*Al-Quds*, 26 April 1996). The committee's statement and its lines of action matched the plans that had been previously prepared by the Orient House staff (*Ha'aretz*, 28 June 1996).

On the parliamentary level, the Palestinian Authority Legislative Council decided in mid-May 1996 that its permanent seat would be in Jerusalem and that until it could be established it would migrate between Gaza, Ramallah, and El-Bireh. This was a symbolic decision, to which an organizational decision was appended. The Council established a committee for Jerusalem affairs for the purpose of tracking the permanent status talks, to oversee the activities of the Jerusalem Affairs Ministry, and to take part in determining "a comprehensive national strategy on Jerusalem that will take into consideration the city's needs and reinforce the steadfastness of its inhabitants" (*Al-Quds*, 17 May 1996; Ahmad, 1997). This definition of roles and powers was supported by a majority in the Legislative Council, winning out over a formulation proposed by one of the Jerusalem representatives, Hatem Abd al-Qadr Eid, who demanded that the statement of appointment declare explicitly that Jerusalem is an inseparable part of the territories occupied in 1967. This was not Hatem Eid's only "hawkish" position. He also said that when the Jerusalem question was placed on the negotiating table, at which time Israel would demand that the permanent agreement guarantee Israeli sovereignty over East Jerusalem, the Palestinians must, in response, state their demands regarding Palestinian claims to property that Palestinians had left behind them in West Jerusalem in 1948. This position did not, however, win broad support (*Ha'aretz*, 17 May 1996). The high level of activity of the Legislative Council members from Jerusalem with regard to their electoral district, and their stand against the national leadership, led Palestinian public opinion to identify the Legislative Council as an institution that was fighting for Jerusalem. According to a CPRS survey conducted in September and October 1996, Jerusalem was the issue on which the Legislative Council received the highest marks. Nationally, 70.8 per cent of those surveyed claimed that the Council's accomplishments in this area were "good" or "very good," which was 10.9 per cent higher than the marks it received on its handling of the settlement issue. The Council received high marks from the residents of Jerusalem as well, even if considerably lower than its rating on the national level – 58.2 per cent.

On the whole, two approaches can be discerned within the Palestinian establishment. The first is that of the Jerusalem delegation to the Palestinian Legislative Council and of the local political establishment centered on Orient House – in particular Hatem 'Id, Hanan Ashrawi, and Faisal Husseini. They seek to limit the distinction between Jerusalem and the rest of the 1967 territories to a single principle: preventing the physical division of the city by a wall like the one that divided it between 1948 and 1967. The border should be the one that preceded the 1967 war, and Palestinian political sovereignty over East Jerusalem should, they feel, be complete.

Knowing that Israel would demand that its annexation of East Jerusalem be recognized and grounded in the permanent settlement, Faisal Husseini remarked that the Palestinians would counter with a demand that Palestinian property in west Jerusalem be returned to them. Husseini stated that the permanent status talks would discuss west as well as East Jerusalem; according to him, 70 per cent of the land in west Jerusalem is Palestinian property (*Al-Ayam*, 27 Sept. 1999). In keeping with this, two Palestinian institutions, the Institute for Land and Water Research and Legal Services and the Association for the Protection of Human Rights, began collecting material for a database that would serve as the basis for claims to ownership of this property (*Ha'aretz*, 8 Feb. 1996, 19 Feb. 1996, 22 Sept. 1997, 24 Sept. 1998).

These moves should be viewed as being aimed at providing a card to play and not as a new Palestinian strategy for taking over large parts of west Jerusalem. Israel will concede all or most of its claims in East Jerusalem and the Palestinians will do the same with their claims in the west side of the city. If the area subject to negotiation is just East Jerusalem, the compromise lines will pass through the Arab part of the city and the Palestinians' gains in Jerusalem will be negligible. For this purpose, Husseini has invoked Israel's classic, almost mythic, claim that Jerusalem is and must forever be a single and indivisible city. If the principle is that sovereignty over the city cannot be divided, then the two sides of the city must then be discussed together. If Israel should refuse to do so, the Palestinians would be able to argue that Jerusalem is not one city but two, and that sovereignty should be divided according to the 1967 lines (Abd al-Hadi, 1996: 213–22; *Al-Ayam*, 27 Sept. 1999; *Al-Quds*, 14 May 1996; Husseini, 1996: 203–8; Musallam, 1996: 121–6).

The major Palestinian national institutions in Gaza advocated the second approach. In his speech at the opening ceremony of the talks, Abu-Mazen explicitly stated that the Palestinian capital was East Jerusalem alone. "We are eager to live in peace in the framework of an independent Palestinian state whose capital is East Jerusalem, and whose borders are secure and recognized, the June 4, 1967 borders" (*Al-Quds*, 6 May 1996). Arafat also stated more than once that "the Jerusalem that we are speaking of is East Jerusalem (*Al-Quds al-Sharqiyya*), the capital of the Palestinian state" (*Al-Ayam*, 6 Dec. 1998; 2 Nov. 1999; *Ha'aretz*, 30 Nov. 1998). In their opinion, Jerusalem is one of several issues to be resolved in the permanent status negotiations. It is not an issue that stands above all other issues; it is of equal importance and can therefore be discussed in the framework of a deal with Israel over a set of issues. It was this approach that in fact stood at the basis of what is called the Beilin/Abu-Mazen document (Beilin, 1997: 167–70).

The Beilin/Abu-Mazen understandings

In secret negotiations that were conducted in 1994–5, Israeli and Palestinian teams formulated an unofficial statement of understanding on the parameters of the permanent agreement. Their goal was to finish the job by May 1996, the official opening of the permanent status talks. At that time, according to the plan, this framework agreement would be produced and initialed by both sides. Israel would hold national elections that would also serve as a national plebiscite on the framework agreement, making it possible to reach a full agreement within a short time (Beilin, 1997: 180). Most of the discussions were conducted between the Israeli team that had originally been involved in the Oslo initiative – Dr. Ron Pundik and Dr. Yair Hirschfeld, under the direction of Yossi Beilin – and two academic figures from England – Dr. Ahmed Khalidi and Hussein Agha, under the direction of Abu-Mazen. Dr. Khalidi and Agha, Fatah members since the 1960s, had been members of the advisory team to the Palestinian delegation to the Madrid conference, and Khalidi had also participated in the negotiations at Taba over the Oslo II agreement (Beilin, 1997: 183, 195). In these talks, Jerusalem was one of the issues on the agenda, but not the most important or most fundamental of them. The difficulty of reaching agreement on Jerusalem was no greater than that of agreeing on the future of Israel's settlements in the territories. Even when agreement was not reached on various constituent questions of the Jerusalem issue, it did not keep the teams from progressing towards solutions to other questions (Beilin, 1997: 174, 193, 200).

The concluding session of the discussions on the document took place on October 30, 1995. It was not an official agreement, but rather an academic and non-binding understanding formulated with the knowledge and under the direction of Beilin and Abu-Mazen, from which the political leadership could continue with the negotiations. The first section of the document deals with the establishment of a Palestinian state, which had, for the Palestinians, become a touchstone for which they were prepared to pay with other issues, including Jerusalem. The Beilin/Abu-Mazen understandings expanded Jerusalem's borders and redivided the expanded territory into five political–municipal areas: the capital of Israel, the capital of Palestine, the Temple Mount, the Old City, and the Arab and Jewish neighborhoods on the east side of the city. In these five areas there was a variable, differential level of Israeli and Palestinian sovereignty.

The proposal was to expand the city's territory and establish an umbrella municipality for the Jerusalem area. The umbrella municipality would be administered by a Jewish majority and would be headed by a mayor. Two sub-municipalities would function under the umbrella municipality: a Jewish sub-municipality, which would provide services to and be responsible for all the Jewish neighborhoods in the west and east of the city, including in the Old City, and an Arab sub-municipality, which would provide identical services to the Arab residents in the new and expanded part of Jerusalem. The jurisdiction of this sub-municipality would extend over areas that are not currently part of Jerusalem's municipal territory: Al-Azariya and Abu-Dis, alongside the rest of the more distant suburbs of East Jerusalem. This sub-municipality would be called Al-Quds and would be the capital of the

Palestinian state. The Israeli part of the city would include west Jerusalem and Ma'aleh Adumum and Givat Ze'ev, which would be annexed to the city. Each side would recognize the other's capital. Israel's recognition of the capital of Palestine, after long years of denying the Palestinians' nationality and their tie to Jerusalem, would be an historic achievement. Palestinian recognition of west Jerusalem as the capital of Israel would allow the Arab and Islamic states and the rest of the world's countries to follow suit and recognize Israel's capital, which most countries now refuse to do. East Jerusalem as it is now defined – the Arab and Jewish neighborhoods on the east side of the city, with the exception of the Old City – would remain an area that both sides would continue to claim for themselves and over which Israel would be prepared to negotiate. In practice, however, this area would continue to be under Israeli sovereignty until such time as the two sides reach an accommodation. Israel would argue that there had been no return to the 1967 borders, in Jerusalem in particular, and that Jerusalem was not under divided sovereignty, since the Palestinian capital would be established outside the current borders of the city in an area that is now under the rule of the Palestinian Authority. The Palestinians could claim that their recognition of west Jerusalem as the capital of Israel is acknowledgement of an established fact, and that they had, by negotiation, succeeded in removing East Jerusalem from Israel's hands and annulling its annexation, even though they would not receive full sovereignty over the area that Israel had occupied in 1967.

The question of territorial sovereignty was deliberately left undecided. The sovereignty that would prevail in the current East Jerusalem would be, in Palestinian eyes, a temporary and unrecognized continuation of the forced annexation of 1967. Palestinian citizenship would be extended to Palestinian residents of this area and, in certain matters, Palestinian citizens residing in this area would be subject to Palestinian law. The Palestinians would continue to demand that the area be transferred to their sovereignty, and a joint commission would deliberate the issue without setting a deadline for finishing its job. Israel saw this as a long-term solution, in the framework of which the question of sovereignty would remain without any final resolution. In the meantime, the existing situation would continue to prevail, and Israel could continue to manage the affairs of this area. Israel would claim that the retention of the *status quo* meant that Israel was sovereign, because the Israel police would continue to keep public order; the Palestinians, for their part, could present the establishment of the commission and its mandate to address the issue as an Israeli retreat from the annexation of East Jerusalem. This arrangement would not include the Old City, which would receive a special status; complete and absolute freedom of worship would be guaranteed to the members of all religions at their respective holy sites, with preservation of the *status quo* with regard to Jewish worship on the Temple Mount.

According to the understandings reached by the two teams, the Palestinians would be allowed to raise their flag over al-Haram al-Sharif as an expression of the Palestinian Waqf's autonomous administration of the site, and the compound would be declared extra-territorial sovereignty. Administration of the Islamic holy sites by the Palestinians would not denote their sovereignty, but at the same time Jordan, Saudi Arabia, and Morocco, for example, could not gain a status equal to that of the Palestinians. If they participate in administration of the site it will be because the Palestinians allow them to do so. Of course, the Palestinians would have right of access to the Islamic and Christian holy sites in the Old City, and for this purpose they would be given a corridor between Al-Quds and Al-Haram al-Sharif. In an effort to reduce the expected opposition from Jewish extremists, it was proposed orally in the talks that the Palestinians agree to set aside a small and defined place on the edge of the compound for Jewish prayer, in the area which orthodox Jewish religious law states is undoubtedly outside the ancient Temple Mount, but this proposal was not included in the written document, which emphasizes the preservation of the *status quo*. Unlike the Temple Mount, the Church of the Holy Sepulcher would fall under the jurisdiction of the Palestinian sub-municipality and would not be declared an extra-territorial zone.

In fact, the Beilin/Abu-Mazen understandings expand the bounds of the Old City beyond the area inside the walls, and include the Jehoshaphat Valley and the Mount of Olives with their sites holy to the three monotheistic faiths. Sovereignty over this area would remain in practice in Israeli hands, a kind of continuation of the current situation, but daily life would be managed jointly with the Palestinians. Of course, the Palestinians would not recognize Israeli sovereignty in principle. Moreover, it was possible that there would be equal Israeli and Palestinian representation on the administering body. The zone would be declared a holy area and designated for preservation not only because of its sacred and historic sites, but also in order to prevent national and religious competition over it.

With the exception of the holy area, the entire Jerusalem region would be administratively restructured into a framework of boroughs that would have independence in municipal administration. The boroughs of Al-Quds would comprise its sub-municipality, and the boroughs of Jerusalem would comprise its sub-municipality. The boroughs would be geographic, functional, and national–ethnic units. Palestinians and Israelis would each elect the mayor of its own sub-municipality. It is important to mention that the Arab residents of East Jerusalem would participate in the election of the mayor of Al-Quds, thus expressing their distinct identity. These areas, such as the neighborhoods of Sheikh Jarah and Wadi Joz, would be administered as a borough of the Al-Quds sub-municipality, even though they would not be under Palestinian sovereignty. In this they would be unlike Al-Azaria and Abu-Dis, in which both day-to-day administration and sovereignty would be Palestinian. The understanding that the present residents of East Jerusalem would vote for the mayor of the Palestinian sub-municipality was a Palestinian gain. Unlike the situation in which they were annexed to Israel and could only participate in the elections to the Israeli municipality, they would be able to vote for and be elected as the mayor of Al-Quds. The Palestinians would see this as an expression of their national sovereignty over East Jerusalem, while Israel would claim that the matter was undecided, and that the elections signified only day-to-day administration.

Above the sub-municipalities would be the umbrella municipality, with a city council containing one representative from each of the city's boroughs. This body would choose the mayor. Since, the number of Israeli boroughs and Palestinian boroughs would reflect the present demographic balance of 2:1, it was reasonable to assume that the mayor of "Greater Jerusalem" would be an Israeli. However, the demographic proportions would be updated, in accordance with agreed procedures, in the light of any subsequent changes. The umbrella municipality would assume authority over matters affecting both the sub-municipalities, such as master development plans, main roads, sewerage, and so on. Finally, the Palestinians would be able to use the Atarot (Kalandia) airport without passing through an Israeli border check.

The beauty of the Beilin/Abu-Mazen document is its integration of different elements, such as achievements that both sides share equally, mutual recognition of each other's capitals, the dismantling of the Jerusalem issue into its principal components, and the game of give and take between the sides. This means insisting on an important principle in exchange for the other side's agreement to compromise on a principle that is less important for it, and vice versa. So there would be no Palestinian sovereignty within the boundaries of Jerusalem as established by Israel in 1967, nor on the Temple Mount, while the Palestinians could fly their flag over the Islamic holy sites. Certain municipal functions now exercised by the Israeli municipality of Jerusalem would be transferred to the Al-Quds municipality, and the Arabs of East Jerusalem would participate in the election of the Al-Quds city council, thus connecting them to the Palestinian capital – unlike the current situation, in which they are allowed to vote only for the Israeli city council and mayor on the local level and for the Palestinian Authority on the national level. In exchange, Israel would enjoy control of the umbrella municipality. Furthermore, the Beilin/Abu-Mazen understandings use a range of means to mitigate the dispute over Jerusalem, for example by postponing the resolution of sovereignty over the annexed part of Jerusalem, the declaration of a holy zone so as to prevent extremists from using religious fervor to ignite a nationalist conflagration, the blurring of the term sovereignty, and distinguishing between its legal–official aspects and its political, symbolic, and functional aspects. Each one of the characteristics of sovereignty is divided differently between the sides in the Jerusalem region.

The understandings also make extensive and sophisticated use of the functional approach, focusing on the particular arrangements required by day-to-day life rather than seeking overarching decisions and resolution on the symbolic level. But it is important to emphasize that the understanding achieved by Beilin and Abu-Mazen does not neglect the symbolic. Instead, however, of allowing this aspect to be dominant and to determine the lines of the arrangement, there is a hierarchy of institutions and solutions providing symbolic satisfaction as needed. In other words, the Beilin/Abu-Mazen understandings also use the differential approach, which distinguishes between partial and full realization of rights, aspirations, and symbols, and different levels of municipal administration and definition of the municipal space (for the conceptual basis of the document, see Hasson, 1997).

The Beilin/Abu-Mazen understandings can be seen as preserving the city's unity on a variable basis, yet also as demarcating different levels of the division of Jerusalem. Neither side will fulfill all its dreams, but neither will either side be forced to abandon its viewpoint, which it will realize in some way. Here is the balance sheet for each side: Israel achieves recognition of its capital. There is no Palestinian sovereignty over East Jerusalem as Israel defined it in 1967, nor is there a return to the 1967 borders in Jerusalem. Jerusalem is not divided physically nor with regard to sovereignty. There is no Palestinian sovereignty on the Temple Mount, but rather a *de jure* confirmation of the *de facto* status that has prevailed since 1967. The umbrella municipality is under Israeli control and the mayor will be Israeli; Ma'aleh Adumim and Givat Ze'ev, outside Jerusalem's municipal borders, are annexed to Israel with Palestinian consent. The Palestinians, for their part, achieve recognition of their capital. Israel consents to re-examine the annexation of East Jerusalem, thus placing a question mark over Israeli sovereignty there. A Palestinian flag flies over al-Haram al-Sharif and the Palestinians receive a preferential position there, taking from Israel the power to grant any sort of status to other Arab and Islamic states. There is a safe passage between Al-Quds and the al-Haram al-Sharif compound and joint administration of the Old City. East Jerusalem Arabs participate in the Al-Quds municipal elections, and the Al-Quds sub-municipality runs the day-to-day municipal affairs of the Arabs, in coordination with the umbrella municipality.

The agreement on the outline of the framework and the guiding principles allowed Abu-Mazen to make an optimistic assessment that it would take only a month for Rabin and Arafat to approve the document and its accompanying maps. The assassination of Prime Minister Yitzhak Rabin on November 4, 1995 and the election of a Likud government in May 1996 prevented the plan from being realized. Beilin and Abu-Mazen separately presented the plan to Prime Minister Shimon Peres and to Chairman Arafat a week after the assassination. Arafat and Peres, each for his own reasons, did not accept the document. Peres did not want a quick agreement with the Palestinians – for electoral reasons he preferred to defer negotiations. He believed that the document was premature and that Israel's citizens were not yet prepared to consent to it. He thus rejected Beilin's position that the document should be incorporated into Labor's election platform and that it would help Labor win a majority. Peres preferred to receive a general mandate from the Israeli citizenry for conducting negotiations, rather than for approval of a specific plan. Instead of intensifying the discord in Israeli society he preferred to try to heal the wounds created by the conflict between the supporters of the peace process and its opponents from the national–religious right.

To this should be added the huge responsibility that fell on Peres after Rabin's murder. This was the first time in the country's history that a prime minister or cabinet member had been assassinated, and that after a campaign of defamation, divisiveness and animosity by his political and ideological opponents. After Rabin's assassination no Israeli prime minister can afford not to fear another political murder. This was not just a personal consideration – what another assassination was liable to do to Israeli democracy also had to be taken into account.

As for the document itself, Peres felt that it left the issue of sovereignty over East Jerusalem too open, and he also opposed allowing a Palestinian flag to fly over the Temple Mount. Furthermore, Peres sought a way to include Jordan in the permanent settlement. He wanted to give it an institutionalized and agreed status on al-Haram al-Sharif. Over and beyond all this was the question of the electoral timing (Beilin, 1997: 210–18; Galili, 4 Aug. 1996; *Ha'aretz*, 19 Feb. 1996, 22 Feb. 1996, 31 July 1996, 1 Aug. 1996, 2 Aug. 1996, 10 Oct. 1996, 7 March 1997). The news reports in Israel in August 1996 on the Beilin/Abu-Mazen understandings roused the anger of the Palestinian establishment in Jerusalem (Sokol, 4 Aug. 1996) and embarrassed the Palestinian national establishment. Since the new Israeli government elected in Israel in June 1996 considered the document irrelevant, even Abu-Mazen disassociated himself from it, denying its very existence in a meeting of the Fatah central committee that convened at the beginning of August 1996 (Sokol, 4 Aug. 1996).

Since 1996, a revised version of the Beilin/Abu-Mazen plan has been discussed unofficially by academics from both sides, who have reported their discussions to their respective political leaderships. According to this "improved" proposal, a network of roads, tunnels, and bridges will tie all the pieces of Al-Quds together. The major innovation in the revised plan is a call for Israel to allow Palestinian sovereignty in the Arab neighborhoods within the current Jerusalem boundaries, alongside the Arab suburbs now outside the city. In return, the Palestinians will consent to leave vague or defer the issue of sovereignty in the "holy basin" – the Old City and the surrounding sacred and historical areas. Special arrangements will be made for the "holy basin," including the option of allowing both sides to display their respective national symbols (*Jerusalem Report*, 28 Feb. 2000).

The opening of negotiations on the permanent settlement, in May 1996, sharpened the differences that had been evident earlier between the national Palestinian leadership, which was negotiating with Israel, and the local Jerusalem leadership. The opposition was led by Hatem Abd el-Qadr Eid, a member of the Jerusalem delegation in the Palestinian Legislative Council. He was the moving force behind a leaflet published on May 15, 1996, which stated that "Arab Jerusalem is shrinking … Jerusalem will not return to our hands by negotiation alone" (*Yerushalayim*, 10 May 1996). The Palestinians had to take action, such as finding housing solutions within the Old City; renovating its dilapidated homes; setting a rent ceiling for the city; imposing rules on homeowners who preferred to rent their property to diplomats, foreign journalists, and UN representatives for high prices; and organizing mass demonstrations and strikes. Eid was also behind the protest activity organized in March 1998 by the Fatah's Jerusalem branch against Israel's policy in Jerusalem. Under the direction of the local Fatah, a commercial and school strike was organized, but Arafat clipped Eid's wings and did not permit the protest he had organized to take off. In protest, Eid resigned his chairmanship of the Jerusalem committee in the Legislative Council (*Kol Ha-Ir*, 6 March 1998, 27 March 1998) and stated that "the Palestinian Authority has conceded Jerusalem" (*Kol Ha-Ir*, 27 March 1998). "It looks to me as if they prefer a Palestinian state without

Jerusalem to the opposite," he added (Cohen, 29 April 1998). The elections to the Fatah leadership in Jerusalem, conducted on November 16, 1998, honed its activist profile. Sixty-two candidates competed for 17 seats and fought for the support of some 2,000 voters who gathered for the election. Those elected were young, largely between the ages of 25 and 35, former Intifada and field activists with "hawkish" views (*Kol Ha-Ir*, 20 Nov. 1998). These positions were what led Arafat to declare in his speech to the assembly that if the way of peace did not lead to the realization of the Palestinian right to a state with Jerusalem as its capital, "our rifles are ready, and we are prepared to use them against all who might try to prevent us from praying in Jerusalem" (*Ha'aretz*, 16 Nov. 1998).

A countervailing statement was not long in coming, and was made in Stockholm at an event marking the tenth anniversary of the PLO's recognition of Israel and condemnation of terror. In his speech, Arafat set out the guiding principles for a permanent settlement, and with regard to Jerusalem he stated that the city should remain open "to all its inhabitants without prejudice. The city must remain physically undivided by roadblocks and fortifications. There is no solution to the Jerusalem question unless the interests of all sides are taken into account, together with standing firm on halting the Judaization of Jerusalem and the preservation of the rights of all communities and of adherents of all the monotheistic faiths equally" (*Al-Ayam*, 6 Dec. 1998).

The events and developments in the Jerusalem area since 1967 that affect the form of the permanent status may be categorized in accordance with the following questions: Is there a functional or geographic division between Jews and Arabs? Is there competition between them? If so, in what area and what level of competition?

Areas of functional division between Jews and Arabs

THE SPATIAL IDENTITY OF THE RESIDENTS OF EAST JERUSALEM

Culturally, linguistically, and religiously, the identity of East Jerusalem's inhabitants is Muslim or Christian Arab. Their spatial identity is unique and manifestly distinct from that of Jerusalem's Jewish inhabitants. Even though city ordinances require shopkeepers to display a Hebrew sign alongside those in other languages, the signs in East Jerusalem have no Hebrew, only Arabic and English, with the exception of certain areas frequented by Israeli Jewish customers. Like other foreign languages, Hebrew is an elective, not a required course in East Jerusalem schools and at Al-Quds University. Israeli institutions that function in East Jerusalem have no choice but to use Arabic in order to provide services to the local residents, although Arabic is used alongside Hebrew or English. ATMs, bank statements issued by Israel's Bank Discount, bank forms, municipal forms, and health plan forms are bi- or trilingual (English being the third language), as are the road signs. True, the Hebrew font is larger than the Arabic one on official forms and signs, but this cannot hide the fact that East Jerusalem has its own independent linguistic milieu (al-Qaq, 1997).

Culturally and religiously, it is not only the Muslim religious institutions that create the different character of East Jerusalem. Businesses and commercial establishments are open and public transportation functions on the Jewish Sabbath and holidays, in glaring contrast to the situation in Jewish Jerusalem. Even the entry of Jewish settlers into East Jerusalem Arab neighborhoods has not changed this situation in any fundamental way – the settler homes are few relative to the majority population. There is considerable friction between them. The change that this penetration seeks to make in the spatial identity causes the Palestinian populace to close ranks to repel the threat.

ISRAEL'S POSSESSION OF THE OFFICIAL SYMBOLS OF IDENTITY, AFFILIATION, AND SOVEREIGNTY

There are two facets here – one symbolic and one practical. On the symbolic level, sovereignty is expressed by the simple fact that the inhabitants of East Jerusalem bear Israeli identity cards. The practical side is the benefits, payments, and services that the holders of Israeli ID cards receive, alongside the obligations and payments imposed on them. An Israeli ID card brings with it a variety of benefits inasmuch as it implies official affiliation with Israel. These benefits include the right to vote in municipal elections, social benefits, health and welfare payments, at an average of $354 per person per year in 1999 prices, from Israel's social security system, residential rights in Jerusalem, freedom of movement into and out of the city in times of closure, freedom of employment inside and outside the city, including freedom of movement and of employment in Jewish Jerusalem. The East Jerusalem Arabs consider these rights to be very important since they grant them an economic, social, and employment advantage over their peers in the West Bank. Even though this freedom is interfered with at times by security checks and harassment, these do not detract from the difference in status between East Jerusalem Arabs and the rest of the Palestinians in the West Bank. Israel has exclusivity in these matters; the Palestinian Authority is not a competitor. Israel views the symbolic aspect as the most important, whereas the inhabitants of East Jerusalem accept their Israeli identity in a pragmatic sense.

In this context there is a difference, first and foremost, between the official and functional–local identity of the East Jerusalem Palestinians and their political and national identity. Only 2.3 per cent of them are Israeli citizens; the rest have only resident status. Legally, their national identity is not Israeli and they do not have the political rights that citizenship brings on the national level, the most important of which is the right to vote for and be elected to the Knesset. Likewise, it is important to distinguish between the "strong," full symbolic identity of citizens of Israel and the "weak" symbolic identity of the residents who are not citizens. Holding a resident ID card creates but a "weak" symbolic link with Israel. The Israeli resident status of East Jerusalem Palestinians establishes nothing about their political ties or their national identity.

INSTITUTIONS AND SERVICES

Israeli currency has been the principal legal tender in East Jerusalem since 1967, with the Jordanian dinar functioning alongside it. The dinar's status in East Jerusalem's commercial, economic, and financial life was prominent until its value plunged in 1991. If a currency is not only a means for the development of economic and commercial life but also a national symbol, it was clear that the dominant symbol was the Israeli shekel, but that its status was not exclusive.

Culture and media.   East Jerusalem's culture and media are Arab and Palestinian, functioning in the framework of Israeli law, which subjects them to Israel's censorship office. The over-arching framework is Israeli, but a different linguistic, cultural, and historical identity beats underneath. It should be kept in mind that the national movements in the Middle East built their political consciousnesses and national ideologies on their linguistic–cultural distinctiveness and on consciousness of their historical uniqueness. In most cases this consciousness led them to demand its expression in a separate political structure and national institutions. While it is not necessarily the case, in general, national movements demand full independence for their peoples, and this is the case with the Palestinians. The linguistic, cultural, and historical identity of the Palestinians in East Jerusalem cannot be detached from their political and institutional expression. It is impossible to maintain for any length of time a system in which people of Arab–Palestinian cultural, linguistic, and historical identity remain without national rights, and are discriminated against in the distribution of services and resources, in access to centers of power, and in the operation of the city's control mechanisms. The arrangements for the elections of the Palestinian Authority's president and Legislative Council opened a door in this direction, but they also created a situation that differentiates between East Jerusalem and the rest of the West Bank.

The freedom of the press that the Palestinian media enjoys is a right that it pays for by being subject to Israeli censorship. Being under Israeli law gives Palestinian journalists and intellectuals greater freedom of action than that of their colleagues in the other parts of the West Bank once under Israeli control, and they are more able to criticize central Palestinian institutions. The restraint evident in East Jerusalem media and cultural criticism of the PA and the PLO is a product of self-censorship. Furthermore, during the Intifada, the Israeli framework in East Jerusalem made it easier for the Palestinian institutions there to express their national identity. Israeli civil law, which applies to East Jerusalem, tied the hands of the military in East Jerusalem more than military law did in the rest of the West Bank.

Education. With regard to education, there is an arrangement whereby on the symbolic level (such as the stickers on the bindings of textbooks), and on the organizational level (such as upkeep of municipal school buildings and payment of salaries), the public schools in East Jerusalem are tied to Israel, while the Palestinian Authority determines most of the curriculum, chooses textbooks, and supervises diploma examinations – roles previously filled by Jordan. This arrangement applies only to the public schools that function under the sponsorship of the Jerusalem municipality, not to private schools or those operated by religious institutions. For these, the organizations that operate them have organizational and administrative responsibility. Their symbolic association with Israel is more limited and their links with the Palestinian Authority are tighter. In the transition period between the functional relationship with Jordan and the identical arrangement with the Palestinian Authority, the two national establishments, the Israeli and the Palestinian, both tried to change the rules of the game and open education in East Jerusalem to competition between them. The principal actors were the Israeli municipal and national authorities, which sought to expand their involvement in the determination of curriculum and examinations. This attempt was, however, unsuccessful and as a result they have, for the time being at least, desisted.

Higher education in East Jerusalem is also party to this arrangement, but in this case the link to Israel is very weak. Like the private schools, Al-Quds University operates in East Jerusalem without a permit and without the oversight of Israel's Council for Higher Education, the statutory accrediting and funding body for Israel's colleges and universities. Instead, the standards are set by the parallel Palestinian body. Right-wing groups in Israel have petitioned Israel's High Court of Justice to change this situation but, for the present, Israel's accrediting procedures have not been fully articulated. In any case, there is no competition in this field.

Transportation.   Israeli law sets the standards and licensing procedures for vehicles and traffic in all of Jerusalem, but there are separate and non-competing systems of public transportation in the two parts of the city. The distinction is not only organizational (different service providers) but also in destinations, quality of service, price, and passenger population.

Electricity.   Following the 1967 war, the East Jerusalem Electric Company continued to function as an independent firm. The Jerusalem municipality's attempt to claim that it was the legal successor of the Jordanian municipality and thus had the right to name two members of the company's board of directors was rejected by Israel's High Court of Justice. Israeli construction of housing for Jews in the eastern part of the city, where the East Jerusalem Electric Company's franchise applied, raised the question of who would supply electricity to the new neighbor-hoods. Israel announced that its electric utility would do so, but the East Jerusalem company objected. In January 1970 Israel decided that all its settlements and military installations in the West Bank would be connected to the Arab electricity grid, in return for which the East Jerusalem Electric Company would provide a level of service identical to that provided by its Israeli counterpart and would issue bilingual bills to its Israeli customers. A new generator was purchased to meet the rising demand for electricity but it was never put into operation because Israel found a legal excuse for preventing this. It was agreed that the Arab com-pany would buy electricity from Israel. Because of the mounting demand for electricity from both its Arab and Jewish customers, by the mid-1980s about 90 per cent of the electricity supplied by the East Jerusalem company was purchased from Israel, three times as much as in 1967. The East Jerusalem company's own generators were in a bad condition and the company received no aid from the Israeli government, as the Israeli company did. Like-wise, the East Jerusalem company was unable to raise its prices because, in 1967, it had obligated itself to supply its services at a low price, whereas it paid full price for the electricity it bought from Israel. The East Jerusalem company thus had financial prob-lems and in 1998 became unable to continue to exist as an inde-pendent provider. For all intents and purposes it is now simply an agent of the Israeli company (al-Qaq, 1997; Cheshin et al., 1999: 137–144).

Health.   Israeli law applies to the health system in East Jerusalem. Under its provisions the inhabitants of East Jerusalem are insured by one of the Israeli health plans and receive care in clinics and hospitals on both sides of Jerusalem.

ISLAMIC HOLY SITES AND INSTITUTIONS

Sharia' Courts.   The Sharia' courts of East Jerusalem are not under the jurisdiction of Israel's Ministry of Religious Affairs, under which the Sharia' courts in Israel operate. The State of Israel does not recognize the rulings of the East Jerusalem Sharia' courts for the purposes of registration of personal status (mar-riage, birth), unless they have been ratified by the Sharia' court in west Jerusalem or in Jaffa. For the Israeli authorities, the ratifica-tion document is the binding one. This technical ratification arrangement solves the problem of public records, protects the inhabitants of East Jerusalem, and preserves the independence of the Sharia' courts of East Jerusalem, especially since it is not the court that transmits its rulings to the parallel court on the western side of the city but rather the applicant himself. The west Jerusalem Sharia' court views the application as a purely technical matter, automatically issuing the required document, without considering itself a superior bench to that in East Jerusalem.

Al-Haram al-Sharif. The Islamic holy site compound and its immediate surroundings has, since 1967, been subject to a functional and geographical division between Israel and Islamic religious authorities such as the High Muslim Council, the Waqf, and the mufti of Jerusalem, as well as to the relevant political institutions in Jordan and the Palestinian Authority. The authority for overseeing routine public order, the security of the Islamic holy sites, their religious management, prayer services, and tourism is in the hands of the appropriate religious bodies. Construction and reconstruction in the compound are carried out without permits from the Jerusalem municipality. There is an Israeli police station on al-Haram al-Sharif itself, but its presence is not at all indicative of Israeli involvement in policing the compound. Beyond the symbolic dimension of paramount sovereignty, the Israeli police presence is required mainly when there are problems with right-wing Jewish groups who have to be kept from disturbing the public order. The Israeli authorities allow Jews to visit the site as tourists, but not to pray there, and anyone suspected of having ritual intent will be blocked or find himself with a police escort to ensure that he does not violate the rules for visitors. Most of the supervision of public order and protection of the area from the inside, as well as responsibility for all the entry gates save one, is in the hands of the Waqf guards. The Israel police are responsible for external security and they supervise the entrance at the Mughrabi gate, adjacent to the Western Wall. Israel may have paramount sovereignty, but this is not felt in the day-to-day functioning of the site. The entry of large police contingents at times of disturbances and demonstrations, as occurred in October 1990, has led to bloody clashes. In general, however, the entry of police forces is prevented through prior negotiation with Palestinian political and religious authorities.

Since the Declaration of Principles of September 1993, competition has developed between Jordan and the Palestinian Authority over control of the functional space of al-Haram al-Sharif and the operation of the site. Israel has tried to intervene in the debate, on Jordan's side. In its peace treaty with Jordan in the summer of 1994, Israel promised to grant Jordan a preferred status in the Islamic holy sites when the permanent agreement between it and the Palestinians came into effect. This commitment was based on a common Israeli and Jordanian desire to separate the religious and political functions of the Temple Mount/al-Haram al-Sharif. The Palestinians succeeded, however, at the end of 1994 and beginning of 1995, in garnering the support of important countries in the OIC and stripping Jordan of the potential right that Israel had granted it. This led to an important change in the administrative status of Jordan in Jerusalem as a whole and al-Haram al-Sharif in particular. In 1997 responsibility for the Waqf in Jerusalem was transferred, by consensus, from Jordan to the Palestinian Authority. Jordan continued to operate within al-Haram al-Sharif, trying its best to take advantage of the fact that the Palestinian Authority was forbidden from operating officially in Jerusalem. In practice and unofficially, however, the Palestinian Authority took control of most of the key positions in the Waqf and in the Supreme Muslim Council. Arafat loyalists now serve as chairman of the council and are a majority of its members, and Arafat's appointee to the position of mufti of Jerusalem was able to displace his Jordanian-appointed colleague. In all things connected to al-Haram al-Sharif, Jordan's status is largely symbolic and the religious powers it wields are very limited.

Areas of low-level competition

LAW AND ORDER

Israeli law has applied in East Jerusalem since the annexation. In general, public order has been preserved in East Jerusalem through loose supervision from above by the Israel police, with the exception of a few instances of unlicensed nationalist demonstrations, some of which proceed quietly and others which lose control and descend into violence. Civil and criminal law enforcement is, however, inadequate. There is no real war on crime, especially against drugs, prostitution, theft, and pickpocketing.

Only some civil disputes reach the Israeli courts. Many Palestinians prefer to seek compromise or arbitration, acting in accordance with customary law and avoiding the Israeli judicial system.

The various Palestinian security systems function in the criminal and civil fields in East Jerusalem. They work in civilian clothes, and without weapons, or at least with weapons concealed. This prevents any infringement on Israel's symbols of identity. It could be said that there is no competition between the Israel police and the Palestinian security forces in the classic areas of police activity. However, the Israel police is, of all Israel's security forces, the body that most actively opposes the activity of the Palestinian security forces in East Jerusalem in the national area. Competition with the Israel police arose largely as a result of the expanding activity of the Palestinian forces, such as their enlistment of agents and their fight against real-estate brokers who sell Arab land and homes to Israeli settlers or their surrogates. To a lesser extent competition has increased also because of the national significance of the classic policing activity of the Palestinian security forces. The Likud government that came to power in May 1996 decided to compete with the Palestinians in this sphere and to assert Israeli sovereignty in East Jerusalem by assigning 400 new policemen and building several new police stations in East Jerusalem, but at the this time the decision has only been partially implemented.

THE AUTONOMY OF THE LOCAL PALESTINIAN ESTABLISHMENT

The activity of Palestinian institutions in East Jerusalem was addressed in a letter from Foreign Minister Shimon Peres to Norwegian Foreign Minister Holst in September 1993. In it, Peres promised not to infringe on, and even to encourage, the activity of all the existing Palestinian institutions in East Jerusalem, including economic, social, educational, and cultural institutions, as well as of the Christian and Muslim holy places. A range of unwritten understandings about the operation of the Palestinian institutions grew up alongside this official commitment. Functionally, the Palestinian institutions handle issues that are not properly dealt with by Israeli institutions. The division is not only of areas of activity, but also of the population that the Palestinian institutions deal with, as this population constitutes a distinct sector whose status in the institutions of the majority population is *a priori* inferior because it is an ethnic–national, linguistic, and religious minority. Furthermore, it does not receive its proportionate share of budgets, resources, and services from the Israeli authorities. It should be noted, however, that the symbols of sovereignty remain in Israeli hands. Israeli law stipulates the framework in which the Palestinian institutions operate, while imposing severe restrictions on them, including the prohibition against Palestinian Authority governing institutions from functioning within East Jerusalem. In this context, it is important to recall that a consensus was reached on the activity of Orient House as a Palestinian political center at the beginning of 1991, even before Peres's commitments to Holst. Orient House has expanded its areas of operation since then, and deals also with reducing and resolving problems that arise between individual Palestinians and the Israeli authorities, with municipal matters, and with finding legal solutions to civil disputes.

The phenomenon that distinguishes the competition between Israel and the Palestinians regarding the Palestinian institutions in East Jerusalem is the mutual penetration into areas that, in other cases, would be functionally divided. As noted, most of the paramount sovereignty and ownership of symbolic assets is Israel's, while routine operation in various minor areas is in Palestinian hands. The picture is somewhat different with regard to some of the Palestinian institutions in East Jerusalem. The Palestinians are penetrating the symbolic area, for example by flying the Palestinian flag at Orient House, policing it with its own guards, and conducting diplomatic meetings there. Israel, for its part, is penetrating the functional realm and restricting the Palestinian institutions' freedom of action through legislation. The Palestinian institutions that Israel demanded shut down have had to halt or restrict their activities, to satisfy a symbolic demand that implies recognition of Israeli sovereignty. However, the mutual penetration is not deep, and thus competition over the extent of the autonomy of the Palestinian institutions remains mild. Israel's requirement that the Palestinian Authority not operate openly and officially in East Jerusalem is generally abided by, and the Palestinian institutions in the city have assumed only a limited symbolic status. On the other hand, in practice the Palestinians are circumventing Israel's restrictions and building a foothold for their institutions in the city, and Israel is not interfering with these activities in any significant way. The political establishments on both sides are in a competition of mutual penetration on both the national and the municipal levels, seeking to alter the *status quo*, but so far they have not been able to bring about any far-reaching changes.

POLITICAL TIES AND POLITICAL PARTICIPATION

In these areas the level of competition is low. The first reason for this is the fact that most East Jerusalem Palestinians boycott the Israeli municipal elections. Second, in 1991 the Israeli government tacitly permitted the East Jerusalem leadership to develop a political link to the PLO, concurring that the political center for the West Bank and Gaza Strip would be established in East Jerusalem. The link has grown tighter since then, and the PLO has gone from "outside" to "inside," not only from Tunis to the West Bank and Gaza Strip, but also from those areas to Jerusalem. Third, in October 1995 electoral procedures were established for the Palestinian Authority presidency and Legislative Council, and in January 1996 East Jerusalem Palestinians participated in those elections.

The participation of East Jerusalem inhabitants in the Palestinian elections was unique in a number of ways, including the election procedures, the manner of voting, polling stations, the establishment of candidate slates, campaigning, the right to vote and to run for office, voter registration, candidates' level of expenditure, voter turnout, and Israeli action to minimize turnout. These are not artificial differences, but rather an official manifestation of the unique political profile of the East Jerusalem Palestinians and of East Jerusalem's special place in Palestinian and Israeli reality. The arrangements agreed upon in these areas restricted Israel's symbolic and political sovereignty in East Jerusalem, as well as that of the Palestinian Authority. So, for example, the vote was conditioned on having polling staions in post offices, and being a candidate on having a second address outside Jerusalem. Mutual restrictions created a reality of symbolic and political duality in East Jerusalem, and of a "gray area" that is not under the control of either side. The existence of a gray area was expressed, for example, in the struggle between the Israeli and Palestinian authorities over the level of voter registration and the participation rate in the actual elections. Each side tried to take control of the gray area, trying either to encourage or discourage the inhabitants of East Jerusalem to vote.

The competition over areas of political affiliation and participation was not conducted only between the national Israeli and Palestinian establishments, but also within them. The Israeli government, led by the Labor Party, wanted to achieve legitimacy for the agreements it had made with the PLO, whereas the subsequent Likud government, and the mayor of Jerusalem, used the agreements and understandings on Jerusalem as a means of canceling the Oslo accords. Indeed, with the accession of Binyamin Netanyahu's Likud government in June 1996 the disparity between the municipal and national establishments narrowed, and the debate between them became merely personal and tactical rather an argument over principle. The competition within the Palestinian establishment was different in character, even though it was also conducted between the establishment in Jerusalem and the national political establishment. The subject of contention was the preservation of the status and independence of the East Jerusalem establishment on the Palestinian political map. The local establishment in Jerusalem opposed giving preference to the general interest over Jerusalem's interests, and of course did not consent to the absolute authority of the national establishment and its executive arm. But as the national conflict in Jerusalem grew sharper, after Israel's opening of the Western Wall Tunnel in October 1996 and with Israel's initiation of the Har Homa construction project at the beginning of 1997, Arafat's national establishment was able to shunt aside the local forces headed by Husseini.

Finally, the level of competition between Israel and the Palestinian Authority in matters of political affiliation and participation is not high. This is because elections to the Palestinian institutions were held in 1996 and no date has yet been set for the next elections, and because Jerusalem and a Palestinian state and its sovereignty are key issues that will be discussed in the permanent status talks. It would, however, be a mistake to view the arrangements for electing the Palestinian Authority's political institutions during the interim period as artificial. The Palestinian elections did not create the link between East Jerusalem's Palestinians and the Palestinian Authority *ex nihilo*. The procedures were based on the reality that prevailed in East Jerusalem for many years; they merely arranged, established, and institutionalized it. Election procedures, campaign rules, and deciding who will be candidates, including the composition of the slate of winning candidates and their social and biographical background – these are all expressions of Jerusalem's unique reality. The elections brought about a situation in which the Palestinian Authority's Legislative Council and its executive arm, like the PLO Executive Committee before them, include a significant number of senior East Jerusalem representatives, who personify the linkage between the residents of East Jerusalem and the Palestinian political system.

Areas of high-level competition

PLANNING AND CONSTRUCTION

There is no understanding between the two sides regarding construction and planning, so competition is now intense. For many years, however, up until the mid-1990s, there was not a great deal of competition in these fields. As in other areas, there was a functional and geographical division between Israel and the Palestinians. There was a great deal of Israeli construction for Jews on the eastern side of Jerusalem, around the Arab city, but not within it. Similarly, there was Palestinian construction in the East Jerusalem suburbs, outside the limits of the territory annexed to Israel. But in the mid-1990s, as the permanent status talks approached, the Israeli authorities began to make a point of the fact that, according to Israeli law, these Palestinian suburbs were outside the boundaries of Israeli Jerusalem, and it also began the construction of the new Jewish neighborhood of Har Homa. Furthermore, in 1997–8 the first steps were taken towards carrying out a plan to build the first Jewish neighborhood in the heart of an Arab neighborhood, in Ras al-Amud. The competition in planning and construction was expressed in the deep penetration by each side into territory that had previously been populated exclusively by the other side. Israel acted to expand its hold on manifestly Arab residential neighborhoods and planned to construct new residential areas on open land separating Palestinian population concentrations. The Palestinians sought to take control of these very same areas via construction, so each side strove to create contiguous built-up areas in the open spaces between their neighborhoods. This turned into a free-for-all, since there was no agreement even on a symbolic level. The Palestinians built illegally, and the Jerusalem municipality and the Israeli Ministry of the Interior demolished the illegal construction. Another sign of the increased competition has been the local Palestinian establishment's attempt to broaden the competition to include Jewish neighborhoods in western Jerusalem. As a counter to Israel's construction in East Jerusalem, the Palestinian side has sought to purchase homes in Jewish Jerusalem. These attempts have, however, failed because of a lack of funds, bad organization, or lack of enthusiasm. The Palestinian establishment in Jerusalem has been able to do no more than promise that the subject will be raised in the permanent status talks in the form of a demand for the return of Arab property abandoned or occupied in the 1948 war. The national Palestinian establishment has scored some successes, however, in the purchase of properties in East Jerusalem. At the end of 1997 and the beginning of 1998 the Palestinian Authority was able to purchase several East Jerusalem lots and houses that had been offered to Jewish settlers, thus frustrating plans to settle Jews there.

While Israel's national and municipal establishment is competing for control of Arab areas with its construction and planning activities, the Palestinian authorities are doing little other than encouraging illegal construction and offering legal and financial aid to those affected by Israel's actions. Palestinian illegal construction is spontaneous and not coordinated with nor planned in advance by the national or local Palestinian leadership. Unlike other areas, in which the competition takes place only in annexed East Jerusalem, the competition in building and planning is conducted throughout the Jerusalem area, and has intensified because of Israel's supplementary actions. Israel has not sufficed itself with building new homes for the Jewish population. It has also begun destroying unlicensed Palestinian buildings in Jerusalem and its surrounding suburbs and revoking the resident status of Palestinians who have moved from within the city to the suburbs. Furthermore, the Israeli authorities have adopted the plan to "strengthen Jerusalem" and create a Jerusalem umbrella municipality that will have construction and planning powers in the entire metropolitan area. The annexation of Israeli West Bank settlements to the Jerusalem municipality's construction and planning space will, so the authorities hope, give the municipality the means to win the construction race with the Palestinians. Despite this broadening competition, Israel knows that it must halt at the gates to the Temple Mount and not impose its construction and planning laws there.

In the final analysis, Israel has not succeeded in winning the battle. The Palestinians have made considerable gains in construction and planning. In the symbolic area, the Palestinian Authority has become the address to which Arab and American leaders turn to discuss the issue, and Arafat as the deed-holder when it comes to planning and construction issues in East Jerusalem. Furthermore, most of the unlicensed structures and homes built by Palestinians in the Jerusalem area remain standing, and it has been proven that the Palestinian presence is a critical mass that cannot be overcome by force, only by negotiation. Moreover, at the beginning of 1998, only the first stage of the Har Homa project had got off the ground. The other neighborhoods that Israel had planned to build are still in the planning stages. The umbrella municipality has not been established either.

POPULATION AND DEMOGRAPHIC BALANCE

Just as the permanent status talks were to begin, in the mid-1990s, Israel discovered that its demographic superiority had been eroded considerably during the previous 20 years, and that the Jewish proportion of Jerusalem's population was projected to decline even further. This meant that one of the touchstones of Israeli policy had been whittled away to the Palestinians' benefit, and this, from Israel's point of view, created a threat to its continued claim to the eastern part of the city. In response, Israel took a number of steps to tip the demographic balance in its favor. It began to revoke resident status from Palestinians who no longer fulfilled the legal requirements for holding it. At the same time, it made plans for large-scale construction in the Jerusalem region and prepared to create a Greater Jerusalem municipality that would establish Israel dominance in the entire area.

Israel's side of the demographic contest is carried out by its national and municipal authorities. Moreover, the minister of the interior in 1996–9 had previously been the chief of the ministry's Jerusalem district office. On the Palestinian side there is a very low level of coordination and organization, as is illustrated by the story of the Palestinian census in East Jerusalem.

In December 1997, the Palestinian Authority launched a census in the West Bank and Gaza Strip. Israel had conducted the last census of the West Bank in the summer of 1967 and there had been no census in the Gaza Strip since 1948. The Palestinian political leadership viewed the census not just as a professional need to provide vital information for its bureaucracy, but also as an expression of the establishment of national institutions and as a stage along the way to full independence. Palestinian political representatives announced that the census would be conducted in East Jerusalem as well. However, the body carrying out the census did not make the necessary preparations and did not distribute forms to the Palestinian households in Jerusalem as it had done a month before the census in other areas. This may have been due to inefficiency or because it was assumed that the response would be low. The Palestinian Authority's officials had no contingency plan for how to get around the Israeli authorities and conduct a census in Jerusalem by remote control, such as by fax, or secretly. The conferences held to mark the census, which the Palestinian establishment considered a milestone in the building of the Palestinian state and its institutions, were held in the suburbs of East Jerusalem, beyond Israeli jurisdiction.

Since the Palestinian Authority is forbidden to operate in Jerusalem, the Jerusalem municipality announced that it would act against any attempt to count the city's households. There were differences on the issue between the cautious statements of the professionals in the Palestinian Authority's Central Bureau of Statistics and the pronouncements of the political leadership of Jerusalem. The former said that they had not coordinated their actions with Israel and that the census could thus not be conducted in East Jerusalem; the latter said unambiguously that the census would be carried out there. These lofty statements had, however, no basis in reality (*Ha'aretz*, 10 Dec. 1997, 11 Dec. 1997). As a rule, it was easier for the Palestinian Authority and Israeli political leaderships to turn the struggle into a matter of principle and symbols. The Palestinian Authority made no preparations to conduct the census in Jerusalem, while Israel, under its Likud government, preferred, as in the past, the politics of symbols over pragmatic arrangements. The Palestinian Authority left the symbolic field to Israel, to the intense displeasure of the local Palestinian leadership, which tried to save what it could by issuing extravagant statements. Since, however, it was the Palestinian Authority and not Orient House that was conducting the census, the local leadership could not create a confrontation with Israel, even on the symbolic front.

Israel took action on several levels. As happened during the Palestinian elections of January 1996, rumors were spread through East Jerusalem that Israel would rescind the Israeli identity cards and resident rights of anyone who participated in the census. Second, the police deployed large contingents to arrest the census-takers should they begin to work. In the event, only a single young Palestinian woman suspected of having participated was detained briefly for interrogation (*Ha'aretz*, 11 Dec. 1997). Third, the Knesset amended the law to forbid "activity of a political or governing nature, or other activity inconsistent with respecting Israel's sovereignty" – in other words, the conducting of a census (*Ha'aretz*, 11 Dec. 1997). Finally, Israel made a low-key declaration that it would grant the Palestinians access to information it had gathered in East Jerusalem during the population and housing survey it had conducted in 1995, information which was in any case slated for publication. In the end, Israel's efforts to prevent the census in Jerusalem went far beyond what was necessary on the practical level, but were in keeping with its view of the census as a symbolic demonstration of sovereignty.

As in the areas of construction and planning, the demographic contest was conducted over the entire region and not limited to the East Jerusalem that Israel had annexed. Likewise, there was no unambiguous resolution in Israel's favor. Resident status was rescinded from only a relatively small number of Palestinians, and many Palestinians moved back into the city itself. The confiscation of identity cards also roused Arab and international protest, which underlined the Palestinian identity of the East Jerusalem Arabs and depicted Arafat and the Palestinian leadership as the injured parties that needed to be consulted on the issue.

The expansion of the contest to include Jerusalem's Arab suburbs in the West Bank is worth examining from three vantage points. First, under the annexation, Israel enjoyed an advantage in Jerusalem that it did not have in the larger surrounding region, as the annexation supplied Israel with control mechanisms that it did not have in the West Bank. It was precisely for this reason that the Palestinian advantage was in the area that had not been annexed.

Difficult competition in the region near Jerusalem meant competing in an area where the Palestinians had an advantage. Nevertheless, Israel broadened the area of competition, because the area surrounding Jerusalem served the Palestinians as a staging ground for their activity in the city.

Second, expanding the dimensions of the competition blurred Israel's annexation line. To put it another way, Israel was tacitly acknowledging that the annexation lines were no longer relevant. This served the Palestinians, and at the same time weakened their steadfastness about the June 4, 1967 lines, since Jerusalem was expanding rather than shrinking. Finally, the competition being conducted throughout the Jerusalem area had affected power relations within the Palestinian establishment. Since the power base of the local leadership was within the annexed city, the interest of that leadership was to see the annexation lines as a filter that weakened the national Palestinian leadership's effectiveness within Jerusalem, as had happened when the Labor Party controlled the Israeli government and the municipality. Strengthening the competition while the annexation lines were weakening made it easier for the national Palestinian establishment to penetrate Jerusalem and allowed it to conduct the contest in Jerusalem at the expense of the local leadership.

Peace in small doses

Israel has ruled both west and East Jerusalem for more than 30 years. It has ruled the Arab part of Jerusalem longer than either Jordan or the British. Despite the length of time that has elapsed since Israel's occupation of East Jerusalem, the Jerusalem area is not bounded by rigid borders. A rigid border exists only in the declarations of the Israeli establishment, which seeks to obtain Palestinian and international consent to make the annexation line the permanent peacetime border. The municipal border is meant to close the city off and disconnect it from the West Bank; within, it is meant to create a single integral unit, united Jerusalem. The municipal border is almost completely identical to the boundary of the military closure that has been imposed on the West Bank since 1991, and its importance both to Israel and to the Palestinians who must cope with it day after day is not open to doubt. But the municipal border is only one of the elements in Jerusalem's character. In practice, there is a deep fissure between the Israelis and the Palestinians in Jerusalem. At its foundation it is a national–ethnic fissure that takes manifestly political form in the contest over the future of East Jerusalem: demographic competition between the two populations, a contest for control of the unpopulated space, a challenge by extremist elements in Israel over the character of the Arab part of East Jerusalem, and a dispute over control of the Islamic holy sites on the Temple Mount. In other words, the line that in the past divided the city continues to exist. It is not a physical boundary, but rather one that has spread and separated, as by a prism, into multiple lines. The inhabitants of the Jerusalem region have many borders in their daily lives and in their consciousness. Alongside the municipal border is the Green Line, the border that split the city between 1948 and 1967, no longer visible but palpably felt. There is the ethnic–national line that divides the Israeli neighborhoods built in East Jerusalem after the 1967 war from their Palestinian neighbors. There is also the larger border that defines the city's space as a focus of employment and services for the population that depends on it, and there is a whole gamut of functional relationships within Israeli Jerusalem that divide areas of responsibility and operation between the Jewish and Arab populations. The application of Israeli law, jurisdiction, and administration has not succeeded in separating East Jerusalem from the West Bank. Nor has it led to full integration between the city's Jews and Arabs. Instead of a rigid border splitting the city or cutting off its eastern boundary from the Palestinian rear, there are a number of borders, and all of them are permeable and soft. Luckily for the inhabitants of Jerusalem, both Israelis and Palestinians, the fissures in Jerusalem are varied and only partially congruent. It is easer to bridge over a "soft" fissure than a "hard" one that concentrates in one spot all the contentious issues and dividing lines between the two populations.

In practice, the huge physical changes that Israel has brought about in East Jerusalem make it impossible to return to the Green Line. Similarly, it is impossible to make the municipal borders into permanent borders because the lines cut through several neighborhoods and even buildings. Moreover, East Jerusalem is a center of employment, tourism, and services, a commercial hub, political focal point, and the most important religious site in the Palestinian Authority. For all these reasons East Jerusalem cannot be cut off from the Palestinian body to which it is connected, while at the same time it cannot be detached from its economic dependence or other ties to Jewish Jerusalem. Over the years, the Palestinians in Jerusalem have turned from a passive population into an active society. Paradoxically, Israel's high level of activity in its capital has turned Jerusalem into a magnet and a metropolitan center for the Palestinians.

What emerges is that both sides have succeeded in braking each other and in vetoing the maximalist goals of the other side. So long as Israel assumes that it can compel the Palestinians in Jerusalem, the Arab world, the Islamic states, and the international community to give their blessing to the annexation of East Jerusalem despite their resolute opposition, it must maintain a vertical segregation of Jews and Arabs in Jerusalem and inequality in the distribution of and access to resources and power. Only thus can it attempt to defeat those who oppose the application of Israeli law, jurisdiction, and administration in East Jerusalem. But this makes the wedge between the city's Jews and Arabs all the more substantial, making it even more necessary to provide an official foundation for the functional and geographical segregation arrangements that have developed in the city.

In contrast, the peace process has grown out of a recognition that a new arrangement must be found, one based on the heterogeneous and multi-dimensional reality that has come into being in Jerusalem. This was the foundation of the Oslo accords and of the understandings reached between the teams under the direction of Yossi Beilin and Abu-Mazen. Contrary to Israel's naïve hope, the peace arrangements in Jerusalem did not and will not sprout from below, from coexistence in the city and from Palestinian acceptance of Israel's annexation, but rather from the various fault lines that have developed in Jerusalem. Recent experience teaches us that only when the political leaderships on both sides have understood that they must address all the fault lines that surround and cut through Jerusalem, have they achieved breakthroughs and agreements. Reality has also proven that arrangements in Jerusalem have grown out of a series of ostensibly small decisions on clearly defined issues, and not from inclusive large-scale decisions that solve all the issues in conflict in one fell swoop. The questions of what elements of the complex reality will be included in the permanent agreement, and which ones will be given precedence over which others, will be the subjects of fierce debate between Israel and the Palestinians during the negotiations.

Furthermore, moves towards peace have not come out of local leadership circles in the Jerusalem municipality and in Orient House, but from the national leadership. This was the case in the confrontations of 1997, in the wake of the opening of the Western Wall Tunnel and the launching of construction of the Jewish neighborhood of Har Homa. It was the national leaderships that resolved the conflicts then, and the local leaderships fell in behind them. The two national leaderships are unwilling to allow the local leaderships to determine the contours for the solution of the Jerusalem question, nor are they willing to be dragged by them into a head-on Israeli–Palestinian confrontation. The national leaderships view Jerusalem as a national issue. They will make the decisions on its future.

In the negotiations the national leaderships conducted on the first and second Oslo agreements, the Jerusalem question was one of the topics discussed, one of several national interests. Had the national leaderships handed the issue over to the local leaderships, they would not have been able to maneuver among different issues and so maximize their negotiating power. But this should not lead to the conclusion that the local establishments are not partners in shaping the arrangements in Jerusalem. The local leaderships affect the city's future through their influence on their national leaders, not by circumventing them and negotiating independently with the other side. Every so often the local leadership, whether Orient House under Husseini or the Jerusalem municipality under Olmert, functions as a vanguard in order to make local gains and influence the national leadership. This happens when they feel that the national leadership is making too many concessions and is not acquainted with, or is cut off from, the reality in Jerusalem.

At times when there was increasing agreement between the national leaderships and a reduction of competition between them, as was the case when the two sides proceeded along the lines set out in the Oslo agreements, there was a significant increase in the oversight and control that the central governments imposed on the local establishments and on the national agencies operating in Jerusalem, such as the police and security services, which opposed the process entirely or in part and blocked its implementation. In parallel, the two national leaderships made an effort to enlist the support of the local elements that favored the process. In this situation the importance of the "gray area" in Jerusalem – those issues over which there is no agreement – declined. The two national leaderships have been inclined to reduce the disagreements between them via temporary or limited arrangements, or have disregarded the disputed subjects entirely. Another method of reducing tensions in Jerusalem has been to expand achievements at the national level and to "import" them into Jerusalem. This, for example, is a way of understanding the agreements on the framework of activity of Palestinian institutions in East Jerusalem and on arrangements for the Palestinian elections in Jerusalem. In this way the national leaderships sought to prove that they made no concessions but, on the contrary, made gains for the city. There is no basis for the claim by the local leaderships that their national counterparts paid in local currency for broader agreements on issues other than Jerusalem.

When there was increasing competition between Israel and the Palestinian Authority and a reduction of the areas of agreement, as under Israel's Likud government, the importance of the "gray area," where competition takes place, increased, and became the pivot of attention and action. With the increase in competition between Israel and the Palestinians in 1996, the local elements have served as the central regime's fighting forces.

The construction of bridges in Jerusalem is not an easy task, and it has yet to be completed. Contrary to the common assumption that there has been no negotiation over the future of Jerusalem, and that no understandings or agreements have been reached about it, this work argues that, in a pragmatic and cumulative way, many foundation stones have already been laid for the solution of the Jerusalem question. The steps taken so far lead to several conclusions:

Collective political organizations, whether the UN, the Arab League, or the OIC, play no significant role in mediating between Israel and the Palestinians. While UN Security Council resolutions 242 and 338 are the source of authority for the peace conferences, talks, and agreements that Israel has had with the Arab states and the Palestinians since 1977, the role of these organizations is merely to provide an official and collective seal of approval to agreements worked out between Israel and the Palestinians.

Israel and the Palestinians do not discuss the Jerusalem question as a religious issue and do not focus on the Temple Mount/al-Haram al-Sharif. The status of the Islamic holy sites is but one of the constituent issues of the Jerusalem problem. Both the Israeli and Palestinian leaderships have an interest in keeping Jerusalem a political rather than a religious problem, knowing as they do that giving free rein to the religious extremists who seek to challenge this is liable to ignite a conflagration that neither side could control. The danger is greater on the Israeli than on the Palestinian side, since Jerusalem is a center for extremist Jewish religious organizations. On the Palestinian side, the fundamentalists, such as Hamas, tend to be relatively weak in Jerusalem and unaccepted by the established religious administration of the holy sites.

The Camp David model, which postponed consideration of the Jerusalem problem until the end of the negotiating process, has proved itself. According to this model, when solutions have been found to the other issues in dispute, neither side will want to put the entire peace process at risk and will thus seek an accommodation in Jerusalem. However, when negotiations between Israel and the PLO began in the early 1990s, it became clear that the Jerusalem issue could not be circumvented, and a process of bargaining and compromise began. The problem with the Camp David model is that it assumed that at the end of the process all the elements of the Jerusalem problem could be taken up and solved at once. The negotiations between Israel and the Palestinians have shown instead that Jerusalem can be discussed and bargained over bit by bit during the course of negotiations on other issues.

The negotiations leading up to the Madrid Conference, and the negotiations that took place in the framework of that conference, demonstrated that Jerusalem could not be excluded from the peace process. Israel's attempts to ensure that Jerusalem's future status will not be a subject of discussion, and to prevent even a symbolic or procedural acknowledgement that East Jerusalem was part of the West Bank, were countered by Palestinian measures that emphasized their claim to East Jerusalem. The Oslo process demonstrated that Jerusalem is not taboo and could be discussed as part of the range of issues that need to be resolved between Israel and the Palestinians. While the Palestinians were willing to exclude East Jerusalem from the interim agreement, this was in no way a concession of their claim to East Jerusalem or of their intention of including it in the permanent settlement.

Both the Israeli and Palestinian leaderships have recognized that East Jerusalem is unique, and that a resolution of its status will have to be unique and creative. Foreign Minister Peres's letter to his Norwegian counterpart, Holst, in September 1993, recognized East Jerusalem as a distinct entity defined not only by geography but also by a separate demography, social reality, and thus political status that applies not just to religious sites but also to other Palestinian institutions in the city. The Declaration of Principles of September 1993 signaled a change in the Palestinian view of East Jerusalem. Whereas the Palestinians had previously insisted that East Jerusalem is an integral part of the West Bank and that all arrangements applying to the West Bank and Gaza Strip should apply to East Jerusalem as well, Arafat and other PLO leaders now began speaking of a separate, creative solution for East Jerusalem. They began to distinguish between Israeli settlements in the West Bank and Gaza Strip, which, they demanded, be dismantled, and the new Israeli neighborhoods on the east side of Jerusalem. Their approach indicates that they recognize that the new neighborhoods represent irreversible changes and that they will ultimately accept the annexation of these new neighborhoods to Israel. Both sides now accept that the city cannot be divided again as it was between 1948 and 1967. They also recognize that the current municipal border cannot become an international boundary because of the interdependence of the city and its Palestinian hinterland. The only option open to both sides in the permanent status talks is a redefinition of the city's boundaries. This can be done in one of several ways: by enlarging the city and establishing an agreed border, agreement on the non-existence of such a border while leaving the issue open for future resolution, or a variable division with a number of borders defining divisions of different kinds of authority.

The Oslo II agreement of September 1995, which established the procedures for East Jerusalem's participation in the Palestinian elections, institutionalized the political link between the inhabitants of East Jerusalem and the Palestinian Authority. At the same time, it was an official recognition on the part of the

Palestinians of the unique, different nature of that connection, which is unlike the relationship between the Palestinian Authority and the Palestinians of the West Bank and Gaza Strip. While nearly all East Jerusalem Palestinians have avoided any identification with Israel (for example, only a fraction vote in municipal elections despite their legal right to do so), their Palestinian political identification is distinct from that of Palestinians in the West Bank and Gaza Strip. East Jerusalem has its own local Palestinian leadership, based in Orient House and in the Jerusalem delegation to the Palestinian Legislative Council, that has taken positions opposed to those of the national Palestinian leadership, especially as regards the negotiations over Jerusalem. However, the national Palestinian government has slowly infiltrated East Jerusalem and seems to have gained the upper hand over the local leadership. The participation of East Jerusalem representatives in the Legislative Council and in the Palestinian executive has both strengthened the political link between East Jerusalem and the Palestinian Authority and granted more authority to the agencies of the Palestinian Authority in East Jerusalem, giving them precedence over the local institutions.

The Oslo process has produced competition as well as consensus between Israel and the Palestinians. Israel has accepted the existence of Orient House as a local political center, as well as the activity of national Palestinian religious institutions in East Jerusalem. But it has taken measures to assert its sovereignty in the city, for example by shutting down Palestinian Authority institutions operating in Jerusalem. Another major means of asserting sovereignty, on the part of the city's Likud Mayor, Ehud Olmert, and the Likud government of 1996–9, has been municipal and national construction and planning powers. These include the demolition of unlicensed Palestinian buildings and the approval of plans for further Jewish construction in the city, including, for the first time, Jewish neighborhoods in the heart of concentrations of Palestinian population. The plan for a Jerusalem umbrella municipality that would include Jewish suburbs of Jerusalem in the West Bank is another example. In reality, however, these attempts to alter the city's demographic balance and reverse the Jewish population's declining proportion of the city's population have had little success. The Palestinian leadership has encouraged unlicensed Palestinian construction in open areas in order to create a contiguous area of Palestinian habitation from East Jerusalem to Ramallah in the West Bank. It has successfully used public and international protest to counter Israeli initiatives such as the opening of the Western Wall Tunnel and, in doing so, has made President Arafat the internationally recognized representative of the Palestinians of East Jerusalem. Israel's attempts to impose its sovereignty unilaterally have been unsuccessful; it must reach an agreement with the Palestinians.

The geographic–municipal and political reality surveyed in this book shows that Israel and the Palestinians are inextricably caught in each other's embrace in East Jerusalem. The simplistic but common wisdom is that this is a boxer's clutch, but that is only partially true. The foundation for an accord on Jerusalem has already been laid, and the competition is partial and limited. The first condition for reaching an agreement is that both sides recognize that they will not be able to win by a knockout. The way to reach an agreement is to stabilize the existing situation, not to upset it. Better to acknowledge the reality in Jerusalem than to bang one's head against it until the blood flows. Current arrangements should be institutionalized, official expression should be given to tacit understandings, to *ad hoc* agreements, and to reality in the street. This is the starting point from which both sides may progress. Businesslike, detailed, and pragmatic negotiations can lead to a permanent settlement that will express Jerusalem's special status and unique character. Negotiations over Jerusalem are not doomed to failure. On the contrary, the key is already in the door.

BIBLIOGRAPHY

SOURCES IN ENGLISH

Abas, Mahmud [Abu-Mazin]. 1995. *Through Secret Channels*. Reading: Garent.

Abdul Hadi, Mahdi (ed.). 1997. *Documents on Palestine*. Vol. I & II. Jerusalem: PASSIA.

Abu-Odeh, Adnan. 1992. "Two Capitals in an Undivided Jerusalem." *Foreign Affairs* 17: 183–8.

Ahmad, Hisham H. 1994. *Hamas From Religious Salvation to Political Transformation: The Rise of Hamas in Palestinian Society*. Jerusalem: PASSIA

Albin, Cecilia. 1992. *The Conflict Over Jerusalem, Some Palestinian Responses To Concepts of Dispute Resolution*. Jerusalem: PASSIA.

American Foreign Policy, Near and Middle East Documents. FRUS (Foreign Relations of the United States) 1949.

Applied Research Institute Jerusalem [ARIJ]. 1998. *Environmental Profile of Jerusalem*. http://www.arij.org

Ashrawi, Hanan. 1995. *This Side of Peace: A Personal Account*. New York: Simon & Schuster.

Awartani, Faisal. 1998. *Labour Force Indicators in the District of Jerusalem: An Unpublished Report*. Jerusalem Institute for Israel Studies and Arab Studies Society.

Ayalon, Ami (ed.). 1993. *Middle East Contemporary Survey XV (1991)*. Boulder: Westview Press.

Baker, James A. III and Deframk, Thomas M. 1995. *The Politics of Diplomacy, Revolution, War and Peace*. New York: G. P. Putnam's Sons.

Barth, Fredrik. 1969. *Ethnic Groups and Boundaries: The Social Organization of Culture Difference*. Boston: Little, Brown.

Bollens, A. Scott. 1998a. "Urban Planning Amidst Ethnic Conflict: Jerusalem and Johannesburg." *Urban Studies* 35: 729–50.

——. 1998b. "Urban Policy in Ethnically Polarized Societies." *International Political Science Review* 19, 2: 187–215.

Brynen, Rex. 1995a. "The Dynamics of Palestinian Elite Formation." *Journal of Palestine Studies* 24: 31–43.

——. 1995b. "The Neopatrimonial Dimension of Palestinian Politics." *Journal of Palestine Studies* 25: 23–36.

Cheshin, Amir S.; Hitman, Bill, and Melamed, Avi. 1999. *Separate and Unequal: The Inside Story of Israeli Rule in East* Jerusalem. Harvard University Press.

Choshen, Maya; Khamaisi, Rasem; Hirsch, Moshe, and Nasarallha, Rami. 1998. *Planning, Building and Development in the Jerusalem Area: An Unpublished Report*. Jerusalem Institute for Israel Studies and Arab Studies Society.

Choshen, Maya and Korach, Michal. 1999. *Jerusalem: Facts and Trends*. Jerusalem Institute for Israel Studies.

Cohen, Shaul Ephraim. 1993. *The Politics of Planting: Israeli–Palestinian Competition for Control of Land in the Jerusalem Periphery*. The University of Chicago Press.

Demant, Peter. 1997. "The Jerusalem Question in the Light of the Brussels Experience." In *Brussels–Jerusalem: Conflict Management and Conflict Resolution in Divided Cities*. Jerusalem and Brussels: IPCRI and VUB: 468–85.

Dumper, Michael. 1997. *The Politics of Jerusalem*. New York: Columbia University Press.

Friedland, Roger and Hecht, Richard. 1996. *To Rule Jerusalem*. Cambridge University Press.

Friedman, Rami. 1998. *Jerusalem Economy: An Unpublished Report*. Jerusalem Institute for Israel Studies and Arab Studies Society.

Garfinkle, Adam. 1992. *Israel and Jordan in the Shadow of War*. New York: St. Martin's Press.

Gutmann, Emanuel, and Klein, Claude. 1980. "The Institutional Structure of Hetrogeneous Cities: Brussels, Montreal and Belfast." In Kreamer, Joel (ed.). *Jerusalem: Problems and Prospects*. New York: Praeger, 178–207.

Hanf, Theodor. 1993. *Coexistence in Wartime Lebanon: Decline of a State and Rise of a Nation*. London: I. B. Tauris.

Hasson, Shlomo. 1996. "Local Politics and Split Citizenship in Jerusalem." *International Journal of Urban and Regional Research* 20: 116–33.

——. 1998. *Jerusalem as a Hybrid City: An Unpublished Report*. Jerusalem Institute for Israel Studies and Arab Studies Society.

Hazboun, Samir. 1998. *Jerusalem Economic Profile: An Unpublished Report*. Jerusalem Institute for Israel Studies and Arab Studies Society.

Hirsch, Moshe; Hausen-Koriel, Devora and Lapidot, Ruth. 1995. *Whither Jerusalem? Proposals for the City's Future*. Jerusalem Institute for Israel Studies.

Hirschfeld, Yair. 1998. From Oslo to Jerusalem. Unpublished manuscript.

JMCC. 1996. *The Palestinian Council*. Jerusalem Media and Communication Center.

Kamil, Muhamed Ibrahim. 1986. *The Camp David Accords: A Testimony*. London: Kogan Page International.

Kamil, Sufian, and Reiter, Yitzhak. *Higher Education in Jerusalem: An Unpublished Report*. Jerusalem Institute for Israel Studies and Arab Studies Society.

Khalidi, Rashid. 1992. "The Future of Arab Jerusalem." *British Journal of Middle Eastern Studies* 19: 133–44.

Khalidi, Walid. 1978. "Thinking the Unthinkable: A Sovereign Palestinian State." *Foreign Affairs* 56: 695–713.

———. 1988. "Toward Peace in the Holyland." *Foreign Affairs* 66: 771–89.

Kimmerling, Baruch. 1977. "Sovereignty, Ownership and Presence in the Jewish–Arab Territorial Conflict," *Comparative Political Studies* 10: 155–75.

———. 1989. "Boundaries and Frontiers of the Israeli Control System: Analytical Conclusions." In Kimmerling, Baruch (ed.). *The Israeli State and Society*. Albany: State University of New York Press, 265–82.

Kimmerling, Baruch, and Migdal, Joel. 1994. *Palestinians: The Making of a People*. Harvard University Press.

Klein, Kerwin. 1997. *Frontiers of Historical Imagination: Narrating the European Conquest of Native America 1890–1990*. Berkeley: University of California Press.

Klein, Menachem. 1996a. "Competing Brothers: The Web of Hamas–PLO Relations." *Terrorism and Political Violence* 8: 111–32.

———. 1996b. "The Islamic Holy Places as a Bargaining Card (1993–5)." *Catholic University of America Law Review* 45: 745–63.

———. 1997. "Quo Vadis? Palestinian Authority Building Dilemmas since 1993." *Middle Eastern Studies* 33: 383–404.

———. 2000. "The 'Tranquil Decade' Re-examined: A New Assessment of Israel–Arab Relations During the Years 1957–67." *Israel Affairs* 6, 37: pp. 68–82.

Kliot, Nurit, and Mansfield, Yoram. 1997. "The Political Landscape of Partition: The Case of Cyprus." *Political Geography* 16: 495–521.

Kliot, Nurit, Mansfield, Yoram and Kotek, Joel. 1999. "Divided Cities." *Progress in Planning*. 52, 3: 167–237.

Kotek, Joel. 1997a. "The Disappearance of Belgian Iconography and its Consequences." In *Brussels–Jerusalem Conflict Management and Conflict Resolution in Divided Cities*. Jerusalem and Brussels: IPCRI and VUB: 427–42.

———. 1997b. "Frontier Cities: A Major Stake at World Level." In *Brussels–Jerusalem Conflict Management and Conflict Resolution in Divided Cities*. Jerusalem and Brussels: IPCRI and VUB: 165–72.

Krystall, Nathan. 1998. "The De-Arabization of West Jerusalem 1947–1950." *Journal of Palestine Studies* 17: 5–22.

Kuttab, Daud and Kaminker, Sarah. "Palestinian–Israeli Contacts on the Municipal Level." In *Brussels–Jerusalem Conflict Management and Conflict Resolution in Divided Cities*. Jerusalem and Brussels: IPCRI and VUB: 221–40.

Laqueur, Walter and Rubin, Barry (eds). 1995. *The Arab–Israeli Reader: A Documentary History of the Middle East Conflict*. New York: Penguin Books.

Lauren, G. Ross and Nader, Izzat Sa'id. 1995. "Palestinians: Negotiations with Violence." *Middle East Quarterly* 2: 15–23.

Legum, Colin; Shaked, Haim, and Rabinivich, Itamar (eds). 1979–80. *Middle East Contemporary Survey*. Boulder: Westview Press.

Lustick, Ian S. "Has Israel Annexed East Jerusalem?" *Middle East Policy* 5: 34–45.

Makovsky, David. 1996. *Making Peace with the PLO: The Rabin Government's Road to the Oslo Accord*. Boulder: Westview Press and the Washington Institute for Near East Policy.

Moore, John Noton (ed.). 1974. *The Arab–Israeli Conflict 3: Documents*. Princeton University Press.

Musallam, Sami F. 1996. *The Struggle for Jerusalem: A Programme of Action for Peace*. Jerusalem: PASSIA.

Muslih, Muhammad. 1996. "Palestinian Images of Jerusalem." In Rosovsky, Nitza (ed.). *Great King: Jerusalem from David to the Present*. Harvard University Press, 178–201.

PASSIA. 1996. *Documents on Jerusalem*. Jerusalem: PASSIA.

Pundik, Ron. 1994. *The Struggle for Sovereignty: Between Great Britain and Jordan 1946–1951*. Oxford: Blackwell.

al-Qaq, Zakariya. 1997. "Post-1967 Palestinian Strategies for Jerusalem?" 339–68.

Quandt, William B.; Jabber, Fuad, and Lesch, Ann Mosely. 1973. *The Politics of Palestinian Nationalism*. Berkeley and Los Angeles: University of California Press.

Robinson, Glenn E. 1997. *Building a Palestinian State: The Incomplete Revolution*. Bloomington and Indianapolis: Indiana University Press.

Roman, Michael. 1997a. "Comparing Jerusalem and Brussels: A Conceptual Framework." In *Brussels–Jerusalem Conflict Management and Conflict Resolution in Divided Cities*. Jerusalem and Brussels: IPCRI and VUB: 173–80.

——. 1997b. "Managing Conflict in Jerusalem." In *Brussels–Jerusalem Conflict Management and Conflict Resolution in Divided Cities*. Jerusalem and Brussels: IPCRI and VUB: 241–57.

Romann, Michael and Weingrod, Alex. 1991. *Living Together Separately, Arabs and Jews in Contemporary Jerusalem*. Princeton University Press, New Jersey.

Ross, Leonard and Sa'id, Nadir. 1995. "Palestinian Attitudes Amidst the Peace Process." *Middle East Quarterly* June: 3–150.

Rubinstein, Danny. 1995. *The Mystery of Arafat*. Vermont: Steerforth.

Sabella, Bernard. 1997a. "East Jerusalem Elites." In *Brussels–Jerusalem Conflict Management and Conflict Resolution in Divided Cities*. Jerusalem and Brussels: IPCRI and VUB: 191–206.

——. 1997b. "Managing Conflict in Jerusalem." In *Brussels–Jerusalem Conflict Management and Conflict Resolution in Divided Cities*. Jerusalem and Brussels: IPCRI and VUB: 258–75.

Sayigh, Yezid. 1997. *Armed Struggle and the Search for State: The Palestinian National Movement 1964–93*. Oxford: Clarendon Press.

Segal, Jerome M. and Nader, Izzat Sa'id. 1997. *The Status of Jerusalem in the Eyes of Palestinians*. Center for International and Security Studies, University of Maryland.

Segal, Jerome M. 1997. *Is Jerusalem Negotiable?* Jerusalem: IPCRI.

Sharabi, Hisham. 1988. *Neopatriarchy: A Theory of Distorted Change in Arab Society*. New York: Oxford University Press.

Shikaki, Khalil. 1996. *Transition to Democracy in Palestine: The Peace Process, National Reconstruction, and Elections*. Nablus: CPRS.

Shlaim, Avi. 1988. *Collusion Across the Jordan, King Abdullah, the Zionist Movement and the Partition of Palestine*. Oxford: Clarendon.

Shultz, George P. 1993. *Turmoil and Triumph: My Years as Secretary of State*. New York: Charles Scribner's Sons.

Sprinzak, Ehud. 1991. *The Ascendance of Israel's Radical Right*. New York: Oxford University Press.

State of Israel. 1995. *Israeli–Palestinian Interim Agreement on the West Bank and the Gaza Strip, Washington, September 28*. Jerusalem: Ministry of Foreign Affairs.

Steinberg, Matti. 1994. "You Can't Clap with Only One Hand: The Dialectics Between the PLO 'Inside' and 'Outside.'" In Rubin, Barry; Ginat; Joseph and Ma'oz, Moshe (eds). *From War to Peace, Arab–Israeli Relations 1973–93*. Brighton: Sussex University Press, 112–36.

Steinberg, Paul and Oliver, Ann Marry. 1990. *The Graffiti of the Intifada*. Jerusalem: PASSIA.

Stotkin, Richard. 1996. *Gunfighter Nation: The Myth of the Frontier in the 20th Century America*. New York: Atheneum.

Tamari, Salim. 1999. *Jerusalem 1948 – The Arab Neighbourhoods and their Fate in the War*. Jerusalem: The Institute of Jerusalem Studies and Badil Resource Center.

Yiftachel, Oren and Meir, Avinoam. 1998. *Ethnic Frontiers and Peripheries*. Boulder: Westview Press.

Yiftachel, Oren. 1996. "The Internal Frontier: Territorial Control and Ethnic Relations in Israel." *Regional Studies* 30: 493–508.

Bibliography

Zilberman, Ifrah. 1997. "From Intifada to Political Agreements: Palestinian Social Change in East Jerusalem." In Abraham Ashkenasi (ed.). Forthcoming.

SOURCES IN ARABIC

BOOKS AND ARTICLES

Abas, Mahmud [Abu-Mazin]. 1994. *The Oslo Channel*. Beirut: Sharikat al-Matbu'at.

Abd al-Hadi, Mahdi. 1996. "Reading the Jerusalem File." In Khuri, Dr. Jiries Sa'ad, Musallam, Dr. Adnan, and Darwish, Musa (eds). *Jerusalem: Palestinian Islamic and Christian Research*. Jerusalem: al-Liqa, 213–22.

Abd al-Jawad, Salah. 1998. *Towards a Palestinian Strategy on Jerusalem*. Bir Zeit: Palestinian Society and Documentation Research Center at Bir Zeit University.

Abu-Arafa, Abd al-Rahman. 1985. *Jerusalem, the New Formation of the City: Research on Israeli Plans to Judaize Jerusalem*. Jerusalem: Arab Studies Society.

Ahmad, Aisha. 1997. "The Building of the Palestinian Legislative Council." In Shikaki, Khilal (ed.). *The First Palestinian Elections: Political Context, Electoral Behavior, and Results*. Nablus: CPRS, 185–202.

al-Maqadma, Ibrahim. Undated. *The Gaza and Jericho Agreement: An Islamic View*. No publisher.

al-Nakhal, Muhammad Matar. 1993. *Metropolitan East Jerusalem: Research on Commuting in Jerusalem*. Jerusalem: Arab Studies Society.

——. 1994. *The East Jerusalem Suburbs*. Jerusalem: Arab Studies Society.

——. 1996. *Residence and Housing in the East Jerusalem Suburbs*. Jerusalem: Arab Studies Society.

al-Shikaki, Khalil and Qasis, Mudar. 1997. "The Political Structure of the First Palestinian Political Elections." In Shikaki, Khilal (ed.). *The First Palestinian Elections: Political Context, Electoral Behavior, and Results*. Nablus: CPRS, 7–26.

al-Shikaki, Khilal (ed.). 1997. *The First Palestinian Elections: Political Context, Electoral Behavior, and Results*. Nablus: CPRS.

al-Shikaki, Khilal. 1997. "The Political Affiliation of the Palestinians." In Sa'id, Nadir 'Izat and Hamami, Rima (eds). *Analytical Study of Political and Social Trends in Palestine*. Nablus: CPRS, 136–64.

al-Takruri, Nawaf Hail. 1998. *Martyrdom Operations according to Islamic Law*. Damascus (no publisher).

al-Tal, Tarik. 1996. "Myth and Misunderstanding in Jordanian–Palestinian Relations." *al-Siyasa al-Filastiniyya* 12: 152–65.

al-Tufakji, Khalil. 1996. "The Settlements in the City of Jerusalem." In Khuri, Dr. Jiries Sa'ad, Musalam, Dr. Adnan, and Darwish, Musa (eds). *Jerusalem: Palestinian Islamic and Christian Research*. Jerusalem: al-Liqa, 359–74.

———. 1997. "The Settlements in Jerusalem: Outcomes and Goals." *Majalat al-Dirasat al-Filastiniyyat* 32: 133–59.

Awartani, Fisal. 1997. "The Demographic Uniqueness of Palestinian Voters. In Shikaki, Khilal (ed.). *The First Palestinian Elections: Political Context, Electoral Behavior, and Results*. Nablus: CPRS, 61–84.

Halabi, Usama. 1993. *The Arab Jerusalem Municipality*. Jerusalem: PASSIA.

Hilal, Jamil. 1997. "The Palestinian Legislative Council: Political and Social Structure." In Shikaki, Khilal (ed.). *The First Palestinian Elections: Political Context, Electoral Behavior, and Results*. Nablus: CPRS, 115–40.

Husseini, Faisal. 1996. "The Israelis Should Terminate Their Occupation of the City of Jerusalem." In Khuri, Dr. Jiries Sa'ad, Musallam, Dr. Adnan, and Darwish, Musa (eds). *Jerusalem: Palestinian Islamic and Christian Research*. Jerusalem: al-Liqa, 203–98.

Naufal, Mamduh. 1995. *The Oslo Agreement Story: Seeing the True Complete Oslo Dish*. Amman: al-Ahaliya.

Ode, Adnan. 1997. "Electoral Districts: The Social and Political Structure." In Shikaki, Khilal (ed.). *The First Palestinian Elections: Political Context, Electoral Behavior, and Results*. Nablus: CPRS, 141–84.

Ukal, Talal and al-Surani, Ghazi. 19 Jan. 1996. *Analytical Research on the Palestinian Elections*. *al-Quds*.

SOURCES IN HEBREW

ARCHIVES, WEB SITES, AND COMPENDIUMS

B'tselem Archive
Archive of the Jerusalem Center for Israel Studies
Laws of the State of Israel
Judgments of Israel's Supreme Court
www.pna.net
www.pcbs.org

PERIODICALS

Davar
Ha'aretz
Yediot Aharonot

Kol Ha-Ir
Ma'ariv
Iton Yerushalaim

BOOKS AND ARTICLES

Algazi, Yosef. 19 June 1998. "The City Mouse of Ramallah." *Ha'aretz*.
——— 9 Sept. 1998. "No Residency, No Health." *Ha'aretz*.
Arens, Moshe. 1995. *War and Peace in the Middle East, 1988–92*. Tel Aviv: Yediot Aharonot.
Arnon-Ohana, Yuval. 1989. *The Sword At Home: The Internal Struggle in the Palestinian National Movement*. Hadar and the Dayan Center, Tel Aviv University.
B'tselem. 1995. *A Policy of Discrimination: Land Confiscation, Planning and Construction in East Jerusalem*. Jerusalem: Israeli Information Center for Human Rights in the Territories.
———. 1997. *Demolishing Peace: The Policy of Mass Demolition of Palestinian Homes in the West Bank*. Jerusalem: Israeli Information Center for Human Rights in the Territories.
———. April 1997. *The Silent Transfer: The Revocation of Residence Status from Palestinians in East Jerusalem*. Jerusalem: Israeli Information Center for Human Rights in the Territories.
———. 1998. *The Silent Transfer Continues: The Revocation of Residence Status and Social Benefits from East Jerusalem Residents*. Jerusalem: copublished with the Center for the Defense of the Individual.
Baron, Arieh. 1997. *Personal Seal: Moshe Dayan during and after the Six Day War*. Jerusalem Institute for Israel Studies.
Beilin, Yossi. 1997. *To Touch Peace*. Tel Aviv: Yediot Aharonot.
Ben-Elissar, Eliahu. 1995. *No More War*. Or Yehuda: *Ma'ariv*.
Bentzur, Eitan. 1997. *The Way to Peace Goes through Madrid*. Tel Aviv: Yediot Aharonot.
Benvenisti, Meron. 2 Nov. 1995. "The Keys are Inside." *Ha'aretz*.
———. 22 Aug. 1996. "On the Verge of Breaking." *Ha'aretz*.
———. 12 Dec. 1996. "A Dangerous Game with Matches." *Ha'aretz*.
———. 1996. *A Place of Fire*. Tel Aviv: Dvir.
Benziman, Uzi. 1978. *Prime Minister Under Siege*. Jerusalem: Dvir-Adam.
———. 26 June 1998. "War of Delusion." *Ha'aretz*.
———. 14 May 1999. "Last Minute Acrobatics." *Ha'aretz*.
Berkowitz, Shmuel. 1997. *The Legal Status of the Holy Places in Jerusalem*. Jerusalem Institute for Israel Studies.
Bialer, Uri. 1985. "The Way to the Capital: Turning Jerusalem into the Official Seat of the Israeli Government in 1949." *Katedra* 35: 163–91.
Blum, Yehuda. 1971. "Zion by International Law was Redeemed." *Ha-Praklit* 27: 315–24.

——. 1972–3. "East Jerusalem is not Occupied Territory." *Ha-Praklit* 28: 183–90.

Cheshin, Amir. 1992. "East Jerusalem: Policy versus Reality." *Ha-Mizrach He-Chadash* 34: 179.

Choshen, Maia and Korach, Michal (eds). 1999. *On Your Data Jerusalem*. Jerusalem Institute of Israel Studies.

Choshen, Maia and Shachar, Na'ama (eds). 1998. *Jerusalem Statistical Yearbook 1997*. Jerusalem Institute of Israel Studies.

Choshen, Maia. 1998. *On Your Data Jerusalem 1997: Existing Situation and Trends of Change*. Jerusalem Institute of Israel Studies.

Cohen, Chaim. 1998. "The Status of Jerusalem in the Law of the State of Israel." In Yehoshua Praver and Ora Achimeir (eds). *Twenty Years in Jerusalem 1967–87*. Tel Aviv and Jerusalem: Ministry of Defense and Jerusalem Institute of Israel Studies, 246–67.

Cohen, Hillel. 19 Jan. 1996. "Silwan Goes to the Polls." *Kol Ha-Ir*.

——. 26 Jan. 1996. "The Elected." *Kol Ha-Ir*.

——. 29 Nov. 1996. "Exposé: This is How We Redeemed the Land of East Jerusalem." *Kol Ha-Ir*.

——. 29 April 1998. "Shake-up in the Territories." *Kol Ha-Ir*.

Cohen, Shmaryahu and Mazor, Adam. 1994. *The Jerusalem Metropolitan Area: Master Plan and Development Plan*. Jerusalem Institute of Israel Studies.

Dinstein, Yoram. 1971. "Zion by International Law Will Be Redeemed." *Ha-Praklit* 27: 5–11.

——. "It Really Wasn't Redeemed, or: Not by Demonstrations but by Action." *Ha-Praklit* 27: 519–22.

Eisenstadt, David. 1999. *Changes in Jerusalem's Municipal Boundaries 1863–1967*. Master's thesis, Bar-Ilan University, Ramat Gan.

Eldar, Akiva. 14 Nov. 1996. "Who Knows the Jordanians." *Ha'aretz*.

——. 13 Feb. 1997. "Negotiating Booth Forever?" *Ha'aretz*.

——. 17 March 1997. "City Engineer vs. Har Homa." *Ha'aretz*.

——. 6 April 1998. "Get Down Har Homa without being Hurt." *Ha'aretz*.

——. 26 May 1998. "A Matter of Weeks." *Ha'aretz*.

——. 22 June 1998. "Expanded Jerusalem: Albright's Document." *Ha'aretz*.

——. 11 March 1999. "Netanyahu Internationalizes Jerusalem." *Ha'aretz*.

——. 10 May 1999. "If I Forget Thee, O Jerusalem, I am no Rightist." *Ha'aretz*.

——. 11 May 1999. "Who Will Land Mordechay." *Ha'aretz*.

Galili, Lili. 4 Aug. 1996. "Enlarging the Cake Instead of Dividing It." *Ha'aretz*.

——. 30 Aug. 1996. "Divide and Rule in Old Jerusalem." *Ha'aretz*.

——. 12 Jan. 2000. "The Righthand Sidewalk is in the Territories, the Lefthand Sidewalk is in Jerusalem." *Ha'aretz*.

Galili, Orit. 5 Aug. 1996. "Jerusalem Has Two Faces." *Ha'aretz*.

Gal-Nur, Yitzhak. 1995. *And the Sons Returned to Their Borders: The Decisions on State and Territory in the Zionist Movement*. Sde Boker and Jerusalem: Ben-Gurion Heritage Center and Magnes.

Ganim, Asad. 1996. *The First General Palestinian Elections Jan. 1996: Test of Democracy*. Givat Haviva: Institute for the Study of Peace.

Gazit, Shlomo. 1985. *The Carrot and the Stick: The Israeli Administration in Judea and Samaria*. Tel Aviv: Zemora Bitan.

——. 1999. *Fools in a Trap*. Tel Aviv: Zemora Bitan.

Gemer, Moshe (ed.). 1981. *The Negotiations on the Establishment of the Autonomy: Principal Documents*. Tel Aviv: Moshe Dayan Center.

Giladi, Rotem and Merchav, Reuven. 1998. *The Hashimite Jordanian Kingdom and its Role in a Future Peace Arrangement in Jerusalem: Legal, Political, and Practical Aspects*. Jerusalem Institute for Israel Studies.

Gilbar, Gad. 1992. "Demographic and Economic Developments as Causes of the Intifada." In Gilbar, Gad and Susser, Asher. (eds). *In the Eye of the Conflict: The Intifada*. Tel Aviv: Dayan Center of Tel Aviv University and Ha-Kibbutz Ha-Me'uchad, 20–39.

Golani, Moti. 1994. "Zionism without Zion? The Position of the Leadership of the Yishuv and the State of Israel on the Question of Jerusalem 1947–9." In Avi Brali. ed. "Divided Jerusalem." *Eidan* 18. Jerusalem: Yad Ben-Zvi: 32–3.

——. 1998. "Separating Yearnings and Action: Israeli Policy on the Question of Jerusalem 1948–67." In Anita Shapira (ed.). *Independence: The First Fifty Years*. Jerusalem: Merkaz Zalman Shazar, 267–96.

Grossman, David. 1987. *The Yellow Time*. Tel Aviv: Siman Kriya and Ha-Kibbutz Ha-Me'uchad.

Haber, Eitan; Schiff, Ze'ev, and Ya'ari, Ehud. 1980. *The Year of the Dove*. Tel Aviv: Zemora-Bitan-Modan.

Halberstam, Malvina. 1988. "The Jerusalem Embassy Law: U.S. Recognition of Undivided Jerusalem as the Capital of Israel." *Mechkarei Mishpat* 32: 391–407.

Hareuveni, Eyal and Dayan, Arieh. 1 Aug. 1997. "The Ras al-Amud Incident: Everyone's Involved." *Kol Ha-Ir*.

Harkabi, Yehoshafat (ed.). 1975. *Arabs and Israel 3–4: Decisions of the Palestinian National Council*. Tel Aviv: Am Oved.

Hasson, Shlomo. 1993. *The Municipal Organization of Metropolitan Jerusalem: Alternative Ideas*. Jerusalem Institute of Israel Studies.

Hatina, Meir. 1994. *Palestinian Radicalism: The Islamic Jihad Movement*. Tel Aviv: Moshe Dayan Center of Tel Aviv University.

Hess, Amira. 1996. *To Drink from the Sea at Gaza*. Tel Aviv: Ha-Kibbutz Ha-Me'uchad and Siman Kriya.

——. 30 March 1997. "The Green Light Was Given by Netanyahu."
    Ha'aretz.

——. 2 July 1997. "Raising Up Jews." *Ha'aretz*.

——. 25 March 1998. "A Few Steps Too Far." *Ha'aretz*.

——. 14 May 1998. "Preventative Document." *Ha'aretz*.

——. 22 Oct. 1999. "Infiltrators from Wadi Hummus." *Ha'aretz*.

Hirsch, Moshe; Hausen-Koriel, Devora and Lapidot, Ruth. 1994.
    Whither Jerusalem? Proposals for the City's Future. Jerusalem Institute for
    Israel Studies.

Ir Shalem. 1998. *East Jerusalem: Planning Status*. Jerusalem.

Jerusalem Municipality. 25 Oct. 1994. *Background Paper for Discussion in
    the Ministerial Committee on Jerusalem Affairs*.

Karpel, Dalia. 13 Oct. 1995. "The History of a Fantasy." *Musaf Ha'aretz*.

Kazin, Orna. 27 July 1999. "The Boundaries of Education." *Ha'aretz*.

Klein, Menachem. 1988. *A Dialogue and Its Breaking: Jordan-PLO Relations
    1985–8*. Hebrew University, Davis Institute for International
    Studies.

——. 1995. *Jerusalem and the Negotiations for Peace: Arab Positions*. Jerusa-
    lem Institute of Israel Studies.

Koren, Dani. 1994. *Time in Gray: The National Unity Governments, 1984–
    90*. Tel Aviv: Zemora-Bitan.

Lapidot, Ruth. 1997. *Jerusalem: Legal Aspects — Background Papers for Policy
    Makers*. Jerusalem Institute of Israel Studies.

—— 1999. *Basic Law: Jerusalem the Capital of Israel*. In commentary on
    basic laws edited by Yitzhak Zamir. Jerusalem: Faculty of Law,
    Hebrew University.

Levi, Gidon. 4 April 1997. "The Time of the Siren." *Ha'aretz* weekly
    magazine.

Litani, Yehuda. 3 Sept. 1996. "Tel Aviv of the Palestinians is a Golden
    Cage." *Ha'aretz*.

Mana', Adel and Yehiye, Kusai Haj. 1995. *Mabruk: The Arab Wedding Cul-
    ture in Israel*. Ra'anana, Center for the Study of Arab Society in Israel.

Ma'oz, Moshe. 1985. *The Palestinian Leadership in the West Bank*. Tel Aviv:
    Reshafim.

Markus, Yoel. 27 Aug. 1996. "Even If It Takes Six Months." *Ha'aretz*.

Melman, Yossi. 29 Aug. 1995. "The Geometry of the Cairo Agree-
    ments." *Ha'aretz*.

Mishal, Shaul and Aharoni, Reuven. 1989. *Stones Are Not Everything: The
    Intifada and the Leaflet Weapon*. Tel Aviv: Ha-Kibbutz Ha-Me'uchad &
    Revivim.

Morris, Benny. 1991. *The Birth of the Palestinian Refugee Problem 1947–9*.
    Tel Aviv: Am Oved.

——. 1996. *Israel's Border Wars 1949–56*. Tel Aviv: Am Oved and the
    Truman Institute of the Hebrew University.

Narkis, Uzi. 1975. *Jerusalem is One*. Tel Aviv: Am Oved.

——. 1991. *Soldier of Jerusalem*. Tel Aviv: Ministry of Defense.

Nesher, Merav. 6 Sept. 1996. "War of Symbols on Book Bindings." *Ha'aretz*.

Nevo, Yosef. 1977. The Political Development of the Arab–Palestinian National Movement 1939–45. Ph.D. diss. Tel Aviv University.

Nir, Ori. 15 Jan 1996. "Who is a Candidate? Where is the Polling Station? Why Vote?". *Ha'aretz*.

Office of the Prime Minister and the Central Bureau of Statistics. 1998. *Population and Housing Census 1995* (Jerusalem data). Jerusalem.

Paz, Reuven. 1988. *The Islamic Covenant and Its Meaning: Data and Analysis*. Tel Aviv: Dayan Center, Tel Aviv University.

Paz, Yair. 1997. "The Hebrew University on Mount Scopus as a 'Sanctuary.'" In Shaul Katz and Michael Hed (eds). *The History of the Hebrew University of Jerusalem: Roots and Beginnings*. Jerusalem: Magnes, 281–308.

Peace Watch. 1995. *What are the Palestinian Authority Institutions in Jerusalem?* Jerusalem.

Pedhatzur, Reuven. 1995. "The Closing of a Circle: Back to the Palestinian Option." *Medina, Mimshal, Ve-Yachasim Beinle'umi'im* 40: 31–66.

Porat, Yehoshua. 1978. *From Riots to Rebellion: The Arab–Palestinian National Movement 1929–39*. Tel Aviv: Am Oved.

Qashu'a, Sayed and Cohen, Hillel. 19 June 1998. "A District Commander for You." *Kol Ha-Ir*.

Quandt, William B. 1988. *Camp David: Peace and the Political Game*. Jerusalem: Keter.

Rabin, Yitzchak. 1979. *Service File*. Tel Aviv: Ma'ariv.

Rabinowitz, Itamar. 1991. *The Peace That Got Away: Israel–Arab Relations 1949–52*. Jerusalem: Keter.

Ramon, Amnon. 1997. *The Attitudes of the State of Israel and the Jewish Public of All Stripes to the Temple Mount (1967–96)*. Jerusalem Institute of Israel Studies.

Reiter, Yitzhak. 1997. *The Temple Mount — al-Haram al-Sharif: Points of Agreement and Dispute*. Jerusalem Institute of Israel Studies.

——. 1991. *The Waqf in Jerusalem 1948–90*.

Rekhes, Eli. 1992. "The Arabs of Israel and the Intifada." In Gilbar, Gad and Susser, Asher (eds). *In the Eye of the Conflict: The Intifada*. Tel Aviv: Dayan Center of Tel Aviv University and Ha-Kibbutz Ha-Me'uchad, 99–127.

Roman, Michael. 1992. "The Intifada's Effect on Jewish–Arab Relations in Jerusalem." *Ha-Mizrach He-Chadash* 24: 162–77.

Rosenthal, Rubik. 17 April 1995. "Flapped Wings in the Air. Almost." *Ha'aretz*.

Rubinstein, Dani. 10 Jan. 1995. "The End of the Consensus." *Ha'aretz*.

——. 11 Aug. 1995. "The Compromise Will Come from Jerusalem." *Ha'aretz*.

——. 15 Oct. 1995. "Close–Near Border." *Ha'aretz*.

——. 27 Oct. 1995. "Here the Palestinian Tel Aviv Will Rise." *Ha'aretz*.

——. 25 Dec. 1995. "On the Way." *Ha'aretz*.

——. 27 May 1996. "Jerusalem Outside of Jerusalem." *Ha'aretz*.

——. 9 July 1996. "Two Flags at Orient House." *Ha'aretz*.

——. 15 July 1996. "Collision Course." *Ha'aretz*.

——. 23 Aug. 1996. "The Temptation: American Citizenship." *Ha'aretz*.

——. 30 Aug. 1996. "Between Explosion and Restraint." *Ha'aretz*.

——. 24 Sept. 1996. "Renewal of the Trauma." *Ha'aretz*.

——. 29 Sept. 1996. "An Islam-Skirting Tunnel." *Ha'aretz*.

——. 20 Nov. 1996. "Thirty Percent of the Residents, Only Seven Percent of the Money." *Ha'aretz*.

——. 13 Dec. 1996. "Two Floors for Arabs, Four for Jews." *Ha'aretz*.

——. 6 Jan. 1997. "The Jordanian Withdrawal." *Ha'aretz*.

——. 26 Jan. 1997. "Eighteen Appointments for the Temple Mount." *Ha'aretz*.

——. 3 Feb. 1997. "Preparations for a Struggle on Identity Cards." *Ha'aretz*.

——. 16 May 1997. "Neither Green Nor Red." *Ha'aretz*.

——. 23 June 1997. "Top-Level PLO in a Pique." *Ha'aretz*.

——. 18 Sept. 1997. "The Temptations of a Rent Control Tenant." *Ha'aretz*.

——. 22 Sept. 1997. "Struggle in the Same Coin." *Ha'aretz*.

——. 12 Feb. 1998. "Banging Your Head on the Western Wall." *Ha'aretz*.

——. 22 June 1998. "Busy Weekend in Al-Aqsa." *Ha'aretz*.

——. 23 June 1998. "The Refugees of '98." *Ha'aretz*.

——. 20 July 1998. "At the End of the Withdrawal the Temple Mount Towers." *Ha'aretz*.

Savir, Uri. 1998. *The Process: Behind the Scenes of a Historic Decision*. Tel Aviv: Yediot Aharonot.

Schiff, Ze'ev and Ya'ari, Ehud. 1990. *Intifada*. Jerusalem: Shocken.

Schiff, Ze'ev. 23 Feb. 1996. "Beilin's Permanent Solution." *Ha'aretz*.

Segev, Amira. 4 July 1995. "In East Jerusalem They Study in Palestinian." *Ha'aretz*.

——. 19 Feb. 1997. "Among the Hills and Mountains." *Ha'aretz*.

——. 1 April 1997. "The Affront to Jibril Rajoub." *Ha'aretz*.

——. 23 Feb. 1999. "The Mufti's New Offices." *Ha'aretz*.

——. 29 March 1999. "Unremittingly Neglected." *Ha'aretz*.

Seideman, Daniel. 17 Aug. 1997. "Before Beginning to Destroy." *Ha'aretz*.

Sela, Avraham. 1983. *Unity Within Division: Arab Summit Conferences*. Jerusalem: Magnes.

——. 1984. *The Palestinian Ba'ath*. Jerusalem: Truman Institute of Hebrew University & Magnes.

——. 1990. "The Attitudes of King Abdallah and the Israeli Government in the War of Independence: A New Look." *Katedra* 57: 120–62, 172–93.

Shabbat, Yechezkel. 1997. *Hamas and the Peace Process*. Givat Ze'ev: published by the author.

Shamir, Shimon. 26 Oct. 1997. "Every Possible Error." *Ha'aretz*.

Shamir, Yitzchak. 1994. *Summing Up*. Tel Aviv: Yediot Aharonot.

Shashar, Michael. 1997. *The War of the Seventh Day: Diary of the Military Administration in Judea and Samaria — June–Dec. 1967*. Tel Aviv: Sifriyat Po'alim.

Shavit, Ari. 7 March 1997. "Yossi Takes Off His Glasses." *Ha'aretz*.

Shchori, Dalia. 21 Oct. 1996. "The Tunnel is Opening Under our Home." *Ha'aretz*.

Shiloah Institute for the Study of the Middle East and Africa, Tel Aviv University. 1978. *The Peace Initiative: The Diplomatic Negotiations Nov. 1977– July 1978: Principal Documents*. Tel Aviv University.

Shragai, Nadav. 20 Jan. 1995. "Half Jerusalem Half Autonomy." *Ha'aretz*.

——. 2 Nov. 1995. "Lists of Give and Take." *Ha'aretz*.

——. 1996. *The Mount of Dissension, the Battle for the Temple Mount: Jews, Muslims, Religion, and Politics since 1967*. Jerusalem: Keter.

——. 17 May 1996. "The Intifada of Negotiations. *Ha'aretz*.

——. 9 July 1996. "Two Flags in Orient House." *Ha'aretz*.

——. 19 Sept. 1996. "Who's the Master of the Mount." *Ha'aretz*.

——. 15 Oct. 1996. "Until the Mount Moves." *Ha'aretz*.

——. 23 Dec. 1996. "Barrier on the Way to the Mount." *Ha'aretz*.

——. 19 Feb. 1997. "From the Sacrifices and from the Paschal Offerings." *Ha'aretz*.

——. 4 July 1996. "The Anteroom beyond the Corridor." *Ha'aretz*.

——. 25 Feb. 1997. "Entry is Forbidden, but Why?" *Ha'aretz*.

——. 27 Feb. 1997. "The Announcement on Construction for Arabs — Misleads." *Ha'aretz*.

——. 1 Aug. 1997. "The Battle for the Wide-Open East." *Ha'aretz*.

——. 25 Sept. 1997. "Longing for the Refined Consensus." *Ha'aretz*.

——. 30 Dec. 1997. "Pig on the Mount." *Ha'aretz*.

——. 31 Dec. 1997. "Stop It Rabbi." *Ha'aretz*.

——. 18 Jan. 1998. "How Much Are They Really Building Settlements." *Ha'aretz*.

——. 8 June 1998. "The Rule of the Mufti." *Ha'aretz*.

——. 27 July 1998. "Cracks in the Glass House." *Ha'aretz*.

——. 18 Aug. 1998. "The Arabs Will Prevent Olmert From Making a Profit." *Ha'aretz*.

Sofer, Sasson. 1986. *Menachem Begin at the Camp David Conference: A Chapter in the New Diplomacy*. Jerusalem: Davis Institute for International Relations, Hebrew University, policy publications.

Sokol, Sami. 4 Aug. 1996. "The Cards Have Been Shown and Reshuffled." *Ha'aretz*.

Sprintzak, Ehud. 1995. *Political Violence in Israel: Between Extra-Parliamentary Protest and Terrorism*. Jerusalem Institute of Israel Studies.

State of Israel. 1973. *The Interministerial Committee for the Examination of the Development of Jerusalem: Recommendations for a Coordinated and Integrated Rate of Development*. Jerusalem.

Steinberg, Matti. 5 Sept. 1994. "You Can't Clap Just One Hand." *Davar*.

Susser, Asher. 1985. *The PLO after the War in Lebanon*. Tel Aviv: Ha-Kibbutz Ha-Me'uchad.

—— 1995. "Demographics and Politics in Jordan." In Ami Ayalon and Gad Gilbar (eds). *Demographics and Politics in Arab States*. Tel Aviv: Dayan Center of Tel Aviv University and Ha-Kibbutz Ha-Me'uchad: 131–52.

Temkin, Moshe. 9 April 1999. "A Second Via Dolorosa." *Ha'aretz*.

Weksler, Uzi. 15 April 1997. "Demographic Wall." *Ha'aretz*.

Ya'ari, Ehud. 6 Oct. 1995. "Oslo II: A Palestinian Reading." *Davar*.

Yisraeli, Rafi. 1982. *Anwar Sadat on War and Peace 1970–1980*. Jerusalem: Magnes.

Zak, Moshe. 1996. *Hussein Makes Peace*. Ramat Gan: Bar-Ilan University.

Zinger, Yoel. 18 Sept. 1998. "Peace Diary." *Ha'aretz*.

INDEX

360

Index

Qria', Ahmad *see* Abu-Ala (Ahmad Qria')
Quandt, William B., 90, 91, 92, 95, 243

Rabin, Yitzhak, 65, 137, 153, 291
  assassination, 306, 307
  Declaration of Principles and, 149
  Israeli peace plan (1989) and, 114
  Israeli policy towards East Jerusalem after Oslo Accords and, 251, 258, 261
  Oslo talks and, 140, 141, 142–3, 147, 148, 150, 151
  Palestinian security forces and, 192
  permanent settlement issue and, 293
  Washington Declaration and, 162, 163, 165, 166
Rabinivich, Itamar, 97
Rabinowitz, Itamar, 45, 49, 50
Rajoub, Jibril, 190, 191, 192, 198, 224, 248
rallies, elections to Palestinian Authority and, 229
Ramallah, 21, 35, 37–8, 39
  elections to Palestinian Authority, 228
Ramon, Amnon, 60, 64
Ramon, Haim, 147–8
Ramot, 27
Ramot Eshkol, 27
Ras al-Amud, 203–4, 261–2, 321
Reagan, Ronald
  London Agreement and, 109
  peace initiative (1982), 107–9
  refugees, 32, 48
Reiter, Yitzhak, 55, 60, 72
Rekhes, Eli, 84
resident status, 267–70, 311, 322, 323, 325
road system, 26, 73, 74, 75
  bus transport, 35, 36–7, 313
Robinson, Glenn E., 184, 242, 243, 244
Roman, Michael, 12, 13, 81, 82
Romann, Michael, 66–7, 72, 83, 186

Ross, Dennis, 135, 285
Ross, Leonard, 207, 208
Rubin, Barry, 42, 43, 44, 90, 100, 108, 111, 113, 117, 130
Rubinstein, Dani, 33, 37, 38, 40, 70, 71, 75, 181, 201, 202, 223, 227, 245, 257, 261, 263, 270, 272, 277

Sa'ad al-Din al-Alami, 56–7
Sabagh, Hasib, 265
Sabella, Bernard, 31, 52, 185
Sabri, Akaramah, 176, 260, 274
Sadat, Anwar
  negotiations with Israel, 86–9, 95–6, 98, 99–100
    Camp David conference, 90–4, 102
  visit to Jerusalem, 86, 101
Safia, Afif, 137
Sa'id, Nader Izzat, 1, 34, 57
Sa'id, Nadir, 207, 209
Sa'ih, Abd al-Hamid, 181
Salah, Abd al-Jawad, 238
Saudi Arabia, 55, 169, 171
Saunders, Harold, 95
Savir, Uri, 142, 144, 145
Sayigh, Yezid, 184, 215
Schiff, Ze'ev, 91
security services *see* police and security services
Segal, Jerome M., 1, 34, 57
Segev, Amira, 70, 71, 280, 284
Seideman, Daniel, 28, 29
Sela, Avraham, 45, 160
sewage system, 73, 74, 75–6
Sha'ar Mizrach, 256, 257
Sha'ath, Nabil, 223, 242
Shachar, Na'ama, 20, 22, 31, 70
Shahal, Moshe, 258
Shaked, Haim, 97
Shamir, Yitzhak, 109, 110, 111
  Baker plan (1991) and, 120–2, 123–5, 126, 128
  Israeli peace plan (1989) and, 114, 118
Sharabi, Hisham, 245
Sharia' courts, 55–6, 176, 314–15
Sharon, Ariel, 264, 279